Small Business

Small Business

an entrepreneur's plan

Fifth Canadian Edition

Ron Knowles
Algonquin College

Australia   Canada   Mexico   Singapore   Spain   United Kingdom   United States

THOMSON
NELSON

Small Business: An Entrepreneur's Plan, Fifth Canadian Edition

by Ron Knowles

Associate Vice President, Editorial Director:
Evelyn Veitch

Publisher:
Veronica Visentin

Senior Developmental Editor:
Elke Price

Permissions Coordinator:
Indu Ghuman

Production Service:
GEX Publishing Services

Copy Editor:
GEX Publishing Services

Proofreader:
GEX Publishing Services

Indexer:
GEX Publishing Services

Manufacturing Coordinator:
Joanne McNeil

Design Director:
Ken Phipps

Interior Design:
Tammy Gay

Cover Design:
Johanna Liburd

Cover Image:
David & Les Jacobs/Getty Images

Compositor:
GEX Publishing Services

Printer:
Thomson/West

Library and Archives Canada Cataloguing in Publication Data

Knowles, Ronald A
  Small business: an entrepreneur's plan/Ron Knowles.—5th ed.

Includes bibliographical references and index.

ISBN-13: 978-0-17-625240-3
ISBN-10: 0-17-625240-1

1. New business enterprises—Planning. 2. Small business—Planning. I. Title.

HD62.5.K568 2006   658.1'141
C2006-906036-3

Brief Contents

Contents

Chapter 4

PROFILING YOUR TARGET CUSTOMER 77

Chapter 5

LEARNING FROM THE COMPETITION: YOUR COMPETITIVE INTELLIGENCE 99

Chapter 6

PRICING AND PROMOTING YOUR PRODUCT OR SERVICE 123

Chapter 7

DISTRIBUTION AND LOCATION 151

Chapter 10

THE POWER OF NUMBERS   233

Chapter 11

FINANCING YOUR BUSINESS   275

Chapter 15

PULLING THE PLAN TOGETHER   389

E-Module 1

EXPORTING: ANOTHER ADVENTURE BECKONS   M1-1

E-Module 2

FAST-START BUSINESS PLAN   M2-1

E-Module 3

BUSINESS PLAN OUTLINE, TEMPLATES, AND EXAMPLES   M3-1

Welcome to the Fifth Canadian Edition of *Small Business: An Entrepreneur's Plan*. This book and our extensive online resources were created for you and thousands of dreamers like you who want to start your own business. Most first-time entrepreneurs start out with little more than an idea. By combining your vision and talents with a practical approach, we will show you how to take your idea and form it into a functional Business Plan.

Every great adventure begins with a map. This book serves as your map and your navigator. The Business Plan Building Blocks and Action Steps provide you with direction and tasks to accomplish along the way, while the vignettes and case studies give you a firsthand look at the trials, tribulations, and successes of other entrepreneurs.

By following these Building Blocks and Actions Steps, you learn how to develop a business plan from the inception of the idea, how to find your target customers, and how to market to them successfully.

Fasten your seatbelt, and prepare to embark on your great entrepreneurial adventure!

TARGET THE CHAPTERS THAT CALL TO YOU

This new Fifth Canadian Edition contains 15 chapters that will guide you along the way to owning or managing a small business.

The textbook contains some 75 Action Steps and Building Blocks apportioned across 15 chapters, from Chapter 1, "Your Great Adventure: Exploring Your Options," to Chapter 15, "Pulling the Plan Together."

- Chapters 1, 2, and 3 help you focus on yourself and your ideas; they explain how to develop and test your ideas in the marketplace before you spend your money. If you are just exploring entrepreneurship, concentrate on these chapters, accompanying Action Steps, and online exercises. You are designing not only your business but also your life.
- Chapters 4, 5, and 6 help develop, locate, and satisfy the key to your success in small business—your target customer. Here you'll learn how to profile your target customer; develop a competitive strategy; and price, promote, and market your product or service.
- Chapter 7 helps you develop your distribution strategy and find a location—at home, on the street, or at the crossroads in cyberspace.
- Chapter 8 helps you untangle and understand the legal red tape of starting and running a business. We help you decide which legal form (sole proprietorship, partnership, or corporation) is best for you and your business, help you understand bankruptcy and its danger signals, and show you how to find the right lawyer and professional advice.
- Chapter 9, "Risk Management Issues," starts you thinking about protecting yourself and your business. It considers matters such as insurance, health and safety, employee fraud, and the basic principles of patents, copyrights, and trademarks.
- Chapters 10 and 11 plunge you into the world of finance. You learn how to formulate a personal financial vision, get your personal finances in order, and determine how much money you'll need to start your business and finance it. By the time you finish Chapter 11, you'll understand financial statements and be able to put together a financial plan to start and run your business.

- Chapter 12 starts you thinking about the basic management functions, organizational structure, and leadership and helps you begin building a winning team.
- Chapter 13 offers tips and advice to those who want to buy an existing business. If your goal is to be the "happy franchisee," turn to Chapter 14. Franchisees are on every corner, but, as we caution you, not all of them are happy with their lot.
- Chapter 15 asks you to gather all of your Action Steps to form the basis for your business plan. We provide you with one detailed business plan example. On the book's support Web site we have provided you with another completed business plan: "Business Plan Proposal for Specialty Chocolates and Candy Concession" and you can also access a detailed business plan template.

FEATURES THAT HELP

The Action Steps and E-exercises, Checklist Questions and Actions to Develop Your Business Plan, and our new online modules help you determine what belongs in your business plan.

ACTION STEPS

Our road to success in small business is marked by 75 Action Steps and supporting E-exercises. Completing these steps should significantly help your chances of reaching your business goals. If the world of business is like a maze— a series of challenges and obstacles—then the Action Steps are designed to lead you through. Each Action Step is an exercise that accompanies our explanation of a particular portion of the maze.

OPENING WINDOWS

In each chapter, figures, charts, tables, and online resources provide useful information and concepts to illustrate the text. Examples include Internet databases (throughout the book), tips for developing strategic alliances (Chapter 4), the best places to set up your booth at a trade show (Chapter 6), and a strategy for selecting your mentor (Chapter 12). All of these offer the new entrepreneur windows onto the world of small business.

ENTREPRENEURIAL VIGNETTES

At the beginning of each chapter and throughout the text we present you with brief case studies full of strategies, real-world applications, and lessons that provide insight into entrepreneurial minds and ventures. We have modified the stories for simplicity and clarity. Some vignettes are composites of several case studies and others are purely fictional.

STAYING ON TRACK

Other features help you stay on track and focus on the task at hand. Learning Opportunities at the beginning of each chapter identify the learning outcomes of the chapter. Margin definitions help you build your business vocabulary.

NEW AND REVISED FEATURES OF THE FIFTH CANADIAN EDITION

New resources and Web sites have been added throughout the chapters. We have also included in this new edition a number of improvements such as comprehensive case studies and online modules designed to make *Small Business* the most exciting, current, comprehensive, and useful small business and entrepreneurship textbook available.

E-MODULES

New to this edition are three comprehensive online instruction modules to further assist you as you enter the world of small business. On the Knowles book support site: (www.knowles5e.nelson.com) you'll find the following comprehensive support modules:

E-Module 1—Exporting: Another Adventure Beckons

Many of you have expressed interest in the export market. And yes, exporting your product or service is an adventure you might want to think about before you start your business. So, in this module, we provide the start-up fundamentals and encourage you to become export-ready.

E-Module 2—Fast-Start Business Plan

If your business idea is very simple or short-term, perhaps you don't need a fully developed business plan. In this module, we help you write a fast-start business plan—one that enables you to respond quickly to an opportunity and to show yourself that the venture is viable.

E-Module 3—Business Plan Outline, Templates, and Examples

If you decide to "take the plunge" and write a detailed business plan—and we strongly recommend you do—you're going to need to follow an outline. In this module, we provide you with a detailed outline of a business plan—including all the questions you must address. If you follow this template, and address all the questions, you will be ready with a solid plan that will guide you through your first year of operation.

This module also includes a business plan template compliments of the Royal Bank and a comprehensive retail business plan outline entitled "Business Plan Proposal for Specialty Chocolates and Candy Concession."

COMPREHENSIVE CASE STUDIES

At the end of each chapter we provide a comprehensive case study to help you put to practice the key learning outcomes. Here we help you understand and learn from successful entrepreneurs, such as Janet and Greta Podleski in Chapter 3 or Robert Murray and Mike McCarron in Chapter 12. By researching the cases and answering the case study questions, you will learn the keys to small business success.

But wait—there's more! Over the course of the next three years of this edition we are going to add additional comprehensive case studies, which will be available on the book's support site. New success stories keep emerging, and this is one way we can help keep you in the loop.

VIDEOS AND WEB CASTS

This Fifth Canadian Edition is also supported by a series of small business videos available in DVD format. Select videos of our extensive end-of-chapter case studies—such as the Garrison Guitars and My Virtual Model cases in Chapters 1 and 5— can be also viewed on the book's Web site at www.knowles5e.nelson.com. A brief summary of the videos, and case study questions with answers, can be found in the online Instructor Video Guide.

E-EXERCISES AND BOOKMARK THIS BOXES

As we move through the book, we offer many current links to the Internet. We encourage linking to the Web in our E-Exercises. Here you can test your entrepreneurial acumen through personal assessment, trend analysis, number-crunching, and even preparing your business plan. We also highlight key sites in our "Bookmark This" boxes. These boxes provide you with the most up-to-date information on small business.

All of the links in the text are provided on book's support site (www.knowles5e.nelson.com). As we all know, Web sites come and go. As a result, we will update the sites on a regular basis.

WEB SITE

www.knowles5e.nelson.com

This Fifth Canadian Edition is supported by our comprehensive support Web site to help you as you begin your entrepreneurial trek. Here you'll find self-study questions, e-exercises, key terms with definitions, PowerPoint® slides, Internet links, and more.

THIS BOOK IS FOR YOU

TO DREAMERS AND BEGINNING ENTREPRENEURS

As you're reading the book, keep your computer or pencil and paper close by so that you can take notes or jot down ideas. Get used to brainstorming and mind mapping. Also, it's not a bad idea to carry a cassette recorder in your car so that you can record ideas that occur to you while you're driving. The inspiration that you get from a highway billboard 400 kilometres from home might be the seed from which your winning business grows.

Our point is that this is *your* book. Use our Web site and the book in whatever way suits your needs. Make notes in the margins, mark it up with a highlighting pen. Use the book as a handbook, a textbook, or both. This small business package is designed for a wide range of creative, energetic people who want to own their own business, and someplace in that range of people is *you*. Good luck!

Figure 1.1   Women Drive Self-Employment

About 12 years ago, Vancouver's Mindy Tulsi-Ingram lost her job, but before long, she had created her own gift services business, Green & Green. Alone, she assembled custom baskets and corporate gift packages in the back of her brother's movie rental shop. "I just did it for fun," said the 43-year-old married mother of one, who has double majors in economics and communications from Simon Fraser University.

As of 2005, Ms. Tulsi-Ingram had four employees and her own warehouse, and is on the hunt for more help. "Women are becoming more and more confident and assertive," she said. "They are now saying, 'Yes I can do it too.'"

A recent *CIBC World Report* highlights a number of trends developing among women who run small, typically one-person, businesses. Female entrepreneurs are on average highly educated and usually gain experience in a paid position before starting their own venture. Here are more key findings from the CIBC report.

- Since 1989, the number of woman-run businesses has risen 60 percent faster than those run by men.
- The number of woman-run enterprises is expected to exceed the 1,000,000 mark by the end of this decade, up from the 800,000 reported in 2005.
- More than 70 percent of female entrepreneurs are married, and a third have children under the age of 12.
- Sixty percent of female entrepreneurs are "lifestylers," who prefer a balance of work and family to business growth.
- Women over age 55, or the so-called "seniorpreneurs," represent the fastest growing slice of self-employed Canadians.
- Between 2001 and 2004, the revenues for firms run by single women grew three times faster than those of their married counterparts.
- Fewer women (38%) than men (55%) who are self-employed believe that they earn more money than they would if they worked for someone else.
- Twenty-five percent of Canada's self-employed women were not born in Canada.
- More than 80 percent of women entrepreneurs are satisfied with their decisions to become business owners. If they had to do it over again, they would choose to start a business.
- If you want to learn more about how woman are changing the entrepreneurial landscape, we encourage you to link on to Roaring Woman—a wonderful grassroots organization headed up by Mandie Crawford.

Source: CIBC, *Women Entrepreneurs: Leading the Charge*, http://www.cibc.com/ca/small-business/article-tools/women-entrepreneurs.html; *The Globe and Mail*, "Small Business Driving Growth, and Women are in Control" by Rob Shaw, http://www.theglobeandmail.com/servlet/story/RTGAM.20050629.wxrsmallbiz29/BNStory/specialSmallBusiness/; *Roaring Woman*, http://www.roaringwomen.com/ (accessed June 2006).

- The vast majority of employer businesses (98%) have fewer than 100 employees. Nearly 75 percent have fewer than 10 employees, and 57 percent have only 1 to 4 employees (see Table 1.2).
- About five million employees, or 49 percent of the total private labour force, work for small enterprises (those with fewer than 100 employees). About 75 percent of these small business employees work in the service sector (See Table 1.3).
- On average, over the past 10 years, small businesses have accounted for about 25 percent of our Gross Domestic Product—a key measure of economic production (see, for example, Statistics Canada, http://strategis.ic.gc.ca/epic/internet/insbrp-rppe.nsf/en/rd01838e.html).

Table 1.2 Number of Canadian Business Establishments by Sector and Firm Size (Number of Employees), December 2004

Number of Employees	Cumulative Percent of Employer Businesses	Number of Business Establishments		
		Total	Goods-Producing Sector	Service-Producing Sector
Indeterminate[1]		1,334,791	351,202	983,589
Employer Business Total	*100.0*	*1,042,316*	*240,537*	*801,779*
1–4	56.6	589,777	146,065	443,712
5–9	73.9	180,345	35,551	144,794
10–19	85.9	125,561	24,483	101,078
20–49	94.6	90,436	19,363	71,073
50–99	97.6	31,323	8,060	23,263
100–199	99.0	14,791	4,247	10,544
200–499	99.7	7,223	2,159	5,064
500+	100.0	2,860	609	2,251

Source: Statistics Canada, *Business Register*, December 2004. Available at http://strategis.ic.gc.ca/epic/internet/insbrp-rppe.nsf/en/rd01226e.html (accessed June 2006).

[1] Note: As of December 2004, there were nearly 2.5 million business establishments in Canada, as shown in Table 1. About half are called "employer businesses," because they maintain a payroll of at least one person (possibly the owner). The other half is classified as "indeterminate," because they do not have any employees registered with the Canada Revenue Agency (CRA). Such businesses might have no work force (they might simply be paper entities that meet one of the criteria for being recognized as a business establishment) or they might have contract workers, family members, and/or only the owners working for them. Information about their work force is not available.

Now we want you to try this line of thought: What do you want to be doing in the year 2010? In 2015? What's the best course of action for you right now? What might be the best business for you? What are your strengths? What skills will you need? What do you want out of life? What are your dreams? Most of all, what are your passions?

Table 1.3 Number of Private-Sector Employees by Industry and Size of Business Enterprise, 2004

Industry	Total	Size of Business Enterprise (Number of Employees)								
		0–4	5–19	20–49	50–99	Small (<100)	100–299	300–499	Medium (100–499)	Large (500+)
Percentage in goods-producing sector	28.9	20.8	22.4	26.7	29.5	24.7	36.3	40.4	37.4	30.8
Percentage in service-producing sector	71.1	79.2	77.6	73.3	70.5	75.3	63.7	59.6	62.6	69.2
Industry aggregate total	10,317,481	889,599	1,798,100	1,337,419	996,999	5,022,118	1,206,141	437,748	1,643,889	3,651,474

Source: Statistics Canada, *Survey of Employment, Payrolls and Hours (SEPH), March 2005*. Available at http://strategis.ic.gc.ca/epic/internet/insbrp-rppe.nsf/en/rd01229e.html (accessed June 2006).

Hundreds of research studies have attempted to determine the common skills, personality, and behavioural traits of successful entrepreneurs. The simple deduction from all this research is that entrepreneurs cannot be cloned. They tend to defy stereotyping and broad-brush labelling. "I have seen people of the most diverse personalities and temperaments perform well in entrepreneurial challenges," concludes business guru Peter Drucker.[6]

Nevertheless, if generalizations must be made, we can say that most of our entrepreneurs possess the following characteristics:[7]

- **Passion.** Entrepreneurs are driven by a compelling vision.
- **Persistence.** Entrepreneurs don't give up easily when things look bleak.
- **Opportunity seeking.** Entrepreneurs are idea generators with a great capacity to dream up and carry out projects. They see problems as opportunities for creative solutions.
- **Vision.** Successful entrepreneurs have learned to visualize. They have a complete mental picture of where they and their ideas are going.
- **Goals.** Entrepreneurs set short- and long-term goals and are committed to meeting objectives.
- **Independence.** Entrepreneurs have a need for freedom—a need to control their destiny and "be their own boss."
- **Idea generators.**
- **People orientation.** Entrepreneurs are not loners. They have to like people—after all, people are what drive business.
- **Desire to share.** As old-fashioned as it sounds, entrepreneurs believe in sharing.
- **Ability to get things done.** Entrepreneurs are doers and invariably identify their primary motivations as "seeing a need and acting on it."
- **Willingness to take moderate risks.** Successful business entrepreneurs are moderate risk takers. They gather as much information and support as possible before making a move. In this way, they build a safety net and decrease the amount of risk involved.

In a groundbreaking PROFIT 100 study of successful Canadian business entrepreneurs, Rick Spence, editor of *PROFIT* magazine, concluded that most of the above entrepreneurial traits represent behavioural characteristics "that can be learned, as opposed to inherited abilities (an affinity for math, say, or an outgoing personality) that confer ongoing advantages on just a lucky few."[8] A recent study and extensive survey by the CFIB came to the same conclusion—entrepreneurship styles are more learned than innate." [9] According to these two studies of successful growth firms, most entrepreneurs are *made*, not born. This is good news for the thousands of Canadians who don't think they have the innate abilities to start up on their own.

REV UP

"If life is a tree, find the passion to play on the ends of the branches and beyond. That's our passion. It has kept my husband and me going and made us successful." So says Adrienne Armstrong, owner of Arbour Environmental Shoppe, a small business in Ottawa, Ontario, that just keeps on growing.

Armstrong's business goal is to help others respect the earth with planet-friendly products—an idea that took shape in the late 1980s. "While studying in France, I saw many small stationery stores selling recycled paper. These were little stores with pride and strong ties to the environment. I felt at home in these businesses. Even back then, I knew where I belonged and what I wanted to do. I kept a diary. I called it my **24/7 Adventure Notebook.** I would wake up at night and mind-map

24/7 ADVENTURE NOTEBOOK

A storage place in which to organize your personal and business ideas

my ideas like crazy. I remember writing letters to a friend—now my husband and business partner—Sean. The idea of protecting the environment consumed me, and I could not wait to get started. Fortunately, I married a man who shared this same vision."

Adrienne and Sean spent months writing and fine-tuning their business plan. "That was our first 'road map,' and we wanted to get it right," she recalls. "Today our plan has become fluid, almost alive. Every three months we revisit it. If we are on target, we celebrate. If we are drifting off course, we get to work and correct it. Over the years our first plan has changed gradually as we discovered new opportunities, grew our business, and moved toward our planet-friendly vision."

Today, Arbour Environmental Shoppe is a successful retail outlet boasting a host of environmental and community service awards. "I'm very proud of these awards," says Adrienne Armstrong. "They remind all of us at Arbour Environmental Shoppe that we are making a difference…We display all our achievements behind the cash desk for everyone to see. We call this our 'Eco Wall of Fame.'"[10]

If you're thinking about owning a business like Adrienne Armstrong does, come along with us! We'll help you accomplish your vision by showing you how to build a road map. But to decide which road to take, you're going to have to do some research and define your personal goals.

You can start the process by getting organized. Some people believe that getting organized stifles creativity. "No way," says Adrienne Armstrong. "My *24/7 Adventure Notebook* was and still is the place where I can organize and channel my thoughts and get creative. As a matter of fact, I woke up one night thinking 'Why are we not on the Web?' In my New Ideas section, I started scribbling down all the things I'd need to do. It took a while since that night. I even had to take a course at a local college. But we did it. Arbour Environmental Shoppe is now on the Web (http://www.arbourshop.com). E-commerce has given our small business tremendous global exposure and has resulted in new sales. Just over 20 percent of our retail sales are Internet generated."

Now it's your turn to get organized and start your creative juices flowing by completing Action Step 1.

WHY DO YOU WANT TO BE AN ENTREPRENEUR?

After racing for Canada in the Summer Olympics and winning 150 times worldwide, cyclist Louis Garneau realized it was time to do something else. He still had a passion for cycling, and so, using his experience in sports and interest in art as a basis, he started his own company.

As with most start-ups, the launch was modest. Garneau began with a sole proprietorship, working out of his father's garage. When the time was right, he moved out of the garage and incorporated. Today, the Louis Garneau Group (http://www.louisgarneau.com) is a multimillion-dollar company with six factories and more than 400 employees.[11]

Self-employment allowed Louis Garneau the freedom to pursue his interest in art and cycling. For Adrienne Armstrong, becoming a "planet friendly" entrepreneur was a lifelong dream. Chris Griffiths, in the opening vignette, wanted to pursue his passion to make a better guitar. According to a CIBC survey, most small business owners (about 60%) consider themselves "lifestylers," whose primary reason for "opening up shop" was to do something they loved.[12] They value their independence and choose the small business career path to pursue their passion and interests—be it building bicycles, saving the planet, or manufacturing a better guitar.

ACTION STEP 1

Compile your 24/7 Adventure Notebook

If you're a typical aspiring entrepreneur, you probably write 90 percent of your important data on the back of an envelope. That might have been OK in the past, but now that you're doing this for real, get yourself some kind of container (a shoebox, briefcase, or folder) to put those envelopes in. Even better, compile a **24/7 Adventure Notebook**, ideally using something with pockets so that you can keep track of small items, such as brochures. Some of you might wish to use a notebook computer or a personal digital assistant (PDA) to organize data.

Your 24/7 Adventure Notebook should include

- a 12-month calendar;
- an appointment calendar;
- a priority list of things you need to do;
- your name, phone number, and e-mail address (at the front, in case you leave it somewhere);
- a New Ideas section (continue to add ideas to this section throughout your search);
- a mind map section to help you picture new opportunities;
- a "new-eyes" list for keeping track of successful—and not-so-successful—businesses you come across, plus notes about the reasons for their success or failure;
- a list of possible team members (Who impresses you and why? What are their key attributes?);
- a list of possible experts to serve as resource people when you need them, such as a lawyer, an accountant, some bankers, and successful businesspeople;
- articles and statistics that serve as supportive data;
- a Bookmark This list of helpful Web sites; and
- a list of potential customers.

ACTION STEP 2

Find out why you want to be an entrepreneur

In your 24/7 Adventure Notebook, list all of your reasons for wanting to become an entrepreneur. Think about your personal and professional lifestyle, as well as your social, spiritual, financial, and ego needs.

Now prioritize the items on your list. Spend a few minutes right away, and many more hours in the next few months, reviewing how several businesses would fit into your prioritized list. What fits? What doesn't? If you have a job, review your current situation. Is your job secure? Are you happy and/or excited about going to work each day? Is there something else you'd rather be doing? If you didn't need the money, would you quit your job? As you explore various businesses, use these lists and questions to determine whether your selected business ideas meet your entrepreneurial focus and passion.

Next, list all of your reasons for not wanting to become an entrepreneur—your roadblocks. Review the list and think about what you can do to minimize these obstacles. When you honestly review the advantages and disadvantages of being an entrepreneur, you'll discover they are the flip side of each other. For example, many people want to become entrepreneurs in order to be their own boss, only to discover that they will have many bosses—customers, suppliers, and investors! Be as realistic as possible as you refine these lists during your exploration of different businesses.

However, there might be all kinds of other motivations for taking the entrepreneurial plunge. Some of you will choose to become an entrepreneur because you want the potential to earn a huge income, build a legacy, or experience the thrill of developing an innovative service or product. We want you to begin thinking about your entrepreneurial motives. Completing Action Step 2 will help you do this.

WHAT DOES IT TAKE TO BE AN ENTREPRENEUR?

As we found out earlier, entrepreneurs cannot be cloned or replicated. Even so, certain characteristics are associated with entrepreneurial success. Action Step 3 (see page 12) will help you discover if you have what it takes to make it in small business. Remember, though, entrepreneurs are made, not born, so if you find that you are lacking in the skills department, you can always make a plan to learn and get more experience.

To discover more about your personality profile, complete the short questionnaire in the E-Exercise, Box 1.2. As you work your way through these exercises, remember that you won't be a perfect entrepreneurial (or "E") fit, because there's no such thing.

What did you learn about yourself? File the results of this E-Exercise in your 24/7 Adventure Notebook. Now, armed with this self-knowledge, you are ready to try your hand at Action Step 4 (see page 13).

Box 1.2 E-Exercise

Do you have a "Type-Entrepreneurial" personality?

If you're thinking about starting a business, online self-assessments are a great place to test your entrepreneurial quotient. To learn more about yourself, check out the following Web pages.

- **Take a self-employment quiz** (Service Canada): http://www.jobsetc.ca/content_pieces.jsp?category_id=371&lang=e—Two online quizzes that can help you assess whether your skills and traits are those that are needed to achieve success.

  1. *Do you have what it takes to be an entrepreneur?*
     A 25-question quiz provides an answer to this question.
  2. *Am I an entrepreneur?*
     A 75-question quiz allows you to take an in-depth look at personal areas such as achievement drive, adaptability, decisiveness, social skills, and intuition.

- **Entrepreneurial self-assessment** (Business Development Bank of Canada [BDC]): http://www.bdc.ca/en/business_tools/entrepreneurial_self-Assessment/selfassessment.htm?iNoC=1—A 50-question "yes or no" assessment will help you learn more about your personal background, behaviour patterns, and lifestyle factors.

- **Are you the entrepreneurial type?** (BDC): http://www.bdc.ca/en/business_tools/entrepreneurial_self-Assessment/Entrepreneurial_self_assessment.htm—This self-assessment will help you measure your entrepreneurial potential. It includes 50 statements and will take about 15 minutes to complete.

- **Self-assessment** (Canadian Foundation for Economic Education): http://www.mvp.cfee.org/en/—Three online assessments help you to find out how you measure up and to learn where you have to improve and how you can build on your strengths.

- **Replacement Business Start-up Quiz:** http://www.yesmontreal.ca/yes.php?section=entrepreneurship/quiz

Are you ready for self-employment? Take the Youth Employment Services interactive entrepreneurship quiz to find out! Answer the questions honestly, then click **How'd I Do?** to find out whether you're ready to become an entrepreneur.

- **Take the TypeE Quiz:** http://www.typeepersonality.com/typeequiz.htm—Alex Giorgio is a practicing psychotherapist and CEO/Founder of The Giorgio Group, Inc. According to Giorgio, "TypeEs who are out of balance in their lives are often mislabelled as having a Type 'A' personality." Do you have a Type "E" personality? Take this simple 10-question assessment and find out.

WHAT IS AN INTRAPRENEUR?

Let's assume that you've just graduated. You decide to put your plans for a small business on hold for a while and find employment with a large national firm. Better still, let's suppose you start your own business and your entrepreneurial venture takes off. A few years down the road, you find yourself heading up a 300-employee multinational firm. By now, your business has become established, and the growth rate starts to level off a little. For either of these situations, does that mean you are no longer an entrepreneur? Not at all. We are now fully entrenched in a "change" economy. To grow and compete, you are still going to have to foster entrepreneurship in a larger company—whether you own it or work for it. This process of making change in a large company is called intrapreneurship.

Intrapreneurs are agents of change who own or work in medium-sized or large organizations. The skills intrapreneurs must acquire are a little different from entrepreneurial skills, but the prime objective stays the same. The main objective of an intrapreneur, as a corporate agent of change, is to take a new idea and translate it into a profitable product or service. Managing and stimulating people to make change will be one of your major preoccupations. Here's a brief list of the sorts of things you'll be doing in your new intrapreneurial role:

INTRAPRENEURS

Agents of change who own or work in medium-sized or large organizations

1. encouraging and rewarding individual and team risk taking,
2. looking for opportunities arising out of failure,
3. disseminating to everyone the vision and goals of company,
4. rewarding employees who make changes,
5. encourage brainstorming and new idea generation,
6. empowering teams to make decisions and rewarding them when they do.
7. encouraging teams to take ownership and work together as their own small business,
8. encouraging employees to set goals and share their vision of company's future,
9. encouraging employees to take ownership of their ideas, and
10. openly encouraging innovation and news ideas.

"INC." YOURSELF

So far, you have explored why you want to be an entrepreneur. You've reviewed your skills, accomplishments, and passions. It's now time to think about what success means to you. Think of yourself as a product you want to create. To help you think of yourself as a business—to "Inc." yourself, figuratively speaking— we are going to introduce you to a technique called mind mapping. A **mind map**—also known as a spoke diagram, a thought web, or a clustering diagram—

MIND MAP

An idea-generating sketch—also known as a spoke diagram, a thought web, or a cluster diagram—that features circled words connected by lines to form units

ACTION STEP 3

Assess your interest and abilities

Do you have what it takes to make it in small business? To find out, profile yourself as an entrepreneur. You won't be a perfect fit—no entrepreneur is. Nonetheless, you will get much more out of this book if you can picture yourself in the role of a successful entrepreneur. Keep your mind open and your pencil sharp. Opportunities are unlimited.

- How would your best friend describe you?
- How would your worst enemy describe you?
- How would you describe yourself?
- How much money do you need to survive for six months? For a year?
- How much money can you earn in your present position in three years? Five years?
- What is the maximum potential of your earning power?
- Are you comfortable taking moderate risks?
- Are you constantly looking for newer and better ways to do things?
- What can you do better than most people?
- Where do you live now? (Describe your home, residential area, geographical area, amenities, etc.)
- What changes would you like to make to any of the above?
- Do you enjoy being in control?
- How do you spend your leisure time?
- Do you look forward more often than backward?
- How important is winning to you?
- Do you know anyone whose strengths complement some of your weaknesses?

This Action Step will help you assess your abilities and interests, and get your creative juices flowing. Make sure you file this information in your 24/7 Adventure Notebook. You will probably come back to this step several times.

is a sketch that features circled words connected by lines to form units. Mind mapping is a form of doodling, only it has a purpose—to generate ideas. It works like this:

1. In the centre of a page, you write your main theme (e.g., your vision or goal), then draw a circle around the word.
2. Every time you get an idea related to your main theme, you write it down, circle it, and draw a line connecting it to the theme.
3. You keep adding new ideas to your mind map. Before you know it, you have a gigantic spider web or idea tree full of opportunities.

Most entrepreneurs do mind mapping naturally. Entrepreneurs are visionaries, and mind maps help them picture what they want to become. A mind map that might have been devised by Adrienne Armstrong, owner of Arbour Environmental, is presented in Figure 1.2. To create your own mind map, along with a success checklist, go to Action Step 5. Once you have completed the first five Action Steps, you will be ready to enter the small business arena of entrepreneurism—the engine of our economy.

WHAT IS A SMALL BUSINESS?

If entrepreneurs are the fuel or driving force of the third millennium, **small business** is the engine. About 15 percent of our labour force is self-employed—that is, they earn an income directly from their own business as opposed to a salary or wage from an employer (See Table 1.1). According to Statistics Canada, about 135,000 new corporations are established each year.[13] As shown in Table 1.2, there are about a million employer businesses in Canada; about 55 percent of these firms have 1 to 4 employees, and most of these small businesses provide services. For example, the service-producing sector houses almost 80 percent of all micro businesses (see Table 1.2).

So exactly what is a small business? Do you define a business as small by the number of employees? Are small businesses those that are run by people classified as "self-employed"? Strange as it might seem, there is no standard Canadian definition. Most Canadian institutions define small businesses in terms of their particular needs, such as financing or exporting. Here are four interpretations.[14]

- According to Industry Canada, a small business is any firm with fewer than 100 paid employees in the goods-producing or manufacturing sector and fewer than 50 paid employees in service-producing firms.
- The Canadian Bankers' Association classifies a business as "small" if it qualifies for a loan authorization of less than $250,000.
- The Small Business Loan Act, one federal government small business program, defines an eligible small business as one that has annual revenue of less than $5 million.
- The Export Development Corporation defines small businesses or "emerging exporters" as firms with export sales under $1 million.

Over the past few years, we have begun hearing about so-called **micro businesses** and **SMEs (small and medium-sized enterprises)**. According to Industry Canada, micro enterprises are most often defined as businesses with fewer than 5 employees, and the term SME normally refers to businesses with fewer than 500 employees. Firms with 500 or more employees are classified as "large" businesses.

As for defining small business, we tend to like the rather open definition provided by the Canadian Federation of Independent Business, which describes a small business as "a firm that is independently owned and operated and is not

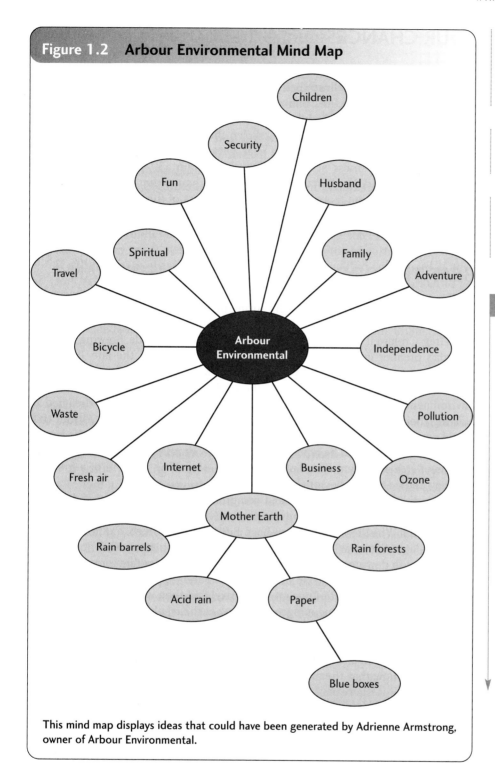

Figure 1.2   Arbour Environmental Mind Map

This mind map displays ideas that could have been generated by Adrienne Armstrong, owner of Arbour Environmental.

SMALL BUSINESS

Any venture with spirit, any business you want to start, or any idea you want to bring into the marketplace

MICRO BUSINESS

Usually refers to a businesses with one to four employees

SME (SMALL AND MEDIUM-SIZED ENTERPRISE)

Normally refers to a businesses with fewer than 500 employees

ACTION STEP 4

Expand your self-assessment

Use your information from Action Steps 2 and 3, and Boxes 1.2 and 1.3, to build on your self-assessment by compiling a list of

- things you love to do,
- skills you have acquired through the years,
- things you are good at,
- the times you were happiest in your life,
- your achievements and failures,
- your passions, and
- your past dreams and dreams for the future.

In Action Step 5, you will be pulling together all your information. Keep your answers in a "Me" section of your 24/7 Adventure Notebook. Add new information whenever it occurs to you, and continue to refine your answers as you work on your business plan.

dominant in its field of endeavour." A typical small business owner, according to this description, would employ anywhere from 1 to 20 employees. This represents at least 85 percent of all businesses in Canada today (see Table 1.2).

The small business we are talking about in this book is any venture with spirit, any business you want to start, or any idea you want to bring into the marketplace. It might be part-time, something you do at home, something you try alone, or something you need a team for. The ideas for a small business are almost limitless.

ACTION STEP 7

Take your "new eyes" into the marketplace

Your community and workplace are your marketing labs. It's time for you to open your mind to all of the information around you. Time to head out!

First stop (large bookstore with lots of magazines): Select and read five distinctly different magazines that you've never read before. What did you learn? Did you read about a target market that you didn't know existed? Next, review the top 10 best-sellers: fiction, nonfiction, children's, trade, and paper-backs. What do they tell you about your current world? Any new genres?

Second stop (music store): What's hot? What's not? Are there any new music styles?

Third stop (local mall): What new stores are opening? Which department store has the best service? Highest prices? Best selection? Which restaurants are hot? Where are the longest lines?

Fourth stop (your favourite store): Compile a list of the products and services that weren't there a year ago (if you are visiting a computer store, shorten the time to 3 or 6 months). Can you guesstimate shelf velocity? What's hot?

Fifth stop (television time): Spend an hour watching *CNN World Report*. Make a list of the stories. Did any surprise you? Are there any opportunities?

Final stop (log on): Surf the Internet for at least two to four hours on topics you know nothing about.

Your brain should now be in high gear—and suffering from information overload! Use this information as you continue to explore opportunities.

Cohen, who found a niche in the travel business. Her idea germinated from a great deal of soul-searching and reading *Equinox*. The point is, keep reading with your new eyes. Look for articles on new trends, new ideas, and new opportunities.

Trade Journals

These are a valuable source once you know what industry and business you're in. Use your new business letterhead to write to trade associations. You can find these listed at your local library. You might also want to try, for example, *Associations Canada*, the *Encyclopedia of Associations*, or the *Gale Directory of Publications and Broadcast Media*, also available at most libraries.

Banks

Banks are in the business of lending money. Banks have economists, marketing experts, and individuals who evaluate, research, and write forecasts and reports about economic trends. Ask to see those reports. Most major banks also have a number of publications and brochures on starting and operating a small business.

Planning Offices

Cities and regional municipalities employ planners to chart the future and plan for growth. Check the city and regional offices listings in the phone book to find out where these offices are. Ask for a copy of the profile on your city. For the best service, however, you'll need to visit the office, make friends with the staff, and be pleasant and patient.

Reports from Colleges, Universities, and Investment Firms

Many colleges and universities publish annual and semiannual reports on economic conditions in the province. You can probably get copies of these by writing to the university public relations office. Reports are also published by private institutions of higher learning with special interests in business.

Real Estate Firms

Large commercial and industrial real estate firms have access to developers' site research. The more specific you can be on what you want to know, the easier it will be for them to help you. Familiarize yourself with the dynamics of the area. What firms are going into business? What firms are leaving business? (For more details on this, see Chapter 7.) Realtors can also supply you with a listing of rental space in your community.

The Business Development Bank of Canada (BDC)

The BDC publishes all kinds of materials of interest to small business. It also provides a wide range of financial alternatives (see Chapter 10) and sponsors numerous seminars on small business. For information, call or visit your nearest BDC office. You can also write to Business Development Bank, 5, Place Ville-Marie, Suite 400, Montreal, QC, H3B 5E7; or visit the BDC Web site (http://www.bdc.ca).

Industry Canada

Industry Canada (http://www.ic.gc.ca) has specific federal responsibilities in the area of small business. The Canada Business Service Centres of Industry Canada should be one of your first stops for small business information. There are 11 CBSCs—one located in each province and the Northwest Territories. Key activities of each centre include toll-free telephone help; CBSC Web sites (see discussion below); CBSC resources and information, with in-person service, directories, publications, and access to external databases; a toll-free, fax on-demand service; and *Pathfinders*—brochures organized by topic, with overviews of services and programs.

Statistics Canada

Statistics Canada (http://www.statcan.ca) produces a large volume and variety of statistics that are available to all Canadians. For most subjects, Statistics Canada will probably be one of your major sources of secondary information. How reliable is this information? *The Economist* asked a panel of experts from various countries to rank statistical agencies. All agreed that Canada has the best statistics in the world. Yes, our number crunchers were ranked number one.

If you haven't used Statistics Canada before, you might find it a little overwhelming. Our advice is to persist—it's well worth the effort. You might want to start with its Catalogue No. 11-204, which provides a guide listing more than 1,000 reports and documents, as well as numerous electronic databases. It's even available on CD-ROM. Their annual publication *Market Research Handbook* (Catalogue No. 63-224) is also a useful starting place. In Chapter 7, we will introduce you to Census of Population data.

Internet Sources and Computer Databases

In the past few years, the Internet has become a predominant source of secondary business information. There are hundreds of Web sites that can help you start and run your business. Here are some major sites.

- **Strategis:** http://strategis.ic.gc.ca—Industry Canada, in partnership with the business community and universities, has created the largest, most comprehensive business information Web site in Canada. It contains more than 75,000 reports, 600,000 pages of text, and two gigabytes of statistical data. You can also get updated information ranging from business diagnostic and benchmarking data to all of the government forms you need to incorporate.
- **Canadian Company Capabilities:** http://strategis.ic.gc.ca/sc_coinf/ccc/ engdoc/homepage.html—This database of more than 50,000 Canadian company profiles allows you to search for a firm by product, geography, or activity. You can also register your company and promote your products or services worldwide in cyberspace.
- **Online Small Business Workshop:** http://www.cbsc.org/osbw/workshop .html—This online site covers all the basics in "how-to," from fashioning the initial product idea to marketing, research, sales forecasting, financing, planning, and everything in between.
- **Contact! The Canadian Management Network:** http://strategis.ic.gc.ca/SSG/ me00062e.html—This is the primary Canadian source on the Internet for business management information and advice. It gives access to a full range of small business support organizations in Canada and provides a wide range of educational materials and tools to help entrepreneurs start a business.

ACTION STEP 8

Begin your industry research

1. To locate the names of trade associations in your area of interest, consult the *Gale Encyclopedia of Business and Professional Associations* or *Associations Canada*, or visit Associations Canada online: http://www.micromedia.ca/Directories/Associations.htm

   • Make note of the associations, addresses, phone numbers, and Web sites.

   Contact the associations that interest you and request information and membership details. Mention that you are a student—they might surprise you by providing you with information that you hadn't thought to ask for.

   You can go further on this assignment by contacting associations that your potential suppliers and customers might belong to.

2. Locate a chapter of a national association and attend a meeting as a guest.

3. Visit your local resource centre or link on to online sources such as http://magazinescanada.ca or JournalismNet (www.journalismnet.com/mags/canada.htm)

   • Locate magazines or journals that are associated with your selected industry,

   • reach your potential customers, and

   • are directed at your suppliers.

   • Spend some time on the Net or at the library researching your list and delving deeper into the information.

4. After completing your industry research, select at least one magazine or journal from each of the categories and request a media kit. The kits will help you fine-tune your research.

• **Canadian Technology Network:** http://ctn-rct.nrc-cnrc.gc.ca/—Here is a site that helps Canadian businesses find technological assistance. Advisers work with individual entrepreneurs to identify needs and to find the right source of assistance for almost every technology imaginable.

• **Business Development Bank of Canada (BDC):** http://www.bdc.ca—According to the BDC, this is a cyber-destination that small and medium-sized Canadian businesses can call their own. The Web site includes more than 300 hyperlinks to small business resources, coast to coast.

Following are some other secondary research online sources.

• **Associations Canada:** http://www.micromedia.ca/Directories/Associations.htm

• **ACNielsen Canada** (tracks retail store sales movement to consumers): http://www.acnielsen.ca

• **Canadian Innovation:** http://www.innovationcentre.ca

Here are some online government databases.

• **Canadian Company Capabilities:** http://strategis.ic.gc.ca/sc_coinf/ccc/engdoc/homepage.html

• **Federal Corporations Data Online:** http://strategis.ic.gc.ca/cgi-bin/sc_mrksv/corpdir/dataOnline/search.cgi?lang=e

• **Strategis, Business Information by Sector:** http://strategis.ic.gc.ca/sc_indps/engdoc/homepage.html?categories=e_bis

• **Strategis, Canadian Industry Statistics:** http://strategis.ic.gc.ca/sc_ecnmy/sio/homepage.html

• **Trade Data Online:** http://strategis.ic.gc.ca/sc_mrkti/tdst/engdoc/tr_homep.html

• **Canadian Importer's Database:** http://strategis.ic.gc.ca/sc_mrkti/cid/engdoc/

• **Statistics Canada, Merchandise Trade Database:** http://www.statcan.ca/trade/scripts/trade_search.cgi

Now is a good time to start researching your chosen industry. Complete Action Step 8.

In a Nutshell

It is the age of the entrepreneur. Small business owners are the fuel of our private enterprise system. Our goal in this book is to encourage you to join the ranks of some two million self-employed Canadians. To begin, we asked you to get organized by creating a 24/7 Adventure Notebook. Next, we advised you to test your entrepreneurial quotient. To help you find out if you are prepared to live the life of an entrepreneur, we encouraged you to take a good hard look at your dreams and passions, your interests and abilities, your strengths and weaknesses. Ultimately, we want you to think of yourself as a future product—that is, to "Inc." yourself.

If you take the entrepreneurial highway, there can be wonderful personal and financial rewards. But you'll also pay a price. You'll work long hours and run into your share of disappointments. Are you prepared to take this roller coaster ride? Or do you need a 9-to-5 job and some semblance of security? We'll help you come to grips with these types of questions.

If you decide that becoming a small business entrepreneur is the right option for you, you'll need to develop a business plan that is backed up by primary, secondary, and new-eyes research. Your success as an entrepreneur cannot be guaranteed, but a business plan will improve your chances of success. This book will provide you with a business plan road map and the ideas and tools to succeed...but the research and the challenge are yours!

Key Terms

24/7 Adventure Notebook

business plan

entrepreneurs (small business)

intrapreneurs

intrapreneuring

micro business

mind map

new-eyes research

primary research

secondary research

shelf velocity

small business

SMEs

target customers

Think Points for Success

✓ Change is accelerating everywhere, and that includes the world of business. Change creates problems. Problems are opportunities for entrepreneurs.

✓ To find the doorway into your own business, gather data and keep asking questions.

✓ Be creative on paper, organize your ideas, test your assumptions, and develop your business plan for the marketplace. Create and maintain a 24/7 Adventure Notebook. Mind-map. Confirm your venture with numbers and words before you enter the arena.

✓ Even though you might not be in business yet, you can intensify your focus by writing down your thoughts about the business you think you want to try. Stay flexible.

✓ Be clear on who you are and what you want to become.

✓ Develop a business plan.

✓ Do your primary and "new-eyes" research. Get out and talk to people. That's the way most entrepreneurs learn.

✓ Do your secondary research.

✓ Always be on the lookout for opportunities.

✓ Above all, follow your passions.

Business Plan Building Block

WHERE AM I NOW?

From the point of view of the potential readers of your business plan (bankers, loan officers, rich relatives, close friends with money, venture capital professionals), the most important part of the plan is you, the entrepreneur who wrote the plan.

Your goal, from the very first sentence on the very first page, is to inspire confidence. Before you write your business plan, study how you look from some of your old résumés. What picture do the résumés present? Who are you? Where have you been?

The résumé work is for your eyes only. Jot notes to yourself about strengths and weaknesses. To trigger your brain to perform this task, review the seven Action Steps in this chapter as you search for ways to transfer your skills and aptitudes to an entrepreneurial situation. If you already have a business up and running, use this same start-up energy to improve it.

No one is perfect. Recognize your shortcomings and make a list of people who have talents that you might lack. It's never too early to think about team building. With hard work and an honest look at your personal skills picture, you'll be able to fine-tune this information when you showcase your founding team in your final business plan.

WHERE AM I GOING?

Now that you've looked at the past and the present, think about where you are going. How do you see yourself in the future? How do you want to be known? Take a closer look at your personal goals. What are your likes and dislikes? Are you passionate about what you want to do? Are you ready to put in the long hours?

Checklist Questions and Actions to Develop Your Business Plan

Your Great Adventure—Exploring Your Options
Ask yourself...

❏ Am I organized? Do I have a central deposit for all my ideas?

❏ Do I have what it takes to be an entrepreneur?

❏ Have I assessed my interests, abilities, and weaknesses as they relate to owning a business?

❏ Have I assessed my past accomplishments and shortcomings?

❏ Do I have a list and a plan of new skills that I will have to work on?

❏ Is my family or those I live with "on board"?

❏ Am I prepared to take the time and do the necessary research before writing a business plan?

❏ Have I interviewed entrepreneurs to see what it is really like to be in business for myself?

❏ Do I have any business ideas that I am passionate about?

Case Study

We want you to go back and quickly reread the Chris Griffiths story in the opening vignette. Chris Griffiths was a successful entrepreneur who had POP—he was passionate, opportunity seeking, and persistent. Chris recognized a market need, satisfied it, and translated it into a financial benefit.

We can all learn from Chris Griffiths's successful entrepreneurial experience. Now we want you to dig a little deeper and link onto the following Web sites.
- Innovation in Canada: Garrison Guitars case profile:
  http://innovation.ic.gc.ca/gol/innovation/site.nsf/en/in04209.html
- Innovation in Canada, The Practice of Innovation Facilitator's Guide, Module 4:
  http://innovation.ic.gc.ca/gol/innovation/site.nsf/en/in04194.html
- Web cast video profile of Garrison Guitars, based on interviews with principals of the company: http://innovation.ic.gc.ca/gol/innovation/site.nsf/en/in04697.html
- Garrison Guitar: http://www.garrisonguitars.com
- Fast Company's profile of Chris Griffiths:
  http://www.fastcompany.com/fast50_05/profile/?griffiths219

We suggest you bookmark these sites. You'll need them again when we continue with this case in Chapter 2.

Case Questions

1. Mind mapping

   Mind mapping is a great way to get and record ideas. Many entrepreneurs like Adrienne Armstrong of Arbour Environmental (Figure 1.2) do mind mapping naturally. They are visionaries, and they think in pictures. But mind mapping is an entrepreneurial skill that can also be learned. In Action Step 5, we encouraged you to do a mind map of your future, or "what you want to become." We now want you to hone this skill further. View the Garrison Guitar case. Then click on to the other sites provided above. Why was Chris Griffiths so successful? Mind-map your reasons.

2. Entrepreneurial and intrapreneurial skills

Many people have an idea for an invention, but it never sees the light of day. Why is that? As we learn from this case, inventing a product and bringing it to market can be a risky and lengthy undertaking requiring entrepreneurial and, eventually, intrapreneurial skills.

What entrepreneurial skills and personality traits helped Chris Garrison launch his successful invention? To refresh your memory about entrepreneurial skills and personalities, you might want to go back to the section in the textbook (page 3) entitled "The Age of the Entrepreneur" or link on to the CFIB report at http://www.cfib.ca/research/reports/rr3000.pdf.

As the company grew, Chris began to take on more of an intrapreneurial role. Briefly describe the meaning of the term *intrapreneur* and explain how Chris used his intrapreneurial skills in the production phase.

3. Roadblocks

Along the way to success, Chris Griffiths was challenged with many barriers. Briefly describe how he overcame three major roadblocks.

4. Entrepreneurs are not loners

As we learned in this chapter, entrepreneurs are not loners. They constantly learn and get help from others. Briefly explain the help that Chris Griffiths received from various people and organizations along the way.

5. Market research

Successful entrepreneurs need to carry out extensive and intensive market research, because research opens doors to knowledge and opportunities. Three approaches to research are primary, new-eyes, and secondary.

Briefly describe or explain these three types of research.

a. What is meant by the term "target customer"? Explain how Chris Griffiths used primary research to find his target customer and get the much-needed start-up capital.

b. New-eyes research played a major role in the Garrison Guitar success story. Give one example of how Chris Griffiths used this type of research.

6. Business plan

In this case study, start-up financing required a comprehensive business plan.

a. What is a business plan?

b. What is the purpose of a business plan?

c. When Chris Griffiths submitted the first draft of his business plan to the Genesis Centre, what was its response?

Notes*

1. Sources: Innovation in Canada, http://innovation.ic.gc.ca/gol/innovation/site.nsf/en/in04217.html and http://innovation.ic.gc.ca/gol/innovation/site.nsf/vDownload/Pra_Innov/$file/F694_IC_Case_Studies_E.pdf, and Garrison Home page, www.garrisonguitars.com/history.html.

2. Canadian Business Online, http://www.canadianbusiness.com/entrepreneur/index.jsp.

3. From CIBC, *For Love or Money? A Study of Entrepreneurship in Canada*, http://research.cibcwm.com/economic_public/download/sb-flom-10112005.pdf; and CIBC, *Women Entrepreneurs are Leading the Charge*, http://www.cibc.com/ca/pdf/women-entrepreneurs-en.pdf.

4. Corrine Pohlmann and Andreea Dulipovici, "Fostering Flexibility: Work and Family, *CFIB Research*, November 2004. Available at http://www.cfib.ca/research/reports/pdf/WFB_e.pdf.

5. See, for example, the CFIB *Study on Workplace Satisfaction in Private, Public Sectors*, http://www.cfib.ca/research/reports/aspects_e.asp; and Wells Fargo/Gallup *TITLE OF REPORT*, http://www.prnewswire.com/cgi-bin/stories.pl?ACCT=104&STORY=/www/story/08-09-2005/0004084922&EDATE=.

* All sites accessed July 4, 2006.

PACIFIC WESTERN

Back in the early 1990s, the Pacific Western Brewing Company closed its doors. This small brewery, located in Prince George, British Columbia, could not compete with the likes of Labatt and Molson. That's when Kazuko Komatsu, a seasoned businesswoman with 20 years of successful marketing, brewing, and exporting experience, came to the rescue. Kazuko bought the company and began by retraining the staff and improving the quality of the beer. By the mid-1990s, Pacific Western became the first brewery to achieve ISO 9002 certification from the International Standards Organization, the most respected quality assurance program in the world. Then, in the late 1990s, Pacific Western became the first Canadian brewery to produce a 100 percent certified organic beer.

Today, Pacific Western (http://www.pwbrewing.com/) produces 13 different types of beers to satisfy a diverse range of tastes, and exports to markets that include China, Taiwan, Argentina, Brazil, Russia, France, and the United States; its beer is the third most popular imported beer in Japan, behind the giant Budweiser and Heineken brands. Pacific Western adheres to a few carefully chosen guiding principles: quality of ownership, quality of product, and quality of service.[2]

Connie van Reenen of Labelle Florists saw the market opportunity for e-commerce in the floral business. Kazuko Komatsu found a way to capitalize on the market need for quality beer. Successful entrepreneurs like Connie and Kazuko recognize market trends and resulting opportunities. But remember: These two women not only recognize opportunities but also respond to them with passion and persistence. As we learned in Chapter 1, winners have POP—they're **P**assionate, **O**pportunity Seeking, and **P**ersistent.

Chapter 2 is designed to help you recognize emerging business trends and opportunities, so you can put your passion and persistence to work. We'll help you to brainstorm and to keep mind-mapping and researching your ideas. We'll encourage you always to be on the lookout for emerging trends in exporting, technology, the Internet, changing demographics, and consumer values. After we have persuaded you to be a trend spotter, we'll introduce you to the life cycle concept, segmentation, and gap analysis, all of which will help you to focus on specific industry opportunities. Then we'll encourage you to step back and refine your business idea.

RECOGNIZING OPPORTUNITIES

What are the best business ventures to pursue today? Where can you find a business that will really pay off? One that will make you rich? One that you will enjoy?

Only you can answer the question, because the best business for you is one that you enjoy. The best business for you uses those experiences, skills, and aptitudes that are unique to you—as we learned from the Chris Griffiths experience in the opening vignette of Chapter 1 and Connie van Reenen's new venture at the beginning of this chapter. The early Action Steps in this book are designed to help you discover what is unique about you. Who are you? What are your skills? What excites you? What do you already know that distinguishes you from others?

Let's back up and get the big picture. Before the Industrial Revolution, most people were self-employed. In this so-called agricultural or first wave, farmers and sheepherders were risk takers, because they had to be. There were few other options. The second wave, or the industrial age, began with the Industrial Revolution and was characterized by machine power and mass production.

We are now firmly entrenched in the so-called information wave. Some have termed these times the knowledge-based era. Others have even called this the mass customization era. We like to think about it as the entrepreneurial age. These times, to a large extent, are marked by the growth of a new craft economy distinguished by quality; small, customized quantities; technology; and service. As in the first wave, working from home has again become both popular and common, as we will see in the Tanya Shaw Weeks story, below, and again in Chapter 7.

The existence of the mega corporation in the new millennium should be considered not a threat to the small entrepreneur but an opportunity. Many large corporations outsource many of their products and services to small businesses. **Outsourcing** refers to the contracting of outside specialists to perform functions that are or could be performed by company employees. This outsourcing trend is going to continue in the years ahead. Large companies know that this is a more efficient and effective way to do business. And this spells opportunity for enterprising small business entrepreneurs who can latch onto this trend.

OUTSOURCING

Contracting outside specialists to perform functions that are or could be performed by company employees

Let's pause for a moment and see how Tanya Shaw Weeks, of Halifax, Nova Scotia, took advantage of the outsourcing trend.[3] Tanya's a classic serial entrepreneur with POP who always knew that she wanted to start her own fashion business. At age 14, she was already hand-sewing for her friends and earning a little spare cash. After graduating, she founded her first business, XZEL Designs, and began sewing clothes in the basement of her parents' home, before she moved the business into her own home. Eventually, Tanya moved XZEL Designs out of her house and into an industrial park and today is owner/partner in at least three interrelated businesses. Today Unique Solutions Design Limited (http://www.uniqueltd.com/main_company.html) is the parent company staffing 46 employees—about half of whom work out of their homes across Canada. Some work on a contract basis; others are full-time employees. In recent years, Tanya's business has gone high tech. The flagship product is the bodyskanner,™ which takes an accurate set of body measurements in less than a minute. It's like a dressing room in a store. The customer walks into a portable kiosk, and the scanner takes 40 body measurements using patented laser technology. Another major product is The Virtual You™—Web-based software for apparel retailers. The Virtual You™ allows customers to go to a Web site, create their own images on the screen, and then try on the clothes without leaving their computer.

When one of the largest sewing pattern companies in the world—Butterick® and McCall's®—wanted customized patterns for each customer, it partnered with Unique Solutions and outsourced the bodyskanner™ technology it needed. Unique Solutions became the customer service arm of Butterick® and McCall's®. It was a winning solution for everyone. In one fell swoop, Shaw Weeks aggressively tapped into the outsourcing trend and the massive U.S. market. With moves like this, it's no wonder that Tanya Shaw Weeks has won a number of national awards and is almost a legend in parts of Nova Scotia.

The exploding need for specialized products and services—from customized sewing patterns to flowers and beer—is mind boggling. You'll probably see as much change in the next 10 years as your parents have seen in their lifetime. Such change creates opportunities for fast, flexible, and focused firms like Unique Solutions. If you stay in touch with change and the exploding market niches that change creates, you will always see more opportunities than you can pursue.

To help jumpstart your mind, we want you to have fun and begin with some new-eyes research. It's a great way to find opportunities. Action Step 9 will help you get some new perspectives on change. As you work through this, and all our other Action Steps, we want you to allow yourself to dream. You might not open a

ACTION STEP 9

Travel back in time and observe a marketplace of the past

Place yourself in a time warp, and take a look at a marketplace of the past. What was selling 25 years ago? 50 years ago? 100 years ago?

To get this picture, look at old magazines, catalogues, movies, TV shows, high-school yearbooks, and family photographs. What do you see? Are all of the people dressed alike? Does everyone have the same smile, the same frown, the same serious look? How small is their world? How small is their horizon?

Study the advertisements in old magazines and newspapers and then

1. list the products that are still around today and
2. list the products that are no longer on the market.

Which list is longer? What does this tell you about the changing marketplace?

BRAINSTORMING

A free and open exchange of ideas

business immediately after reading this text or taking this class, but don't let this discourage you. By keeping an open mind and training your research skills, chances are, sometime down the road you will latch onto an incredible opportunity—like Connie van Reenen in the opening vignette and the many students who have worked their way through this text over the past 10 years.

Now we want to introduce you to brainstorming—a powerful entrepreneurial technique for discovering opportunities that are right for you.

BRAINSTORM YOUR WAY INTO SMALL BUSINESS

Pete and Geoff loved to snowboard. For seven years, they looked for opportunities to make a living from doing what they loved.

At a local college, Pete and Geoff discovered the technique of mind mapping—a method of note taking that involves using clusters and bubbles, letting the information float along its own course (see Chapter 1). They also learned a new technique called brainstorming—an open exchange of ideas. The goal of brainstorming is to come up with as many ideas as possible related to a specific topic.

Now it was time for them to put their brainstorming skills to practice and record their ideas in a mind map. They just knew they could brainstorm and mind-map their way into the snowboarding business!

Pete and Geoff gathered a few friends together, found a comfortable spot, and ordered some pizza. Soon, ideas began to flow. In the centre of a large sheet of paper, they wrote "snowboarding." In a bubble next to "snowboarding," they wrote "segments," which led to bubbles with the words "skateboarders," "teens," "families," and "adults." "This is fun," Pete said, as the momentum built up. "This smells like money and fun," Geoff added.

Pete, Geoff, and their friends kept on brainstorming, mind-mapping, and eating pizza until they developed an idea for their business: Snowboard Express, which would provide roundtrip weekend bus transportation to various mountain ski resorts from five local pickup points. Pete and Geoff's completed mind map is shown in Figure 2.1.

The point of this example is to show what can result from **brainstorming**—a free and open exchange of ideas. If you gather people around you with wit, spark, creativity, positive attitudes, and good business sense, the synergy will almost always surprise you and could lead to new ideas, company growth, expanded profits, or perhaps the information for a new industry. The possibilities are limitless, but the trick is to structure brainstorming sessions in a way that maximizes creativity. A few suggestions follow.

1. Pick a Saturday, Sunday, or other day when everyone has some free time.
2. Find a site where you'll have few interruptions.
3. Invite 10 to 15 people (some will drop out, and you want to allow for no-shows).
4. Schedule the starting time at 9:00 a.m., serve coffee and doughnuts, and really begin at 9:30.
5. Allow time for self-introduction. Tell participants not to be modest. They're getting together with winners. Have them talk in terms of accomplishments.

Here are some tips.

- Have everyone arrive with a potential business idea.
- Before the close of the first meeting, select one or two hot ideas (take a vote), and ask participants to prepare a one-page checklist summary and analysis of the ideas.

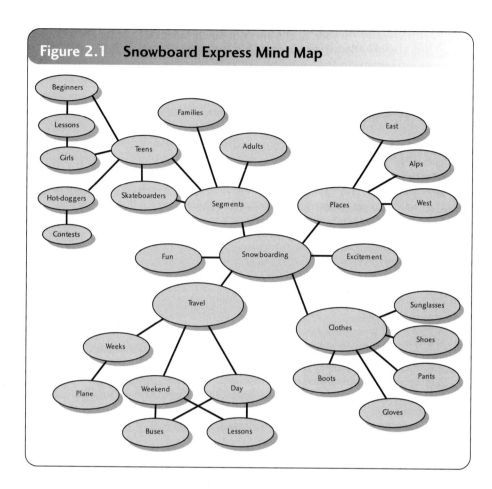

Figure 2.1   Snowboard Express Mind Map

- Get together again and brainstorm the hot ideas. Make it clear that the basic purpose is to spin ideas off one another, not to form a huge partnership.
- The best brainstorming sessions occur when you come brain-to-brain with other creative, positive people. Brain energy is real, and you need to keep tapping it.

Here are some things to remember when gathering participants and planning your meeting,

- Try to find imaginative people who can stretch their minds and who can set their competitive instincts aside for a while.
- Remember that in brainstorming sessions, there's a no-no on no's. You're not implementing yet, so don't let skepticism kill an idea.
- Find a neutral location.
- Try to focus on one problem or opportunity.
- Encourage the members of a group to reinforce and believe in one another.
- Use helpful equipment, such as an audio recorder and a flip chart. And don't forget to bring a supply of paper and pencils.

BE A TREND WATCHER

Industry or market trends reflect our economy's response to change. And change creates entrepreneurial opportunities. As an entrepreneur, you will want to make sure that your business serves a need. Knowledge of market trends will help you identify growth opportunities.

Major trends creating opportunities for enterprising entrepreneurs are shown in Box. 2.1. Even more trends are provided in the E-Exercise, Box 2.2. Five of the

ACTION STEP 10

Investigate the new technologies

If you're a tech expert, share your insights with others. Bring them up to speed! Technology affects every aspect of small business today—distribution, marketing, products, and so on. If you're not tech savvy, it's time to shift gears.

- **Do a Google™ search.** Start by entering the names of the industry gurus listed. See what they have to say about technology and the new economy.
- **Read magazines.** *Wired* (http://wired.com), either online or in hard copy, would be a good place to start. Read several copies of *The Futurist, Science,* or high-tech magazines in your selected industry. List all of the new, developing technologies. Can you spot any trends or opportunities?
- **Surf the Internet.** You might want to start with some of the secondary sources of information listed in the last section of Chapter 1. Visit your local resource centre or library, and find five articles on new technologies. Can you discover any trends developing? Future opportunities? Share your findings with others. A technological breakthrough in one industry will often lead to breakthroughs in other industries.
- **Link to the CATA*Alliance* Web site** (http://www.cata.ca). What does the Canadian Advanced Technology Alliance, "Canada's high-tech voice," have to say about emerging technologies and resulting opportunities?

With this information in hand, you will be better prepared to focus on the opportunities within these changing technologies.

E-COMMERCE

Any business function or business process performed over electronic networks

our "industry gurus." Read everything they have to write. These are people who make a business out of trend watching. Here's a short list to get you going.

- Don Tapscott: international authority, consultant, and speaker on business strategy and organizational transformation
- Nuala Beck: influential economist, researcher, author, and columnist
- Faith Popcorn: renowned consumer trend expert, industry advisor, and author
- Dr. David Foot: world-renowned demographics expert and professor of economics at the University of Toronto
- Martha Barletta: internationally recognized expert and consultant on successful marketing to women
- Watts Wacker: lecturer, best-selling author, political commentator, and social critic
- P. J. Wade: leading authority on retirement, housing, boomers, and the maturing marketplace

Action Step 10 asks you to do a "Google™ search" and explore new technologies in more depth.

INTERNET AND E-COMMERCE

Matthew von Teichman is a shrewd entrepreneurial twentysomething who knows that market trends create opportunities. Having successfully owned and operated several small businesses in the food service and home decor industries, in addition to working as a marketing consultant for a major Canadian winery, von Teichman, along with other visionary partners, turned his attention to the Internet and the online recruiting trend. His company, JobShark Corporation (http://www.jobshark.ca), was recognized by *PROFIT* magazine as one of the 50 fastest-growing Canadian companies. JobShark's rapid growth, from 6 to 75 employees, mirrors the explosive growth of the online recruiting industry, which is expected to grow by 300 percent to about $2 billion in 2005. Furthermore, JobShark has pursued the lucrative international market by expanding its operations to England, Ireland, Mexico, Chile, Argentina, Brazil, Peru, Colombia, Mexico, and Venezuela.[6]

The Internet is a ubiquitous part of Canadian life, business, and culture. It almost goes without saying that most Canadian households and business are now connected to the Net. As shown in Figures 2.2 and 2.3, almost 65 percent of Canadian households and 82 percent of private businesses are connected.

The question now facing the business community is, How do you profit from this connectivity? And this is a challenge. Most Canadian businesses, especially small enterprises, have been slow to use the Internet for online sales. Although Canadian households spend more than $3 billion online, only about 7 percent of Canadian businesses sell goods and services over the Net.

But the Internet can provide many more benefits than just online selling. It's more than a sales tool. Successful companies like JobShark, Webview 360, and Labelle Florists are launching **e-commerce** (or e-business) strategies. E-commerce is a catchall term that includes any business function or business process performed over electronic networks. In other words, suppliers, distributors, and customers use the Internet as the basis for their operations. E-commerce business functions would include[7]

- advertising, customer relationships, and after-sales service;
- managing supplies and internal operations;
- communication;

- payments and financial services;
- online collaboration; and
- receiving orders, distribution, and delivery.

E-commerce accounts for less than 1 percent of total operating revenues for private firms (2004). Clearly, the e-commerce trend is just beginning. We know the mega sites like eBay and Amazon will continue to grow. But there is a growing trend for small, successful niche firms like Webview 360 and Labelle Florists, operating on small budgets (for example, "Five E-Commerce Trends to Watch": http://www.ecommercetimes.com/story/16967.html). If you want your new business to be successful, you're going to have to start thinking about your e-commerce strategy. According to Industry Canada, your plan should be composed of five stages.

Stage 1: COMMUNICATING—E-mail and Internet Access

If your firm never goes any further than hooking up to the Internet, you will be well ahead of the game. Your staff will be able to communicate inexpensively and precisely with suppliers, customers, and others by e-mail while creating instant records of the exchanges.

Stage 2: PROMOTING—Create Your Own Web Site

Even at its most basic, the Web is like a 21st century Yellow Pages,™ used regularly by growing numbers of well-informed browsers with money to spend. Even if you don't take the next step and turn your Web site into an interactive forum or an order site, at the very least it can serve as a great place to strut your stuff.

Stage 3: LINKING INTERNALLY—Communicate Better within Your Firm

Using an intranet, you can improve company processes such as project management, payroll, human resources, purchase orders, and inventory. By sharing information, your team members can leverage one another's insights and efforts.

Stage 4: LINKING EXTERNALLY—Bring in Suppliers and Customers

The really exciting payoff comes when a business uses the Internet to link with suppliers and customers (extranet). The Internet can serve both as an inexpensive way to increase sales and a cost-effective way to link with suppliers. Firms that introduce internal systems that are open to suppliers and/or customers can orchestrate production and delivery to minimize delays, shrink inventories, and eliminate mistakes.

Stage 5: CREATING NEW BUSINESS MODELS—Share Resources and Risk with Virtual Business Partners

The Internet has the potential to act as a central nervous system coordinating the business activities of new types of corporate organisms. Imagine setting up an arrangement whereby sales information is shared instantaneously with wholesalers, shippers, manufacturers, designers, and even suppliers of raw material. Suddenly you have an integrated supply chain. Administrative responsibilities and even marketplace risks can be shared.[8]

Box 2.4 will help you learn more about e-commerce. At the very least, you're going to have to have an e-mail account and Internet access (Stage 1) before your start your business. But we also want you to begin thinking about building a Web site (Stage 2), which will allow you to sell your products over the Net. Fortunately, most college and university business programs include Web site development courses, so many of you have a head start.

Figure 2.2 Percent of Canadian Households with at Least One Regular Internet User

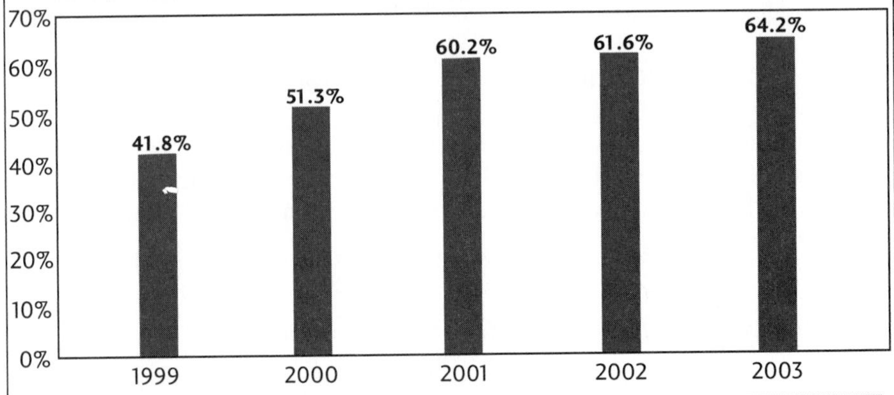

Source: Statistics Canada, *Highlights from the 2003 Household Internet Use Survey (HUIS)*: http://e-com.ic.gc.ca/epic/internet/inecic-ceac.nsf/en/gv00254e.html (accessed July 2006).

Figure 2.3 Some E-Commerce Facts

- Private businesses using the Internet—82% (2004)
- Private businesses that have a Web site—37% (2004)
- Private businesses using the Internet to purchase goods/services—43% (2004)
- Private businesses using the Internet to sell goods/services—7% (2004)
- Private business e-commerce sales—$28 billion (2004)
- E-commerce accounted for less than 1% of total operating revenues for private firms (2004)
- Household Internet spending—$3 billion (2003)

Sources: Industry Canada, *Highlights from the 2004 Survey of Electronic Commerce and Technology*: http://e-com.ic.gc.ca/epic/internet/inecic-ceac.nsf/en/gv00316e.html; *Canadian e-Commerce Statistics*: http://e-com.ic.gc.ca/epic/internet/inecic-ceac.nsf/en/gv00163e.html (accessed July 2006).

Box 2.4 E-Commerce Revolution

Begin learning more about e-commerce by checking out these sites.*

1. Take the interactive E-Commerce Quiz:
   http://strategis.ic.gc.ca/epic/internet/inecom-come.nsf/en/h_qy00034e.html
2. Building an Effective Website:
   http://www.e-future.ca/manitoba/en_CA/pdf/building_an_effective_website.pdf

3. Setting up an e-business—The Basics:
   http://www.cbsc.org/servlet/ContentServer?cid=1102698522519&pagename=OSBW%2FCBSC_WebPage%2FCBSC_WebPage_Temp&c=CBSC_WebPage
4. Industry Canada, Ebiz.enable:
   http://strategis.ic.gc.ca/epic/internet/inee-ef.nsf/en/Home
5. Doing Business via the Information Highway:
   http://strategis.ic.gc.ca/SSG/me00097e.html
6. e-Commerce—Exporting Your Options:
   http://www.cbsc.org/servlet/ContentServer?pagename=CBSC_SK/display&c=GuideFactSheet&cid=1081945275887&lang=en
7. Federal E-Forms and E-Services:
   http://canadabusiness.gc.ca/gol/cbec/site.nsf/en/bg00254.html
8. E-Business Info-Guide:
   http://www.cbsc.org/servlet/ContentServer?pagename=CBSC_ON/display&c=GuideInfoGuide&cid=1085667968794&lang=en
9. CBSC's Doing Business on the Internet:
   http://bsa.cbsc.org/gol/bsa/site.nsf/en/su04935.html

* All sites accessed July 2006.

THE BOOMER TREND

The **baby boomers**, those born between 1947 and 1966, numbering about 10 million Canadians (30 percent of the total population), are now hitting the "big 6-0." By 2010, half of them will be over 55, and 18 percent will be over the age of 60. An excellent animated graphic of Canada's changing population structure can be found by linking onto Statistics Canada (http://www12.statcan.ca/english/census01/products/analytic/Multimedia.cfm?M=6). Moreover, the boomer trend is not unique to Canada, as boomers are getting set to retire in major countries across the world. We caution you, however, that each country has its own distinct boomer patterns. If your business plan is depending on American boomer information, we strongly suggest you back it up with Canadian demographic statistics (see Table 2.1).

The boomer trend is one that no self-respecting, opportunity-minded entrepreneur can ignore. Soon the front end of the boomer generation will be looking for things to do in their "new job"—retirement. A wave of retirement will sweep across Canada and other major countries. Boomer retirement needs—many of which might not be obvious—will create all kinds of opportunities for enterprising entrepreneurs. Oh my! We just remembered, it won't be long before Ron Knowles, the author of this book for the past 10 or so years, will be looking to retire. Now there's an opportunity: Who is going to be the next author?

Real opportunities will be found by those who dig a little deeper into this retirement wave. Tanya Shaw Weeks of Unique Solutions knew that home sewing was a fast-growing North American leisure activity of the aging female boomer market. We did some of our own secondary research and found out that education and health care will likely be two of the first industries to feel the retirement crunch. If you are looking for a new business idea, maybe education and health care industry segments would be a good place to start.

Catering to the needs of retiring boomers is only one opportunity. There are all kinds of opportunities resulting from this trend. As this segment ages, not only in Canada but around the world, boomer needs will have a profound impact on sectors such as real estate, when boomers begin selling their homes; finance, as they begin cashing in their RRSPs; and health care, as boomers will be living longer and healthier. We encourage you to do your research. How can the boomer needs help you find a new profitable business?[9] How about considering the needs of the boomer children—the so-called **echo boomers**, as we describe next.

BABY BOOMERS

Those born between 1947 and 1966 (about 10 million Canadians, or about 30 percent of the total population)

ECHO BOOMERS (MILLENNIALS, OR Y GENERATION)

Those born between 1980 and 1995 (about 6 million Canadians, or about 20 percent of the total population)

Table 2.1   Canada's Changing Population Profile (Millions)

Age	1996	2001	2011
0–4	1,991.5	1,924.3	1,980.1
5–9	2,036.9	2,082.2	2,016.6
10–14	2,035.2	2,124.8	2,104.8
15–19	1,996.3	2,124.5	2,259.2
20–24	2,027.0	2,115.2	2,332.3
25–29	2,217.5	2,177.7	2,392.8
30–34	2,615.4	2,366.4	2,416.1
35–39	2,657.3	2,723.4	2,443.0
40–44	2,377.8	2,716.3	2,544.5
45–49	2,146.6	2,399.6	2,801.9
50–54	1,667.4	2,140.1	2,722.0
55–59	1,327.3	1,651.4	2,362.2
60–64	1,209.4	1,300.9	2,063.6
65–69	1,129.7	1,154.0	1,544.5
70–74	980.4	1,027.1	1,142.5
75–79	704.9	831.9	906.1
80+	842.9	1,017.7	1,398.1
Total	29,963.7	31,877.3	35,420.3

Source: Statistics Canada, *Population Projections for Canada, Provinces and Territories, 1993–2016* (Catalogue 91-520, January 23, 1995).

THE SPLINTERING OF THE MASS MARKET

Today's consumers are informed, individualistic, and demanding. Their buying habits are often difficult to isolate, because they tend to buy at several levels of the market. For instance, a materials management person might buy the office copier from Xerox but the paper from a discount office supply warehouse. Some high-fashion, high-income consumers patronize upscale boutiques yet buy their household appliances at discount outlets. They may even buy clothing at the "GT" (Giant Tiger) boutique.

For the consumer, five key factors have splintered the mass market.

1. **A shrinking middle class.** There are more high-end, affluent consumers and an increasing number of consumers (for example, part-time workers, single parents, and contract workers) who live at or near the poverty level.

2. **Shifting sizes of age groups.** Each group has particular well-defined needs. How about the echo boomers (or Y generation)—about 6 million Canadians born between 1980 and 1995 (approximately 20 percent of the total population)? They have been given many names: the Nintendo Generation, Generation Y, the Millennial or Digital Generation, and the one we like best, the Sunshine Generation. You find them smiling on their cell phones and happily cruising and buying on the Net with the same ease as their boomer parents accessed "dead wood" information like magazines and newspapers. And what about the so-called *tweens*—8- to 14-year-olds—or the affluent over-80-year-olds? All of these changing segments have specific needs.

3. **Living arrangements are changing and evolving.** These include stepfamilies, dual-career families, single parents, grandparents raising grandchildren, three-generation households, more adult children returning to the nest, and empty nesters. Each of these groups has different needs for such things as furniture, housing, transportation, and food preparation.

4. **Ethnic groups are shifting and growing.** Our visible minority population has tripled since 1981. More facts on this growing trend are provided in Box 2.5. Furthermore, ethnic diversity will continue to increase, leading to more opportunities for those who can cater to this trend.[10]

5. **Improved information access.** The new electronic, digital economy means that Canadians are far better informed than they once were. They can search the Net, get product and company information from around the world, and make purchases with the click of a button. The mass production era is on the decline. We have now entered into what some experts have called the **mass customization** era. Successful companies customize their products and services efficiently and cost-effectively and then sell in large quantities. This is another trend that Tanya Shaw Weeks of Unique Solutions took advantage of. She found a way to provide individualized sewing patterns for the mass market of women who wanted to customize their sewing creations.

MASS CUSTOMIZATION

The ability of companies to customize products and services efficiently and cost-effectively in large quantities

---

Box 2.5   Our Growing Ethnocultural Profile

Over the next decade, Canada's minorities will continue to grow in size and in the share of the population. Successful companies like The Kumon Institute (http://www.kumon.com/)—a Japan-based franchise operation that offers after-school help in math and language arts for kids—has taken advantage of this changing and growing Canadian ethnocultural trend. And so can you!

Here are a few facts about our changing mosaic.

- About 4 million individuals (13.4 percent of the total population) identify themselves as visible minorities—persons, other than Aboriginal peoples, who are not white. This proportion has increased steadily over the past 20 years—from 4.7 percent of the total population in 1981.

- Chinese, South Asians, and Blacks are the three largest visible minority groups accounting for two-thirds of the visible minority population. The Chinese are the largest visible minority group, accounting for about 25 percent of the visible minority population.

- Of the 1.8 million immigrants who arrived between 1991 and 2001, 58 percent came from Asia.

- Nearly three-quarters (73 percent) of the immigrants live in just three metropolitan census areas: Toronto, Vancouver, and Montréal.

- Of the 1.8 million immigrants who arrived during the 1990s, 309,700, or 17 percent, were schoolchildren aged between 5 and 16. Most of these immigrant children (69 percent) lived in Toronto, Vancouver, and Montréal.

- In 2001, 61 percent of the immigrants who came in the 1990s used a nonofficial language as their primary home language.

Not only will many of our new young entrepreneurs be coming from this growing segment, new product and services will be required to satisfy ethnic needs. How about after-school language training—especially targeted to the fast-growing Asian segment? What about new food opportunities? Some food companies are already taking advantage of these trends by introducing new products such as wasabi-flavoured potato chips and sour cream. If you are thinking about starting a restaurant, how about having an ethnic theme? What city would you want to be located in (remember what we said about Vancouver, Toronto, and Montréal)?

Source: Statistics Canada, *2001 Census: Analysis Series, Canada's Ethnocultural Portrait: The Changing Mosaic* (Catalogue 96F0030XIE2001008, January 21, 2003): http://www12.statcan.ca/english/census01/products/analytic/companion/etoimm/contents.cfm (accessed June 2006).

TRENDS CREATE OPPORTUNITIES

Discover how changes = trends = opportunities

Get started on your Industry secondary research. Pick up the six most recent issues of magazines such as *Maclean's, Canadian Business, or Time* (your local resource centre should have copies) and your notes from Action Steps 9 and 10, and begin reading. What's happening in the world? Fill in the chart below with the areas that are changing within each environmental variable. If you are fortunate and have done your research, you'll spot the changes before trends start to develop. Being at the forefront of trends has made business-savvy people rich. Remember when the biotechnology industry began? How about the cell phone industry? Or digital photography? If you had spotted the changes within these technologies, hopped onto one of the trucks, and ridden the opportunities to success, where would you be today?

The six "S E P T I C" environmental variables

Social/cultural
Environmental Variables:
Changes:
Trends:
Opportunities:
Economic
Environmental Variables:
Changes:
Trends:
Opportunities:
People (Demographics)
Environmental Variables:
Changes:
Trends:
Opportunities:
Technology
Environmental Variables:
Changes:
Trends:
Opportunities:
International (Legal/Political)
Environmental Variables:
Changes:

(continued)

Change creates market trends that lead to opportunities for innovative entrepreneurs. We want to encourage you to become a "trend tracker" and take advantage of the resulting business opportunities. Now let's dig a little deeper. How can all these trends help you find a profitable business?

Industry or market trends reflect our economy's response to change. And these changes create entrepreneurial opportunities. Take a minute and return to the opening vignettes. The e-commerce strategy of Connie van Reenen allowed her to expand her local market, but she could also communicate with her suppliers and significantly reduce her transaction costs and the time involved in ordering products. Kazuko Komatsu of Pacific Western Brewing Company found a way to capitalize on the fast-growing exporting trend. Chris Griffiths (Chapter 1) latched onto the technology trend with his Griffiths Active Bracing System.™ This new technology allowed him to improve manufacturing efficiency and quality.

Changes within the business and social world can be grouped into six major environmental categories:

1. **social/cultural**—immigration, single parents, religion, ethnic shifts, and aging population;
2. **economic**—recessions, inflation, changing income levels, cost of housing, food, and energy;
3. **people (demographics)**—the boomers, the echo boomers, and changing ethnic and multicultural patterns;
4. **technology**—biotechnology, the Internet, nanotechnology, personal genomics, and universal translation;
5. **international (legal/political)**—who is in power and changing rules locally, provincially, and nationally, tax laws, and where the growing export markets are; and
6. **competition**—deregulation, the impact of the so-called big-box stores, foreign companies.

Each change within these six environmental categories and the subsequent market trends signals possible opportunities that will need further research. Your research for opportunities should begin with an environmental scan of the big picture. Action Step 11 will help you get started on the process of identifying change, subsequent trends, and market opportunities.

We encourage you to scrutinize boomers carefully. Determine if you can develop products or services that will make money. The following list of opportunities should help you get started.

- **Technology coach.** The boomers need help understanding and making use of new technologies. How about helping them find "e-friends" over the Net? How many "older" people are familiar with MSN? What about helping them access electronic libraries? How about e-shopping? Or helping them create digital photo albums? The list goes on.
- **Upmarket travel advisor/agent.** Boomers will be travelling and they'll be looking for unique travel experiences—for example, trips that focus on world sporting events, native culture, or spirituality. How about ecotourism? This is a combination of nature appreciation and cultural exploration in wild settings—bird watching and whale watching, to name a few obvious examples.
- **Lifestyle coach.** Boomers are looking for help and advice to improve their lifestyle and well-being—spiritual advisors, diet coaches, or personal trainers are examples.
- **Financial advisor/retirement planner.** Boomers will need help managing their wealth.

- **Concierge service agent.** Help boomers to take care of all the little things they don't have time or desire to do—fix the stove, clean the windows, pick up the dry cleaning, and the list goes on.
- **In-home service provider.** Help the parents of boomers to keep living in their homes and maintain their independence—shopping, going to the doctor, cleaning, food preparation, animal care, and so on—a concierge service for boomer parents. Many boomers will not have (or be willing to make) the time they need to help their aging parents—but they will have the money.

The needs of the aging boomers will create a litany of opportunities for enterprising entrepreneurs. But that's not the only demographic trend creating business opportunities. Think about where some other openings might exist. Obvious business opportunities to meet the needs of dual-income families and single parents include child care, home security systems, and home pet care, to name a few. Those caught up in the "poverty of time" trend are also likely to be favourably disposed toward easy-to-fix meals, fast food, teleconferences, feel-good products for stressful times, and in-home services. Here are other trends and corresponding business opportunities.

- **Ethnic trend.** Canadian society will evidence a growing ethnic diversity. *Opportunity*: Help schools and business integrate.
- **Fitness trend.** More and more people are concerned about their fitness. *Opportunity*: For those who want to look good while sweating, sell attractive sports clothes. How about e-shopping services for those who have little time?
- **The health-consciousness trend.** *Opportunity*: For those who care about what they eat, how about selling or growing organic foods? *Other opportunities*: homeopathy, naturopathy, chiropractic, and herbal medicine.
- **Employment trends.** Jobs are changing more quickly than they used to. As a result, there is a growing need for retraining. *Opportunity*: businesses related to education, training, and career planning.
- **Environmental trend.** People are becoming more concerned about the environment. *Opportunity*: ecotourism agent, as we previously noted, or *ecoretailing*—selling planet-friendly products that do not contain materials that are harmful to the body or environment.
- **Energy conservation trend**. Most Canadians have become very concerned about the high cost of energy. *Opportunity*: There is a need for energy efficiency businesses that do caulking and insulation, replace windows, and upgrade furnaces.

Many more ideas and opportunities are contained in Box 2.6 and the E-Exercise in Box 2.7.

Now it is your turn. Action Step 12 will help you come up with your own list of trends and opportunities. But we want to caution you: Once you figure out an opportunity, you will have to make sure that your have the talent, skills, and interest to take advantage of it.

Box 2.6 Ten Trends and Opportunities According to P. J. Wade

1. **On the maturing market (= boomers + seniors).** "Enabled by the Internet, maturing consumers will band together and have business work for them, instead of adapting their lives to what business will provide. Successful businesses and professionals will join in and gain consumer-partners in the process..."
2. **On leisure time.** "People will be attracted to shopping and transacting online once they realize how much time and stress can be saved. This freedom from repetitive tasks and mundane buying will transform shopping into the ultimate

ACTION STEP 11

Discover how changes = trends = opportunities *(continued)*

Trends:
Opportunities:
Competition
Environmental Variables:
Changes:
Trends:
Opportunities:

Let's look at the well-known boomers trend. This is a social trend you could have identified in this Action Step. We know that about 55 percent of Canadian disposable income and about 80 percent of savings account dollars are controlled by the 50+ age group. Chances are, many of these boomers will have lots of money to buy your product or service. Therefore, knowing the needs of this growing demographic force can result in huge benefits for the imaginative entrepreneur.

ACTION STEP 12

Compile a list of trends and opportunities

It's time for you to start developing a list of trends. Review this section (including Boxes 2.2, 2.5, and 2.7). Brainstorm with your friends. Form a focus group of your friends or colleagues and ask them about their wants or needs. Do some electronic research. Visit your local malls.

We want you to write down five or six trends that appeal to you and then list a few opportunities arising from those trends. Here are a few examples to get you started.

(continued)

ACTION STEP 12

Compile a list of trends and opportunities (continued)

TREND	OPPORTUNITY
Information	Information broker
Cocooning	Home security
Home-based	Networking business home computers
Internet	Online shopping
Downsizing	Downsizing consultant
Dual-income	Pet-sitting earner services

Now it's your turn!

TREND	OPPORTUNITY
1. _____	_____
2. _____	_____
3. _____	_____
4. _____	_____
5. _____	_____
6. _____	_____

Add your trend/opportunity list to your 24/7 Adventure Notebook.

leisure experience and leave people free to enjoy the search for unique, personalized treasures..."

3. **On neighbourhoods.** "As neighbours become electronically interconnected, human bonds will become even stronger. The result? Super-neighbourhoods like the city-states of old..."

4. **On entertainment.** "Adventures and experiences will overshadow consumerism as people spend to enjoy life, not to accumulate stuff..."

5. **On housing.** "The demand for houses and condominiums built for people, not for the convenience of builders and developers, will result in wide acceptance of universal, barrier-free design—the first housing revolution of the next millennium..."

6. **On retirement housing.** "No more warehousing the elderly, communes are just one people-friendly alternative to watch for when considering our oldest old…"

7. **On careers.** "Occupations will be replaced with play-occupations and the four-letter word 'work' will be replaced by satisfaction and fulfillment for the well-educated and electronically connected..."

8. **On mega shopping malls.** "As online shopping reduces the need for mega-stores, these major malls will become 'people meeting and merchandising' sites where people will come to learn, to swap experiences, to pitch their skills and to sell their goods and services. Covered malls will be converted into select year-round residential communities..."

9. **On food.** "Those who want to live vibrant active lives well past 100 will lead a revolution of good health. With healthcare becoming so expensive, preventative 'medicine' through good nutrition will make good food the new consumer craze in ways we have never dreamt of..."

10. **On the future.** "This is the best time in history for 'the ordinary guy.' Opportunities galore, technology to make you look successful before you are and everything up for grabs. Dive in there and invent the future of your dreams..."

Many more trends and opportunities provided by P. J. Wade can be found by linking onto P. J. Wade, *Future Thoughts*: http://www.thecatalyst.com/futurethoughts.html (accessed July 2006).

Box 2.7   E-Exercise

Link onto the Canada Business Service Centre's *Forty Concepts for a Small Business*: http://www.cbsc.org/servlet/ContentServer?cid=1102594897591&pagename=OSBW%2FCBSC_WebPage%2FCBSC_WebPage_Temp&c=CBSC_WebPage

Here you'll find 13 ways to take advantage of the market. Do a mind map of these ideas and opportunities. These ideas will help you complete Action Step 12. Make sure you put this in your 24/7 Adventure Notebook.

THE LIFE CYCLE STAGES

LIFE CYCLE

Four stages, from birth to death, of a product, business, service, industry, or location

When you've produced a long list of trends, divide them into four groups according to the stage of their **life cycle** (see Figure 2.4 on page 41). If a trend is just beginning, label it an *embryo*. If it's exploding, label it *growth*. If it's no longer growing and it's starting to cool, label it *mature*. If it's beyond maturity and is feeling chilly, label it *decline*. You don't necessarily have to create a new life cycle chart with a new set of trends. Many of you might choose to start with Figure 2.4 and begin adding new products services within each of the four stages. Perhaps you might open a new section of your 24/7 Adventure Notebook. Keep adding your new products or services into your life cycle chart.

The point is everything changes—products, needs, technology, neighbourhoods —so we want you constantly to be thinking about categorizing these changes in life cycle stages. Looking at the life cycle diagram, you can see, for example, that the auto industry as a whole is very mature. Nonetheless, some of its segments are promising—for example, minivans, sports models, and upscale imports. Convertibles are back, and in the suburbs you see young mothers driving around in Jeep® four-by-fours. Despite traffic jams, people are still driving. But the cars they drive reflect changing lifestyles. What you have with this example is a growth segment in a mature industry.

How do consumer habits determine trends? Well, people are keeping their cars longer, so one growth segment in the auto industry would be the **aftermarket**. Examples of business in that segment would be paint, detailing, electronic accessories, and engine rebuilding. If you're interested in the auto industry, consider the aftermarket.

Where can you find gaps in the life cycle diagram? Where is your business in its four-stage cycle? Action Step 13 will get you to match the life cycle stages with trends you have discovered.

AFTERMARKET

The marketplace where replacement items, such as auto tires and sewing machine belts, can be purchased

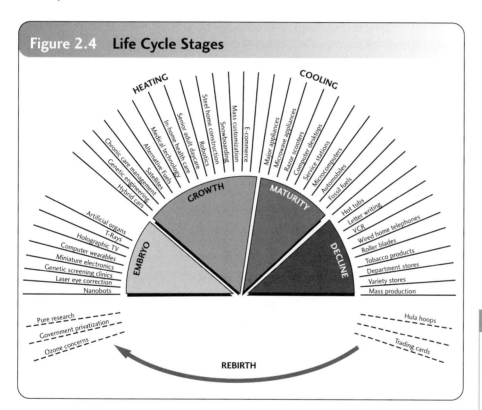

Figure 2.4   Life Cycle Stages

WATCH FOR MARKET SIGNALS

Market signals are everywhere: on the Internet, in electronic display bulletin boards, in the newspaper (classified ads, bankruptcy notices, display ads), in the lines at the theatre, in the price slashing after Christmas, and in discount coupons, rebates, store closings, and grand openings. With practice, you can follow a product in the market right through its life cycle.

For example, consider designer jeans. In the early 1980s, massive ad campaigns convinced otherwise-sane Canadians they should pay $40 and up for jeans carrying designer labels. These jeans were available only in the posh stores. A year later, designer jeans had reached the discount stores. Jeans that had sold for $55 were now going for $9.99. A bargain? Yes, and also a trend. But what has now replaced that trend? Custom-fit jeans with more than 440 combinations to ensure the exact fit.

ACTION STEP 13

Match trends with life cycle stages

By now, you will have identified a number of emerging market trends. Review Figure 2.4 and determine where the trends that you've discovered belong on the life cycle. How many of your listed trends belong in the embryo stage? The growth stage? The maturity stage? The decline stage?

Next try to discover opportunities that exist within the relevant stages. If you're entering the embryo stage, be prepared to "beat the pavement" for new business. If you're entering the maturity or decline stage, you must be ready to meet—and beat—the competition head on!

What items have you seen go through their life cycle, from upscale to deep discount?

Now go back to the life cycle and see if you can add some products and industries to it.

HOW DEEP IS DEEP?

When merchandise slides into deep discount, the profit party is over. The air is cool. The market is flooded, sinking is likely, and drowning is possible. The product is at the end of the life cycle. If that's happened to your job—or to your business—it's time for you to find a **growth segment** of a **growth industry**.

GROWTH SEGMENT

An identifiable slice of an industry that is expanding more rapidly than the industry as a whole

GROWTH INDUSTRY

An industry whose annual sales increase is well above average

Experts tell us that the average worker will have at least seven kinds of jobs in his or her lifetime and several careers. No one's job is completely secure. Rhonda Van Warden thought hers was, until the school system eliminated her position. When that happened, she started to look at the trends in her community and in the country. Rhonda has some great assets, including intelligence and being a good listener, and she has the flexibility to see herself in a totally new role when opportunity knocks.

After being downsized from her job as a school counsellor, Rhonda started to attend seminars, read books about job hunting, surf the Internet, and network with her friends for leads. One day she was talking to two friends, and their conversation turned to lingerie.

"What I wish," said Kary, "is that I could buy some of that semi-sexy stuff without having to go into Le Sex Shoppe to buy it."

"There're always the catalogues," Marsha pointed out, "and there are ads in the back of every magazine I subscribe to."

"I don't trust those catalogues," Kary replied. "When I pay that much money for something that small, I want to see what I'm getting!"

Marsha turned to Rhonda. "You're sitting there not saying a word, Rhonda. What're you thinking about?"

"I think," Rhonda said, "I've just discovered the business I want to be in."

Rhonda's idea was to tap her women friends for potential target customers who would like to come to her home for a private showing of women's intimate undergarments. Rhonda named her business Private Screenings (fictitious name) and had letterhead stationery printed. Then she began to contact suppliers and manufacturers' reps. They were interested in her idea.

Her first "private screening" was well attended. Only women were present, and Rhonda sold almost a thousand dollars worth of merchandise. The women loved what they saw, and they had fun. Ten years earlier, they probably wouldn't have considered buying the things they bought that night, but times and people change.

Rhonda went on from her success in selling to develop a line of products that she markets through her own catalogue and on her Web page. Her husband has joined her in the business, and she has hired a woman to present her intimate merchandise through seminars. (The seminars also are held in private homes.) Rhonda spends most of her time recruiting personnel and developing new products.

"When I started in this business," Rhonda admits, "I thought it might help to supplement my husband's income. But it's expanded so much that we have to scramble to keep up with orders. We travel a lot, talking to manufacturers about trends, picking up ideas. This business is a full-time job for both of us."

Rhonda was a sharp reader of market signals—the trends that reflect changes in how people think. What trends have helped to make Rhonda's business successful?

1. **Specialized consumer tastes.** Rhonda's target customers are discreet middle-class women in their 40s and 50s, many of whom would be uncomfortable walking into a specialty shop to see intimate apparel. When Rhonda brings the merchandise to them, they feel comfortable, special, and adventurous.
2. **High tech/high touch.** We can't stop the entry into our lives of computers and the information age. But we all try to balance the electronic effects of whirring machinery with human responses—just look at EST, dance, the arts, and anything feeding our fantasies. Private Screenings capitalizes on the desire for softness in these high-tech times.
3. **Relaxing attitudes about sex.** Private Screenings was founded in the 1990s, a time when attitudes toward sex were becoming much more relaxed.

What other trends do you see contributing to the success of Private Screenings?

SEGMENTATION AND GAP ANALYSIS

The idea of **market segmentation** is to keep breaking down potential markets into as many similar subsegments as possible. The more you learn about an industry, the better informed you will be to write your business plan. This procedure will help you identify opportunity gaps and see combinations of gaps that might constitute markets. Segmenting the consumer market can be done geographically (e.g., by province), demographically (e.g., by age under 20, 20–30, and so on), psychographically (e.g., concern for safety), by benefits sought (e.g., sports utility in cars), and by the rate of product/service usage (e.g., one-time purchase for a number of years of a vacuum cleaner or weekly purchase of dry cleaning service). Figure 2.5 illustrates a mind map that dissects one segment of the health care industry into subsegments. This is the kind of thinking we want you to do in Action Step 14. It's another brainstorming activity, so have fun with it.

KNOW YOUR REAL BUSINESS

Watch a carpenter framing a new house, working close to the wood, nailing with quick hammer strokes. But to get a view of the total house—the structure that will become someone's home—the carpenter must step back from the detailed work, cross the street, and examine the shape of the whole.

What business is the carpenter in? The nail-driving business? The framing business? The home-building business? Or the business of satisfying the age-old "nesting" need?

Only by stepping back can you answer the question of what business you are in. Once you know who your customers are and what satisfies their internal and external needs, you can move forward. Mary Clark's experience illustrates the importance of understanding what business you are really in.

Mary Clark was a 40-year-old teacher who had always been more interested in riding her prize-winning saddle horses than in teaching school. When her grandmother died and left her $200,000, Mary made a down payment on a boarding stable and left teaching forever, or so she thought.

The boarding stable was run down. It had stalls for 100 horses, but only 40 were occupied. Mary did everything she could think of to make the place better for horses. The $57,000 she spent on rebuilding,

MARKET SEGMENTATION

Breaking down potential markets into homogeneous groups with similar characteristics and qualities

ACTION STEP 14

Have some fun with segmentation and gap analysis

Form some of your friends into a focus group and poll them about gaps in the marketplace. Ask them to respond to the following questions:

- What frustrates you most about your daily life? Shopping? Banking? Dating? Living? Buying a car? Grocery shopping? Other kinds of shopping?
- What products do you need that you can't get?
- What products or service would enhance your quality of life?
- How could you increase your productivity without working more hours?

Make a list of the gaps that the group identifies. Then project the list out as far as you can, and follow the wants and frustrations of your friends into the marketplace. Are any of the needs they mentioned national in scope? Global?

Figure 2.5 A Mind Map

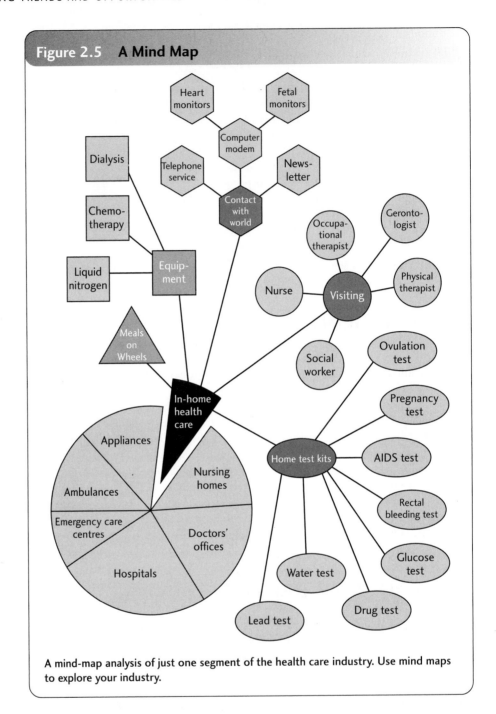

A mind-map analysis of just one segment of the health care industry. Use mind maps to explore your industry.

painting, and grading made Clark's Stables a very attractive place. She bought the highest quality of feed and gave the horses the best care money could buy.

So when owners began to move their horses to other stables, Mary couldn't understand. She hadn't increased her fees, and she treated the horses like friends. Six months later, only three customers remained. In 9 months, she was behind on her mortgage payments. In her 10th month, Mary had to sell the stables. What went wrong?

Mary had made the simple mistake of thinking that horses were her target customers. She thought she was in the business of stabling horses. In fact, the business she was in was providing service for girls between the ages of 7 and 14 who rode horses. The girls wanted recreation, training, and social activities. Mary's customers left because other stables were providing lessons, trail rides, barbecues, and a fun experience. Today, Mary is back in the classroom, wondering why people don't care more about their horses—and why they didn't care about the quality of her stables.

DEFINE YOUR BUSINESS

Having defined a specific industry segment, you're ready to define what you do. Naming anything is a game of words, and a small business is no exception. If you're hesitant about defining it at this early stage, remember what happened to Mary Clark's stable.

When defining your business, keep in mind that people don't buy products or services—they buy what the product or service will do for them (for example, make their lives easier, safer, or more fun). Cosmetics firms frequently say they are in the business of selling "hope in a jar." The examples in Table 2.2 can help you define your business.

Now complete this sentence:

I'm in the business of _____.

Explain why you chose this definition and how it relates to your target customer (include benefits).

Keep honing your definition of your business. Once a month is not too often to redefine it, especially before the start-up. Check your definition against the signals you get from your potential target customers, as they might perceive your business differently. You might have to print new letterhead stationery printed after you talk to them, but as business expenses go, that's a small price to pay to prevent customer confusion. By developing a questionnaire about your business idea and getting feedback from a number of potential customers, you'll be able to redefine the business you are in.

DEVELOP YOUR PITCH

In addition to looking at what business you are really in, you should also consider how your business definition can impress not only your prospective customers but also your suppliers and potential investors. We suggest that you begin to formulate your "**elevator pitch**," or speech that can hook your listener into responding, "Tell me more." It's a clear, concise description of your business idea, the market need, how your business will satisfy that need, and how your business, the customer, and your investors will benefit. It should last only a few minutes— some say the time it takes to ride up in an elevator. This short description or pitch should answer three major questions.

ELEVATOR PITCH

A clear, concise description of your business idea that can hook your listener into responding, "Tell me more"

1. What is the market?

   What is your product or service?
   What are the features and benefits?
   What are the driving trends? Why does your target market need that product or service?
2. How does your business satisfy this market need?

   What is your competitive advantage?
   Who is your competition, and why will your customer buy from you?

CURRENT POSITION AND FUTURE OUTLOOK

Example:

This is what you learn about Big Wheels, a growing bike shop in town. The two owners are well-known trail bike riders who, for the past two years, have been repairing and servicing all kinds of bicycles out of the oversized garage of one of their partners. In the past 12 months, this part-time venture grossed $161,000 without the benefit of advertising or a retail location.

The market for high-quality and custom-made bicycles has grown by more than 10 percent per year over the past 10 years, and industry observers expect the trend to continue. The new retail store will have 5,000 square feet in showroom space and another 3,000 square feet for doing repairs and stocking goods. Big Wheels will also have a Web site, where customers will be able to purchase customized bikes and have them delivered within two weeks.

The bicycle industry in North America sells two dollars' worth of accessories and clothing for every dollar spent on bicycles. Between the store and the Web site, Big Wheels expects sales to at least double in the first year (they previously had not sold clothing) and to reach $1 million in three years.

It's your turn again. Develop your section on the current situation and future outlook. It's important to demonstrate an understanding of growth problems (such as choosing the right location and attracting customers), as well as cash management, gross margins, inventory control, and vendor sources. Ready or not, start writing down what you already know and what you need to know. You will have many opportunities to upgrade this section as you gather data. Your primary research, when complete, will help.

_____

_____

_____

_____

_____

MANAGEMENT AND OWNERSHIP

Needed now is a mini-résumé of the key player (or players) you'd like to have on your founding team. Lenders, capital firms, and vendors consider the founding team to be the most important factor in a business plan.

At this point, keep the résumés brief, focusing on the past experience that will give this start-up a competitive edge. (Save the full-blown résumés of the management team for the appendix at the back of the plan.) Explain your business form (that is, corporation, partnership, or sole proprietorship) and, if you have more than two people on the team, include an organizational chart.

Your turn again. Who are the players?

_____

_____

_____

_____

_____

DESCRIPTION OF YOUR BUSINESS

Think of yourself riding up 50 floors in an express elevator. You have 30 seconds to explain to a stranger what your business is about.

Example:

My partner and I retail high-end bicycles from our store in Halifax. We repair, service, and modify off-road bikes for the serious trail rider. Ninety percent of our customers are from Halifax, and they see us as a valuable resource in helping them to achieve a healthy and enjoyable exercise lifestyle.

Note that this description is short and to the point, but it also includes important customer benefits.

Now it's your turn.

My business is

_____

_____

_____

_____

_____

Checklist Questions and Actions to Develop Your Business Plan

Spotting Trends and Opportunities

❑ What trends will influence your small business?

❑ What business are you really in?

❑ What segment of the market will be your niche?

❑ Is it a growth segment in a growth market?

❑ Initially define your target market, and determine how large that customer base is.

❑ Identify the secondary sources you will use as part of your market research.

❑ Does this business fit your vision and values?

❑ Other than making money, what are the goals of your proposed venture? (You should be able to establish four to six over the next three years.)

❑ For your business, what objectives do you wish to achieve this next year?

Case Study

As we discussed in the opening vignette and Chapter 1 case study, Garrison Guitars has become a raging success story. We can all learn from Chris Griffiths's experience.

Now we want you to dig a little deeper, go back and link onto the following sites:

• Innovation in Canada: Garrison Guitars case profile: http://innovation.ic.gc.ca/gol/innovation/site.nsf/en/in04209.html

• Innovation in Canada, "The Practice of Innovation Facilitator's Guide": http://innovation.ic.gc.ca/gol/innovation/site.nsf/en/in04194.html

• Web cast video profile of Garrison Guitars, based on interviews with the company's principals: http://innovation.ic.gc.ca/gol/innovation/site.nsf/en/in04697.html

• Garrison Guitars: http://www.garrisonguitars.com/history.asp

Case Questions

1. Entrepreneurial skills (e-skills)

   We introduced you to an e-skill called mind mapping in Chapter 1. In this chapter, we learned about brainstorming as an entrepreneurial skill that will help you discover trends and business opportunities (page 28).

   a. Briefly, what is brainstorming?

   b. Trends create opportunities. Brainstorming is a skill that can be learned with practice. Get together with a group friends or classmates. Brainstorm the possible trends that would help Chris Griffiths be successful in the manufacturing and distribution of guitars? Record your results in the form of a mind map.

2. Trends create opportunities

   Industry or market trends reflect our economy's response to change. And change creates entrepreneurial opportunities. A knowledge of market trends will help you identify growth opportunities.

   a. Briefly, what is a trend? What's the difference between a trend and a fad? (Hint: Link onto ACOA's, "From Ideas to Business Opportunities" site provided in Box 2.2, page 30.)

   b. Faith Popcorn is the author of *The Popcorn Report*, a best-selling book on market trends. She tells us that ideally, a winning business idea should include or encompass at least three major trends. Five pervasive macro trends that Canadian small business must embrace were discussed on page 33. Briefly describe these five trends. Which of these five trends did Chris Griffiths take advantage of?

3. Mass customization

   The new electronic era means that Canadians are becoming far better informed, with a resulting trend toward individualism. Many Canadians search the Net, get product and company information from around the world, and buy what they want at the click of a button. Electronic access to information is a key factor in the splintering of the mass market. We have now entered a growing trend called mass customization.

   In this chapter, we learned how Tanya Shaw Weeks took advantage of mass customization (page 27). Go to the Garrison Web site. Show how Garrison Guitars has now begun taking advantage of this new mass customization trend.

4. Outsourcing and contracting out

   a. Click onto "What Is Outsourcing?" (http://www.outsourcing-faq.com/1.html) and watch the video. According to Peter Bendor-Samuel, a top authority on outsourcing, what is his distinction between outsourcing and contracting out?

   b. What are the possible major benefits of outsourcing?

   c. In the commercialization stage, did Chris Griffiths choose to take advantage of the outsourcing or contracting out trend? (See http://innovation.ic.gc.ca/gol/innovation/site.nsf/en/in04198.html)

5. Building an effective Web site

   Link onto the Manitoba efuturecentre's Building an Effective Web Site: http://www.e-future.ca/manitoba/en_CA/pdf/building_an_effective_website.pdf. Go to page 6, "What Should You Have on Your Website?" What are eight common sections and pages that should be contained on an effective Web site? Evaluate the Garrison Guitars home page based on these criteria.

6. What business are you really in?

   In this chapter, we have encouraged you start thinking about the needs of a customer. We wanted you to start thinking about defining your business in terms of the benefits to your target customer.

   a. Who is the target or major customer of Garrison Guitars?

   b. What business is Garrison Guitars really in?

7. Pitching your product

   Chris Griffiths spent several years perfecting and developing his idea. When it came time to manufacture his guitars, he needed venture capital—$250,000—to build his prototype and a further $3 million to build a factory and complete the commercial implementation phase. Assume for a moment that you are Chris Griffiths of Garrison Guitars and you now need the $3 million. You have to satisfy the needs of your potential venture capitalists, and you don't have much time to convince them. You need an elevator pitch.

a. What is an elevator pitch?

b. What are the basic needs of your venture capital investors?

c. What are the key issues you would address in your elevator pitch?

Notes

1. Canada/Manitoba Business Service Centre, *e-Business Case Study—Labelle Florists*: www.cbsc.org/servlet/ContentServer?pagename=CBSC_MB/display&c=GuideInfoGuide&cid=1099919464397&lang=en (accessed September 2005).

2. Pacific Western Brewing Co., "About Us": http://www.pwbrewing.com/ (accessed September 2005); and Daphne Bramham, "Japan Taps into Pacific Western Beer: The Various Brands Are Brewed to Suit Japanese Tastes, Entrepreneur Says," *The Vancouver Sun*, March 7, 1997.

3. Unique Solutions Design Ltd. home page, Media link: http://www.uniqueltd.com/index.html/ (accessed February 2006).

4. See, for example, Canadian Business Online: http://rankings.canadianbusiness.com/Profit100/list.asp?type=p100&listType=&year=&page=1&content= (accessed May 2006).

5. Manitoba efuturecentre, *e-Business Case Study—Webview 360*: http://www.e-future.ca/manitoba/en_CA/pdf/cs_webview360.pdf (accessed July 2006).

6. Jobshark.Com, Web site (http://www.jobshark.com); and Canadian Business Online, "Best Businesses to Go into Now": http://www.canadianbusiness.com/entrepreneur/index.jsp (accessed September 2005).

7. Industry Canada, *E-Commerce in Service Industries*: http://strategis.ic.gc.ca/cgi-bin/sc_indps/service/siec/tabulate (accessed September 2005).

8. Industry Canada, *Doing Business via the Information Highway*: http://strategis.ic.gc.ca/SSG/me00097e.html (accessed September 2005).

9. Statistics Canada, *The Aging Workforce*: http://www12.statcan.ca/english/census01/products/analytic/companion/paid/canada.cfm#5; and The Retirement Wave: http://www.statcan.ca/Daily/English/030221/d030221f.htm (accessed September 2005).

10. http://www12.statcan.ca/english/census01/products/analytic/companion/etoimm/canada.cfm/three_largest_urban_centres (accessed June 2006).

11. Business Know-How, "The Art of the Elevator Pitch": http://www.businessknowhow.com/money/elevator.htm; and "Pinpoint Connections": http://socialsoftware.weblogsinc.com/entry/8435544887719633/ (accessed September 2005).

SUGGESTED READING

McGee, Kenneth G. *Heads Up: How to Anticipate Business Surprises and Seize Opportunities*. Boston: HBS Press, 2004.

Linn, Susan. *Consuming Kids: The Hostile Takeover of Childhood*. New York: New Press, 2004.

Nyce, Steven A., and Sylvester J. Schieber. *The Economic Implication of Aging Societies: The Costs of Living Happily Ever After*. Cambridge, UK: Cambridge University Press, 2005.

Tapscott, Don, and David Ticoll. *The Naked Corporation: How the Age of Transparency Will Revolutionize Business*. New York: Simon and Schuster, 2003.

Barletta, Martha. *Marketing to Woman: How to Understand, Reach, and Increase Your Share of the World's Largest Market Segment*. Chicago: Dearborn Trade, a Kaplan Professional Company, 2002.

Mathews, Ryan, and Watts Wacker. *The Deviant's Advantage: How to Use Fringe Ideas to Create Mass Markets*. Three Rivers, MI: Three Rivers Press, Popcorn, Faith, and Adam Hanft. *Dictionary of the Future: The Words, Terms, and Trends That Define the Way We'll Live, Work, and Talk*. New York: Hyperion, 2001.

Marigold, Lys, and Faith Popcorn. *EVEolution: The Eight Truths of Marketing to Women*. New York: Hyperion, 2000.

chapter 3

Positioning Yourself as an Entrepreneur for Market Opportunities

This chapter will help you prepare part B of your business plan, The Market and the Target Customer.

In the mid-1990s, Cathy Waters owned and operated a small store called Timeless Books in Victoria, British Columbia. She was paying the bills and making a modest living, but small bookstores like Cathy's were feeling the heat. She just did not have enough customers, and in many cases, she could not service the customers she had. If someone wanted a rare book that she did not stock, Cathy could spend hours searching catalogues from other book sellers. Rifling through circulars to find rare books was a time-consuming art form. Even if she found the needed book, it just wasn't worth the effort. To make matters worse, some experts were predicting the end to the small bookseller, claiming that the so-called e-books would eventually do away with the "dead tree" media.

These were trying times for Cathy. She had a passion for used and rare books—and she wanted to help people find the books they wanted to read. But how could she reposition the business and translate her love for books into a profitable business?

These were also challenging times for Cathy's husband, Keith. He was working for the British Columbia government, and she knew he wasn't that happy with his job. Boredom was setting in. He needed a new challenge. So, one night when the two of them were out for dinner with a techie friend, Rick Pura, and his significant other, Cathy popped the question. "You guys need a new challenge, so why don't you find a better way for me to sell my books? I want to do it better and cheaper." The brainstorm began. The entire meal was taken up by ideas—many of which had to be recorded on a napkin.

Keith was a Web site developer, and his friend Rick was a database manager. Cathy had told them that other small booksellers were having the same problems. Small "mom-and-pop" book retailers had to rely on cumbersome and sometimes dated used book catalogues. Why not use their skills to put these circulars into a Web-based electronic catalogue? This would allow used book people, many of whom operated out of their homes, to buy and sell books from around the world at the speed of e-mail. At the very least, they could reduce paper and save a few trees.

The idea inspired them, and within a year both Keith and Rick quit their "real" jobs. AbeBooks, a company that provided an efficient and cost-effective way for sellers of used books to connect with buyers,

LEARNING OPPORTUNITIES

After reading this chapter, you should be able to

- connect your personal and business values with market opportunities;
- mesh your personal business objectives with one of the many opportunities in the marketplace;
- understand that your business objectives provide a positive and unique thrust to your business;
- narrow your industry research until viable gaps appear;
- gain insight into hidden pockets of the life cycle by using an industry chronology;
- understand how problems can be turned into opportunities;
- combine demographic (population) data with psychographic (picture of a lifestyle) data to produce a customer profile;
- identify heavy users of your product or service;
- brainstorm creatively;
- develop a strategy for your business using a SWOT analysis;
- use a matrix grid for blending your objectives with your research findings to produce a portrait of a business; and
- create a mission statement for your business.

ACTION STEP
PREVIEW

16. Clarify your values.
17. List your business goals for the next three years.
18. Collect secondary data on your favourite industry segment.

(continued)

ACTION STEP 17

List your business goals for the next three years

What do you want from small business? Money? Fame? Job security? To be your own boss? Freedom to explore the marketplace? Control of your own destiny? Just want to be a president?

Think back to the forces that made you interested in small business in the first place. What were those forces? Where were you when you first thought about owning the store? How have circumstances changed your goals?

List everything you want, even if it seems unreasonable or embarrassing to you. This is your personal list, after all, and you will sift through the ideas later.

4. **Safety**. There was no way they wanted to lose money now. They had a family to think about.
5. **Growth industry**. They wanted to find a booming segment of a growth industry (an industry whose annual sales growth is considerably above average).
6. **Time**. They knew that getting a business up and running could take a year at the very least. They wanted to define and develop their business so that they could make a little money in the first year, get their feet wet, and then go bigger in the next two to four years, once they knew what they were doing and what the market really wanted.
7. **Key people**. They wanted to operate the business themselves for the first year. But as the business grew over the next four years, they wanted to be able to attract the best people to work with them.
8. **Fun, adventure, and excitement**. They knew that starting a small business, even in a growth or glamour industry, would involve hassles, problems, and surprises. So they decided to make sure their business would be one with which they would have some fun.

Now it's your turn. Why do you want to start your own business? What are your goals? Action Step 17 will help you work through this.

Box 3.3 Small Business Tips

Ultimately, each of your broad goals will boil down to a set of specific business objectives. These objectives should be S M A R T:

- **Specific,**
- **Measurable,**
- **Action based,**
- **Realistic, and**
- **Time framed.**

SMART objectives can be applied to your personal life as well as your business planning. For example, here is a simple example of a possible SMART personal objective for a student:

- I (name) will graduate from this course (specific name) on (provide exact date) with a grade of (provide grade level) as determined by (name of professor).

We encourage you to get started using SMART goals. What is your goal for this course?

STEP 2: LEARN MORE ABOUT YOUR FAVOURITE INDUSTRY

As you searched for trends in Chapter 2, you probably found a dozen industries that seemed interesting. Now it's time to explore one of them in more depth. The industry should be the one that interests you most and about which you have at least some knowledge, whether it's genetics, robotics, entertainment, food service, travel, education, publishing, retailing, construction, manufacturing, information, or whatever. Here, trade associations can be a valuable source of information. For example, if you plan to be in the gift business, you will want to check out the Canadian Gift and Tableware Association (http://www.cgta.org). If you're planning to start a restaurant business, you would certainly connect with the Canadian Restaurant and Foodservice Association (http://www.crfa.ca). As we note in Chapter 5, Associations Canada (http://www.micromedia.ca/Directories/Associations.htm) would be a good starting point if you're looking for an association related to your particular industry.

As you move into your selected industry, collect information from previous Action Steps. For secondary data, the Internet is probably the best place to start, but you need to sift through a lot of information. Be sure to check out

Strategis: It's a very useful source of industry research (see Box 3.4). Visit a resource centre or library; study periodicals like *The Globe and Mail*, *Canadian Business*, the *National Post*, *PROFIT* magazine, and other general business or news sources. Most libraries have computer databases to help you search. In addition, the Canadian Business Index and other such sources will point you to dozens of articles in your field. Is there a trade show you can attend? What you're looking for is an accurate picture of trends in the industry that interests you. You need to learn what's breaking, what's cresting, and what's cooling down.

Box 3.4 Bookmark This

Strategis (http://strategis.ic.gc.ca)

As we noted in Chapter 1 the Industry Canada, Strategis Web site is a great source of secondary research. It is devoted to providing information, resources, contacts, and hard-to-get information in a prearranged, easy-to-use format. On its "Researching Markets" page, you'll find the following industry information for foreign and domestic markets.

Foreign

- **STAT-USA Market Research Reports:** http://strategis.gc.ca/epic/internet/inimr-ri2.nsf/en/gr-01000e.html—Access current country profiles, analyses, and guides supporting international market research, business intelligence, and trade opportunity identification. Get brief, factual summaries concerning the people, history, government, economy, and foreign relations: Country Analysis Briefs, Country Background Notes, Country Commercial Guides, Foreign Labour Trends, Industry Sector Analysis, International Market Insight, and the CIA's *World Fact Book*.

Domestic

- **Canadian Company Capabilities**: http://strategis.ic.gc.ca/sc_coinf/ccc/engdoc/homepage.html—This site enables you to find out what others are doing by searching an online database with more than 50,000 Canadian companies and 200,000 products and services.

- **Federal Corporations Data Online**: http://strategis.ic.gc.ca/cgi-bin/sc_mrksv/corpdir/dataOnline/search.cgi?lang=e—Access information on hundreds of thousands of federally incorporated companies in Canada by searching this database.

- **Canadian Industry Statistics**: http://strategis.ic.gc.ca/sc_ecnmy/sio/homepage.html—This site provides information on various aspects of Canadian economic activity. Areas of special emphasis include economics, employment, international trade, investment, public equity financing, and growth indices.

- **Trade Data Online**: http://strategis.ic.gc.ca/sc_mrkti/tdst/engdoc/tr_homep.html—This page provides import and export statistics by commodity (product), industry, and geographic location for a 10-year period. This yields detailed and aggregate Canadian and U.S. information concerning trade trends and market shares.

- **Canadian Importers Database**: http://strategis.ic.gc.ca/sc_mrkti/cid/engdoc/index.html—This Web site offers a list of major importers either by product/commodity or by city. The final report—generated using the latest year's data collected by the Canada Customs—will give you names and postal codes of the top 80 percent of import companies in your specified sector.

Source: Industry Canada Strategis Web site: http://strategis.ic.gc.ca/sc_x/engdoc/researching_markets.html?guides=e_res

ACTION STEP 18

Collect secondary data on your favourite industry segment

What industry segment really attracts you? What's out there that has a magnetic pull that you can't resist? To help you get started, recall what you discovered in Action Steps 9 through 15.

Start with a wide-angle view by looking at two or three segments that interest you. After you've decided on "your" segment, research in depth. It might help to organize your research into categories such as life cycle, speed of change, history, competition, recent industry breakthroughs, costs of positioning yourself, customer base, and so on.

If you're working alone, it will help to write your industry overview. If you're working with a team, you'll save yourself some confusion if each team member writes an overview and later shares his or her perspective with the others.

This is a never-ending Action Step. Once you are in business, you will have to be as diligent in keeping up with the industry segment as you were in your initial research.

In focusing on your industry, break down your search into categories such as life cycles, speed of change, history, competition, recent industry breakthroughs, costs of positioning yourself, target customers, and so on. Later, after you've gathered the data, you can use these categories as idea filters for sifting information through the power marketing funnel.

For example, using the life cycle concept discussed in Chapter 2 will sharpen a first look at any industry. When you're reading a newspaper and you see the headline "CBC tries to shed stodgy image in prime time—but can it be hip?" you make three fast-reflex judgments. First, the industry is entertainment. Second, the segment is network television. Third, the shows are in the mature phase, on their way to decline.

And when you're driving down the street and see a shopping mall being renovated, you know that the face-lift is an attempt to move the mall back from a mature or decline phase into a growth phase. The point of all this is to find an industry segment where there is room for growth.

A second helpful category is competition, which we'll be analyzing in detail in Chapter 5. Competition, which varies with each stage of the life cycle, is an idea filter that can save you years of grief.

A third helpful category is the concept of industry breakthroughs, or hot buttons. What really hums in your industry or segment? Remember, the first computers filled large rooms and ran on punch cards. The first industry breakthrough was the printed circuit. The second was the microchip. And the third was computer networks. Could the fourth be the network computer—a personal computer with no hard drive?

Let's return to Anne and Steve. They had a firm idea of their favourite industry. They had done a lot of primary and secondary research and had decided to focus on the information industry. All the numbers told them this was still a growth market. On a personal level, Steve loved the technical world, whereas Anne knew there was a real need for marketers in the technology sector, and she liked working with techies. They had chosen a growth industry that meshed with their personal visions and goals.

Now it is your turn. Research your favourite industry. Is it in a growth phase? What breakthroughs are occurring? Does your business capitalize on the latest advances in technology and imagination? Put this kind of thinking into Action Step 18.

STEPS 3 AND 4: IDENTIFY PROMISING INDUSTRY SEGMENTS AND PROBLEMS THAT NEED SOLUTIONS

MARKET GAP

An area of the market where needs are not being met

When you write your business plan, you'll need to explain why you've chosen a particular **market gap** and what you believe the resulting business opportunity is. If you have selected a promising opportunity and have communicated your excitement about it, you'll have developed a "hook" for the banker or investor who will read your plan. As we discussed in Chapter 2, e-commerce is one example of an industry where market gaps will abound. More evidence of this trend is provided in Box 3.5. In the opening vignettes, Cathy and Keith Waters found their niche selling used books over the Web, whereas Ted Wolff von Selzam of Kinnikinnick Foods found his in the e-retailing of alternative food products.

Anne and Steve had done a lot of primary and secondary research. They knew that computers and the Internet were explosive market segments (see Figure 3.3). They also learned that there was a growth market for computer networks—especially for small businesses. From their research, they had isolated four breakthrough segments: the home computer market, the Internet, intranets, and computer networks. It would be hard to argue that any of these is not a growth segment. The numbers

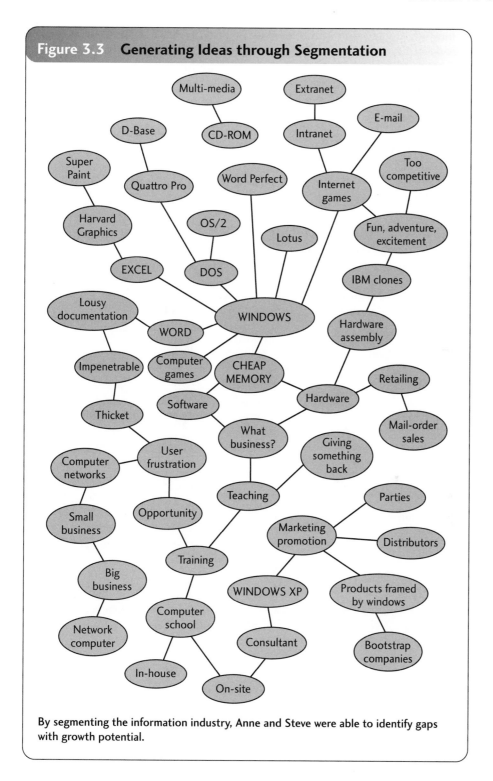

Figure 3.3 Generating Ideas through Segmentation

By segmenting the information industry, Anne and Steve were able to identify gaps with growth potential.

are quite clear—at least for the next couple of years. Wisely, Anne and Steve also listed some of the major problems in the industry: consumer distrust of products and services, speed change, information overload, security, cost, and so on.

The secret to focusing on market gaps is to find a target customer—a person or business that needs a particular product or service that you could provide. You then profile your target customer (we do this in detail in the next chapter), and that profile becomes one of your idea filters. Now it's your turn to focus on the segments

ACTION STEP 19

Identify three or four market gaps that look promising

Now that you're hip-deep in your industry, scrutinize segments where you think you could survive and prosper. It's time to begin to profile your target customer.

Prepare a combination demographic-psychographic checklist to help you explore target markets. Include items for evaluating

- demographic data—age, sex, income, family size, education, socioeconomic status, place of residence, religion, political affiliation, and so on; and
- psychographic data— occupation, lifestyle, buying habits, dreams, interest and leisure activities, ambitions, and so on.

Or, if you're going after a commercial/industrial market, use company size, type of industry, number of employees, location, departments of large companies, and so on.

Tailor your checklist so that it provides a thorough profile of your target customer.

ACTION STEP 20

List problems that need solutions

When you surveyed your friends in Action Step 12, you were approaching the list of problems you need to develop now. The difference is that the problems you are seeking now are those that are unique to the industry you've been exploring.

Get together with people who know something about your industry. Ask them for input and write down everything. Use this input to develop your list.

Each problem you identify multiplies your opportunities to prosper in your segment.

within your industry and spot some that look promising. Complete Action Step 19. Action Step 20 will help you spot opportunities in your industry segment. If this exercise draws a blank, go back and do some more brainstorming. Remember, the process of idea generating is not linear. You might have to bounce around for a while.

Box 3.5 Internet Commerce in Canada—10 Key Metrics

1. Value of online sales (private and public) in 2004 = $28.3 billion
2. Value of online sales (private only) in 2004 = $26.4 billion (2003 = $18.6B)
3. Value of business-to-consumer (B2C) sales in 2004 = $6.6 billion
4. Value of business-to-business (B2B) sales in 2004 = $19.8 billion
5. Percentage of firms (connected to the Internet) using high-speed Internet access in 2004 = 72%
6. Percentage of firms (connected to the Internet) using low-speed Internet access in 2004 = 18%
7. Canadian e-commerce household spending in 2003 = $3.0 billion
8. Households using Internet regularly from home = 54%; from any location = 64.2% (with high-speed Internet access from home: 65%)
9. Regular use households purchasing good/services from home = 47% (purchasing using high-speed Internet access: 72%)
10. Percentage of firms, by size, using different technologies in 2002–2004

	Small Firms		Medium Firms		Large Firms		All Firms		
	2002	2003	2002	2003	2002	2003	2002	2003	2004
Internet access	73.1	75.9	91.8	93.7	99.0	97.2	75.7	78.3	81.6
Web site presence	26.6	29.0	61.8	66.1	77.1	77.2	31.5	34.1	36.8
Purchasing online	29.3	35.1	46.5	50.1	56.6	60.5	31.7	37.2	42.5
Selling online	6.6	6.0	12.9	14.2	16.2	15.5	7.5	7.1	7.0

Source: Statistics Canada, *Survey of Electronic Commerce and Technology, 2005*: http://e-com.ic.gc.ca/epic/internet/inecic-ceac.nsf/en/h_gv00032e.html (accessed September 2005).

STEP 5: BRAINSTORM FOR SOLUTIONS

In Chapter 2, we introduced you to brainstorming. It's a process used by many groups—think tanks, middle managers, major corporations, and, especially, small businesses—to generate fresh ideas (see Box 3.6 on page 65). What follows is a short recap of the brainstorm held by Anne and Steve—with their best friends, Carol and Rick—as they started to transform problems into business opportunities.

"Anne and I have invited you over for a pizza and to get some ideas on business opportunities," Steve began.

"As you all know," said Anne, "we are thinking about starting our own business. We have done all kinds of research and have decided to focus on the information industry. We have even identified a few hot segments. We want to brainstorm for more ideas and some solutions to industry problems."

The four spent the first hour tossing around ideas. Some of these did not appear at first to be going anywhere. Rick, for example, thought the company should design computer games and go head-to-head with Sega® and Sony. Ideas kept coming out—virtual training, leveraged buyouts, virtual games, software manufacture, hardware assembly, retailing, Web design, and on and on. Anne wrote them all down on a flip chart. Finally, she said, "I'm exhausted. Time for a break."

When they came back, it was Steve's turn to keep track of the ideas. He flipped to a clean sheet on the chart. Over the next hour, the four friends created a mind map loaded with ideas for a business (see, for example, Figure 3.3).

By the time the brainstorm session wound down, they had identified two areas to explore. The first area was the installation of and training for network computing systems. Their target market would be small business. Steve had just finished reading about a Statistics Canada survey that said computer networks (especially LANs) were now being installed in small businesses at a record pace. Their second option was intranet design and installation for small and medium-sized businesses.

"Well, this about wraps it up for tonight. Anne and I have a lot of ideas to mull over," concluded Steve. "We're going have to think about these two options."

"Wait a minute. How will you decide?" asked Carol.

"We'll have to do more research, then use a matrix grid. We learned about the matrix grid in class last week," Anne responded.

It's helpful—and, in most cases, necessary—to summarize after a brainstorming session so that you can identify the useful ideas. Let's review what happened in this session.

1. Using brainstorming, the team identified problems and possible solutions.
2. Most ideas were good ideas.
3. The two ideas that looked best involved computer networks and intranet systems.
4. It did not seem that Anne and Steve could pursue both ideas at once. They had two different target customers. This meant that one idea might have to go on the back burner. (This isn't a bad thing. It's always helpful to have budding ideas in your pocket, as every product or service has a life cycle.)

Box 3.6 Brainstorming—The Rules

Brainstorming requires an environment and attitude in which innovative thinking can occur. In a brainstorming session, everyone is encouraged to contribute ideas. Stimulation is provided by the ideas of others. The goal is to come up with lots of ideas, some of which might seem far-fetched or even erroneous, and then, as momentum grows, to see where concepts develop. A key to brainstorming is to reserve judgment initially so that creativity is not stifled. Finally, brainstorming must be conducted in an environment in which "anything goes." People must not be made to think that their ideas are silly or stupid. Negative statements or actions, reservations, or criticisms are not allowed.

Now that you understand what brainstorming is and what it can accomplish for a business, give it a try with your own business. Assemble your partners or friends and go for it. Action Step 21 gives you some directions.

ACTION STEP 21

Brainstorm for solutions

Now you need to get really creative. Dig out the list of problems in your industry that you made in Action Step 20. Every problem can be turned into an opportunity.

You'll generate better ideas in the long run if you just let your imagination roll. Don't be concerned with a lot of logic and reason—not at this stage. You might begin with a quick overview of what you know so far and then slide into possible (and impossible?) solutions. An audio recorder can be useful.

Have fun.

STEP 6: MESH POSSIBLE SOLUTIONS WITH OPPORTUNITIES IN THE MARKETPLACE

MATRIX GRID

A screen through which ideas are passed in order to find solutions

ACTION STEP 22

Mesh possible solutions with your goals and objectives, using a matrix grid.

A matrix analysis will help you focus, especially if you're working with a group and have diverse objectives to satisfy. If you prepare a large grid and put it on the wall, all members of the team can participate.

Down the left side, list the goals you brainstormed in Action Step 17. Along the top, list the possible solutions you came up with in Action Step 21. Select a rating system to use for evaluating the match of each possible solution with each of your goals. It could be a 10-point scale or a plus-zero-minus system:

Plus (+) = 3
Zero (0) = 2
Minus (−) = 1

When you've rated all of the combinations, find the total for each column. The totals will indicate your best prospects. The rest is up to you.

Some people like to use lists or mind maps for arriving at opportunities, but others prefer a more systematic method. A **matrix grid** can provide the desired structure for decision making. After you have brainstormed some possible solutions, you need to improve your focus on them and evaluate them. The matrix grid in Figure 3.4 helped Steve and Anne do this. The next day, after their brainstorm with Carol and Rick, they reviewed the various criteria on the list. Then, they ranked the top three in order of greatest importance and the bottom three in order of least importance. The top 3 were then assigned a value of 3, whereas the bottom 3 were given a value of 1. This way, each criterion did not receive the same value.

The group voted on several of the possible solutions they brainstormed. When the numbers were tallied, they decided the network computer business was the preferred option. They liked the idea of working with small businesses. This segment was really starting to heat up. They would provide advice and consulting in computer networks. Their target market would be smaller, independent business that wanted growth. If they succeeded, the intranet would be the next focus.

Now prepare a matrix grid, and weigh your criteria to help you focus on the best course of action. Action Step 22 tells you how to do it.

STEP 7: TAKE STOCK AND FOCUS

What have you learned about the opportunity selection process? Before you answer this, take some time to rethink what you want to achieve in your small business. If you feel a little uneasy about how fast you've run the last couple of laps, perhaps it's because you haven't yet identified your industry. It's time to take stock.

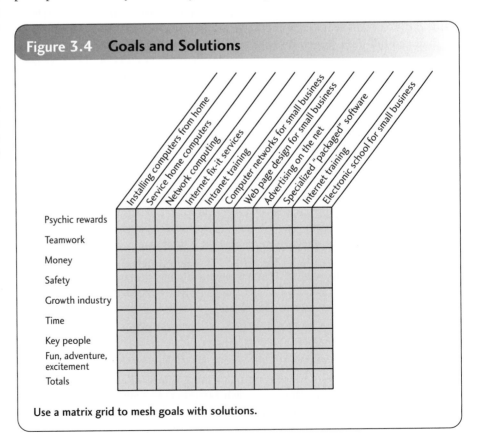

Figure 3.4 Goals and Solutions

Use a matrix grid to mesh goals with solutions.

What is your industry?

_____

What is your market gap?

_____

What are some opportunities for you?

_____

MISSION STATEMENT

Now that you have identified your market opportunity—one that reflects your values—you need to think about a business mission.

Your personal vision and values give you guidance and direction in the conduct of your life. In much the same way, a business mission—the **mission statement**—is a statement of your company's purpose and aims. Mission statements are normally connected to the values and vision of the business owner. In small business, a mission statement is concise (about 25 words or fewer) and briefly describes the product or service, who the target customer is, and what niche or segment is the focus.

MISSION STATEMENT

A statement of your company's purpose and aims

YOUR MISSION

Your mission is your road map. First, it states what you believe in—the difference that the organization makes. Second, it becomes a way of measuring your success as you evaluate your results over time against what you stated you wanted to do. Third, it becomes your promotional message, as you incorporate it as part of your printed material.

A mission statement expresses the nature and raison d'être, or purpose, of the business. According to Industry Canada, it usually covers the major functions and operations of the organization and answers the following questions:[5]

- What are the products and services?
- Who is the expected or target customer?
- What industry is it in?
- Which markets does it serve? and
- What is its major driving force?
- Why will this business be successful?

Peter Drucker, in his book *The Practice of Management*, notes that we should think about a number of factors in developing a mission statement.[6]

1. **Customers**. Who is your target customer?
2. **Product or service**. What is your business all about—in a sentence or two?
3. **Geographic market**. Are you serving your local city, the province, Canada, or—if you are exporting—maybe even world markets?
4. **Concern for financial contribution and growth**. What returns do you expect on your investment, and what growth pattern do you expect to achieve (e.g., growth of 5 percent per year)?
5. **Core values and beliefs**. Look back at the list of values you created earlier in this chapter. Are these values consistent with what you want to do?
6. **Self-concept**. Because of knowledge and expertise, you may bring to the business a special skill that will give you a unique niche.
7. **Concern for public image and stakeholders**. Are you an environmentally friendly business? Will you be contributing a percentage of all sales to charity? Are you actively involved in your community?

8. **Concern for employees**. Are you planning to run your business on a team basis? Or will you alone be it?

9. **Technology and systems**. Does your business offer a value-added benefit by using technology or a particular system?

Your mission statement is unique. Some people capture their thoughts in a few words; others take pages. Some people express them in poems, some in music, and some in art. Some experts advise that an empowering mission statement

- represents the deepest and best within you,
- fulfills the contribution your business will make, and
- deals with your vision and principle-based values.[7]

For example, Anne and Steve's mission statement for their business might read like this:

> To help growing small businesses improve their profitability, effectiveness, and long-term growth through the implementation of, and training in, computer networks.

Here are a few other examples of mission statements:

> To own a flower and gift shop that specializes in highly stylized floral arrangements for "special occasions," and that services the local community.
>
> To be a proud and profitable home-based business providing responsive and efficient word-processing services and laser-quality correspondence to local small businesses.
>
> To sell environmentally friendly cleaning products to convenience stores in our city in order to reduce our growing dependence on chemicals.

In some cases, the mission statement is embedded in or followed up with a set of guiding principles or personal beliefs of the company/owner. For example, Vivienne Jones operates a by-appointment jewellery studio out of her Victorian home in downtown Toronto.[8] Her mission—to create a very personal form of expression through her jewellery—is rooted in her statement of personal beliefs about the way she does business:

> Jewellery to me is much more than "decoration." I see it as a very personal form of expression, both for the maker and for the wearer. I make jewellery for personal creative expression, and my work is an expressive and versatile medium into which I can put my thoughts and ideas and aesthetics. Intrinsic to the way I work is my imagining that the pieces I make will be worn and valued and hopefully will become a meaningful object in someone's life. It is perhaps because of the very personal attributes of jewellery that, when asked, I will enjoy working with a client to create a piece for them.

Vivienne Jones's beliefs help her stay true to herself, and to her vision of providing individualized jewellery that is both wearable and meaningful.

If you have been able to isolate an opportunity gap in your industry, it is now time to begin drafting your mission statement. Complete Action Step 23.

YOUR BUSINESS STRATEGY

BUSINESS STRATEGY

The broad program for achieving an organization's objectives and implementing its vision

A **business strategy** is a broad program for achieving an organization's objectives and thus implementing its vision. It creates a unified direction for the organization in terms of its many objectives. It also guides those choices that determine the nature and direction of an organization.

Before you start developing the strategy for your business, it's helpful to have a context or framework in which competitive strategy is formulated. A number of business models can help you begin to formulate your business strategy. An excellent positioning tool is the **SWOT** approach. SWOT is an abbreviation that refers to an analysis of internal **s**trengths and **w**eakness; and external **o**pportunities and **t**hreats.

The strengths and weaknesses are factors that are internal to the business. Here, you would be evaluating the strengths and weaknesses of both owner(s) and the business itself. Doing a strengths and weaknesses evaluation of yourself is an important piece of advice provided by successful entrepreneurs like Mike McCarron of MSM Transportation Incorporated (See, for example, E-Exercise, Box 3.7). Let's say that you wanted to open a new restaurant. If you had extensive experience in the food business (product knowledge), this would be an internal strength. If you had no demonstrated teamwork (managing skills) abilities, then this would be an internal weakness. As for the business, it might be short on cash. This would be an internal weakness of the business. On the other hand, if you had found a wonderful location, this would be an internal strength of the business.

Now let's go to the external aspects of a SWOT. External opportunities are those factors that are outside the control of the owner and the business. These would include aspects such as new distribution channels, changing tastes, or technology improvements. As a new restaurant owner, for example, an external opportunity might be a growing demand for ethnic foods or healthy eating. External threats relate to outside forces such as competition or a declining trend for restaurant patrons to consume alcohol.

An underlying weakness of the SWOT approach is its subjectivity. There is a tendency for an enthusiastic entrepreneur to overvalue the strengths and opportunities and undervalue the weaknesses and threats. To reduce this evaluative risk, you might want to get a "reality check" by asking knowledgeable people to do a SWOT on both you and your business idea. Another suggestion might be to apply a particular weighting factor (say 1 to 10) to each of your SWOT elements. Nevertheless, SWOT is an excellent way to position your business idea and begin your strategic thinking process. We will return to this SWOT framework when it comes time to talk about the competition, in Chapter 5, and your human resource requirements, in Chapter 12. In the meantime, if you want additional information on SWOT, a good Web site is Tutor2u™ (http://www.tutor2u.net/business/strategy/SWOT_analysis.htm).

We encourage you to integrate your SWOT into the kind of strategic model suggested by Michael E. Porter of the Harvard Business School. This framework (Figure 3.5) can be very helpful in building a sound strategy for your business. As you review the Porter model, you'll see that the left side refers to "Factors Internal to the Company." As an entrepreneur, you are required to look at your own strengths and weaknesses—after all, you are the company!

Your "Personal Values" will be contained in your value analysis and also in your mission statement. Don't take this section lightly, as it will be your internal guide to your overall business plan.

The right side of the competitive strategic model outlines the two major components to the "Factors External to the Company." "The Industry Opportunities and Threats" are critical to success and survival as a small business. As well, it is important to understand the "Broader Societal Expectations"—the trends discussed in Chapter 2 that your business will face.

Now is a good time to test your business idea. We encourage you to do the "Test Your Business Idea" E-Exercise in Box 3.7.

SWOT

An abbreviation that refers to an analysis of internal strengths and weaknesses, and external opportunities and threats

ACTION STEP 23

Begin drafting your mission statement

In Chapter 2, Action Step 15, we asked you to define your business and begin to develop your "pitch." Now you are ready to begin drafting your mission statement. We will help you to refine this statement over the course of the next few chapters. In Chapter 4, Action Step 27, and in Chapter 5 when we discuss your competition, we'll encourage you to go back and refine this statement.

In a short paragraph, describe the nature and purpose of your business. Try to include the following:

- What are your products and services?
- Who is your expected or target customer?
- What industry is your business in?
- Which markets does the business serve? and
- What is the major driving force of the business? Why will this business be successful?

You might also want to expand your statement by including your core set of values and beliefs, concern for stakeholders and the environment, or concern for employee well-being.

Now go back and revisit your personal vision. Does your personal vision connect with your business mission? It should. If you're having trouble, here is one example that might help.

(continued)

ACTION STEP 23

Begin drafting your mission statement *(continued)*

Beatrice had a personal vision: "To live a life in which others would remember her with dignity and respect." Her business mission was "to be a respected flower and gift shop owner specializing in highly stylized floral arrangements for 'special occasions' and catering to her local community needs."

As her business mission, Beatrice wanted to be remembered with respect and dignity through her gift of flowers.

Figure 3.5   Context in Which a Competitive Strategy Is Formulated

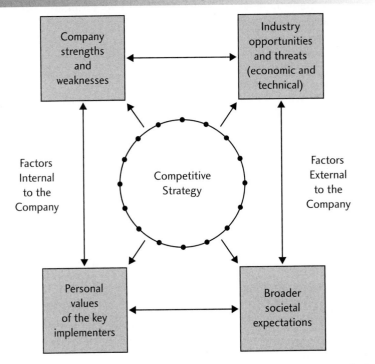

Use this model, developed by Michael E. Porter, to understand the context in which your business strategy will be formulated.

Source: Adapted with the permission of the Free Press, a Division of Simon & Schuster, from *Competitive Advantage: Creating and Sustaining Superior Performance* by Michael E. Porter. © 1985 by Michael E. Porter.

Box 3.7   E-Exercise

Test Your Business Idea

Atlantic Canada Opportunities Agency (ACOA): http://www.acoa.ca/e/business/entrepreneurship/ideas/appendixa.shtml—Visit the "From Ideas to Business Opportunities" page on the ACOA Web site. Test your business idea by exploring these four themes.

1. **Personal considerations.** Does your business idea satisfy your personal goals and objectives?
2. **Marketing considerations.** Is there a market need for your product or service?
3. **Production considerations.** Will you be able to produce the required volume and quality of products and services?
4. **Financial considerations.** Can your operation satisfy the required financial goals?

SWOT Yourself and Others

To understand your competitors, you're going to have to snoop. As we will learn in our Chapter 12 case study, Mike McCarron is a founding partner of MSM Transportation, an award-winning trucking company. Link onto his Streets Smarts article "I've got a Secret": http://www.shipmsm.com/Articles/SS200210%20%20I%27ve%20Got%20a%20Secret.pdf. What advice does he give us on how to learn more about our competition?

In a Nutshell

In the first few chapters, we encouraged you to come to grips with your personal vision and goals and to look at the industry trends with new eyes. In this third chapter, we want you to begin to match your personal vision, values, and goals with market needs. Here, we provide you with a seven-step opportunity selection process and encourage you to brainstorm and complete a matrix grid to help you get your personal vision in sync with your business mission. To illustrate how this process works, we followed the progress of Steve and Anne, who ended up deciding to start their business in the field of network computers. Next we wanted you to begin thinking about your mission statement. We hope that we have helped you connect your personal vision to a mission statement for a new business opportunity and that you are on the way to establishing your strategy for achieving your vision.

Key Terms

market gap	business strategy
matrix grid	SWOT
mission statement	values

Think Points for Success

✓ Your business must reflect your personal values. These values provide you with guidance and direction in the conduct of your business and life.
✓ Select an opportunity by using the seven-step opportunity selection process as a guide.
✓ Align your mission statement with your personal values. The statement must include the purpose and aim of your firm.
✓ Establish a strategy that supports your vision.

Business Plan Building Block

CURRENT POSITION AND FUTURE OUTLOOK

You will need to explain your current position and future outlook for this business projected out three to five years. And you are going to have to back up your explanation with industry research.

What does your secondary research say about your industry and industry segment? Go back to Action Step 18, page 62, and review your results. Consult with industry associations or experts. Review trade magazines.

If you're planning for an existing business, you must perform a critical analysis of your current situation and how you will grow the business over the next few years.

Focus on how you are unique and how to build on your strengths. If this is a start-up venture, base your forecast on industry research and your plans to exploit your market niche.

You began this process of defining your business in Chapter 2. Now it's time to build, correct, and polish your first attempt.

What industry are you in? What is your industry segment? How do you plan to grow your business over the next few years?

_____

_____

_____

_____

_____

Uniqueness and Differentiation

It is important that you demonstrate that you are addressing an unfilled need. You are different and unique, and you understand the meaning of pricing and value from your potential customers' perspective.

Your Business Is Unique Because ...

Your product is smaller, faster, neater, more flexible, lighter, more attractive, stronger, and so on. Or your service is quicker, more reliable, and mobile. Your people are better trained, your location more convenient. Your prices are competitive, and your business has many advantages over existing competition.

Nobody wants to hear about a "me too" business. Stress the ways in which your company is different—then translate these features into benefits for a hungry market. It's important to show how you have an edge over the competition. Try to think in terms of a "personal niche monopoly."

Market Opportunities

Based on your research, arrange the most promising opportunities in the marketplace according to the following categories:

1. new or emerging markets—gaps and niches,
2. neglected customer needs,
3. failing competitors,
4. complementary product mix,
5. expanded use of existing facilities,
6. new geographical and international opportunities, and
7. potential for profits.

Rank by priority order those that are most attractive now and up to five years forward.

Checklist Questions and Actions to Develop Your Business Plan

Positioning Yourself as an Entrepreneur for Market Opportunities

❑ How is your product or service addressing the needs of the target market and offering benefits?

❑ What are your business and personal values?

❑ Define your market niche.

❑ Define the idea filters you used to establish the business viability for your product or service.

❑ Complete your mission statement.

❑ Revisit and update your business goals and objectives under Checklist Questions and Actions on page 49 (Chapter 2).

❑ Identify market segments that have potential.

❑ List industry problems that your business might face, and describe how you would address them.

Case Study

CRAZY PLATES: A WINNING TEAM

Case Background

"Loser." With a small grin curling up on her face, Janet Podleski savoured and stretched out the first syllable. In the late 1990s, we found Janet playfully teasing her sister and business partner, Greta—and not in private. Despite Greta's renowned gourmet abilities in the kitchen, at that time she was without a man in her life and was the subject of her sister's public jibes. It was part of their promotional shtick. And although "loser" was hardly a moniker most people would use to promote themselves, Greta and Janet are not *most people*, as we will soon learn.

The Podleski sisters burst onto the business scene in the mid-1990s. They had joined forces with David Chilton, well-known author of *The Wealthy Barber*, and formed their own publishing company—Granet Publishing Incorporated. Each partner had his or her own role and responsibilities. David, the president, would manage the company, Janet would do the marketing, and Greta was the culinary expert. Their first cookbook, *Looneyspoons*, and its follow-up, *Crazy Plates*, were fun to read and hugely successful (over a million copies sold!). The books, peppered with cartoons and puns, contained healthy recipes with light-humoured names like "Jurassic Pork" and "Yabba Dabba Stew."

By the late 1990s, after their best-selling *Crazy Plates* cookbook hit the market, Greta and Janet felt the entrepreneurial itch and began to hunger for a new challenge. They didn't want to write a third cookbook—at least not for the time being. They also rejected a line of sauces and turned down several book and TV proposals—including a very lucrative U.S. offer. "We didn't care about being household celebrities," recalled Greta. Then, after thorough market research and much soul searching, the trio decided to make the leap from the business of publishing and cookbooks into the highly competitive business of frozen food.

Chilton and the Podleskis planned to target a growing trend of busy, "time-strapped" Canadians living in small family units, who wanted to quickly prepare healthy, delicious meals at reasonable prices. Cookbook buyers had been telling the team that they loved the recipes but didn't have enough time every night to cook from scratch. According to Chilton, "Even the big food companies had told us that fast, prepared and healthy dinners was the direction the industry was heading." The Podleskis and Chilton decided to establish a new company called Crazy Plates Incorporated. The compelling business vision for Crazy Plates was to put fun back into the kitchen and help time-strapped adults to prepare and eat healthy meals. The team's business goal was to combine their entrepreneurial, culinary, and marketing skills and launch a line of healthy, reasonably priced frozen dinners.

But the trio knew from the get-go that the frozen food business was highly competitive and filled with pitfalls—any one of which could put them under. They would have to overcome a litany of issues, such as creating meal kits with mass appeal; establishing and maintaining a pipeline for top-quality ingredients; packaging the food; transporting frozen items; making deals with grocers to get space on store shelves, preferably at eye level; projecting the correct volumes, so the supermarkets would have neither too much nor not enough food; and catching the attention of busy, already bombarded consumers. The team knew that anywhere along the line, a miss could mean a disaster—and all this in a business where even the large, multinational food companies worked on tight margins.

Given all these road bumps, nobody had quite figured out how to make money on this emerging trend. So the Podleskis and Chilton knew they had a tough nut to crack. Still, recalls Greta, as they had with the cookbooks, "we wanted to do something that had never been done before and we wanted to be the best."

The entrepreneurial spirit beckoned the trio. But how would the market respond?

After 15 months of "unpaid" work—developing recipes, testing the products, designing the packages, and finding suppliers and vendors—the first Crazy Plates Meal Kits went on the shelves of selected stores owned by Loblaw Companies Limited in the spring of 2001. Within two months, the market responded—with a thud. "We were on the wrong track," Chilton lamented. The "seminal moment" came in June, following, of all things, a golf tournament. At 1:00 in the morning, Chilton phoned Greta and Janet. "We have to start over," he told them.

According to Chilton, there were two major problems with the initial launch. The packages were unattractive, and, more significant, the meal kits, originally designed to serve families of four or five, were too big and, at $13.95, too expensive. "We needed a new size, a new price point, and new packaging," said Chilton. "It was awful," Greta painfully remembers. There were 50,000 dinners in the freezers at the stores and at the warehouse.

Chilton ended up paying $600,000 to the grocers to buy the food back. Over the summer months, at supermarkets across Ontario, Greta and Janet could be found handing out the Crazy Plates dinners, one by one, along with a letter admitting they'd goofed and asking customers to check out their new product line that fall. It was a costly exercise, but it was critical to maintain goodwill with both their customers and suppliers.

They could have given up, but they didn't. This first disaster actually propelled the team into a higher entrepreneurial gear. In the evenings, Greta, the team's "Chief Culinary Advisor" (CCA), scrambled to rework the kits. Janet, the marketer and self-declared kitchen klutz, created the Web site and planned a new promotional strategy. David renegotiated with suppliers and grocers, and began looking for investors.

Chilton found his answer to the money issues at the first door he knocked on. William Holland, a long-time Chilton fan and the chief executive of CI Mutual Funds Incorporated, drove an hour and a half from Toronto to Kitchener to have dinner at Greta's 1860s farmhouse home and test kitchen. "He didn't ask us many business questions," Chilton said, thinking back. Greta had worried that "maybe we hadn't sold him hard enough." But the next day, Holland told Chilton, "Tell me when you want your cheque."

Although Holland considered the food business "outrageously competitive," he was swayed by the quality of the food and by Chilton's impressive track record. "I didn't even know I was eating the frozen food," Holland recalled. He personally invested $1 million into the Crazy Plates venture, contributing most of the outside capital Chilton had been seeking. A second private investor put up the remaining $250,000. That, with $1 million directly from Chilton, was the company's financial food.

Today, with Chilton and the Podleskis at the helm of Crazy Plates, their Meal Kits have no resemblance to a loser. Crazy Plates Meal Kits take 20 minutes or less to cook but require the consumer to have a hand in their making. Each one is designed to feed two to three people; they are easy to prepare and priced competitively, retailing at stores like A&P for $7.95 and sometimes even a little less. As for quality and taste? Their Meal Kits are an award-winning delight and healthy to boot. According to Greta, "our Meal Kits taste great and they're simple to make. That's my responsibility, and that's one of the reasons I am proud to say our Meal Kits have been voted Best New Grocery Product of the Year by the Canadian Grocery Industry."

Since the speed bumps—some resembling rather large potholes—of the early 2000s, the team has gradually expanded its retail distributorship. In addition to A&P, for example, the Meal Kits are now available at additional Ontario stores like Food Basics, Dominion, Loeb, and The Barn. In the summer of 2005, they added to their product mix, launching a line of multigrain thin-crust pizzas into the market. These were the first multigrain pizzas in the Canadian marketplace. They now sell more pizzas than meal kits! In the fall of 2006, they introduced an exciting new addition to their distribution channel. The Crazy Plates team entered the U.S. market, selling their pizzas in select southeastern states.

As for the Podleskis, in early 2003 they committed to writing another cookbook. According to Greta, "After two years of long days and sleepless nights, we have now released our best book to date." *Eat, Shrink, and Be Merry!* hit the shelves in September 2005. It's another bestseller—of course. The sisters are also working on a TV show and a line of cooking tools and gadgets.

Today, Greta and Janet have become almost as much the product as the food itself. With their sexy appeal and overflowing enthusiasm, the Podleskis still present themselves as a wacky, struggling pair up against the giants. Last time we saw them, they had again plunked themselves in a large retail food outlet, joking, poking fun at each other, and finishing each other's sentences. On their display table were tasty product samples and stacks of *Eat, Shrink & Be Merry!*—each copy ready to be signed with a frilly pen and a thank you. Understandably, we did not hear the word "loser" this time. These are two hard-working entrepreneurs and very shrewd "cookies" who are passionate about healthy food.

Case Resources

Special thanks to Greta Podleski for her input, updates, persistence, wonderful sense of humour, and infectious enthusiasm.

- Katherine MacKlem, "Crazy Like Foxes, The Looneyspoons Team is Putting Its Money Where Your Mouth Is," *Maclean's,* March 4, 2002: http://www.macleans.ca/topstories/business/article.jsp?content=64411 (accessed July 2006).
- Crazy Plates home page: http://www.crazyplates.com/dave.html (accessed July 2006).
- Professional Speakers' Bureau Inc.: www.prospeakers.com/topic/?load=chilton (accessed July 2006).

Case Study Questions

1. Values

   In this chapter, you learned the importance of aligning your personal vision and values with the market opportunities. This "alignment" was a major factor contributing to the success of Cathy Waters of Abebooks and Ted Wolff von Selzam of Kinnikinnick Foods, featured in the opening vignettes.

   a. Briefly describe what is meant by the term *values*.

   b. In the section entitled "Your Values" (page 55), we provided you with a possible list of personal and business values. Based on this list, state four key values that the Crazy Plates team exhibited. For each value, give an example of how the team displayed or acted on this value.

2. Passion and vision

   According to David Chilton and this chapter (see Box 3.2 and http://www.prospeakers.com/topic/?load=chilton), passion and a clear business vision are critical to the success of a new venture. These are two major reasons why Chilton teamed up with the Podleskis. Briefly describe Janet and Greta Podleskis' passion and corresponding business vision for Crazy Plates.

3. Market Segmentation

   Chilton and the Podleskis found a market segment, or niche, that was consistent with their visions and values. What was the Crazy Plates market segment/niche?

4. Mission Statements

   Mission statements help successful entrepreneurs focus on their market niche.

   a. What is a mission statement?

   b. Draft a mission statement for Crazy Plates.

   c. Crazy Plates' first product launch was not successful. Briefly explain why.

5. Trends Can Create Opportunities

   In both this chapter and Chapter 2, we learned that trends can create business opportunities.

   a. Briefly explain how four market trends have contributed, so far, to the success of Crazy Plates? (To refresh you memory on trends, you might want to link onto http://www.acoa.ca/e/business/entrepreneurship/ideas/sectioniv.shtml)

   b. What is a SWOT? If you were to do a SWOT analysis of Crazy Plates, in what sections of your SWOT would you be discussing trends?

6. Problems Create Opportunities

   The first Crazy Plates product launch was a "disaster." But as we've learned in these first three chapters, successful entrepreneurs are those who continually look for opportunities. Chilton and the Podleskis attacked this problem in a positive fashion. They used this "time to start over" as a learning experience and a time to create new opportunities. Briefly describe three opportunities that the Crazy Plates team created as a result of this first product launch.

Notes

1. Adapted from "A New Life for Old Books" by Jack Kohane, Canadian Business Online: http://www.canadianbusiness.com/entrepreneur/index.jsp (accessed September 2005).
2. Kinnikinnick Foods Web site (http://www.kinnikinnick.ca); and Industry Canada, "Electronic Commerce in Canada, Success Stories": http://e-com.ic.gc.ca/english/stories/kinnikinnicksucc.html (accessed September 2005).
3. Canadian Business Online, "CEO Stories": http://www.canadianbusiness.com/entrepreneur/index.jsp (accessed September 2005).
4. Personal contact with Art Coren, Kwantlen University College, British Columbia.
5. An excellent discussion on developing your mission statement can be found by linking onto Industry Canada, "Steps to Competitiveness": http://strategis.ic.gc.ca/epic/internet/instco-levc.nsf/en/h_qw00053e.html (accessed June 2006).
6. Adapted from Peter F. Drucker, *The Practice of Management* (New York: Harper and Row, 1954).
7. Stephen R. Covey, A. Roger Merrill, and Rebecca R. Merrill. *First Things First* (New York: Simon & Schuster, 1994).
8. Vivienne Jones Web site (http://www.viviennejones.com); and Janice Lindsay, "Jewel in Parkdale," *The Globe and Mail*, July 13, 2002, p. L7.

SUGGESTED READING

Kawasaki, Guy, and Michele Moreno. *Rules for Revolutionaries: The Capitalist Manifesto for Creating and Marketing New Products and Services.* New York: Harper, 2000.

Schwartz, Evan I. *Juice: The Creative Fuel That Drives World-Class Inventors.* Cambridge, MA: HBS Press, 2004.

Pink, Daniel. *A Whole New Mind: Moving from the Informational Age to the Conceptual Age.* New York: Riverhead, 2005.

Jackson, Bruce. *Go it Alone! The Secret to Building a Successful Business on Your Own.* New York: Harper Business, 2005.

Gerber, Michael. *E-Myth Mastery: The Seven Essential Disciples for Building a World Class Company.* New York: Harper Business, 2005.

Ray, Michael. *The Highest Goal: The Secret That Sustains You in Every Moment.* San Francisco: Berrett-Koehler Publishers, 2004.

Gunther McGrath, Rita, and Ian MacMillan. *The Entrepreneurial Mindset.* Boston: Harvard Business School Press, 2000.

Kanbar, Maurice. *Secrets from an Inventor's Notebook.* New York: Penguin, 2002.

Kelley, Tom, with Jonathan Littman. *The Art of Innovation: Lessons in Creativity from IDEO, America's Leading Design Firm.* New York: Doubleday, 2001.

Profiling Your Target Customer

Chapter 4 will help you prepare part B of your business plan, The Market and the Target Customer.

Lands' End is a successful multinational retailer that sells clothes, luggage, and household products worldwide through outlet stores, catalogues, and the Web. It's a so-called **direct merchant (intermediary)**, meaning it works directly with mills and manufacturers in an attempt to eliminate the markups of middlemen. In the mid-1990s, Lands' End recognized the power of the Internet and became an "early adopter." Landsend.com was launched, and since then, it has grown to become one of the world's largest (in business volume) apparel Web sites.

What does this successful multinational company have to do with Canadian small business? Much of the Lands' End's dot-com success has do to with the vision, passion, and persistence of two Canadian entrepreneurs—Louise Guay and Jean-François St-Arnaud. Their company, My Virtual Model Incorporated (MVM), which began operation in the late 1990s, now provides much of the technology for Lands' End to sell its apparel online.

At Lands' End, here is how the My Virtual Model works. You log on and fill in a customer-friendly questionnaire. If it's your first time, the idea is to get quick feedback and to understand that the online system is easy, user friendly, and very efficient. When you are finished, your silhouette appears on the screen. You can then go shopping. You click on the garments you want and put them on the model. The virtual model allows you to mix and match different colours, styles, and sizes, and even turn a full circle. It's quite real, and it's fun. You can also add accessories.

Since the early 2000s, MVM has grown into a multimillion-dollar company. Its major clients, beginning with Lands' End, now include retail heavyweights such as Sears, L.L. Bean, and Adidas. The technology has fitted more than 4 million virtual models with 100 million garments, and they are increasing by 300,000 per month. My Virtual Model improves the profitability of e-retailers in three ways. First it increases the online "conversion rate"—the percentage of Web site visits that are converted into purchases. "Customers who use My Virtual Model have a 34 percent higher conversion rate," said Sam Taylor, vice president (in 2002) of e-commerce for Lands' End. In addition, the average order value is increased by as much as 15 percent, and the return rate can be reduced by up to 50 percent.

LEARNING OPPORTUNITIES

After reading this chapter, you should be able to

- understand that your key to survival in small business is the target customer;
- recognize three kinds of customer groups;
- use primary and secondary research to profile your target customer;
- simplify the messages you communicate through your business;
- discover how popular magazines aim at the target customer;
- match your target customer with what he or she reads, watches, and listens to;
- become more aware of, and start being on the lookout for, potential partnerships, alliances, and associations;
- recognize the market and the target customers who are about to surface;
- research your prospective target customers, and refine your mission statement; and
- visualize your business and target customers.

ACTION STEP
PREVIEW

24. Develop your own psychographic profile.
25. Research specific magazines in your business area.
26. Profile three firms using the Canadian Company Capabilities database.
27. Research your prospective target customers, and refine your mission statement

ACTION STEP 24

Develop your own psychographic profile

1. **Profile yourself.** Eventually, you're going to have to do a profile of your target customer. To get some practice—and have a little fun in the process—we want you to profile yourself as a target customer.

   The VALS model places adult consumers into one of eight segments: Innovators, Thinkers, Achievers, Experiencers, Believers, Strivers, Makers, or Survivors. We encourage you to learn more about your own needs and attitudes by taking the following VALS psychographic test. Click on to SRI Consulting Business Intelligence (SRIC-BI, http://www.sric-bi.com/VALS/presurvey.shtml). What is your VALS type?

2. **Profile your target customer using postal codes.** You can get a psychographic (and demographic) profile by postal code. Link onto Generation 5 (http://www.generation5.ca/CAN_insight5_mosaic.html), then type in your postal code or the postal code of one of your customers. Generation 5 will provide you with a psychographic profile of this group of homeowners. What a great way to learn all about your prospective customers—if you know where they live.

3. **Do your own psychographic profiling.** You may even want to invite a few friends to a "psychographic" party, or get together with a group of classmates. Ask questions: What are their motivators? Why does one brand appeal more than another? Is price important? What do they buy most? Do they prefer to buy online? Why? What products do they buy online? This informal primary research will help you understand why people buy specific products and services.

buying. For example, two adults with a combined income of $75,000, but with no children (**D**ouble-**I**ncome-**N**o-**K**ids) have different spending patterns than two adults earning $75,000 to $125,000 but with four children. Why? Because these two groups have completely different wants and values. People now buy products and services that reflect the needs of their lifestyles, not necessarily those of their sex, age, or income group.

Psychographics explores the whys and wants of consumer purchases. It is a process of segmenting the population by lifestyles and values, recognizing that people in each segment or slice have different reasons for making a purchase. Psychographic analysis groups (or segments) individuals into specific categories based on attitudes, needs, values, and "mental postures." It helps marketers, researchers, and business owners understand why people buy specific products and services. What are their motivators? Why does one product appeal more than another?

There are a number of "proprietary" psychographic models in use in North America. Two of the most prominent are the VALS (value and lifestyle model), from SRI International, and the Goldfarb model. In Action Step 24, we encourage you to become more comfortable with psychographics by profiling yourself using the VALS psychographic model.

Several for-profit companies can provide you with a psychographic or lifestyle profile for a specific area. For example, Compusearch or Generation 5 (see Action Step 24) can provide lifestyles data by postal code. The *Financial Post's FP Markets, Canadian Demographics* is another good source of psychographic data as well as demographic information. These kinds of data can be obtained in published form for large areas, but when it comes to a specific neighbourhood, you will most likely have to pay for the data. The cost can range from hundreds of dollars to hundreds of thousands of dollars, depending on the level of detail you need.

You will probably have to do most if not all of your own research to get a psychographic handle on your target customer—mainly because of cost factors. This is your opportunity to practise your new-eyes and primary research, and learn why people buy things. At worst, you will have fun playing marketing detective. In addition, this might be your opportunity to piggyback all of the information gathered for use by media sources. Check out Box 4.4 to see how one entrepreneurial firm, D-Code Incorporated, profiles its target customer—the Nexus generation. Then use Action Step 24 to begin developing your own psychographic profile.

Box 4.4 Target Market—The Nexus Generation

Businesses, governments, or other organizations trying to reach Generation X soon come up against a major roadblock: No one knows exactly who or what Generation X is!

According to some, Generation X is all about the year you were born: 1963, 1969, or (depending on who's talking) 1976. On the one hand, Generation Xers have been described as wanderers, slackers, and couch potatoes interested only in watching Simpsons reruns. On the other hand, they have been portrayed as the most conservative, hard-working generation since those born during the Great Depression. Similarly, some experts say Xers are serious about marriage, whereas others see the X generation as a group reluctant to make commitments.

Robert Barnard feels the term Generation X, as a label, is widely overused, ambiguous, and a cliché. "It means too many things to too many different people," says Barnard, a thirtysomething Xer from Toronto. Barnard founded D-Code, a small consulting firm that helps companies and government departments better understand what makes this group tick. In place of the term *Generation X*, D-Code uses the phrase *Nexus generation* to characterize this target group—those born in the early '60s to late '70s. *Nexus* means a bridge, or connection; in this case, the connection is between the industrial age and the birth of the information age.

D-Code helps its private- and public-sector clients decipher the aspirations, preferences, and unique features of the age group born at this critical nexus. It works with them to design marketing, human resource, or public policy strategies that connect with the Nexus generation consumers, employees, and citizens. In the process, D-Code strives to build bridges across generations.

The Nexus group is a powerful demographic making up about one-third of the Canadian population. According to D-Code, there are a number of key psychographic likes and dislikes of the Nexus generation:

- For Nexus, financial compensation is not as important as it is to the preceding generations. Nexus ranks quality of life (e.g., longer vacations) and opportunities for on-the-job training ahead of a whopping paycheque.

- Nexus is more skeptical about and has less confidence in traditional institutions such as the church, the university, the nuclear family, the state, and the corporation.

- Nexus is more media savvy, techno literate, educated, and worldly than any previous generation.

- Nexus is composed of "experience seekers" who put off marriage, kids, and house payments longer than those in previous generations.

- Nexus is more comfortable—and less anxious—about change.

- Nexus uses the Internet more than do other demographic groups.

- For Nexus, small business ownership is the most desirable occupation.

Sources: Personal correspondence with D-Code Inc. and D-Code's Web site at http://www.d-code.com (accessed October 2005).

WHAT WE CAN LEARN FROM MEDIA SOURCES

Mina Cohen was an archaeologist and teacher by training. She had worked on numerous excavations and had been a pedagogic adviser of Foreign Affairs and a teacher at a local high school. But despite her talents and extensive training, it seemed that she was always worried about her next job. The market just wasn't there for her talents. She even had to take a few secretarial jobs to supplement her income.

One day in late summer, she decided to take control of her life and entered a small business program at a local college. At first the course seemed incomprehensible. Techniques such as brainstorming and mind mapping were foreign to her; up to this point, she had been taught, in a "right-brained" manner, to be logical. In the end, however, she decided to persist and stay in the course. Finally, after a few group brainstorming sessions and extensive primary and secondary research, she had an idea: Why not offer archaeological excursions? She would be in the "holidays-with-a-purpose" business. But who were her target customers?

One fall evening, she was curled up, browsing her favourite magazine, *National Geographic Traveler*. She had been noticing a lot of ads by travel agencies and airlines. For these major advertisers, readers of *National Geographic Traveler* were their target market. It suddenly occurred to her that these readers might just be her target market as well. After all, this was *her* favourite magazine. She began flipping

be found at Home Hardware, in dozens of municipalities, and in health food and environmental companies, eavestrough repair companies, seasonal landscape businesses, and more! Arbour Environmental is now both a B2B and a B2C.

We want to encourage you to think about the opportunity to sell your product or service to businesses as well as to consumers. As we learned from the experience of the Arbour Environmental Shoppe,[7] you can benefit from both worlds. For example, you might start a small gift store. Why not prepare corporate gift packages? Those busy executives with oodles of money and poverty of time can have their special gifts sent out to their loved ones or business associates with a quick telephone call or at the click of a button—if you have a Web site, that is.

PRIMARY RESEARCH CAN HELP TOO

Secondary sources of demographic, psychographic, or business profiling information might be enough to target customers. Chances are, though, that you'll need to test your profile against reality. Field interviewing and surveying are two important primary research tools that can help you get a more accurate profile of your target customer.

FIELD INTERVIEWING TARGET CUSTOMERS

A lot of people go into small business because they don't have much choice. Many of them have to learn new skills and learn them fast. Fortunately, entrepreneurs tend to be bright, creative, and hard working. Julia Gonzales is a good example.

"It's no secret that I was distressed when my husband was transferred. I didn't blame him wanting the transfer; I would have wanted it, too. But I had a terrific job as manager of a full-line baby furniture and bedding store, and to keep both job and husband I'd have had to commute over 160 kilometres daily, five days a week. So, I quit my job.

"But I missed the store, and it was hard living on one salary when we'd gotten used to two. When I started to look for work, I found that my reputation had preceded me. Store owners knew of the place where I'd worked, and they were pretty sure that all I wanted was to work for them to get a feel for the area so that I could open a store of my own and compete with them.

"This gave me an idea. I hadn't *considered* doing that. So when I couldn't find work, I decided to go for it, to go ahead and compete with them. Their fear gave me confidence!

"One thing I learned on my way up from stock clerk to store manager was that it pays to know your customer. So, in the mornings I'd get the kids off to school, do a few chores, and drive to a baby store. I'd park my car a block away, and when customers came out of the store, I'd strike up conversations with them.

"'Hi!' I'd say. 'My name's Julia Gonzales, and I'm doing market research for a major manufacturer who's interested in this area. I'm wondering if you might have a minute to answer a few questions about babies.'

"My enthusiasm must have helped. I like people and babies, and I guess it shows. Being a mother helps me understand other mothers, too. I always dressed up a little bit and carried a clipboard. I'd ask the obvious questions like

- What do you like about this store?
- What things did you buy? and
- Were the people helpful and courteous?

"Sometimes I parked in the alley to research the delivery trucks. At the beach and the shopping malls, I would stop every pregnant woman I saw. I developed a separate list of questions for pregnant women:

- Have you had a baby shower?
- Which gifts did you like best?
- Which gifts seemed most useful?
- What things are you buying before your baby comes?
- What things are you waiting to buy?
- How are you going to decorate the baby's room?
- What do you really need the most?

"The research was time consuming, but after 30 interviews, I had enough information to make some very sound decisions. I also knew the weaknesses of my competition."

One way to get primary data is to interview or conduct focus group discussions among potential target customers, and in some cases, this might be the way to go. You could also interview other businesses if your target customer is the consumer or end user.

We saw how Julia Gonzales used interviewing to help her locate her new store. In the next chapter, we'll come back to interviewing again when we're researching our competition. In the meantime, we'll move on and use another skill: surveying to get a more refined picture of our target customer.

SURVEYING TARGET CUSTOMERS

Let's see how Elizabeth Wood used the survey technique to get her started on her own business.

Elizabeth was a supervisor at a local textile plant. Over the past few years, things had been tough. It seemed that she was always hearing about someone being laid off. She wondered when it would be her turn, but as time rolled on, she was becoming less and less concerned. She loved to be creative with food, and she had set her goal: opening a small neighbourhood restaurant.

For some time now, she had been developing her skills in business. She had taken several courses in restaurant and bar management. Next she took a small business course at a local university. In an attempt to get a handle on her target customer, she read many studies on the eating-out habits of Canadians. She knew that there was a trend to eating outside the home, but what did this mean for her local market? This secondary research was very revealing, but she just couldn't risk her future on someone else's research. She decided to do her own survey. She studied survey design and got plenty of advice from her professor, who had lots of experience in surveying. Crazy's Roadhouse was one of the most popular eating spots in town. Often, Elizabeth would have a bite to eat there, and she got to know Crazy's owner, Max, quite well. She told Max about her dream to open a small restaurant some day, and about how much she was learning in her small business course. They got to talking, and at last Max agreed to let Elizabeth do her survey of his customers. After all, the price was right. She would do the survey free of charge and would give Max her results—a classic win-win proposition.

Elizabeth spent the next few weeks designing her survey. How many customers should she survey? When should she survey? How should she conduct herself? There was so much to do. Fortunately, with the help of her small business teacher, Max, and the team she had been working with

ACTION STEP 27

Research your prospective target customers, and refine your mission statement

Now that you've profiled several target customers, it's time for you to take a big step. It's time to move from the tidy world inside your head to the arena of the marketplace. It's time to rub elbows with the people who'll be buying your product or service.

You know your TC's habits, income, sex, personality, and buying patterns, and can guess at his or her dreams and aspirations. You've identified the heavy users of your product or service. Now you're going to check these things out by interviewing these potential customers.

If you need help in preparing for you field interview, you might want to click onto "Field Research: Conducting an Interview": http://owl.english.purdue.edu/workshops/pp/interviewing.ppt.

Make up some questions in advance. Some of them should be open ended—that is, calling for more than just a simple yes or no. Here are some questions to help get you started:

- Do you like to shop at this store? Why?
- Why do you shop at this location?
- What need is this store satisfying?
- What products did you buy today?
- Are the salespeople helpful and courteous?
- How did you learn about this store?
- Is this your first visit? If not, how often do you shop here?
- What are you looking for that you didn't find in the store today?
- Where do you live?
- What do you read?

Now, we encourage you to return to your draft mission statement (Chapter 3, Action Step, 23, page 69). Refine your discussion on the target customer. What are the needs of your target customer, and how will your business satisfy these needs?

in school, she launched a week-long survey of Max's customers. To Max's surprise, customers wanted to fill out the questionnaire. To Elizabeth's surprise, she heard Max explaining to someone that he thought it was about time he learned a little bit more about what the customer wanted.

Stay tuned. We'll hear more about the results of Elizabeth's survey later on. But for now here are three of the major findings related to Max's target customer:

1. The lunch trade (Monday to Friday) customers were older than expected: Almost 40 percent were aged 35 to 44. In contrast, the weekend customers were younger: Fifty-two percent were 25 to 44 years old. As for the "after five" crowd, the average customer was even younger—almost 33 percent were under 25.
2. Regarding income, Elizabeth found that the major customer base was the affluent (those with $48,900+ in total family income). As a matter of fact, almost 50 percent of the customers had a professional as the head of the family, and 87 percent had two or more wage earners in the family unit.
3. From a psychographic perspective, Elizabeth found that at lunch, Max was getting the business crowd, who were eating salads and sipping Perrier. More than 60 percent ate at a restaurant at least once a week. In the evening, Max's restaurant attracted the bar crowd.

Elizabeth tried to answer a number of questions regarding the customer base: Why did the customer come to Max's? Where did his customer live and work? Who did the customer think the competition was? When her work was completed and she handed Max her results, Elizabeth got a pleasant surprise. She received a cheque from Max. "A small token of my appreciation," Max said. "It's not a lot, but I really did learn something. I thought I knew my customer before you came along."

Elizabeth didn't earn enough to quit her real job, but it was nice to get paid for developing a customer profile, one she could use to help her start her own restaurant. In the next chapter, we'll come back to Elizabeth and find out what her survey said about Max's competition.

When Julia Gonzales and Elizabeth Wood discovered that they would have to work for themselves, they quickly began to research their target customers. The method they chose was interviewing and surveying.

Understanding the needs of the target customer is critical to your business success. You are going to have to do your research. Action Step 27 tells you how to do this. It will also help you refine your mission statement.

VISUALIZE YOUR NEW BUSINESS AND TARGET CUSTOMER

A **business vision** is a mental picture of your business, product, or service at some time in the future. You might not get there, but this vision provides you with guidance and direction, and, in many cases, it's the raison d'être for your persistence and passion. It's the driving force.

Let's return to the My Virtual Model case. To large degree, the success of this business was the compelling vision of its cofounder Louise Guay. A local merchant with deep pockets had challenged her to "come up with an idea that will prove that technology will help women buy, and then I'll create a virtual store." She responded with a visual picture of her new business product—the Virtual Model.

"I thought, wow, I can come back to my passion because I love fashion, art and creativity, stage, to invent things, and I thought, isn't it the right time to start, to come with a neat idea, to solve these problems? So I thought, I have seen this little CD-ROM called Barbie Fashion

Designer. [Mattel's] Barbie was walking in 3-D on the runway and that was very well done. Very impressive. So I thought, it would be fantastic if we could create an experience where the user would fill a questionnaire about her measurements, the shape of her face, the colour of her eyes, her hair, and suddenly, a 3-D silhouette would appear and say: "Hi! I'm your virtual model, and I was born to look like you."[8]

Many e-types like Louise Guay of My Virtual Model and Adrienne Armstrong of Arbour Environmental Shoppe are dreamers. Their best ideas come in the form of visions. If you can identify with this e-type, then we encourage you to have the courage to follow your dreams. But make sure you record them in your 24/7 Adventure Notebook. Visualize your customers—primary, secondary, and even invisible customers, and the type of business you want. It will give you the passion and persistence to succeed. It will help you not only start but also grow your business. Remember, for example, Adrienne Armstrong had a new vision that helped her grow into a B2B rain barrel business. Now let's return to Louis Guay's business vision for My Virtual Model. It's inspiring and a good way to end this chapter.

"In the next five years I really see that we will open new areas. Right now we are in the garment industry but I can see that we will be in the beauty products. We are talking with very big beauty companies in the world where people ... for their hairstyle, their cosmetics, even plastic surgery for sure, reconstructive surgery, and for fitness, for health, for games. Imagine you will be in a video game playing with other people in the world and they will be in the game as you! In movies ... we already have demands to be part of many trailers. So it will diversify the use of the model in other areas and, geographically speaking, we start to work in the Netherlands and in France and the UK and Germany. We are already with Lands' End in the UK, Germany, and Japan. The Japanese people love fashion, they love technology, and I know they will love us."[9]

In a Nutshell

Your target customer is the key to your survival in small business. Constructing a customer profile is like drawing a circle around that customer to turn the circle into a target at which you can aim your product or service. Before you open your doors, you should profile your target customer at least five times. Try to visualize your new target customer and business. After your doors are open, it's a good idea to gather data through surveys, interviews, and so on, and to refine the profile monthly.

An end user profile combines demographic data (age, sex, income, education, residence, cultural roots) with psychographic insight (observation of lifestyle, buying habits, consumption patterns, attitudes). The magazines read by your target customer will reveal a well-drawn profile, because the chasers of this very expensive advertising have already researched the customer thoroughly. What other media sources are important to your target customer? And can these media sources help you with your profile? The Internet is another useful secondary profiling tool, especially if your target customers are other businesses. Surveying and field interviewing are primary research tools that will also help you find your target customers. You might want to go back and revisit Action Step 27 and the online workshop of field interviewing.

Profiling your target customer is important because it shows you

1. how to communicate your message with a minimum of confusion;
2. what additional service your target customer wants, such as delivery, credit, gift wrapping, installation, post-sales service, and so on;
3. how much the target customer can pay;
4. what quality the target customer wants;

BUSINESS VISION

A mental picture of your business, product, or service at some time in the future.

- Innovation in Canada, "Case 6, My Virtual Model Inc." http://innovation.ic.gc.ca/gol/innovation/site.nsf/en/in04211.html
- My Virtual Model Home page: http://www.myvirtualmodel.com/en/index.htm
- Lands' End, About Lands' End: http://www.landsend.com then click on "About Us"
- Lands' End, Direct Merchants: http://www.prnewswire.com/mnr/landsend/11847/

Case Study Questions

1. Customer relationship marketing

    In this chapter, we discussed an important marketing strategy called customer relationship marketing, which emphasizes a market-pull approach and one-to-one marketing.

    a. What is customer relationship marketing? Briefly explain how My Virtual Model made use of this strategy.

    b. Briefly explain the market-pull approach to marketing. How did MVM use this approach to get their first customer, Lands' End?

    c. Explain the term *one-to-one marketing*. How did MVM help Lands' End take advantage of this strategy?

2. Three types of customer groups

    We discussed three types of customer groups. Briefly, describe these three groups, and give an example of each based on the My Virtual Model case.

3. Profiling your target customer

    In this chapter, we broadly distinguished between two types of companies—business-to-business (B2B) and business-to-consumer (B2C).

    a. What type of company is MVM? If you were asked to profile MVM's target customer, what major variables or factors would you consider?

    b. What type of company is Lands' End? If you were asked to profile Lands' End's target customer, what major variables or factors would you consider?

4. Visualize and research your business and target customer

    A major reason for the success of MVM was the compelling vision of its cofounder Louise Guay.

    a. What was Louise Guay's visualization of her business and target customer?

    b. What is a business vision? What was MVM's business vision?

    c. You'll need to test your idea against reality. Field interviewing and surveying are two important primary research tools. Louise Guay had a vision for her new business and her target customer, but also knew she had to do some primary research. What is primary research and what primary research did Louise do before starting MVM?

5. Key success factors

    Market trends and partnerships were two key factors contributing to the success of MVM.

    a. List five market trends contributing to the success of MVM.

    b. As we explained in this chapter, alliances and partnerships are key success factors of fast-growth companies. Give two examples of how partnerships contributed to the success of MVM.

Notes

1. Innovation Canada, "Case 6, My Virtual Model Inc.": http://innovation.ic.gc.ca/gol/innovation/site.nsf/en/in04211.html; Innovation In Canada, "The Practice of Innovation, My Virtual Model": http://innovation.ic.gc.ca/gol/innovation/site.nsf/en/in04706.html: Innovation In Canada, The Practice of Innovation, My Virtual Model: http://innovation.ic.gc.ca/gol/innovation/site.nsf/en/in04712.html (accessed July 2006).
"Lands' End First With New 'My Virtual Model' Technology: Takes Guesswork Out Of Web Shopping For Clothes That Fit": http://www.prnewswire.com/mnr/landsend/11847/; Lands' End, "About Lands' End: http://www.landsend.com/, then click on "About Us"; and My Virtual Model; http://www.myvirtualmodel.com/en/index.htm (accessed July 2006).

2. Critical Mass, Case Studies http://www.criticalmass.com/clients/casestudies (accessed September 2005); Silicon Valley Business Inc., "Reflect.com Shines Despite Slowdown": http://www.svbizink.com/headlines/article.asp?aid=1563 ; and Industry Canada, "Electronic Commerce in Canada, Success Stories": http://e-com.ic.gc.ca/english/stories/criticalmasssucc.html (accessed July 2006).

3. The *Ottawa Citizen*, "From Rinks to Riots," by Janet Eastman, August 31, 2005, p. D1.

4. National Geographic, Bonnier Publications: http://www.bonnier.dk/Crosslink.jsp?d=bohp&d=164&a=184 (accessed July 2006).

5. Ron Truman, "Take It Outside," *Canadian Business* Online, August 4, 2005: http://www.canadianbusiness.com/entrepreneur/index.jsp; and Erik Heinrich, "Online Outsourcing," *Canadian Business* Online, December 2002/January 2003, http://www.canadianbusiness.com/entrepreneur/index.jsp (accessed July 2006).

6. Rick Spence, *Secrets of Success from Canada's Fastest Growing Companies* (Toronto: John Wiley and Sons, 1997), p. 103.

7. Primary research, "Networking and Brainstorming with Adrienne Armstrong, Arbour Environmental Shoppe," February 2006.

8. Innovation in Canada, "The Practice of Innovation, My Virtual Model." http://innovation.ic.gc.ca/gol/innovation/site.nsf/en/in04706.html (accessed July 2006).

9. Innovation in Canada, "The Practice of Innovation, My Virtual Model."

SUGGESTED READING

Blanchard, Ken, Jim Ballard, and Fred Finch. *Customer Mania! It's Never Too Late to Build a Customer-Focused Company.* New York: Free Press, 2004.

Clarke, Irvine, and Theresa Flaherty. *Advances in Electronic Marketing.* Hershey, PA: Idea Group, 2005.

Clegg, Brian. *The Invisible Customer.* Dover, NH: Kogan Press, 2000.

CustomerFAQs. (2004). "Online Customer Service: Making Inroads in the New Millennium." Available at: http://www.customfaqs.com/Press-BusinessServices.html (accessed July 2006).

Deluca, Fred, with John P. Hayes. *Start Small, Finish Big: Fifteen Key Lessons to Start—and Run—Your Own Successful Business.* New York: Warner Books, 2001.

Foot, David, with Daniel Stoffman. *Boom Bust & Echo: How to Profit from the Coming Demographic Shift.* Toronto, ON: Macfarlane Walter & Ross, 1996.

Godin, Seth. *Purple Cow: Transform Your Business by Being Remarkable.* New York: Portfolio, 2003.

Levinson, Jay Conrad, and Al Lautenslager. *Guerrilla Marketing in 30 Days.* Irvine, CA: Entrepreneur Press, 2005.

Ries, Al, and Jack Trout. *Positioning: The Battle for Your Mind.* New York: McGraw-Hill, 2001.

Tapscott, Don, and David Ticoll. *The Naked Corporation.* East Rutherford, NJ: Penguin, 2004.

Weiss, Michael J. *The Clustered World: How We Live, What We Buy, and What It All Means About Who We Are.* New York: Little Brown, 2000.

Zaltman, Gerald. *How Customers Think: Essential Insights into the Mind of the Market.* Boston: Harvard Business School Publishing, 2003.

Learning from the Competition: Your Competitive Intelligence

This chapter will help you prepare part C of your business plan, The Competition.

Ron Taylor's family had been in the business of building new homes until the early 1990s, when there was a recession in the housing market. When the bottom fell out of new-home construction, the family business closed, and Ron was left with the opportunity to find another business. It wasn't easy. It took healing time, a lot of soul searching, and a new skill—competitive intelligence.

In time, his new-eyes research led Ron into the business of renovating basements. People couldn't afford high-priced new homes or high interest rates, so they renovated. Secondary research from Statistics Canada and CMHC (Canada Mortgage and Housing Corporation) told him that this was a growth segment. His psychographic research led him to the conclusion that his primary target customers would be those who couldn't afford to build new homes but who wanted to build a sanctuary for their teenage offspring. He would be in the business of cocooning for teens.

It then came time for him to research his potential competitors. At first, he thought this was obvious. His major competitors were other contractors and builders—after all, if you could build a house, certainly doing a basement renovation would be no problem. But he soon realized that this was the same type of logic that had gotten his family into trouble in the early 1990s. His new business couldn't survive with a market sharing/price-cutting mentality. He could no longer afford to share a market. So, using primary research—interviewing, focus group discussions, and just plain listening—and a new technique called touchpoint analysis, he began to build a list of the benefits that his target customers were looking for, and a list of who, in the eyes of the customer, were the best companies or individuals to satisfy their wants. His first list included benefits such as

- electrical outlets—lots of them for teen toys;
- soundproofing;
- an area equipped for dancing; and
- a bathroom with a full-length mirror.

One night, after a long session with his mentor and some close friends, Ron realized that his competition wasn't other contractors at all. His competition was almost invisible. It was anyone who could provide the same benefits. He began to realize that in a strange way, even his customers could be major competitors.

LEARNING OPPORTUNITIES

After reading this chapter, you should be able to

- use competitive intelligence to collect and use information about your competition for the purpose of growing your business;
- discover how to create and grow your market with the help of your customers and competition;
- define your real competition through competitive touchpoint analysis;
- scout the competitive landscape to research your competition;
- evaluate your potential competitors using a competitive test matrix or SWOT analysis;
- begin your pricing strategy by completing a competitor pricing review sheet;
- define the unique benefits offered by your product or service;
- use the four-phase life cycle to change the arena and establish your competitive positioning strategy;
- discover ways to create uniqueness through service and product change;
- benefit from partnerships and associations with your potential competitors; and
- draft your competitive strategy.

ACTION STEP PREVIEW

28. Conduct a competitive touchpoint analysis.
29. Create a competitor review sheet.
30. Construct a competitive test matrix and competitor pricing review sheet.
31. Develop your competitive positioning strategy.

Back in the late 1990s, while living in a downtown Vancouver condo, Perri Domm was asked by his condo board to look into getting the graffiti removed from the building but could find no one to do the job. That's what gave him the idea. He formed Goodbye Graffiti Incorporated, a community-minded company whose vision was to "clean the world one wall at a time."

Like most start-ups, Goodbye Graffiti had a humble beginning. Perri began with a used truck, a power washer, and a variety of "so-called" graffiti removal products. In the early years, business was brisk. There was little competition, so Perri didn't give much thought to his competitive strategy. "We created an industry when we started our company," recalls Domm. "We never really had to test our ability to compete."

But by the early 2000s, unexpected and fierce competition moved in. The result: a hefty slump in sales. Because he had no competitive plan, Perri had to take swift, unplanned action, and he could only hope to survive. He needed his B2B customers to know the benefits of his service—and fast. Perri launched an expensive name and product recognition campaign. Domm's goal was "to distinguish his company against the low price guy who drives up in the rusty pickup truck with no logo and no insurance." His brand recognition campaign included both reactive and proactive benefits:

- A graffiti removal program would provide ongoing services, such as patrolling a customer's entire property at least once a week (proactive benefit).
- His company would start repairing windows damaged through scratching and acid etching (reactive benefit).
- He developed a proprietary product called Scratchiti, which protected windows against scratching and graffiti (proactive benefit).
- He launched an online graffiti removal program. With the click of a button, building owners could have their buildings inspected and cleaned. Goodbye Graffiti would go out and inspect the building, send (electronically) a detailed estimate (including photos), and, if approved by the owner, do the necessary work. Under this one-to-one marketing program, building owners would never have to leave their office (proactive benefit).

Fortunately for Domm, the benefits strategy worked. Today Goodbye Graffiti (http://www.goodbyegraffiti.com/index.htm) has more than 14 locations throughout Canada and the United States servicing some 3,000 properties. Major B2B customers include building owners, property managers, cities, municipalities, street equipment owners, parks superintendents, and vehicle fleets. But Domm had learned his competitive lesson. He now arms himself with competitive intelligence, has a competitive plan, and keeps a sharp lookout for competition—spending some $150,000 just to maintain and build his unique brand.

Only a few years ago, the subject of competition conjured up warlike terms such as "beat the competition," "disarm your competitor," "take a piece of their market," and so on. This market-sharing mentality assumed that when you went into business, you would take a piece of the action away from someone else. In a steady-state environment in which industries changed at a slow and predictable pace, the focus was on attacking the competition. Because there was little change going on, this strategy seemed to be the only way to drum up new business.

The knowledge-based economy, technology, and the new informed customer have changed the way businesses view competition. Competitive strategy is now about creating your own market niche or brand and continually changing and improving your product or service as the customer dictates. Competition is healthy, but it's not easy to deal with new competitors, and you must be prepared. Competition can come quickly, and it can threaten the life of a business—as Perri Domm learned. In some cases, it might even be difficult to determine who the real competition is—as Ron Taylor learned from his experience in the construction business. Brian Scudamore is founder and CEO of 1-800-GOT-JUNK? It is North America's largest junk-removal service. Brian and GOT-JUNK are highlighted in our opening vignette and case study in the next chapter. His first competitive challenge taught him that you must be prepared to learn from your competitors. A "learning" competitive strategy will help you grow your business.

In this chapter, we will help you understand and learn from your competitor, develop your competitive intelligence, and further define your specific product or service through competitive analysis.

WHO IS YOUR COMPETITION?

Recall in Chapter 2 that we talked about defining your business not in terms of a product or service but in terms of the benefits that your product or service provides to the potential customer. For example, you don't sell a book per se. You are really selling the benefits of information, enjoyment, or pleasant memories. In the same vein, your competition is not necessarily other businesses that provide a similar product or service. So, we now want you to think of your competitor in broader context. Your **competition** includes those companies or individuals that provide products, services or benefits similar to yours, as perceived by your target customer. **Direct (first-level) competitors** are those companies or individuals that offer the same types of products or services as yours, as perceived by your target customer. These are the most obvious types of competitors. They offer a product or service that is potentially interchangeable with yours in the eyes of the consumer. For example, if your business is selling ice cream, your direct competitors would be other ice cream and yogurt stores in your area. In the case of Ron Taylor, in the opening vignette, his direct competitor might be other local building contractors.

When thinking about your competition, you must also consider other so-called **indirect (second-level) competitors**. Indirect competitors are companies or individuals that provide the same benefit as your company does, as perceived by your target customer. Indirect competitors compete with your business for "same occasion" dollars. If you sell ice cream, for example, and the benefit for your target customer is an afternoon treat, then your indirect competitor is anyone who provides those treats. Your customer could stop and buy flowers, specialty coffee drinks, yogurt, sweet rolls, low-carb bars, or cookies. These indirect competitors might not provide the same product or service, but they are providing a competing benefit. Returning to Ron Taylor in the opening vignette, his indirect competitor might very well be a big-box store like Home Depot, which offers all kinds of home improvement services—mainly through outsourcing to its list of local contractors.

COMPETITION

Those companies or individuals that provide similar products, services, or benefits, as perceived by your target customer

DIRECT (FIRST-LEVEL) COMPETITORS

Those companies or individuals that offer the same types of products or services, as perceived by your target customer

INDIRECT (SECOND-LEVEL) COMPETITORS

Those companies or individuals that provide the same benefit, as perceived by your target customers

INVISIBLE COMPETITION

People or businesses that have the capacity or desire to provide the same products, services, or benefits that you do

Now we want to introduce you to a third kind of competitive threat called the **invisible competition**—that is, any business that has the *capacity* and *desire* to provide similar products, services, or benefits to your customer. In a borderless, virtual environment where you can order goods from as near as your next-door neighbour or from a place whose name you can't even pronounce, this type of invisible competition has become a real threat. It is definitely not virtual! Suppose that "Ted," for example, operates "Ted's Maintenance"—a successful building maintenance company in Halifax. He's feeling pretty secure. His equipment is paid for, and he has some healthy corporate clients. He thinks it would be difficult for a new company to invade his turf quickly. Then, almost overnight, a Goodbye Graffiti franchisee enters Halifax with a strong corporate partner; high-tech, efficient cleaning processes, and an online service program. That's right, Goodbye Graffiti, with its head office in Vancouver, is in the franchise business. They have some 14 franchise outlets and have an aggressive program to grow their domestic and U.S. market. If Ted cannot offer at least equivalent services at comparable prices, he is quite likely to begin losing some of his best corporate customers. Your invisible competitor does not necessary have to live on the Internet. For example, imagine you are in the fast-food business in a small town that doesn't have a McDonald's. Then Wal-Mart comes to town. Your invisible competition has just arrived with a McDonald's within its store. We also learned in the opening vignette that Ron Taylor's business had somewhat invisible competition—his customer might be able to the job and not need his services.

We encourage you to define your competition as broadly as possible at the beginning and then work through your industry to identify both direct and indirect competitors—and always be on the lookout for invisible customers. Remember, as well, that your competition is not necessarily who *you* think it is (although your views are important). Your customers define the competition in terms of those who can best satisfy their needs.

COMPETITIVE INTELLIGENCE

COMPETITIVE INTELLIGENCE (CI)

The process of learning, collecting, and using information about your competitors for the purpose of growing your business.

To identify your direct, indirect, and invisible competitors, you are going to need to conduct **competitive intelligence (CI)**. There is a myriad of definitions for the term *competitive intelligence*. A simplified definition is the process of learning, collecting, and using information about your competitors for the purpose of growing your business.[2] Competitive intelligence is proactive—not reactive. Your major objective is to find new customer needs and opportunities as a result of your competition analysis. The objective is not to eliminate your competitors but to learn and benefit from them. CI is future oriented. You are looking to develop and improve your specific niche or position in the marketplace.

Ten common goals of competitive intelligence are to

- improve your product features (especially price) and customer benefits,
- improve your customer service,
- find new ways to distribute your product/service,
- improve your advertising and promotions,
- develop more efficient production processes,
- reduce your reaction and delivery time,
- add value to your product or service,
- find new alliances and strategic partners,
- find new ways to grow your current product/service, and
- develop new product/service opportunities.

Your competitive intelligence will require a well-researched understanding of

- your target customers,
- your current competition, and
- your future competition.

How and where do you find information to conduct your competitive intelligence? Your target customer should be your major focus, so we are going start with your customer research and the resulting competitive touchpoint analysis.

COMPETITIVE TOUCHPOINT ANALYSIS

People don't just purchase products or services—they also buy what the products and service do for them. The customer wants to know, "What's in it for me? How does it make my life better, easier, more effective, and fun?" **Competitive touchpoint analysis** is a way to begin learning about your competition. It involves analyzing customers' perceptions of the competition to find out what benefits and features are important to them. A touchpoint represents an instance when the customer has contact with anything affiliated with a firm: advertising, products, packaging, public relations, receptionists, salespeople, or the building or store. Provided below are a few examples of customer touchpoints that you might look for in your competitive analysis. (Of course, many more possible touchpoints could be added to this list.)

Possible competitor touchpoints:

- **Receive advertising in the mail**. What is the quality of the advertisement? Is it mailed first class? Is it addressed to the right person? How many mailings does the customer receive before he or she responds?
- **Customer inquiries**. How quickly is the phone answered? What is the process for responding to a telephone inquiry? How long is the customer put on hold before being directed to a salesperson? Is there an online help service? Are the salespersons knowledgeable, articulate, and able to answer the customer's questions? Is the receptionist polite and pleasant?
- **Place orders**. Is the order form easy to fill out and understand? Is the pricing clear? Are alternatives clearly spelled out? Is ordering online straightforward and quick?
- **Receive orders**. Does the customer receive the right order at the right time and at the right place? Is there any follow-up?
- **Call to complain or change an order**. Are the customer's complaints or requests to change an order addressed in a timely and considerate fashion? Are follow-up calls made to ensure that the customer's problem has been solved?
- **Price/value**. Are customers looking for a sale, or are they looking for value? How important is the quality factor?

Competitive touchpoint analysis is a primary research tool. You have to talk to customers directly, and there are numerous ways to do this. Here are four possible methods.

1. Gather together a small group of your potential target customers for a "group think" on your competitors. Some would call this a focus group. Walk together through the entire experience your customers encounter with your competition. Make a list of all the customer touchpoints, and rank their importance as perceived by your target customer.
2. A second method of getting touchpoint information is simply to be a customer yourself. Go to competing establishments, and ask a lot of questions. Make sure you bring a pad of paper and a pencil. You don't have to pretend to shop from your competitors. It's okay to buy something. Make a small investment. Not only will you gain firsthand experience of the company's products and services, you will also now understand how they service the customer. And don't forget that many businesses are now selling over the Net. If that's the case, you might want to "Net" buy a competing product. What was your experience? How did they deliver the product? How long did it take you to receive it? What did they charge? Was their Web site customer friendly?

COMPETITIVE TOUCHPOINT ANALYSIS

Analyzing customers' perceptions of the competition to find out what benefits and features are important to them

3. A third approach is to go out and talk to your competitors' customers one on one. This could be a useful approach for retail businesses such as hardware outlets, clothing stores, and restaurants. Normally it involves talking to a customer soon after he or she has made a purchase. Here, you have to be careful and use your discretion. Be truthful. If the customers want to know why you are asking these questions, tell them that you sell similar products and want to improve your business by finding out what your competitors are doing right and doing wrong. We caution you. Be respectful of your competitors, as well. For example, you should not interfere with a competitor's business. You should not be seen as trying to steal business away. And above all, you should not "badmouth" your competitor. If you feel uncomfortable about talking to your competitor's customers, do a site visit. Walk around the competitor's place of business. Use your new-eyes research. Observe the corporate image, product displays, level of service, and corporate ambiance.

4. A final approach is to talk to or survey your own customers. Who do they think your competition is? Where do they shop, eat, or purchase services similar to yours? Now, this might not be a useful technique if you are just starting a business, since you don't have a real customer, but there are still creative opportunities. Let's return to Elizabeth Wood (from Chapter 4) and see how she uncovered the real competitor for Max, the owner of Crazy's Roadhouse, by using a survey questionnaire. Remember, Elizabeth's business was not yet off the ground. She was doing free research for Max to learn more about her favourite industry.

Max, the owner of Crazy's Roadhouse, didn't think he needed to know what the customer thought. He knew who the competition was: that other roadhouse down the street. Fortunately, Elizabeth knew better. In her restaurant questionnaire, she asked the customers who the competition was: "If you did not eat here today, what restaurant would you have chosen?"

The results gave Max a new perspective on his business. He learned that his competition depended on the dining-out time. At noon, his competition was any restaurant within a two-kilometre radius that could serve the customer fast. The noon-hour trade was more concerned with "getting in and out" than with the quality of the food.

Weekdays from 6 to 9 p.m. and weekends, his competition was any restaurant within an 18-kilometre radius of his roadhouse that provided great food and a fun atmosphere. During this period, Crazy's was perceived as a "destination" restaurant. In contrast to the noon-hour trade, these customers did not value quick service as much as quality food and dining atmosphere.

The crowd after 9 p.m. on both weekdays and weekends had a different need: fun time. Max's competition was not the great eateries but establishments that catered to the entertainment side of the business. Customers were prepared to drive as much as 50 kilometres to enjoy a good evening out.

Max was taken aback by the survey results. He didn't have a specific competitor at all. He had a number of potential competitors, depending on the dining-out period. With Elizabeth's help, not only did Max get a much clearer picture of his somewhat elusive competitors, he also began to get some new ideas about how he could promote and grow his business.

DISTINCTIVE COMPETENCY

Unique features and benefits that attract customers and encourage customer loyalty

To compete effectively, you need to stand out! Develop a **distinctive competency** — unique features and benefits that attract customers and encourage customer loyalty. Success in business is not based merely on obtaining customers; true success is achieved by retaining them. So as you do your competitive touchpoint analysis, seek out your competitors' strengths and weaknesses. Look for those features and bene-fits that encourage customer loyalty by continually reviewing your touchpoints. Remember to keep focusing on the benefits your customers receive.

We encourage you to do your own competitive touchpoint analysis by com-pleting Action Step 28.

SCOUTING THE COMPETITIVE LANDSCAPE

Competitive touchpoints are a primary source of competitive intelligence. You get your target customers to help develop your competitive strategy. Now we are going to ask you to research your direct, your indirect, and even your invisible competitors—scout the competitive landscape—to further hone your strategy. There are all kinds of primary and secondary sources that will help you learn more about your competitors. We have listed below a number of these major other sources. To gain the most benefit from these information sources, you will need both your primary and your secondary research skills. The particular source(s) that will be most useful to you will depend on the type of business you are starting, your resources, time factors, and so on.

- **Suppliers.** Suppliers can provide great insight about your competitors and the big picture. Get a list of your major suppliers, maybe even your competi-tors' suppliers, if you have this information. Go out and talk to them. Ask such questions as Who else do they supply? How much do they supply? What are your suppliers' pricing policies? Beware of and remember those suppliers who provide you with "confidential" information—they are likely to provide the same information about you to your competitors in the future!
- **Trade shows and conferences.** Attending trade shows and conferences, and asking questions, provides excellent market information, and if you go with a friend or partner, you can split up so that you can cover the entire show, com-pare insights, and return to ask more detailed questions. No one knows an industry better than the salespeople. The more of your competitors' sales-people you encounter, the more you will learn.
- **Competitors' literature.** Request, as a potential customer, product brochures and price lists from existing competitors. These will give insight into the product concepts, promotion, and corporate image.
- **Industry/association journals.** Read industry journals. What are they saying about your potential competitors? Learn about the publicity competi-tors are receiving on new products and services.
- **Resource centres.** Community resource centres and public libraries are a very good source of commercial and government publications, and the information is usually free. Here you'll find competitive information from industry reports, newspapers, trade journals, and company information and databases. A college or university resource centre can provide you with an even broader collection of competitive intelligence resources, such as *Financial Post—Industry Reports*; Dominion Bond Rating Service; Industry Studies; *Financial Post 500*; *Report on Business* magazine: the top 1000; and Standard & Poor's *Industry Surveys* (a U.S. source that contains some Canadian information). You might want to check out Canadian business directories such as *Blue Book of Canadian Business*, *Scott's Industrial Directory*, and *Fraser's Canadian Trade Directory*.
- **Trade magazines.** Learn about competitors' new products and services. What publicity are they receiving? If you don't know your industry trade magazines, Associations Canada (http://www.micromedia.ca/Directories/Associations.htm) would be a good start.
- **Industry Internet analysis.** Start with one of the more common search engines: AlltheWeb, AltaVista, Excite, Gigablast, or Google. Do a search on

ACTION STEP 28

Conduct a competitive touchpoint analysis

Investigate your customer's per-ception of the competition and what benefits are important to him or her. As you look for a niche in the marketplace, you must review your competitors' actions and products.

Work with a group of your poten-tial target customers; be a cus-tomer, talk to your competitors' customers directly, or do a survey. What is the customer experience of purchasing your competitors' products? Make a long list (as many as 60 items) of touch-points—each time the customer comes in contact with any facet of the competitors' business. Each facet makes up the entire product: the jewel. The more you know about the jewel, the more you can make it shine!

Make a list of your customers' touchpoints, and rank their impor-tance as perceived by your target customer. You need to consider which facets are worth going head-to-head with, which are not worth dealing with, and in which areas you can outperform your competi-tion. Keep your touchpoints handy, because you will return to them in Chapters 6 and 7. When writing your Business Plan, capitalize on the touchpoints that make you stand out in the crowd!

your favourite industry. You might even find specific information on your competitors. Bookmark your competitors who have a Web site.

- **Company Web site analysis**. Many businesses, of course, have their own site. Visit the Web sites of your major competitors. In some cases, this can provide a gold mine of information. What you learn will depend on the company, the type of business, and your information needs. But you should be on the lookout for such information as the company structure, history, location, product prices, mission, and future plans. Who are the owners and major players? What is their experience? Sometimes, in B2B companies you might even be able to get a list of your competitors' major customers. Do your competitors e-retail? If so, you might want to become a Net customer. Buy a product. Evaluate the e-retailing process. If you're satisfied with the process, how can you improve your process to connect with the customer over the Net? Make a list of those competitors who don't have Web sites. If they don't sell over the Net, this might be an opportunity for you to "fill the gap."

- **Franchise information**. Franchises are a fact of business life in Canada. Start with the Canadian Franchise Association (http://www.cfa.ca). Do you have any potential competitors in the franchise business? Are there any franchises that provide the same benefits? Is an invisible competitor looming?

- **Internet news groups**. Call up a search engine, Google for example, and click on the box that points you to groups. With a little Net research and a few clicks, you could land on a Usenet discussion forum related to your industry.

We hope we have encouraged you to start with some rich sources of competitor information. A more comprehensive list and discussion of on- and offline sources of competitive intelligence can be found by linking onto the Industry Canada sites provided in Box 5.1. The kinds of information you will be looking for are shown in Box 5.2.

Next we want you to think about how you can position yourself and your business.

Box 5.1 Bookmark This

What Is Performance Plus?

Found on the Strategis Web site (http://strategis.ic.gc.ca/epic/internet/inpp-pp.nsf/en/Home), Performance Plus is an online performance benchmarking tool that helps small businesses determine how they measure up against their competitors by providing detailed financial and employment data—over several years—on more than 600 business sectors across Canada. This extensive database has been created from a sample of Canada Revenue Agency tax returns for businesses operating in Canada. To learn more about these profiles, visit the "What Is Performance Plus?" page. Click on "Small Business Profiles," and discover the answers to these questions:

- What are the Small Business Profiles?
- How are they derived?
- How can you use the profiles?
- How "small" are the businesses represented in the Small Business Profiles?
- What data items are available?

Now we want you to click onto "View a Sample Case." By following this example, you will learn how to use this "treasure" of an information source to obtain current and historical industry information.

E-Sources of Competitive Information

Link onto Industry Canada's ebiz.enable: http://strategis.ic.gc.ca/epic/internet/inee-ef.nsf/en/h_ee00502e.html.

Here you will find a plethora of helpful competitive information on

- software programs,
- information professionals,
- consulting and research services,
- industry Web sites,
- publications,
- Canadian company information,
- Canadian business directories,
- commercial information and research services, and
- on- and offline sources.

Box 5.2 Elements of a Competitor Profile

A competitor profile will include data needed to identify, classify, and track competitors and their behaviour effectively. You'll be looking for points of comparison regarding your strengths and weaknesses versus theirs.

The following is a comprehensive list of suggested data to consider. We recommend that you use this as a guideline, or checklist, selecting only those elements that make sense for your particular business, industry, or competitive situation. Action Step 29 will help you compile a list of potential competitors.

Company Identification

- **Name.** Full legal name, informal or abbreviated versions.
- **Access information.** Address, office locations, Web sites, e-mail, phone, fax, etc.
- **Company structure.** Organizational structure and legal structure (proprietorship, partnership, corporation).
- **Ownership.** Owners, percentage of ownership and control, form of ownership (common stock, etc.), extent of involvement in company.
- **History.** Background and track record.
- **Corporate culture.** Business philosophy, guiding beliefs.

Stature and Credibility of the Company

- **Size.** Breadth and depth of resources of organization.
- **Stability.** Length of time in business or successful market presence.
- **Reputation.** Ethical conduct (business practices, employee relations, customer relations), government or industry certification, community sponsorship.
- **Credibility.** Market or industry recognition (honours, awards, references), record of effectiveness or success.

Proprietary Assets

- **Patents.** Any registered or pending copyrights, patents, or trade secrets.
- **Proprietary attributes.** Trademarks, processes.
- **Branding.** Recognized brand names or brand loyalty.

Product Design/Services and Innovation

- **Offering.** Product or service lines, features and mix, customer support.
- **Quality.** Perceived quality of products or services, and support (from the customer perspective).

ACTION STEP 29

Create a competitor review sheet

Using sources of competitor information such as those detailed in the section "Scouting the Competitive Landscape," compile a list of your competitors. Boxes 5.1 and 5.2 will also help you get started. Don't worry if your list of competitors gets too long. The more competitors you detect, the more you can learn.

Using your list of touchpoints from Action Step 28 and past research, create a review sheet for each competitor. It should answer such questions as

What is unique about this firm?
Who are its target customers?
What are its strengths and weaknesses?
What needs aren't being met?
What area could you capitalize on?
Where do you see yourself being strong or weak?
What images are your competitors projecting?
What image will you project? and
What price(s) do they charge, and does the consumer feel he/she is getting fair value?

Keep this Action Step on hand, because you will need it to complete Action Step 30.

- **Research and development (R&D) activities.** Anticipated new products/services (consider also new generations of existing products/services, complementary products/services, and replacement products/services). The R&D activities of suppliers and customers might also provide a glimpse of future prospects.

Operations (Production/Service Capability)

- **Internal resources and capacity.** Staff, skills, equipment, facilities, and communication technology. Consider staff's status (union vs. non-union, contract, shift, etc.), qualifications, and experience; condition of equipment and facilities (obsolete vs. leading edge); staff communication and flexibility (telecommuting, remote access, etc.).
- **External resources.** Subcontractors, strategic alliances, etc.

Marketing and Sales Approach

- **Sales.** Expressed either as unit sales (number of product units sold) or dollar sales (sales revenue from units sold or services provided).
- **Market share.** A company's sales expressed as a percentage of total sales in the market. Although several definitions of market share are possible, the most readily available measure is of "overall market share." This is based on total industry sales, which are available from government or industry trade association sources.
- **Sales force.** Internal vs. external representation, size, recruitment and training, compensation.
- **Sales activities.** The process of identifying and qualifying sales prospects, number of sales calls per period, productivity of sales staff, and average size of sale.

Marketing Strategy and Pricing:

- **Target markets.** Primary and secondary market segments.
- **Expansion plans.** Growth objectives (market penetration) and strategy.
- **Communication.** Promotion, advertising, public relations, Internet, publications, and trade shows.
- **Pricing.** Price levels, gross margins, and discount structure (volume, prompt payment, etc.).

Distribution

- **Geographic coverage.** Domestic, foreign, or global.
- **Distribution channels.** Direct, through agents, or retail.
- **Customer support.** Product support, field service, and so on.

Management Resources

- **Key decision makers and operating staff.** Names, positions, primary responsibilities, unique skills and experience, and compensation.
- **Board of directors.** Name, position on board, background, and extent of involvement with company.
- **Planned additions to management team.** Positions, primary responsibilities and authority, requisite skills and experience, recruitment process and timing of opportunities, compensation, etc. (available from recruitment ads and activities).

Finance

- **Financial resources.** Assets, liabilities, inventory, revenue, cost of goods sold, expenses, income, cash flow, profit margins, return on investment, new investment, and so on. Financial data are available from financial statements (included in annual reports or financial analyses). Financial statements comprise the balance sheet, earnings statement (or income statement), retained earnings statement, and changes in financial position statement.

Source: Industry Canada, *ebiz.enable, Elements of a Profile*: http://strategis.ic.gc.ca/epic/internet/inee-ef.nsf/en/h_ee00541e.html (accessed July 2006).

DEVELOPING YOUR COMPETITIVE STRATEGY

Now that you have studied the competition and prepared your competitive review sheet(s), it's time that you begin thinking about your competitive **positioning** strategy. **Positioning** is the process of establishing in the mind of the consumer a unique image or perception of a company, product, or service. **Competitive positioning** is the process of establishing unique benefits and features that the target customer values relative to the competition. What is it that makes your company unique? What is your distinctive competency? What key component will give you the competitive edge? We want you to think of yourself as building a moat around your castle, so that your competitors will find it difficult to enter. The key component you are looking for is what some have termed your company's driving force.[3] All decisions, including those about what products to develop, which customers to target, and which markets to enter, should be based on your driving force (some have called this a value discipline or distinctive competency). For most small businesses, there are three broad competitive strategies that provide a framework for you to home your particular driving force in on.[4]

POSITIONING

The process of establishing in the mind of the consumer a unique image or perception of a company, product, or service

COMPETITIVE POSITIONING

The process of establishing unique benefits and features that the target customer values relative to the competition

NICHE, OR FOCUS STRATEGY

A company carves out a specific or narrow segment of a market. A firm is pursuing a focus strategy if it targets one or more narrow market segments, or "niches," which are segments within segments. This strategy is particularly popular among smaller businesses. Some specialist roles open to niche competitors include the following:

- End-user specialists serve one type of "end-use" customer (consumer).
- Vertical-level specialists limit themselves to one level of the production-distribution chain (i.e., produce raw material but not components).
- Customer-size specialists concentrate on small, medium, or large customers.
- Specific-customer specialists sell to only a few major customers.
- Geographic specialists sell only in a particular area or region.
- Product or product-line specialists produce a single product or line of products.
- Product-feature specialists produce only a certain type of product or product feature.
- Custom specialists create custom products to order.
- Quality/price specialists concentrate on the low or high end of the market.
- Service specialists offer one or more services not available from other firms.
- Channel specialists serve only one channel of distribution (e.g., airline food).

DIFFERENTIATION STRATEGY

A differentiation strategy helps a firm to compete by successfully developing and maintaining a unique perception of its product or service that is valued by the customer. This "uniqueness" may be physical, technological, or psychological. Here are four ways in which a firm can differentiate its offerings from those of competitors:

- product design/quality differentiation,
- services/support differentiation,
- technology differentiation, and
- image differentiation.

ACTION STEP 30

Construct a competitive test matrix and competitor pricing review sheet *(continued)*

analysis. Name and briefly describe two invisible competitors. What two companies do not service your target customer but have the potential to do so?

Invisible Competitor #1. Name/briefly describe: _____

_____

_____

Invisible Competitor #2. Name/briefly describe: _____

_____

_____

Finally, we want you complete the competitor pricing review sheet provided in Box 5.3. You might want to consider this a first draft. In the pricing section of Chapter 6, we'll ask you to return to this analysis and review and refine your results.

Now you're ready to draft the following competitor pricing statement.

The price(s) of my products or services relative to my competitors' will be

_____

_____

_____

My justification is

_____

_____

_____

PRODUCT PENETRATION

A calculated thrust into the market

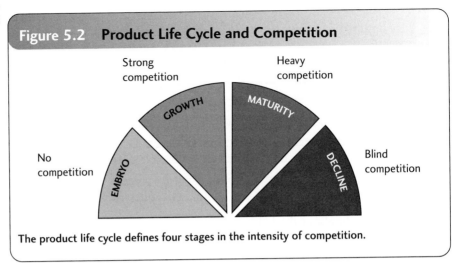

Figure 5.2   Product Life Cycle and Competition

The product life cycle defines four stages in the intensity of competition.

got six months from the birth of an idea to **product penetration**. After six months, competitors have already entered the market, and the product begins to enter the decline phase. What this means is that to survive, you must constantly be in touch with the market and compete with the right strategies accordingly. Figure 5.3 and Box 5.4 will help you understand the life cycle stages more clearly.

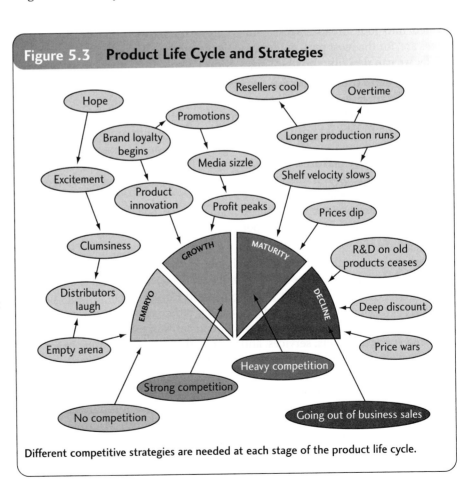

Figure 5.3   Product Life Cycle and Strategies

Different competitive strategies are needed at each stage of the product life cycle.

Box 5.4   The Competition Life Cycle

The Embryonic Stage

The embryonic stage is marked by excitement, naïve euphoric thrust, clumsiness, a high failure rate, and much brainstorming. Competition has not yet appeared. Pricing is experimental. Sales volume is low, because the market is very small, and production and marketing costs are high. It's difficult to find distributors, and resellers demand huge gross margins. Profit is chancy and speculative. Shrewd entrepreneurs, however, can close their eyes and divine the presence of a core market. And persistence can pay off. The authors of the best-selling *Chicken Soup for the Soul* series went to more than 30 publishers before finding the one that launched their multimillion-dollar empire.

The Growth Stage

The growth stage is marked by product innovation, strong product acceptance, the beginnings of brand loyalty, promotion by media sizzle, and ballpark pricing. Product innovation occurs. Distribution becomes all important. Resellers who laughed during the embryonic stage now clamour to distribute the product. Strong competitors, excited by the smell of money, enter the arena of the marketplace, as do new target customer groups. Profit shows signs of peaking.

The Mature Stage

The mature stage is marked by peak customer numbers and zero product modifications. Design concentrates on product differentiation rather than product improvement. Competitors are going at it blindly now, running on momentum even as shelf velocity slows. Production runs get longer, so firms can take full advantage of capital equipment and experienced management. Resellers, sensing doom, are cool on the product. Advertising investments increase, in step with competition. Prices are on a swift slide down. Competitors entering the market now won't survive unless they offer a unique product or service and effectively convey the benefits of that product/service to the target consumer.

The Decline Stage

The decline stage is marked by extreme depression in the marketplace. Competition becomes desperate. A few firms still hang on, but R&D ceases. Promotion vanishes, and price wars continue. Opportunities emerge for entrepreneurs in service and repair. Diehards fight for what remains of the core market. Resellers can't be found—they've moved on.

YOUR COMPETITIVE POSITIONING STRATEGY

In previous chapters, we've learned that a major objective when starting or owning a business is to position your product or service in a growth segment. If your market is growing at 25 percent a year, you might make a lot of mistakes and still succeed. If, however, you're competing in the mature or decline stage, one mistake can spell disaster. In these stages, you'll be forced to lower prices, take business away from others, or invest lots of advertising money. These are market-sharing conditions, and you don't want to—or shouldn't plan to—share a market.

You really don't want to position yourself in an embryonic competitive stage either. In this initial stage, you'll be all alone with virtually no proven market. We know that if you expect to make it, you'll need customers—a receptive market. But this means that you will need some competition, something that is virtually nonexistent in the embryonic stage.

COMPETITIVE POSITIONING

The process of establishing unique benefits and features that the target customer values relative to the competition

In today's changing economy, there are no choices. Your strategy must be a constant "war of movement" (for those of you who still think that your competitive strategy should be warlike) or a constant process of positioning and moving your product or service toward a growth market. The name of the game is change and creating uniqueness as dictated, first and foremost, by your customers and, second, by your potential competitors. Figure 5.4 depicts this new **competitive positioning** strategy. Yes, you will always have competition, because you need their advice. The secret is to learn continually from your competitors and customers, so that you can adjust your product or service to meet the needs and wants of the market. Your competitive strategy is all about changing the arena. By constantly adding benefits to your product or service, you will guide your business into growth segments. Another way to achieve this objective is to strike up partnerships with the competition.

FORMING STRATEGIC ALLIANCES WITH COMPETITORS

You'll recall Mina Cohen from Chapter 4. She decided she wanted to be in the "travel-with-a-purpose" business. Her product was archaeological excursions. The bad news was that she had created an embryonic product. No one else was offering this kind of service, so she was faced with such questions as What price do I charge? and How can I attract customers without massive advertising? To complicate things even more, her competitive analysis told her that her target customers valued their time and would likely get travel agencies to help them plan their vacation experience. Her competition would be travel agencies that could easily enter her market if they wanted to, and they would have a strong customer base to draw from. Here she was with an embryonic product, trying to position herself and do business in the fiercely competitive travel industry. What a challenge!

As Mina sifted through the ideas she had recorded in her 24/7 Adventure Notebook, a creative solution gradually took shape. Why not partner with a travel agency interested in the ecotourism market? She would locate the best travel agency

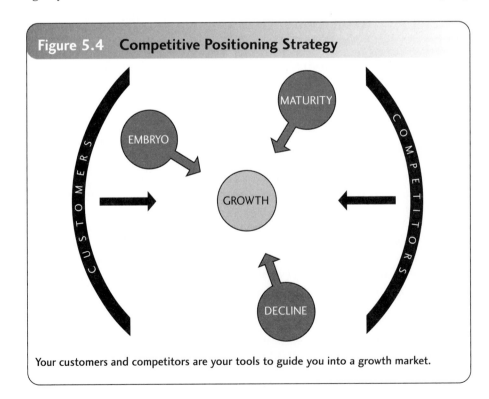

Figure 5.4   Competitive Positioning Strategy

Your customers and competitors are your tools to guide you into a growth market.

in town and offer her excursions as an add-on service. The agents would handle the advertising, pricing, and booking, as this was their strength—organizing and planning. Mina could then focus on her strengths—teaching and archaeology—and get paid from the travel package for her knowledge and expertise.

The lesson from Mina's experience is clear. She moved her embryonic service into a competitive market by creating an association with her potential competitor. By understanding the needs and strengths of her competitors, Mina was able to create a win-win situation by creating a **strategic alliance** with her potential competitors. A strategic alliance is a partnership between one or more organizations that is formed to create a competitive advantage. Partnership between competitors is a growing trend—one that should not be overlooked by small businesses, especially if they find themselves positioned in the embryonic stage.

STRATEGIC ALLIANCE

A partnership between one or more organizations that is formed to create a competitive advantage

CREATING UNIQUENESS THROUGH CHANGE

In today's competitive landscape, "If it ain't broke, don't fix it" has given way to "If it ain't broke, improve or change it, or it *will* be broke." Let's see how James Grenchik, owner of a retail tire company called Tire Pro, used this strategy to revive his flagging business.

It was painfully obvious to James that Tire Pro, a family business serving a large farming community, was in trouble. Every time he turned around, there seemed to be a new competitor setting up shop in his back yard. Canadian Tire, a recent arrival, was starting to cut into his business, and there were rumours that Costco was thinking of moving in. James fought back with price promotions and distress sales, but these traditional strategies just didn't seem to work anymore. Profits were dwindling.

James realized he had two choices—get out of business or change. Before he could make that choice, however, he needed to evaluate his competitors. To get a clear picture of their strengths and weaknesses, he talked to employees and customers, and began to construct a competitive test matrix (see Action Step 30). After months of soul searching, networking, brainstorming, and reviewing his competitive test matrix, James decided to stay in business. To keep Tire Pro viable, he introduced the following unique benefits.

- **An installment plan for farmers**. This add-on service is a major benefit to Tire Pro's target customers—farmers—who need tires early in the growing season, just when they are experiencing cash flow problems.
- **Tires with free rotation and inspection**. Tire Pro's customers now receive a free six-month tire rotation. In addition to the inspection, they get a free report card on potential trouble spots. Every six months, reminder postcards are mailed to customers; this keeps Tire Pro's name and image front and centre in the minds of its customers.
- **A revamped waiting room**. Tire Pro has added some amenities to its shop. While they wait to have their tires serviced, customers can sip free coffee while reading *AgriFamily Business Magazine* or using one of the recently installed computers to search the Internet for the latest commodities report. Another addition to Tire Pro's waiting room is a bulletin board on which notices (ads for used farm equipment, for example) can be posted.

Tire Pro's competitive strategy is not restricted to add-on services and customer service improvements: James is developing a Web site that will allow Tire Pro to build an online relationship with its target customers.

COMPETITIVE ANALYSIS

Summarize the material you have developed in this chapter to demonstrate that you haven't underestimated your competitors. A brief competitive overview could be sufficient for a small firm serving a local geographic area, a specialty distributor, a short-run manufacturer, or a professional service (1–2 pages).

A detailed competitive analysis is needed for larger firms ($2 million to $200 million in projected sales). Write a comprehensive analysis of their market share, marketing strategies, pricing, positioning, promotion, distribution, finances, and customers' perceptions (3–10 pages).

Make sure that you formulate your competitive positioning strategy. Answer the six basic questions provided in Action Step 31.

Checklist Questions and Actions to Develop Your Business Plan

Learning from the Competition

❑ Define and analyze your real competition through competitive touchpoint analysis.

❑ Construct a competitive test matrix or competitive SWOT analysis.

❑ Draft a competitive pricing strategy. Are your prices competitive?

❑ What is your major competitive positioning strategy?

❑ What is unique about your product or service?

❑ Are any invisible competitors ready to invade your territory?

❑ What is the size of the total market? What share do you expect to achieve in the first, second, and third years, and why?

Case Study

MY VIRTUAL MODEL

In the opening vignette of Chapter 4, we highlighted My Virtual Model (MVM), a successful company headed up by two Canadian entrepreneurs, Louise Guay and Jean-François St-Arnaud. MVM's major B2B clients included Lands' End, Sears, L.L. Bean, and Adidas.

In our case study, for Chapter 4, we encouraged you to do some further research into this winning company. Now we want you dig even deeper and consider the competitive environment for MVM. Our Chapter 5 case study questions will help you put to practice what you have learned from this chapter and improve your competitive intelligence skills.

Case Resources

The following sites will help you answer the case study questions. We suggest that you begin with the two case study Web casts listed first.

- Innovation in Canada, The Practice of Innovation: http://innovation.ic.gc.ca/gol/innovation/site.nsf/en/in04697.html—Be sure to view both.
- Innovation in Canada, "The Practice of Innovation, My Virtual Model, Case Profile" (text version): http://innovation.ic.gc.ca/gol/innovation/site.nsf/enin04706.html
- Innovation In Canada, The Practice of Innovation, My Virtual Model, Case Profile (text version): http://innovation.ic.gc.ca/gol/innovation/site.nsf/en/in04712.html
- Innovation Canada, "Case 6, My Virtual Model Inc." http://innovation.ic.gc.ca/gol/innovation/site.nsf/en/in04211.html

- Innovation Canada, "Module 5, Stage 4—the Continuous Innovation Cycle": http://innovation.ic.gc.ca/gol/innovation/site.nsf/en/in04199.html
- My Virtual Model home page: http://www.myvirtualmodel.com/en/index.htm
- Lands' End, "About Lands' End": http://www.landsend.com, then click on "About Us"
- Lands' End, Direct Merchants: http://www.prnewswire.com/mnr/landsend/11847/.

Case Study Questions

1. Types of competitors
   a. On page 101, we encouraged you to think about your competition in a broader sense. Briefly define MVM's competition in terms of this expanded definition.
   b. Briefly describe the difference between a direct and an indirect competitor.
   c. According to St-Arnaud of MVM, "We have the technological base to do everything more cheaply and more quickly than our competitors. It'll take them a long time to catch up" (http://innovation.ic.gc.ca/gol/innovation/site.nsf/en/in04211.html). In Chapter 2 we highlighted Unique Solutions Design. Link onto The Virtual You (http://www.uniqueltd.com/main_products.html). Is Unique Solutions Design a possible MVM competitor?
   d. In Box 4.1 (page 79), we highlighted Critical Mass, a Canadian company that helped Nike build an online one-to-one relationship with its customers. Is Critical Mass a possible MVM competitor? Briefly explain the reason for your answer.
   e. Is it possible for Wal-Mart or IBM to be invisible competitors of MVM? Briefly explain your reasons.

2. Touchpoint analysis
   a. Briefly describe the objective of a competitive touchpoint analysis.
   b. Suppose you are a potential MVM competitor. Get together with three or four of your friends or classmates (or you might want to do this on your own), and link onto the My Virtual Model home page (http://www.myvirtualmodel.com/en/go_shopping.htm). Choose an online MVM shopping site, and each of you go shopping. Begin developing your competitor review sheet (Action Step 29). Evaluate (1 is poor, 10 is great) the following touchpoints: shopping experience, price/value, product availability, customer service, product delivery, and method of payment. What was your average group rating for each category? Would you shop again on this site? Why? Why not?

3. Competitive positioning
   a. What is meant by the term *competitive positioning*?
   b. Based on your analysis in Question 2, above, and a review of MVM, formulate a possible competitive positioning statement for MVM.

4. Competitive strategy
   a. As we described in this chapter, for most small businesses, there are three broad competitive strategies. Briefly describe these three competitive approaches.
   b. What was MVM's major competitive strategy and driving force (or distinctive competency)?

5. SWOT analysis
   a. Briefly describe the components of and rationale for a competitive SWOT analysis.
   b. What are MVM's internal strengths and weaknesses, and external threats and opportunities? (To learn more about SWOT analysis, you might want to link onto Mind Tools, "SWOT Analysis" (http://www.mindtools.com/pages/article/newTMC_05.htm#business).

Notes

1. *Canadian Business* Online, "When Competition Looms" (Web site); and Goodbye Graffiti: http://www.goodbyegraffiti.com/index.htm (accessed October, 2006).
2. A number of definitions competitive intelligence can be found in Richard Combs Associates' *The Competitive Intelligence Handbook*, Chapter 1 (http://www.combsinc.com/chapt1.htm).

3. See, for example, Michael Robert, *Strategy Pure and Simple*, 2nd ed. (New York: McGraw Hill, 1998).
4. Industry Canada, ebiz.enable, "Identifying Strategies": http://strategis.ic.gc.ca/epic/internet/inee-ef.nsf/en/h_ee00542e.html
5. *Fast Company*, www.fastcompany.com/resources/innovation/watson/071204.html (accessed October 2006).

SUGGESTED READING

Berkman, Robert. *The Skeptical Business Searcher: The Information Advisor's Guide to the Evaluating Web Data, Sites, and Sources.* Medford, NJ: CyberAge, 2004.

Chan, Kim W., and Renée Mauborgne. *Blue Ocean Strategy: How to Create Uncreated Market Space and Make Competition Irrelevant.* Cambridge, MA: HBS Press, 2005.

Fishman, Ted. *China, Inc.: How the Rise of the Next Superpower Challenges America and the World.* Princeton, NJ: Scribner, 2005.

Gilad, Benjamin. *Early Warning: Using Competitive Intelligence to Anticipate Market Shifts, Control Risk, and Create Powerful Strategies.* New York: AMACOM, 2003.

Hamel, Gary. *Leading the Revolution.* Boston: Harvard Business School Press, 2000.

Hock, Randolph. *The Extreme Searcher's Internet Handbook.* Medford, NJ: CyberAge, 2004.

Liautaud, Bernard, with Mark Hammond. *E-Business Intelligence: Turning Information into Knowledge into Profit.* New York: McGraw-Hill, 2000.

Porter, Michael E. *On Competition.* Boston MA: Harvard Business School Press, 1998.

Porter, Michael. *Competitive Strategy: Techniques for Analyzing Industries and Competitors, with a New Introduction.* New York: Free Press, 1998.

Tapscott, Don, David Ticoll, and Alex Lowy. *Digital Capital: Harnessing the Power of Business Webs.* Boston: Harvard Business School Press, 2000.

Trout, Jack, with Steve Rivkin. *Differentiate or Die: Survival in Our Era of Killer Competition.* New York: John Wiley and Sons, 2000.

6 Pricing and Promoting Your Product or Service

This chapter will help you prepare Part D of your business plan, Marketing Strategy. You will learn how to price your product or service, refine your product features and benefits, and develop a cost-effective promotional strategy.

Brian Scudamore, like many successful entrepreneurs, thinks in pictures. He's a dreamer. Just before his 19th birthday he was in line outside a McDonald's, dreaming away, waiting for his lunch. A pickup truck filled with trash was waiting in line in front of him at the drive-through. Hungry at the time, and thanks to McDonald's, Brian experienced another one of his business visions—one that would change his life. "Why not 'do real junk'?" he thought.

Brian moved quickly and bought a used pickup truck the very next day. "The Rubbish Boys" was hatched overnight—a junk removal service with the slogan, "We'll Stash Your Trash in a Flash!" Scudamore was a university student at that time. After three increasingly successful summers, he was ready to take his business to the next level, investing in more trucks, hiring student drivers, and setting out to make his company the "FedEx of Junk" throughout the Vancouver area.

In the mid-1990s, an employee and friend named Mike McKee decided to leave The Rubbish Boys and set up his own trash removal service—called the Trashbusters. Brian's warlike competitive juices kicked in, and he spent two years trying to find ways to "take Trashbusters down." Competitive, reactive bashing became an obsession for Brian and his employees—one that, Scudamore recalls, caused him almost to lose his business.

One evening Brian had a business epiphany while at his parents' cottage sketching out his future business dreams. He realized that his experience with Mike, his first direct competitor, could be the start of a long line of direct competitors. This is when Brian found out the importance of learning from the competition. Scudamore learned that he needed a different way to grow his business. Not long after this "magical" evening, he decided that franchising was the way to go. He changed the company name to 1-800-GOT-JUNK? and quickly turned to franchising. With a catchy name, a new distribution channel, and a renewed focus on the customer, Brian outgrew his competition in a short time.

The first GOT-JUNK franchise was sold in 1999, and since then the company has enjoyed exponential growth and widespread recognition for its business achievements. As of 2005, the company had some 150 franchise locations and an estimated $175 million in sales. "We're revolutionizing the way the business is done,"

LEARNING OPPORTUNITIES

After reading this chapter, you should be able to

- understand how to price your product or service;
- develop a pricing strategy;
- understand how to communicate with target customers, using both conventional and guerrilla marketing techniques;
- get free publicity;
- maximize economy in advertising and promotion;
- understand the value of personal selling;
- use creative techniques to arrive at the right promotional mix;
- promote through networking;
- build your own network; and
- attach price tags to your promotional strategies.

ACTION STEP PREVIEW

32. Calculate and justify your product/service price.
33. Build your network.
34. Brainstorm a winning promotional campaign for your business.
35. Attach a price tag to each item in your promotion package.

says Scudamore—who is now in his mid-30s with a corporate nickname, "Junkdog." "This has always been a very fragmented mom-and-pop industry. We're creating the FedEx of junk removal," says Scudamore. Since the early days, Junkdog and his team have been driven to success through their compelling "FedEx" vision to make the collection and disposal of junk a respectable business.

Scudamore has also taken the junk business into Cyberspace. "If you're not comfortable using the Internet, we don't want you as a franchisee," says Cameron Herold, CEO. According to one source, their business model seems to have attracted the attention of more than a few dot-com refugees. The linchpin of the company's business model is an intranet Web-based system that handles all booking, accounting, and dispatching tasks. The software maps each franchise partner's territory. It is a sophisticated system in which all job orders for the company's franchise partners are booked and dispatched by 32 office employees in the Vancouver head office—known as the "Junktion." "We've created a business model that allows franchise partners to work on the junk business, not in the booking and dispatching business," says Scudamore.

GUERRILLA MARKETING

Small business promotional strategy that involves unconventional methods of getting the customer's attention at minimal cost

Guerrilla marketing is a key promotional strategy of Scudamore and his franchisees. Guerrilla marketing is a key small business promotional strategy that refers to unconventional methods of getting the customer attention at minimal cost. The idea is to expend energy and creativity rather than money. According to Scudamore, "Rather than spend a ton of money on advertising, I believe it is better to get out there and promote." For example, franchisees are encouraged to be creative. Waves are a common guerrilla tactic. Franchisees can be seen wearing blue clown wigs, standing on busy roads, waving to motorists, and passing out free lollipops (junk food) or junk bucks. Junk motorcades are also a common practice. For example, the Toronto franchisee has 12 trucks that sometimes travel in a convoy down Yonge Street, in the heart of the city. When not on a job, some crew members go on junk patrol, scouring neighbourhoods for cluttered yards or driveways. The driver knocks or leaves an estimate on the front door.

Service and quality are also key factors to the GOT-JUNK franchise system. As a result, their business format is highly controlled. For example, all franchisees must wear clean apparel, and trucks are to be washed every day. One franchisee in Calgary even lost his franchise rights when he drove a muddy truck with a peeling 1-800-GOT-JUNK? label. Follow-up calls are made to ensure total customer satisfaction.[1] The main job of the franchisee is to staff and run the operation—with an emphasis on promoting their services.

MARKETING STRATEGY

An analysis of four major elements: external market and trends, target market, product/service uniqueness and competitive advantage, and the marketing mix

In our case study section at the end of this chapter we'll ask you to return to this 1-800-GOT-JUNK? vignette, do some research, and learn from the pricing and promotional tactics of this great Canadian success story.

Your business plan **marketing strategy** will include an analysis of four major elements:

(1) external market and trends, (2) your target market, (3) product uniqueness and competitive advantage, and (4) the marketing mix. We have addressed

the first three elements in the first five chapters of this book. In Chapters 2 and 3, we stressed the importance of external market trends. Chapter 4 focused on your target customers. We encouraged you to analyze and learn from your competition to create a competitive advantage in Chapter 5. In Chapters 6 and 7, we turn our attention to the fourth element of your marketing strategy, traditionally called the **marketing mix**—a blend of **p**roduct offering, **p**ricing, **p**romotion, and **p**lace (location). Some refer to this marketing mix as the "Four Ps." Up to this point, we've helped you develop your product offering—your market niche and the product or services that are right for both you and the market. In this chapter, we'll get you thinking about the next two "Ps" of your marketing mix: price and promotion. Then, in Chapter 7, we will help you with your last "P"—your place, or location. We begin with pricing considerations and strategy—a topic we first addressed in relation to your competition (Chapter 5).

> **MARKETING MIX**
>
> A blend of product offering, pricing, promotion, and place (location)

PRICING YOUR PRODUCT OR SERVICE

In principle, the price(s) you charge for your product or service must be acceptable both to you, the seller, and to your customer. From your customers' perspective, an acceptable price depends on competitive alternatives for your product/service in addition to the perceived value. As for you, the supplier of a product/service, your price can be based on any number of pricing considerations. But it's fairly safe to say that ultimately, you will be trying to maximize your sales revenue and profits.

New businesses often make the mistake of charging either too little or too much for their product or service. To help you avoid making one of these mistakes, we're going to outline four basic methods for determining your price. These are the most common methods for small businesses, but we caution you: The process of setting a price can become quite complicated and technical—especially if you are starting up a manufacturing business. Pricing depends on many internal and external factors, and you might have to get some professional help. For example, the process of estimating the price of a product will include product costs as well as labour costs. In contrast, if you are offering a service, you might not have to deal with any product costing. Retail pricing for a storefront with rent considerations will be very different from pricing for a home-based e-retailing operation with little or no rent.

Below are four common small business methods of pricing a product or service. Depending on your business idea, you might need a lot more information and guidance. Should you need more guidance, we have also provided you with a number of sites in Box 6.1 to help you price your specific product or service.

FOUR COMMON METHODS OF PRICING FOR SMALL BUSINESS

1. Competitor-Based Pricing

Recall that in Action Step 30, Chapter 5, we asked you to review your competitor touchpoint analysis and state the prices of your products or services relative to your customers' perception of the competition. In fact, we were asking you to calculate your price relative to the market. We wanted you to find out what prices were acceptable to your potential customers given their possible choices and competitive options. Many new business owners begin their pricing strategy by first determining what prices or price range the target market will accept, relative to the competition. This is often referred to as **competitor-based pricing** (sometimes referred to as market-based pricing or pricing to market[2]).

The price of your product or service depends on your competitors' prices, but you're also going to have to figure out your costs. If the market price cannot cover your costs, then your business is going to lose money. And naturally, you want to make sure that the price you charge is enough to yield a profit. This leads us to a second approach, called **profit-based,** or **cost plus, pricing**.

2. Profit-Based (Cost Plus) Pricing

One of the most common errors new owners make is setting their prices of products based only on the costs to produce them.[3] If you set your price based solely on the cost, your business won't make any profit. The price you charge must also take into consideration your profit expectations. After all, you don't just want to sell your service or product at the price you pay for it. There are different methods for calculating price to take account of profit. A simple and common formula for estimating price (per unit) is

Selling price = total costs per unit + estimated dollar profit per unit

Your costs for producing a particular product (or supplying a service) will include three broad costing groups: (1) direct material costs (or your cost of supplies), (2) direct cost of labour for producing your product or service, and (3) overhead, or fixed expenses (indirect costs), such as rent and advertising.

Your estimated profit will depend on a number of factors, such as the type of product or service, the market demand, your costs, and so on. If possible, you're going to have to rely on your primary or secondary research, such as industry averages, for your type of business (see *Performance Plus*, http://sme.ic.gc.ca/epic/internet/inpp-pp.nsf/en/Home). Some businesses might even set profit targets for each of the three broad costing groups.

According to many industry analysts, pricing based on costs and profit establishes an estimate of the lowest price, or floor price, for your product or service.[4] This is the minimum price that you can accept to meet your profit targets. Second, the price you will be able to charge will be determined by the demand for your product or service as well as by your competition.

3. Industry Norm, or "Keystone," Pricing

Some types of business charge prices according to certain generally accepted or industry standards. This is called **industry norm,** or **keystone, pricing**. Two examples of this type of approach might be setting the price at:

- triple the cost of goods sold or
- two times the labour costs.

The marketing concept of **markups** might also help you determine your price. A markup is a percentage of your cost of sales (sometimes the selling price is used) that you add to the cost to determine your selling price. Note that you don't include overhead costs in your markup calculation. Include only your costs for materials and supplies.

For example, if the selling price is $3, and the cost is $2, the markup is calculated as follows:

Markup = (price − cost) / cost
= ($3 − $2) / $2
= 1/2
= .50 (or 50%)

When it comes to concept markups, you have to be a little cautious. Mark-ups are calculated in some cases as a percentage of costs and in others as a percentage of the selling price. In the above example, the 50 percent markup was calculated as a percentage of cost. If we had calculated the markup as a percentage of selling price, then the markup would be 33 percent, or ($3 − $2)/$3. It is common in the retail industry to calculate markups based on selling price.

If you know what the standard or industry markup is for your product or service, then you can estimate a selling price. For example, if you are selling greeting cards, and you know that the industry markup (on the selling price) is 50 percent, then you can determine your selling price. Your final price will ultimately depend on all of your costs (not just the material cost), the competition, and the market demand.

4. Ceiling, or Premium, Pricing

Ceiling, or **premium**, **pricing** means setting the highest price target consumers will pay for a product or service, given their needs and values and the competitive options.[5] Your ultimate goal or strategy is to try to focus on a specific market segment, create uniqueness, and differentiate your product or service as perceived by the customer. Some pricing analysts refer to this ceiling price as the "highest price the market will bear." This differentiation strategy will make your product or service more inelastic, or less sensitive to price changes. If your product or service is inelastic, it means that your customers, on average, will be willing to buy your product or service even if your prices are on the high side relative to those of your competitors—because your customer values the fact that your product is different. But remember, you must also be able to justify that this ceiling or premium price more than covers your costs and yields the desired profit.

CEILING, OR PREMIUM, PRICING
Setting the highest price target consumers will pay for a product or service, given their needs and values and the competitive options

OTHER PRICING STRATEGIES

These four broad strategies are not the only options available. For example, common pricing strategies used mainly by larger firms include:
- **penetration pricing**—setting the initial or introductory price artificially low to increase sales volume with the intent of raising prices after the introductory period;
- **economy (limit) pricing**—setting "no-frills" low prices to increase volume and discourage competition; and
- **price skimming**—setting prices high initially to appeal to consumers who are not price sensitive, then lowering prices as competitors enter the market.

PENETRATION PRICING
Setting the initial or introductory price artificially low to increase sales volume

ECONOMY (LIMIT) PRICING
Setting "no-frills" low prices to increase volume and discourage competition

YOUR PRICING STRATEGY

The price you will charge for your product or service will depend on a number of factors, including costs of production, market considerations, competitive forces, geography, size of business, the product, service distribution channel, and so on. You are also going to have to think about your pricing strategy in relation to promotional factors (described in the next section), including sales promotions and quantity discounts. Additional information on pricing strategies can be found in Box 6.1. We also encourage you to learn more about pricing by completing the E-Exercises in Box 6.2.

We suggest that you begin your pricing analysis by considering the ceiling price strategy. Then follow up by making sure that this price will cover your costs and lead to a profit. This is the approach used by most of the successful small

PRICE SKIMMING
Setting prices high initially to appeal to consumers who are not price sensitive, then lowering prices as competitors enter the market

ACTION STEP 32

Calculate and justify your product or service price

The marketing section of your business plan should tell the reader (1) what price(s) you are charging; (2) what your pricing strategy is, and; (3) why you chose this pricing strategy. This three-step exercise will help you establish and justify a price for your product or service.

Step 1: Estimate your price based on market considerations

In Action Step 30, Chapter 5, we asked you review your competitor touchpoint analysis and state the prices of your products or services relative to your competitors. We were asking you to calculate your price relative to the market. Now we want you to go back and review your results from Box 5.4, in Chapter 5. We want you to ask yourself again: Is my product unique/distinctive relative to my competitors'? Is my product inelastic? If not, how can I make it more unique and thus more inelastic? Can I charge higher prices relative to my competitors? This process will provide you with a product/service price estimate based on market considerations.

Step 2: Estimate your price based on cost considerations

Now we want you to list all the costs associated with your product or service. Remember, you may have a network of suppliers. Can you find any costing estimates on the Net? This particular exercise might take some time and involve plenty of primary and secondary research, but try not to cut corners. Get the most realistic costs possible.

Once you have the costing numbers, we want you to calculate your product/service price based on the profit-based (cost plus) approach explained above. We suggest you try this costing method, but, if this approach is not right for your business, or if you need more information, check out the sources provided in Box 6.1.

(continued)

businesses like 1-800-GOT-JUNK? Many small business owners think they should start out with low prices to attract customers, but in most cases, this is a mistake. In general, small businesses should not aim to sell products or services at the lowest market price. Strategies such as penetration pricing, economy pricing, and price skimming are approaches that should be reserved for the large firms, such as Coke and Wal-Mart, that want to increase their market share and dominate the market.

It is now time to introduce you to promotion, the next element in our marketing mix. But before we do, we want you to complete Action Step 32—calculate and justify your product/service price.

Box 6.1   Bookmark This

Pricing Your Product or Service

The following sites will help you become familiar with various pricing strategies and concepts.

- Canada Business Service Centres, "Marketing Primer": http://canadaonline.about.com/gi/dynamic/offsite.htm?zi=1/XJ&sdn=canadaonline&zu=http%3A%2F%2Fwww.cbsc.org%2Fservlet%2FContentServer%3Fpagename%3DCBSC_FE%252FCBSC_WebPage%252FCBSC_WebPage_Temp%26cid%3D1102594891135%26c%3DCBSC_WebPage%26lang%3Deng or Google "Canada Business Online Small Business Workshop"
- Marketing Teacher, "Pricing Strategies": http://www.marketingteacher.com/Lessons/lesson_pricing.htm
- Michele Determan, "Marketing: Price Strategies and Adjustments": http://www.determan.net/Michele/mprice.htm
- Mark Deo, "Pricing Strategies for Small Business": http://www.sbanetwork.org/articles/articles_view.asp?id=110
- CCH, Business Owner's Toolkit,
- "The Steps to Pricing Your Product": http://www.toolkit.cch.com/text/P03_5200.asp
- "Researching Product Price Elasticity": http://www.toolkit.cch.com/text/P03_5230.asp
- "Case Study: Whole Planet Beverages": http://www.toolkit.cch.com/text/P03_5310.asp
- "Analyzing Your Costs and Overhead": http://www.toolkit.cch.com/text/P03_5270.asp

Note: All Web sites accessed July 2006.

Box 6.2   E-Exercise

Pricing Strategies

Have some fun. Here are two exercises that will help you learn more about pricing strategies.

- Click onto the Marketing Teacher site, and learn about all kinds of pricing strategies on the "Lesson" link (http://www.marketingteacher.com/Lessons/lesson_pricing.htm). Test your understanding of four of the better known strategies by clicking onto the "Exercise" link. Find out how you did by clicking the answer button.

- Click onto Biz/ed Pricing Strategies. Activity (http://www.bized.ac.uk/educators/16-19/business/marketing/activity/pricingstrat.htm). Here you will find two case studies that will help you learn more about pricing strategies and the factors influencing how firms decide on prices for their products and services.

PROMOTION

PROMOTION—YOUR WAY OF CONNECTING WITH THE CUSTOMER

Promotion is the art and science of moving the image of your business to the forefront of a customer's mind. Recall that in Chapter 4, we discussed three kinds of customers: target customers, secondary customers, and invisible customers. When promoting your business, you need to consider all three types.

Each business is unique, and you don't want to waste money on promotional schemes that won't work. For example, if your target customer is a college-educated, suburban woman aged 45 to 55 who earns more than $100,000, owns three cars, rides horseback 10 hours a week, and reads *Practical Horseman* and *Performance Horse*, your best chance of reaching her is through direct mail. If, on the other hand, your target customers are male and female college students aged 18 to 25 with limited incomes, you'll probably achieve better results by promoting at local colleges.

Developing a promotional plan requires five steps:

1. determining your sales and marketing goals (e.g., sales of $350,000 for the year);
2. developing strategies to achieve a goal (e.g., increase repeat business of best customers by 10 percent);
3. creating specific promotional methods for carrying out one or several of the strategies, and having measurable objectives (e.g., mailer for special Christmas shopping night with a goal of selling $20,000 worth of merchandise during the evening);
4. detailing and enacting a program involving the specific promotion(s) chosen following a predetermined budget (e.g., gold-embossed mailer sent to 300 best customers in November for special Christmas shopping night with free cookies, pastries, cider, and gift wrapping, at a cost of $1,750); and/or
5. evaluating the cost and effectiveness of your promotional vehicles and adjusting as needed (e.g., expected return of $20 in increased sales for every $1 spent on advertising and promotion).

Your promotional efforts should be consistent with your overall image, target market, and business mission. The quality and professionalism of your promotional package is important. Remember to stress customer benefits and your "distinctive competency." Much of your marketing and promotion should be partially developed at this point through the past Action Steps, especially your "customer touchpoints" (Chapter 5). At this point, you know the areas in which you can and must shine. The next step is to begin the promotion selection and process to showcase your strengths.

Any promotion or **promotional mix** that advances the image of your business is worth considering. Survey some of the more common and traditional means of promotion before you decide on your promotional strategy, and be sure you remain open to all options. It is essential to keep an open mind as you brainstorm for strategies, examine promotional campaigns, and come to understand the importance of planning ahead. You will then be able to make wiser decisions on how to connect with the customer.

Several considerations are critical to your campaign, such as what is appropriate for your customer, what you can afford to spend (your budget), and your own

---

ACTION STEP 32

Calculate and justify your product or service price (continued)

Step 3: Determine and justify your pricing strategy

In Steps 1 and 2, you calculated a price based on market considerations and one based on cost considerations. What final price will you charge? This will depend on your choice of pricing strategy. Most successful small businesses use a ceiling (or premium) price strategy.

They charge the highest price the market will bear and one that yields an acceptable profit given cost considerations. However, this might not always be the case, so we want you to review the various pricing strategies provided in Boxes 6.1 and 6.2. To complete the pricing section of your marketing plan, answer the following questions:

- What price(s) will you charge?
- What is your pricing strategy?
- Why have you chosen this strategy?

Keep these pricing results handy. You'll need them when it comes time to forecast your sales (Chapter 10).

PROMOTION

The art or science of moving the image of your business into the forefront of a prospective customer's mind

PROMOTIONAL MIX

All the elements that you blend to maximize communication with your customer

prior experience. Most important, though, is what is *most likely* to give you "the biggest bang for your buck." Here, creativity, consistency, and repetition are key elements for achieving a successful result.

THE PROMOTIONAL MIX

The key to connecting with customers is considering a wide variety of promotional strategies and then choosing the right ones. A number of potential strategies are provided below. As we review these, please keep in mind the touchpoints from Chapter 5. Your research has already shown you the most important areas on which to focus your marketing efforts.

As we learned from the GOT-JUNK opening vignette, customer service and quality are the cornerstones of any marketing or promotional strategy. This is the point at which we begin our promotion discussion.

YOUR PROMOTIONAL CORNERSTONES: SERVICE AND QUALITY

According to Jim Clemmer, author of the classic book *Firing on All Cylinders*, "Customer service and quality are back in vogue." Each year *PROFIT* magazine announces its PROFIT 100 and PROFIT Hot 50. Winning companies like Blueprint Public Relations (http://www.blueprintpr.ca) and Virtual Causeway (http://www.v-causeway.com) consistently remind us that the key to their success is pleasing the customer with exceptional service and quality.[6]

Time and again, surveys have shown that improved customer service and quality are key factors contributing to business profit and growth. Why is delighting the customer with service and quality so important? Here are a few market facts:

- You can charge up to 10 percent more if the customer perceives quality service.
- Firms with high service records are 12 percent more profitable than firms without, and their yearly sales growth is 12 percent higher.
- About 68 percent of customers stop doing business with a particular establishment because the employees appear indifferent toward the customer.
- It costs five times as much to get a new customer than to keep your present customer satisfied.
- A happy customer will tell 5 new people, but an unhappy customer will complain to 10 people.
- What's worse is that only 1 dissatisfied customer out of 26 will bother to tell the owner. This means that if only 1 customer complains, 25 others also have complaints, and each one is telling 10 people.
- Remember, the 80–20 rule: Eighty percent of the world is influenced by the other 20 percent. Word of mouth by the customer is a major way to get your message out once you are established. A customer who is happy because of quality service is the way to make word of mouth work for you.

OTHER MARKETING STRATEGIES

Paid Media Advertising

A sure-fire way to reach out is through advertisements on radio, television, display boards (written or electronic), newspapers, magazines, and trade journals. For some businesses, the Yellow Pages (paper and electronic) can be an effective promotional vehicle. Advertising tickles the customer's mind. With a good ad, you can reach right into your TC and create the desire to buy from you.

Advertising has some obvious drawbacks: (1) it can be expensive to create; (2) if you don't spend a lot of money, your ad won't get wide exposure; and (3) major advertisers get preferred placements (i.e., the best locations within a publication, store, or business area; or the best time slots on TV or radio).

Advice

- Make sure that a large percentage of the listeners, viewers, or readers are in one of your TC groups. Otherwise your message is wasted.
- Your best ad is often yourself. Stay visible, and remember the importance of personal selling.
- Check with vendors. Ask for tear sheets, copy, and cooperative advertising money, and help on advertising design and layout.
- Explore creative co-op advertising, in which suppliers share a portion of the cost.
- Check with marketing departments of newspapers. Ask for help, advice, and information.
- Newspapers sometimes offer advertising in special supplements, such as a small business section, at reduced cost. The offer includes free editorial copy.
- Start small, and test and analyze the results of each promotional campaign.

Business Cards

One restaurant owner we know gave individualized businesses cards to all employees. These employee business cards entitled the recipients to a 10 percent discount on meals. He encouraged the staff to hand them out, and they were rewarded for their promotional efforts. The restaurant would keep track of each card that was redeemed. Every month, the employee who generated the most business through businesses card handouts would receive a special reward, such as free tickets to a National Hockey League game. This strategy worked, generating 10 percent of all new customers.

Business cards are a marketing necessity. At the very least, they are an inexpensive way of improving the effectiveness of your networking and word-of-mouth campaign. Even if you haven't started your business, a business card will help you get the word out. These days, a box of well-designed business cards is very cost effective and quick to have printed. Just Google "business cards Canada" and a number of sites will pop up. Order your cards online or from your local business store, and in no time you'll be ready to market yourself and your business.

Advice

- **Basic information.** Make sure your business card contains such basic information as your name, business Web site, address, fax number (if you have one), mailing address, and telephone number.
- **Image.** Be professional. Typos and bad grammar are a no-no.
- **Keep track.** When you hand out your cards, get the recipients' information. If they don't have a card, write down their name and contact information. Keep a list of all contacts with their e-mail address, telephone numbers, and location.
- **Logo.** Think about designing a logo to go on the card.
- **Use both sides of the card.** Consider including the major benefits you are offering? How about your mission statement?
- **Your picture.** If you want a picture of yourself on the card, make sure it's not *your* ego needs that you are trying to satisfy. Does your photo sell your business? If so, do it. If not, find some image that will. How about using your company logo instead?
- **Promote.** Use your business cards to get customers and actively promote your word-of-mouth campaign.

- **Be creative.** 1-800-GOT-JUNK? in the opening vignette has a "cool" idea—free refrigerator magnets. It's a business card their customers see every day. (http://www.1800gotjunk.com).
- **Web site.** Use your Web site to promote your cards. For example, if you order the 1-800-GOT-JUNK? fridge magnet over the net, you have to complete all kinds of information about yourself. The GOT-JUNK people promote these business card magnets to learn about their target customer.

Point-of-Purchase Displays

POINT-OF-PURCHASE (P-O-P) DISPLAY

A display that acts as a silent salesperson for a specific product

A **point-of-purchase (P-O-P)** is a display that acts as a silent salesperson for a specific product. In the retail businesses, an estimated 70 percent of sales are impulse buys. Entrepreneurs Geoff Moss and David Minister are the owners of Poptech, a Toronto-based company that makes P-O-P displays. They took advantage of this market niche, added new technology and fresh ideas, and launched their business into a *PROFIT* Hot 50.[7]

Point-of-purchase displays, situated usually at or near the checkout counter or front desk, encourage impulse purchases of last-minute items such as paperbacks, pantyhose, candy, magazines, and gum. A sharp P-O-P display can also improve your image, and it serves as a tireless, silent salesperson, always on duty. A good P-O-P can be used for customer education. If it's hard to understand how to use your product or its benefits aren't clear to the TC, your silent salespeople can deliver the message.

There are, at the same time, a few problems with these displays: (1) you can't sell large items, because they crowd customers at the cash register; and (2) the display must sell itself as well as the product. (A tacky P-O-P will turn prospective customers *off* instead of *on*.)

Advice

- Do weekly evaluations of all P-O-Ps. Make certain your silent salespeople are doing their work.
- Ask your suppliers for help. Many suppliers can assist with in-store promotion, signage, and P-O-P displays.
- Some wholesalers will carry racks and displays for their retail partners. Don't be afraid to ask.

Packaging

Don't forget the importance of product packaging. Review your competitors' packaging by purchasing their products and checking out the cost and effectiveness of their product packaging. What can you do better? What can you do more efficiently? What can you do more cost-effectively? How could the packaging be made more attractive? Professionals in the packaging and distribution fields will be able to work with you on the proper sizing of packages and provide you with the benefits of their years of experience. One entrepreneur we know tried to sell her homemade sauces in two-litre jars until one of her retail accounts suggested she sell them in more "shelf friendly" one-litre jars and spiff up her packaging by including her start-up story on the label to distinguish herself in the marketplace. Sales of her gourmet sauces tripled, as more accounts were willing to stock the smaller jars because they fit on the shelves much more easily.

Advice

- Consider environmental, safety, hygiene, and legal issues as well as customer requirements.

Catalogues

This sales tool is just right for isolated shoppers and shoppers in a hurry. Because we are becoming so "time poor," even general items are now being purchased via catalogues. Customers can shop at their convenience and not have to worry about store hours, parking, or traffic. Catalogue houses such as Lands' End don't usually manufacture anything, so they are always looking for good products. Use catalogues as another kind of silent salesperson to reach customers if your TC tends to be a catalogue shopper.

If you try printing your own catalogues, you'll run into at least three problems: (1) cost (they are expensive to print and to mail), (2) size limitations (it's tough to sell anything by catalogue that's big, bulky, or inconvenient to ship), and (3) the challenge of establishing and maintaining a reliable mailing list.

Advice

- Be prepared to take advantage of online catalogues. They are growing in number, especially in business-to-business transactions.
- Let major catalogue houses do your promotion, but make sure you can deliver if your product takes off.
- Before you get in too deep, approach a few major houses with a product description plus photographs. If they don't like your product, they might help you locate a catalogue house that will. The feedback will be invaluable.

Direct Mail

This promotional tool lets you aim your brochures and fliers where they will do the most good. **Direct mail** is very important for small business, because it can go to the heart of your target market.

Direct mail reflects the importance of customer relationship marketing, which we discussed in Chapter 4, page 79. The success of direct mail will depend on your ability to focus on the needs of your target market. For example, a financial advisor might send one type of brochure to his or her clients that have younger children and a slightly different pamphlet to the clients that have grandchildren. If you don't know exactly what the needs of your target customer are—that is, your market is fragmented—the direct mail approach might not be appropriate.

DIRECT MAIL
Advertisement or sales pitch that is mailed directly to target customers

Advice

- Know what the needs of your target customer are.
- Develop customer lists based on customer needs.
- Follow up your direct mail with a short telephone call.

Money-Back Guarantees

You might not have thought of a guarantee as a form of promotion, but it is. You can reach security-minded customers by emphasizing the no-risk features of your product.

The problem is that you must back up your guarantee with time and money. Therefore, if you have a guarantee, don't overlook the cost implications in your income and expense statements.

Advice

- Allow an extra 3 to 5 percent into your pricing to cover returned goods. If the product is fragile or easily misused—and people have been known to misuse just about everything—build in a higher figure.

Free Ink and Free Air

You should be constantly asking yourself, "How can I get my company free publicity?" Brian Scudamore at 1-800-GOT-JUNK? is a master at using guerrilla marketing skills for getting free ink. GOT-JUNK was even able to get Dr. Phil, Oprah, CBS, and CBC to promote their company—all free of charge. Maybe you will never be able to get Dr. Phil and Oprah to talk about your product or service. But remember, it can be done. After all, GOT-JUNK did it.

According to Scudamore, getting free press is a three-step process:

- **Step 1**. Clearly identify your target audience. In the franchise business, it might be franchise business reporters, for example.
- **Step 2**. Develop a hook or angle. Give them the right angle that's newsworthy— a high-profile sporting event or court case, for example.
- **Step 3**. Make calls. Call target reporters and make your pitch. Save your best prospects until the end. By this time, you will have honed your pitch.[8]

Free publicity through reviews, features, interview shows, press releases, and newspaper columns costs you nothing and can be effective. Think about sending out free samples of your product to news outlets. How about delivering free snacks to the media? Then listen to them rave about your treats. **Free ink and free air** are excellent ways to promote, because they establish your company in a believable way. The target customer is likely to attach more credence to words that are not paid advertising. The obstacle here is getting media people to see how your business is unique and noteworthy.

Advice

- Be prepared to spend significant time and effort to get full impact.
- *Every* business is newsworthy in some way. Dig until you find a different twist. Know the media people. Aim your release at *their* target readers, viewers, or listeners.
- Make your press kit visually appealing, include your story, and send accompanying photos of your principals, your facility, and your product being used or your service being performed.
- Caution is advised. Free ink/free air can also have a negative impact. If you are not careful, the "story angle" might not be the one you are hoping for. So, take the time, do your homework, and make sure that your promotional strategy reflects positively on the business.

Freebies

The GOT-JUNK franchisees are constantly looking to help at community events. Sometimes they even pick up junk for community associations. A giveaway, or "freebie," can attract your target customer's attention, get you in the news, stimulate interest in a new product, or help you gather market research. Remember the free fridge magnets. They not only serve as a business card but also help provide customer information and research.

Personal Selling

It doesn't matter if you've never sold before; if you believe in your product or service, no one is a better salesperson than you are. You *are* the business. If you listen carefully, your TCs will *tell* you how to sell them your product or service. That's why a good salesperson is a creative listener, not a fast talker. Most customers like to talk with the owner of the business. Use that to your advantage (see Box 6.3).

FREE INK AND FREE AIR

Information about a business that is published or broadcast free of charge

Unfortunately, **personal selling** is expensive, especially if you have to pay others to do it, and it will boost your overhead unless you pay your salesperson only by earned commission. And if you try to do it all yourself, you won't have the time and energy for other things that only you can do. Still, for small businesses, the best form of promotion is personal selling.

PERSONAL SELLING

The selling and taking of orders by an individual salesperson

Advice

- Make everyone in your business a salesperson: delivery people, warehouse people, computer programmers, bookkeepers, clerical people, and switchboard operators. If nothing sells, they're out of a job. Remind everyone who works for you that your TC needs a lot of TLC (tender loving care).
- Consider developing a network of sales reps who will work on a percentage of sales. Keep cheerleading. Reps need encouragement, too.
- Increase your personal visibility. Join a business or service club and trade associations. Write a newspaper column. Be bold.
- Stay in touch with your customers, and listen to them. If you don't, you might lose your business.

Box 6.3 Direct Sales Is Alive and Thriving

The Direct Sellers Association of Canada (DSA) defines **direct selling** as "the sale of a consumer product or service by an independent sales contractor in a face-to-face manner away from a fixed retail location." Direct sales are still alive and thriving, but few firms make house calls like the Fuller Brush salesman or Avon lady did in the 1950s and '60s. Direct selling mainstays like Avon Canada and Quixtar Canada, or Canadian upstarts like Weekenders have adjusted to the "ding dong" tactics of the past. House parties, offices, and technology are their new stomping grounds—and in many cases, their roads are electronic, and their doors are on computer screens. Here are some facts.

DIRECT SELLING

The sale of a consumer product or service by an independent sales contractor in a face-to-face manner away from a fixed retail location

Direct Selling: Industry Facts
Estimated 2004 Canadian Retail Sales: $1.3 Billion

Location of Sales

Percentage of sales:	
In the home	61.9%
In a workplace	6.7%
Over the phone (in a follow-up to a face-to-face meeting)	15.6%
Via the internet	10.8%
At a fair, exhibition, shopping mall, etc.	3.9%
Other locations	1.1%

Industry Stats

Percentage of Sales by Major Product Groups:	
Home/Family Care Products (cleaning products, cookware, cutlery)	30.4%
Personal Care Products (cosmetics, jewellery, skin care, etc.)	39.9%
Services/Miscellaneous/Other	5.5%
Nutritional/Vitamins/Wellness	17.9%
Leisure/Educational Products (books, encyclopedias, toys/games)	6.3%

Compensation Structure

Multi-level 82.8% of member companies	
Single-level 17.2% of member companies	

Sales Methods	
Individual/Person-to-Person selling:	69.0%
Party Plan/Group Selling:	28.5%
Customer placing order directly with firm (in follow-up to a face-to-face meeting):	1.7%
Other:	0.8%
Estimated Total Retail Sales (2004): $1.3 billion	
Estimated Total ISCs (2004): 898,120	

Source: DSA, "Location of Sales": http://www.dsa.ca/industryfacts-locationofsales.htm (accessed October 2005). Reprinted by permission of the DSA.

Trade Shows

These shows display your product or service in a high-intensity way. Trade shows focus on customers who have a keen interest in your business area. Your appearance at a trade show asserts your position in your industry. The local library or resource centre should have a copy of the publication *Canadian Industry Shows and Exhibitions*. This will help you learn where to display your products. You might also want to check the CARD (*Canadian Advertising Rates and Data*, available online at http://www.cardmedia.com), which lists many publications under various occupational and industrial classifications. Another option is to visit the Trade Show News Network (http://www.tsnn.com).

However, if the show is not in your area, you'll have transportation costs, as well as booths and space to rent. Furthermore, unless you're careful and make a study of the layout, you might end up with a space that is thin on traffic. See, for example, Figure 6.1.

Advice

- Setting clear "show" objectives and having a training session with booth staff before the show can significantly improve effectiveness.
- Know beforehand what you want to achieve from each booth visitor.
- Have a plan in place for "after-show" follow-up—which relates to your show objectives.
- In the early years, at established shows, you might have to settle for low-traffic locations. If that's the case, try to get the show organizer to provide additional promotion in the show guide. Each year, try to obtain space in a higher traffic area.
- Always be on the lookout for cross-promotions. Try to arrange to hand out promotional items at the booth of a related non-competing company.
- Share a booth with another small business owner.
- Get your suppliers to help out—or share a booth with your supplier.
- Combine functions by doing some market research while you're promoting.

Industry Literature

"We're always looking to generate name recognition with as little money possible," says Rudolf Melik, CEO of Tenrox. Melik learned there were no books on new techniques for his business area—streamlining the costing of project-driven businesses—so he and his brother wrote a book, *Professional Services Automation: Optimizing Project and Service Oriented Organizations*.[9] By writing the book, Melik

Figure 6.1   Map of the Layout at a Trade Show

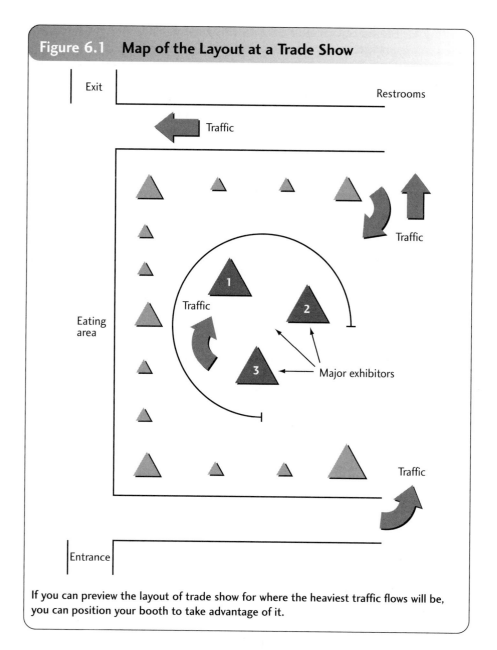

If you can preview the layout of trade show for where the heaviest traffic flows will be, you can position your booth to take advantage of it.

promoted his company as an industry leader and drummed up a lot of new leads. You don't necessarily have to write a book, but you can become an "expert" source of information for your industry by producing brochures, newsletters, handbooks, product documentation, annual reports, newspaper columns for the layperson, or even the "bible" for your industry. Your goal is to be recognized as an expert in your field.

We think this is one of the best promotional devices around if your business lends itself to trade literature promotion. Remember that expertise is admired and sought out by others. As you grow in expertise, you'll also grow in confidence.

Advice

- If you're not a good writer, encourage a friend to help.
- Talk is cheap. If you get your thoughts down on paper, you're two steps ahead of the talkers.
- Sometimes joint advertising with a manufacturer in a trade magazine is possible.
- Use your Web site to inform and help your customers.

Working Visibly

Working visibly is a major promotional strategy of the 1-800-GOT-JUNK? franchise team. Franchisees are encouraged to be creative, take initiative, and be visible. **Impact marketing** is a key strategy. Special events are designed to attract the attention of their target customers. For example, they encourage staff to wear blue clown wigs, stand on busy traffic islands, and wave to passing motorists. One franchisee reported a 20 percent increase in sales due to this high-impact marketing strategy. "Junk motorcades" are a common practice for the Toronto franchise. Here, as many as 12 trucks travel in a row down a busy downtown street. Most good service firms like GOT-JUNK display their presence as they work: They put signs on everything—their business, their trucks, and their work sites. Wherever they're busy, they let people know it. They make themselves visible.

The drawback here is similar to one of the drawbacks with point-of-purchase displays. If the presence you maintain doesn't sell itself—if it is unattractive or if it calls attention to an unappealing part of your business—you will lose potential customers rather than gain them.

> **IMPACT MARKETING**
>
> Conducting special events designed to attract the attention of target customers

Advice

- Exploit your public activities with signs that tell people who you are.
- Be unique and professional in your image and message.
- Make sure the message is working.
- Work visibly. Think about advertising on your car or truck, wearing a distinctive uniform, and placing signs where you work.

Discount Coupons

If you book online at GOT-JUNK, you get a 10-percent-off coupon. In many businesses, a discount attracts a part of your market that "likes a deal." Discount coupons are a special form of freebie, because they give you positive feedback on your promotion. They should have an expiration date and multiple-use disclaimers (as, for example, a disclaimer that the coupon cannot be used in conjunction with other promotions or discounts). They should also be coded to identify the source, so that you can find out where your advertising is paying off, and tested in small quantities before major use.

Everyone seems to like coupons. Even if your product or service is upscale, consider trying coupons as an introduction or at your slow times of the year. Another twist on the coupon is the entitlement card: "Buy five cups of coffee and get the sixth cup free." There are numerous variations on this theme.

Advice

- Consider giving away freebies that will catch your customer's attention. Box 6.6 shows some examples of low-cost promotional strategies.

Branding

The coffee mug you carry often has its own identity—maybe telling everyone, for example, that you're a Tim Horton customer. And maybe it's the same with the baseball cap you wear: The "swoosh" tells everyone who's got you branded. A **brand** is a name, sign, symbol, design, or combination of these used to identify the products of one firm and to differentiate them from competitive offerings. The 1-800-GOT-JUNK? is quickly becoming a brand name. It is their promise of the value their customer will receive from you. Smart entrepreneurs figure out ways to make themselves—and thus their business—distinctive.[10]

> **BRAND**
>
> A name, sign, symbol, design, or combination of these used to identify the products of a firm

Advice

Start with answering the following questions:

- What makes you and your business unique?
- How does your customer benefit from your product or service?
- What would your customers say is your greatest strength?
- What is your most noteworthy personal trait? How is this trait tied to your business?
- Why should your customers buy from you instead of from your competitors?

Promotion in Cyberspace

Now is the time to be on the Web—even if you don't think your target customer is a potential Web surfer. Every business should have a Web site. It's your electronic telephone number and a valuable key to success. If you want to see a Web site that generates business, take a look at the 1-800-GOT-JUNK? site (http://www.1800gotjunk.com). We have provided in Box 6.4 a list of just a few of the retailers who are now online.

Today, anyone can have a Web site, and almost anyone does. But a site with no visitors is of little benefit to you. How do you make your site worth bookmarking? Sites that can help you build your Web presence and stay current were provided in Chapter 2, Box 2.4.

Advice

- Promote your Web site offline. Offline promotion of a Web site can account for a major portion of first-time buyers. Include, for example, your Web site address in your letterhead and business cards. Be innovative; use every opportunity you have to promote your Web site with your company name.
- Get your Web site listed with search engines and directories. This will help your customer find you.
- The title of your Web page should clearly indicate the contents or purpose of the site.
- Design your message so that it is simple and easy to update.
- The Web is good for selective reading. Help your customers quickly select what they want.
- Remember that your customers might not have the most recent Internet technology. If you design a site that requires the latest technology, you are going to lose some customers—how many will depend on your target market.
- Make your Web page action oriented. Provide your customer with the benefits of purchasing from you.
- In the interactive world, the ad is there only if the person finds it. Therefore, promoting on the Internet must give the customer a compelling reason to search out the site. Make your Web site rich and integrated with respect to content, but also make it entertaining.

Box 6.4   Bookmark This

More and more retailers are going online to sell their products. Here are a few examples

- **Canada Shopping Links:** http://www.canadashoppinglinks.com—A directory of Canadian retailers offering online shopping;

- **TownNet.com:** http://www.townnet.com/shopping/olmalls.html—A collection of links to online malls; and
- **Downtown Anywhere:** http://www.awa.com—Links to and descriptions of online retailers.

Sales Reps as Connectors

Suppose you have a new product that has immediate sales potential across the country. How can you connect with the whole country? Should you hire your younger brother to take care of it for you, or should you seek out a professional sales representative, who will act as a commissioned sales agent for you?

An army of sales reps awaits your call. Make your selection carefully. Exercise caution, because the reputation of your sales reps will become *your* reputation.

The best way to find good reps is to interview potential buyers of your goods. Ask them to recommend some reps that have impressed them. When the same name surfaces several times, you will know where to start your contacts. Also, look carefully at who calls most frequently on your TC.

Aggressive reps might contact you. Prepare yourself to ask them the right kinds of questions:

- Who are your customers?
- How many salespeople do you have?
- What geographic areas do you cover?
- What lines have you carried?
- What help can you offer in collecting overdue accounts?
- What ideas do you have for trade show presentations?
- Do you have a showroom?
- Could you work with us on a regional analysis while we get ready for national coverage?
- Do you promote over the Internet?
- What percentage commission do you expect?
- Can I participate in your sales meetings?
- Do you handle competing lines?
- What kind of reports on your sales calls can I expect?
- What kind of performance guarantees do you offer?
- How can the agreement be terminated?
- Can I pay out after I have collected from customers?

Provide all the encouragement and support to your reps that you can, and never stop being a cheerleader. At the same time, insist on sales call reports that will keep you informed on what is going on in the field, and pack your bags and make some calls with your reps. Write monthly sales letters, and encourage feedback from both your reps and their customers. You *could* learn the worst—that a new line has taken your place or that the reps have been sleeping. This feedback will help you evaluate your product line and your reps.

Courtesy as Promotion

A dealer in luxury imported autos mailed 5,000 postcards to high-income prospects. The postcard message read something like, "Come in and test-drive this road warrior and receive a nice gift."

One potential customer travelled 65 kilometres for his test drive. The gift was a good incentive, but he'd been looking at cars for a year and was about to make a decision, so he wanted the test drive. That morning he had transferred funds to his chequing account. "Honey," he said to his wife as he left the house, "I'll be home with a car." His pink slip on his trade-in smouldered in the glove compartment.

Mr. Serious Prospect entered the dealer's showroom wearing old clothes and clutching his postcard. Four dapper salesmen in three-piece suits had seen him coming and had left the showroom quickly.

Without a salesperson in sight, the prospect spent 10 minutes waiting, reading the literature. The demos were locked, so he couldn't even sit behind the wheel for a fantasy drive. At last, a secretary entered the showroom, asked him for his postcard, and gave him the premium gift. About this time, one salesman returned, hands in his pockets and looking bored. The prospect took the opportunity to ask some questions about the car, to which the salesman responded without enthusiasm in monosyllables—and with a yawn.

Mr. Prospect took his business elsewhere that morning. He found the car he wanted and wrote a cheque for $45,000.

The promotion objective was to bring in customers for a test drive, not to give away premiums. Everything worked except the last person in the chain. How many other deals did that dealer lose during the promotion?

Be dramatic. Impress your employees with the fact that you mean business about customer courtesy. Close down your business for a day, and have all employees attend a sales retreat that stresses the importance of potential customers to your remaining in business. Follow up the retreat with incentive programs that reward employees for acts of exceptional courtesy to customers.

NETWORKING

Another source of promotional power is the technique of **networking**. Almost 40 percent of HOT 50 CEOs network report they belong to peer groups of entrepreneurs.[11] Networking carries the image of your business to a support group of non-competitive helpers. Gena D'Angelo speaks for many when she gives this testimonial for networking.

> "When Rob and I decided to go into business for ourselves, we looked around for more than a year. I had some training in graphics and Rob is good with numbers, so what we finally decided on was a franchised mail-box operation. We paid the franchiser a flat fee and agreed to pay a percentage of our gross as well. In turn, we received assistance and a well-developed business plan.
>
> "What they didn't tell us about was networking.
>
> "When you're in the mail-box business, giving good service is how you forge ahead. We knew we had to promote our image, and we tried everything—brochures, leaflets, fliers, and full-page display ads in the local newspapers. But the business didn't start rolling in until I joined my first network.
>
> "It's a sales lead club, and the membership is varied. We have a real estate broker, an insurance agent, the president of a small bank, the owner of a coffee service, a printer, a sign manufacturer, the owner of a chain of service stations, a sporting goods store owner, a travel agent, two small manufacturers, and a contractor. We meet once a week for breakfast. If you don't bring at least one sales lead for another club member, you have to put a dollar in the kitty. I've gotten more business from that club than from all my other promotional efforts combined.
>
> "I then decided to join another club, and I used the contacts I made to build my own network. Business has been good ever since. We

NETWORKING

Communicating through person-to-person channels in an attempt to sell or gain information; talking to people with the purpose of doing business

economy (limit) pricing

free ink/free air

guerrilla marketing

impact marketing

industry norm, or "keystone," pricing

marketing mix

marketing strategy

markup

networking

penetration pricing

personal selling

point-of-purchase (P-O-P) display

price skimming

pricing to the market

profit-based (cost plus) pricing

promotion

promotional campaign

promotional mix

Think Points for Success

✓ Be distinctive, and you can charge a ceiling or premium price.
✓ Be unique with your promotions. Instead of Christmas cards, send Thanksgiving or April Fool's Day cards.
✓ Stand in your target customer's shoes. Think like your TC. Find the need. Find the "ladder" in the TC's mind.
✓ Maintain a visual presence.
✓ A world in transition means opportunities for entrepreneurship. Fast footwork can keep you in the game.
✓ To start your mailing list, give away something for free. In return, potential customers will give you their names.
✓ Rent a Santa. Rent a robot. Rent a hot-air balloon. Rent a talking dolphin.
✓ Brand yourself. Create some excitement, because excitement sells.
✓ When you think you have it made, keep connecting with that customer anyway. You will never be so big that you can afford to disconnect. Remember this, and it will make you rich.
✓ Remember to promote the benefits and value of your product or service.
✓ Use the Internet to promote your business.

Business Plan Building Block

Before you begin these building block exercises, you might want to "look ahead" at the 1-800-GOT-JUNK? case and resources provided the end of this chapter. The GOT-JUNK marketing, pricing, and promotional strategies might help you develop, refine, and clarify your plan.

PRICING YOUR PRODUCT

Describe what prices you will charge, and why, in relation to your customers, potential competitors, costs of production, and expected profit. Describe your pricing strategy and why you have chosen it.

ADVERTISING AND PROMOTION

Describe your advertising and public relations plan. What are the most cost-effective ways to reach your customers? Use the data you have developed from the text. Your final budget and plan might look something like Table 6.1, page xx, depending on your type of business.

Public Relations—Unpaid Advertising
- Sample news releases (attach)
- Research articles or contributions to trade or technical journals
- Participation in or sponsorship of events

- Contributions to local media (air, press, and others)
- Community charities and/or networking activities

Media Advertising and Direct Mail
- Mail list applications
- Advertising space purchases
- Yellow Pages
- Computer bulletin boards and Web sites
- TV and radio commercials
- Point-of-purchase displays, signs, and billboards
- Brochures and selling sheets
- Business cards and ad specials
- Trade shows and informational seminars

Don't be afraid to be different and unique. Your message has to penetrate a lot of clutter.
Now it's your turn: *This will take a page or more.*

SERVICE AND SUPPLY

Once the sale is consummated, explain delivery of the product. Take-out? Will call? UPS? Purolator? FedEx? and so on. Follow up with sales support. What will your customer need from you once the product or service has been delivered? Look for techniques to turn your service into additional sales opportunities.
Now it's your turn.

MARKET STRATEGIES

This is a general statement that demonstrates that your business is customer driven. Use the information in Chapters 4 and 5 and in this chapter to develop a one-page marketing strategy philosophy.

SERVICES AFTER THE SALE

Once you have a customer, what will you do to keep him or her? Phone call follow-up? Correcting shipping or product mistakes? and so forth.

_____
_____
_____
_____
_____
_____

Checklist Questions and Actions to Develop Your Business Plan

Marketing Strategies and Promotion: Connecting with the Customer
- ❑ What is your marketing strategy?
- ❑ What prices will you charge?
- ❑ What is your pricing strategy?
- ❑ What are the promotional mix, goals and objectives?
- ❑ What stimulates your target market to buy or use your product or service?
- ❑ What has the primary and secondary market research told you about promoting your business?
- ❑ Develop a promotional strategy for your business.

❑ What percentage and what amount of your promotional budget will be spent on each of the components of a promotional mix, and why?

❑ Does your business have a unique twist for a possible publicity story?

❑ Why did you select the business name you are using?

Case Study

1-800-GOT-JUNK?

Case Background

At the beginning of this chapter we highlighted 1-800-GOT-JUNK?—a Canadian franchise organization that has experienced meteoric growth. To a large degree, the success of this company can be attributed to its marketing and promotions strategies. GOT-JUNK has put in place a successful pricing and promotions strategy, leading to healthy profits for the franchise system.

Below are additional sources of information and case study questions to help you understand why GOT-JUNK has been so successful and to reinforce the major marketing, pricing, and promotional themes of this chapter.

Case Resources

Refresh your memory and reread the GOT-JUNK vignette at the beginning of this chapter. We also want you to link on to the sites provided below:

- 1-800-GOT-JUNK? home page: http://www.1800gotjunk.com—Be sure to link on to "Media News" and "Web Casting" links.
- *Fortune Magazine*, "Cash for Trash": http://www.1800gotjunk.com/content/tf/blue.asp?action=viewArticle&a=228&z=236&n=Fortune-Magazine-2003 (accessed July 2006).
- Entrepreneur.com, "1-800-Got-Junk?, Company Background": http://www.entrepreneur. com/franchises/1800gotjunk/293278-0.html (accessed July 2006).
- *Canadian Business* Online, "One Deadly Obsession": http://www.canadianbusiness. com/entrepreneur/columnists/brian_scudamore/article.jsp?content=20060210_122709_2608 (Accessed July 2006),

Case Questions

1. **Marketing strategies**
   a. At the beginning of this chapter, we discussed the four key elements of the marketing strategy. What are these four elements?
   b. In Chapter 2 we explained how market trends create opportunities. The 1-800-GOT-JUNK? franchise system has linked on to a number of market trends. List five major trends that 1-800-GOT-JUNK? has taken advantage of.
   c. In Chapter 5, we explained the purpose and importance of competitive intelligence. According to Brian Scudamore, the war on Trashbusters—his first direct competitor—represented "an important chapter in the history of 1-800-GOT-JUNK?" Return to the opening vignette or link onto *Canadian Business* Online, "One Deadly Obsession."
   Explain what happened in the case of Scudamore's first direct competitor. What did Brian learn about the purpose of competitive intelligence from this experience?

2. **Guerrilla marketing**
   a. As we explained in the text, guerrilla marketing is a key promotional strategy of 1-800-GOT-JUNK?. Explain the meaning of the term *guerrilla marketing*, and give three examples of how GOT-JUNK uses this strategy.
   b. GOT-JUNK spent only $1,800 in advertising (2004) to reach potential franchisees. Free ink/free press is a key guerrilla marketing strategy for 1-800-GOT-JUNK?. Scudamore, the founder, recommends a three-step process to maximize this strategy. Briefly explain Scudamore's process.

3. Pricing
   a. In this chapter, we described four of the more common small business approaches to pricing: competitor-based pricing; profit-based pricing; industry norm, or keystone, pricing; and ceiling, or premium, pricing. Briefly explain each of these strategies.
   b. Which of the four strategies in question 3(a) do you think is being used by 1-800-GOT-JUNK?. Briefly explain why.
   c. A major marketing strategy of 1-800-GOT-JUNK? is to focus on a specific market segment, create uniqueness, and differentiate its service as perceived by the customer. Does this strategy lead to a more elastic or inelastic demand for company services? How does this marketing strategy affect GOT-JUNK's pricing policy?

4. Promotional strategies. A number of promotional strategies were discussed in this chapter. Many of these strategies are being successfully used by GOT-JUNK and are listed below. Give one example showing how GOT-JUNK used each of these promotional tactics.

Strategy	Provide a 1-800-GOT-JUNK Example
Freebies	
Free ink	
Free air	
Personal selling	
Working visibly/impact marketing	
Discount coupons	
Branding	
Networking	
Word of mouth	
Recycling and charity	
Community involvement	
Contests	

5. Promotion in Cyberspace. The 1-800-GOT-JUNK? franchisor made heavy use of promoting in Cyberspace. Link onto the Manitoba efuture centre's *Building an Effective Website*: http://www.e-future.ca/manitoba/en_CA/pdf/building_an_effective_website.pdf (accessed July 2006). Go to Page 6: "What Should You Have on Your Website?"
   a. Evaluate the 1-800-GOT-JUNK? home page based on the criteria provided.
   b. Do you think this Web site is an effective promotional tool? Give four reasons.

Notes

1. Fortune Magazine, "Cash for Trash": http://www.1800gotjunk.com/content/tf/blue.asp?action=viewArticle&a=228&z=236&n=Fortune-Magazine-2003; Franchise Zone, "1-800-GOT-JUNK, Company Background": http://www.entrepreneur.com/franzone/details/0,5885,12-12—-293278-,00.html; 1-800-GOT-JUNK?: http://www.1800gotjunk.com; *Investor's Business Daily*, "Three Steps for Getting Free Publicity": http://www.1800gotjunk.com/content/articlefiles/investors%20daily%20article.pdf; *Canadian Business Online*, "One Deadly Obsession": http://www.canadianbusiness.com/entrepreneur/columnists/brian_scudamore/article.jsp?content=20060210_122709_2608 (all sites accessed July 2006).

2. See CBSC's "Marketing Primer, Pricing Techniques": http://www.cbsc.org/servlet/ContentServer?cid=1102940227172&pagename=OSBW%2FCBSC_WebPage%2FCBSC_WebPage_Temp&c=CBSC_WebPage; and CCH, *Business Owner's Toolkit*, "Pricing Your Product": http://www.toolkit.cch.com/text/P03_5200.asp (accessed July 2006).

ACTION STEP 36

Use your new eyes to evaluate business locations

Think about how location affects your spending habits. For example, where do you buy gas for your car? Do you buy it on your way to work or school, or on your way home? Why?

Now, with your 24/7 Adventure Notebook in hand, look through your home. How important was the location of the retailer when you bought the items you see? For example,

- candy or soda;
- prescription drugs;
- washing machine;
- designer clothes;
- paintings;
- wristwatch;
- wall hangings;
- jewellery;
- carpeting;
- paint;
- mail order items, such as books, CDs, magazines, or clothing;
- power lawn and garden tools;
- DVDs;
- collectibles;
- car, motorcycle, or bicycle;
- your home itself;
- custom-made golf clubs; and
- eyeglasses.

A random look through your chequebook might trigger your memory. Feel free to add to this list.

How far did you travel, for example, for your last dinner out with a friend? For a carton of milk? A magazine? A lounge chair? A videocassette rental? How far would you travel to consult a brain surgeon?

What conclusion can you draw about the importance of location in making a purchase or providing a service?

Remember also that the cheapest location might not always be the best location.

You can expand on this Action Step by interviewing purchasing agents and buyers of commercial and industrial goods. Ask them what impact location has on their choice of vendors or on their recruitment of employees.

businesses and you are manufacturing a product, then your wholesaling channel of distribution might dictate warehousing space and transportation costs. Nonetheless, as you plan the location for your business, we do want you to think of the concept of multiple distribution channels and how this will affect where you locate your business.

We now want you to work through Action Step 36. Use your new eyes to examine your consumer's behaviour. This will help you understand the importance of location in making a purchase or providing a service. Will your location be "customer friendly"? Once you are armed with your new-eyes research from Action Step 36, we want you to complete Action Step 37 and brainstorm the perfect location for *your* business.

Now we want you to consider a location filter or checklist.

A LOCATION FILTER

Before you charge out to scout possible locations for your business, you need to decide what you really want from the location. The checklist below will help you zero in on the criteria that are important to your business. Use a scale of 1 to 10 to rate the relative importance of each item in terms of your target customers. When you have finished, go back and note the high numbers, say, anything above 5. Then, after you've read the rest of the chapter, come back to this list to see if your priorities have changed. We also suggest you take a moment and complete the "Which Location Would You Recommend?" E-Exercise in Box 7.1.

RATING IMPORTANCE (1–10)

✓ **Local/municipal licensing.** A wide variety of trades and establishments require a licence fee that can range anywhere from five dollars to thousands of dollars. In many Canadian municipalities, for example, licences are required if you operate a limousine service, refreshment vehicles, auctioneer service, billiard and pool hall, and skateboarding facilities. You'll also want to find out about local regulations on the installation, alteration, and maintenance of exterior signs and parking. We encourage you to begin learning more about your licensing and other local requirements. One option is to link onto Canada Business (http://canadabusiness.gc.ca/gol/cbec/site.nsf/en/index.html) and click on your province or territory. Another option for municipal regulations is to link to Canadian municipalities (http://www.municipalworld.com/hotlinks.htm#mun). Here you can start researching your municipal requirements. For example, if you link onto the City of Hamilton, Ontario, at http://www.myhamilton.ca, you'll find a list and description of the various licences required as well as licensing costs. This site also explains which types of health, police, or fire inspections are required. Zoning, building signage, and other issues are also explained fully.

✓ **Neighbour mix.** Who's next door? Who's down the street? Who's going to help pull your target customers into the area? Which nearby business pulls in the most customers? If you're considering a shopping centre, who's the anchor tenant (the big department store or supermarket that acts as a magnet for the centre)?

✓ **Competition.** Where are your competitors located? Mapping the location of your competitors can sometimes indicate location patterns or illustrate opportunities. Do you want competitors kilometres away, or does your business benefit from the clustering of competitors, as is the case with many "shopping goods" retailers?

✓ **Security and safety.** How safe is the neighbourhood? Is it as safe as a nursery at noon but an urban jungle at midnight? Is there anything you can do to increase the security? To learn more about security, complete the Store Layout Quiz in Box 7.1.

✓ **Labour pool.** Who's working for you, and how far will they have to commute? Does your business require more help at certain peak periods of the year? How easy will it be to find that kind of skilled or technical help you need? How far will they travel? Don't overlook the potential of part-timers, teens, seniors, and homemakers. Are there any zoning restrictions?

✓ **Services.** These include police and fire protection, security, trash pickup, sewage, and maintenance. What is included in the rent, and who pays for those services that are not? Is your location near a bus or subway stop?

✓ **Costs.** What is the purchase price if you're buying, or what are the rent or lease costs (and what is the type of lease)? Insurance, improvements, association dues, and routine maintenance: Who pays for what? Can you negotiate a few months' free rent?

✓ **Ownership.** If you're planning to buy the property, who will you get to advise you on real estate? Consider a lease with an option to buy, but have the contract reviewed by a real estate lawyer.

✓ **Property owner/landlord.** Have you considered the reputation of the property owner? There is no "hotter hell" for some business owners than a landlord who is slow to return calls, make necessary repairs, respond to "common area" issues, and so on.

✓ **Past tenants.** What happened to the past tenants? What mistakes did they make, and how can you avoid those mistakes?

✓ **Space.** If you need to expand, can you do it there, or will you have to move to a new site?

✓ **Accessibility.** Is your business where your target customer might expect to find you? Does your business require the "cumulative drawing power" of a mall or power centre? Is "driving time" rather than distance more relevant to your customer as an indicator of accessibility? Have you considered a Business Improvement Area (available in some provinces)?

✓ **Getting professional advice.** Have you considered using a commercial realtor, advisor, or mentor for help with storefront location selection?

✓ **Parking.** Most people like to park for free and close to your door. Is that possible?

✓ **History of the property.** How long has the landlord owned this property? Is it likely to be sold while you're a tenant? If the property is sold, what will happen to your business? What will happen to your tax obligations? If the property goes on the market, do you want the first right to make an offer?

✓ **Physical visibility.** Does your business need to be seen? If so, is this location easily visible? Can you make alterations to increase its visibility? Can you install the type of sign you want?

✓ **Life cycle stage of the area.** Is the site in an area that's embryonic (vacant lots, open space, emptiness), growing (high-rises, new schools, lots of construction), mature (building conversions, cracked street, sluggish traffic), or declining (vacant building, emptiness)? What will the area be like in five years? What effect would that have on your business? What do the municipal planners have in mind for the area? When will the highway department tear up the street? (See Figure 7.1.)

✓ **Image.** Is the location consistent with your firm's image? How will nearby businesses affect your image? Is this an area where your customers would expect to find a business like yours? (Look for a place that reinforces your customers'

ACTION STEP 37

Fantasize your perfect location

Sit down where you won't be disturbed, and brainstorm the ideal location for your small business. Get a pencil and paper, and let yourself dream. Draw a mind map, or use a list format; the idea is to get your thinking on paper. One example of a location mind map can be found at Biz/Ed's "Business Location Mind Map" (http://www.bized.ac.uk/educators/16-19/business/strategy/presentation/location_map.htm).

Start with your target customer. How will you make it easy for him or her to meet and greet you? Why is your location "customer friendly"? For example, if you were going to open a candy-cigarette-cigar stand, you might want to locate in West Edmonton Mall, where people pass by every hour. Or, if you were going to open an extremely upscale boutique, you might visualize a location in Toronto's Yorkville. Do you really need a storefront operation, or can you meet potential customers online or at craft shows and trade fairs? If you plan to establish a home-based business, consider factors such as the availability of parking in your neighbourhood. What will your major distribution channel be? Remember, we want you to consider multiple distribution channels. How are you going to integrate other channels—especially the Internet? This is why we encouraged you to begin thinking about setting up a Web site in Chapter 3.

Once you have the general idea of the type of neighbourhood and location you have in mind, write down what else is terrific about this location. Writing everything down will give you a starting point as you move out to explore the world.

perception of your business.) Remember, in the case of a home-based business, an important factor is the maintenance of a professional image.

✓ **Hours of operation.** Most municipalities have bylaws regarding the hours of operation. These hours might be different for various areas within a region. If you're planning a retail operation, be sure to look into this detail.

✓ **Utilities.** The high cost for water, sewage, gas, or other utilities might bring some unpleasant surprises. You should list all your utility requirements. Are they adequate? What would you require to upgrade them?

✓ **Local zoning bylaws.** Check out the present and future zoning. What restrictions might apply to your business?

✓ **Taxes.** Property and business taxes can change from street to street. Try to find out if there are any plans for reassessment.

✓ **Approvals.** Have you considered necessary approvals, such as those required from health officials, the fire marshal, the city planning office, and the liquor licensing board?

✓ **Transportation.** How much will your business depend on trucks, rail, buses, airports, or shipping by water? If you're in manufacturing or distribution, you'll need to determine your major transportation channel. It's also a good idea to have a backup system. A good technique here is to make a diagram of the location and all the lines of transportation your business will use in both receiving goods and customers and shipping goods.

✓ **Your target customers.** This is the last but most important criterion. Will your customers—lured by your terrific promotions—find you easily but have no place to park? Consider highway access and potential obstacles that could make coming to your place of business inconvenient or unpleasant. What do your customers really want? Ease of parking? Convenience? Atmosphere? Proximity to work? Even the side of the street is important. (For example, a dry cleaner would want to be on the inbound side of the street, so customers can easily drop off their cleaning on their way into the city to work.) Your location must satisfy the needs of the customer, not your personal needs. This is a particularly important consideration if you're

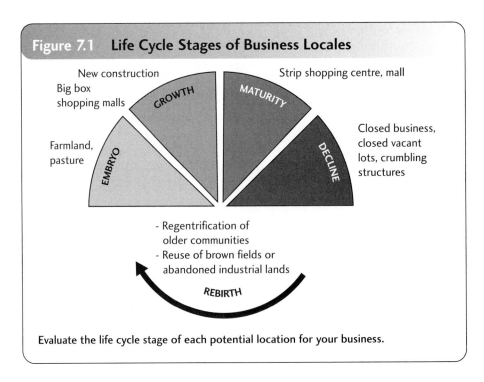

Figure 7.1   Life Cycle Stages of Business Locales

New construction
Big box shopping malls — GROWTH

Strip shopping centre, mall — MATURITY

Farmland, pasture — EMBRYO

Closed business, closed vacant lots, crumbling structures — DECLINE

- Regentrification of older communities
- Reuse of brown fields or abandoned industrial lands

REBIRTH

Evaluate the life cycle stage of each potential location for your business.

planning to operate out of your home. Are you setting up a home-based business because it's convenient to you or your customer? Remember, you work from home, not at home!

Box 7.1 E-Exercises

1. **Which Location Would You Recommend?**
   Visit Marketing Teacher's "Newtown" (http://www.marketingteacher.com/ Lessons/exercise_place.htm). Floor-Mart is considering where to put their new store. You must recommend a location. Which one would you choose?
2. **Store Layout Quiz**
   Visit http://crimeprevention.rutgers.edu/crime/shoplifting/layoutquiz.htm. Many shop owners, eager to sell their wares, jam a lot of stuff into a small space. The store illustrated on this site sells fabric and sewing supplies. It has many problems with poor sight lines and hidden corners. Take the Store Layout Quiz. What are the problems? How would you correct them?

THE RISE OF THE GOLD-COLLAR WORKER

Exercise + people + fun + work + stress = start a physical fitness program in the workplace. Psychographic thinking and the guidance of visionaries such as Faith Popcorn have been put into practice successfully by Sheila Mather. There she was, early on a Saturday morning, sharing her experience with an audience of soon-to-be businesspeople. She operates her business out of her home, but today this seminar was about her location, and she was marketing herself at a local small business seminar called "Look before You Leap."

Sheila began her talk with a few minutes of low-impact aerobics. When everyone was energized, she said, "You don't have to be a rocket scientist. I'm not in the high-tech business per se. But my job is to increase productivity in our growth high-tech sector. I'm in the 'feel good, energy, and people business.' These are the benefits that my customers want. You're also my potential customer, and after exercising, I hope you feel a little better now."

She explained that her home-based location strategy was not about finding a physical site. It was about finding ways to locate herself and her business in front of the customer. "My real location is where I meet and greet my customers. Yesterday, for example, my location was an empty office where I conducted my exercise program for one of my company clients. Today, my location is here at this seminar. Tomorrow, I am giving advice online to my virtual customers. In a home-based business, your location can be very fluid, and one thing is for sure: you should plan to be out meeting people, because it is people who will drive your business."

Working at home has become a major trend in the way Canadians do business. About 2 million Canadian households create jobs, stimulate local economies, and provide a growing commercial market. Most of these home businesses have been in operation for more than a year (44 percent, one to three years; 35 percent, more than three years). Almost half of the home workers are self-employed; 14 percent are substituters (employees who spend part of their day at home); and 39 percent are supplementers (employees who bring work home). According to these statistics, chances are that you will be working out of your home in the future—even if you have another job. In their report on home business, Barbara Orser and Ted James dispel a number of myths about the nature of home-based business (see Box 7.2).

Home business is one of the "golden" industries of the next decade, with the annual growth rate expected to be in the 12 percent range. There are several major reasons for this trend.

- **Cocooning.** Many of us are attempting to reduce outside stresses by spending more leisure and work time at home.
- **Computerization.** New high-tech equipment such as fax machines, personal computers, and modems for e-mail and the Internet have made it a lot easier and more convenient to operate out of the home.
- **Two-income families.** It makes it a lot easier to work out of the home when both parents are trying to raise a family and make a living.
- **Growth of the service industry.** A service business generally has lower start-up costs, operational expenses, and equipment costs, making it much more sensible to run your operation out of the home.
- **Higher productivity.** Studies show that productivity increases by 20 to 60 percent when employees can work during peak times at their own pace. In fact, such statistics have influenced the new knowledge-based companies to encourage telecommuting.
- **Increased efficiency.** The home worker saves on transportation, rental, furniture, and equipment costs.
- **Improved service.** The new consumer demands more individual attention. Home-based businesses are well positioned to adapt to changing and individualized consumer needs.
- **Vigilante consumers.** The new customer is fragile and fickle, and craves superior service. This consumer doesn't tolerate the mediocrity of mass production and sameness.
- **Downsizing.** Today, companies are encouraged to go small and to contract out whenever possible.
- **Mobility.** With the growth in personal care and home care, more and more businesses are going to their customers, which means that a storefront isn't always necessary.

Starting your business out of the home does not mean that your plan is written on the back of an envelope. It takes just as much care to open and operate a home business as it does to establish a traditional retail business. Before you decide on a location, consider the advantages and disadvantages of operating out of your home. Box 7.3 will help you get started. See also Box 7.4 for online resources that could help you run a successful home business.

Box 7.2 Dispelling the Myths about Home-Based Businesses (HBBs)

Myth. HBBs are fairly small in number.
Fact. One in four of all Canadian households operates some form of home business.

Myth. HBBs spend all their time at home.
Fact. Less than 40 percent of the workday is spent at the home base; 30 percent is spent on the road, and 32 percent at the customer's or client's premises.

Myth. HBBs are mostly service providers.
Fact. About 50 percent of HBBs provide service; the remainder are manufacturers and wholesalers.

Myth. HBBs typically occur only in urban areas.
Fact. Nearly half (48 percent) of people primarily running an HBB live in a non-urban area.

Myth. HBBs are motivated by financial reward.

Fact. Intrinsic factors such as independence and flexibility are more important motivators for being home-based than financial rewards.

Myth. HBBs create problems for the neighbourhood.

Fact. The number of registered public complaints about HBBs is so small as to be insignificant.

Myth. HBBs deliberately ignore municipal bylaws.

Fact. In a recent study, 40 percent of home-business owners surveyed were not even aware of existing bylaws regulating their business activities.

Source: Barbara Orser and Ted James, *Home Business: A Report Prepared for the Home-Based Project Committee, Industry, Science and Technology Canada and Employment and Immigration Canada*, p. 8. Reproduced with the permission of the Minister of Public Works and Government Services Canada, 2006.

WHAT HOME-BASED BUSINESS IS BEST FOR ME?

We're often asked, "What is the best home-based business to go into?" Well, that will depend on your ability to connect your values, experience, and knowledge to current market trends—as we talked about back in Chapter 2. You are going to have to figure out your skills and interests, determine what you are good, at and then look for a market opportunity that has confluence with your personal attributes. We're going to provide you with a list of home-based opportunities based on growing market trends as outlined by industry leaders and business experts and our trend analysis in Chapter 2.[2]

Here goes:

- technology coach;
- upmarket travel advisor;
- caterer for a healthy lifestyle;
- eco-friendly cleaning service provider;
- elder services provider;
- concierge service agent;
- personal health or fitness trainer;
- pet sitter/grooming provider;
- life balance, personal, or business coach;
- financial advisor;
- energy efficiency contractor/consultant; and
- home improvement/décor contractor/advisor.

We hope you are ready to start thinking about a home-based business, and we suggest you begin by carefully weighing the pros and cons. Complete Action Step 38.

Box 7.3 Is Home the Best Place? A Location Checklist[3]

The following checklist might help you determine if you should operate your business out of the home.

- **Target market.** How far will your customers be willing to travel to get to you? Can your business travel or deliver to the customer? How efficient is it for you to serve your customer from your home?
- **Neighbourhood mix.** Do you need other businesses to pull your customer to you?

ACTION STEP 38

Decide whether a home-based business is in your future

Before starting a business from your home, answer the following questions: "What are the benefits?" "What are the negatives?" What is my distribution strategy?

1. **List reasons to work at home.** Start with the obvious: low overhead, close to snacks, an easy commute, familiar surroundings. If you have children and want to be near them, working at home is one solution. Keep listing.

2. **List the problems with working at home.** How do you handle interruptions? How do you show that you are serious? How do you focus amidst clutter? If you have clients, where do you see them? What's the zoning situation in your neighbourhood? Keep listing.

3. **List solutions to the problems raised in number 2.** If you're being interrupted, you need to get tough. Set up a schedule and post a notice: "Dad's working from 9–11. Lunch will be served at noon. If Dad does not work, there's no lunch!"

4. **Go technical.** What will it cost you? Consider expenses such as a computer, scanner, modem, printer, answering machine, and so on. Use e-mail to connect with your customers.

5. **Where will your workspace be?** Garage? Basement? Bedroom? Den? How can you keep it yours? What will it cost to make it usable and productive space?

6. **Check out your home insurance.** What does it cover? What additional coverage do you need, and what will it cost? (Check out the Cooperators, "Home Business Insurance" site in Box 7.4, **Commercial Leases.**)

7. **Review your health insurance, if needed.** Can you qualify? What will the cost be?

8. **Get advice.** Talk with your family and friends who own home-based businesses.

- **Physical visibility.** Does your business need to be seen?

- **Competitors.** Why would your target customer deal with you out of your home-based business rather than with your competition? What advantages does your home business offer over that of your competitors?

- **Life cycle stage.** Is your area in an embryonic (e.g., vacant land), growing (e.g., plenty of construction, new schools), mature (e.g., cracked streets, sluggish traffic), or decline (e.g., vacant buildings) stage? Will you want to be doing business in the same location five years from now?

- **Image.** How would your target customers react if they learned that you were operating out of your home? For example, right or wrong, some customers might not take you seriously.

- **Local/municipal regulations.** Do you require a licence to operate out of your home, and can you get one?

- **Local zoning bylaws.** Do local bylaws allow you to operate your business out of your home?

- **Space/physical requirements.** Do you have enough space to serve the customer and your business needs effectively? What are your physical requirements? For example, do you need to add a washroom? Do you have a designated area to work? How will the customer enter your location? Do you need a separate entrance?

- **Approvals.** Have you considered the necessary approvals related to health, fire, transportation, environment, and labour?

- **Insurance.** Will your insurance company allow you to operate a business out of your home? How will this affect your insurance premiums?

- **Utilities.** Are there any extra utilities requirements (e.g., extra telephone line)?

- **Work habits/behaviour.** Do you need to "get away in the morning"? Many businesspeople like to completely separate their business and personal lives. Do you have the discipline to work in your home?

- **Lifestyle.** Will your business disrupt your family and personal lifestyle? How will your neighbours feel about your running your business out of your home?

Box 7.4 Bookmark This

Home-Based Business Resources

These Web sites provide a wide range of resources for people who operate a business out of the home.

- **Business Know-How:** http://www.businessknowhow.com
- **BizOffice.com's "Small and Home-Based Business Resources":** http://www.bizoffice.com
- **Canadian Home and Micro Business Federation:** http://www.homebiz.ca
- **British Columbia, *Starting a Home-Based Business—A Manual for Success*:** http://www.cse.gov.bc.ca/reportspublications/publications/hbb2000.pdf
- **Canada/Newfoundland and Labrador Business Service Network, "How-To Guide on Home Based Business":** http://www.cbsc.org/servlet/ContentServer?pagename=CBSC_NL%2Fdisplay&lang=en&cid=1100003682929&c=GuideHowto
- **Starting a Home-Based Business:** http://www.cbsc.org/servlet/ContentServer?pagename=CBSC_SK%2Fdisplay&lang=en&cid=1102419630189&c=GuideHowto
- **The Co-operators, "Home Business Insurance":** http://www.cooperators.ca/english/products/business/homebased.html—Find out whether you qualify as a home business and learn about the coverage available to protect your business.

Note: All sites accessed July 2006.

GETTING THE INFORMATION YOU NEED TO FIND THE RIGHT LOCATION

Businesspeople tend to stay in a location for a while because it is expensive to renovate and move. Thus, selection of your location will be one of your most important start-up decisions. You'll want to make sure that you are right in the heart of your target market. So, where do you go for information? We'll begin with secondary sources of location information—that is, published data that have been gathered and compiled by others.

LOCATION INFORMATION USING SECONDARY RESEARCH

Data collected by Statistics Canada, in particular, census information, could be one of your major sources of secondary information, especially if you are planning to rent, lease, or buy a retail or manufacturing business. We have already provided you with a number of possible Statistics Canada sources in the demographic profiling section of Chapter 4, pages 82. You might want to go back and check these out again.

We also encourage you to get on the Net. Strategis (http://www.strategis.ic.gc.ca) is probably your best place to start. In Chapter 5, we asked you to use Strategis to seek out competitor information. Now we want you to go back to this research and see if you can discover some valuable information for locating your business.

As we know by now, Statistics Canada and Industry Canada are not our only sources of secondary information. Municipal and regional governments have all kinds of information, such as traffic counts, so a visit to your local planning office is a must. While you're there, check the zoning bylaws and future plans. For example, you might be awfully disappointed if you decide to locate your home-based business in a municipality that forbids home-operated enterprises. Or, locating your business on a road scheduled for sewer work might be your quick ticket to bankruptcy. If you are going into a mall, the mall owners should have a detailed location study. Get their analyses, or don't locate there. Consider potential suppliers. They should know which outlets are doing the greatest business. If you approach them in the right way, they might be pleased to help you. After all, this could mean more future business for them.

Private companies also will, for a price, get you some pretty detailed information. One such firm is MapInfo (http://www.mapinfo.com), which maintains location databases that are highly targeted and include names of facilities and offices within a specific area. Commercial real estate agents can also be very helpful, particularly if you're thinking about a retail or manufacturing operation.

LOCATION INFORMATION USING PRIMARY RESEARCH

In the first six chapters of this book, we have talked about your primary research techniques, such as brainstorming, interviewing, mind-mapping, and so on. As you know by now, we cannot rely strictly on secondary research because it is just that—secondary. For your location analysis, you are also going to have to do some of your own primary research. But the hitch is that there is no formula or set framework to follow. Nevertheless, this is a real opportunity to practise your new-eyes research. To help, we will provide examples of how some enterprising entrepreneurs did theirs. We then encourage you to find your own creative way.

> Ben wanted to start a dry cleaning business. He knew that the success
> of his business would depend on the number of cars that passed by a
> specific point during peak hours. Through experience in the business,
> he had found a direct relationship between the number of cars and the

volume of dry cleaning. What did he do? He did not rely on the traffic counts from his local municipality, although this secondary information was useful in narrowing down possible sites. His answer was to sit in his car for several days and count the number of vehicles that went by his potential sites. After doing this a few times for various locations, he finally found the "perfect" spot. Today, Ben has 15 outlets, and we find him out counting cars, getting ready for his 16th store. He tells us that he is in the business of counting cars, because if he can get that right and competition is not a serious factor, then everything else should unfold nicely.

Now let's see how Lucy did her primary research by counting people.

Lucy wanted to start a gift store that her favourite grandmother would be proud of. The name of her new business would be Gramma's, so the location had to be right, for she wanted to keep this name for a long time. She also knew from working in gift stores that most of the business would come from the impulse buyer.

A new mall was opening down the street, and the manager, fresh from business school, had loaded her down with site plans, traffic studies, and potential store locations. "You had better hurry," he said. "The good spots are being snapped up awfully fast." Fortunately, her small business teacher was close by and added a little sanity to her life. "It's easy," she said. "Just replicate, and you will know for sure. Find a mall that is under construction and tell me how much business the gift store is doing."

"That's crazy," exclaimed Lucy. "You can't possibly know how much a business is doing before the mall is built."

"That's true," said her professor. "Why don't you wait until you know what is going on."

"I'm going to miss this one," protested Lucy.

"Yes, you may, but when you find the right location, you will know it, because you will be able to back up the mall research with some of your own primary research."

About six months later, Lucy finished doing her pedestrian counts in front of an empty store at a more established mall on the other side of the city. Her own traffic counts and the mall studies convinced her that this was the location for her. Today, Lucy's gift store at the better established mall is doing well. She is not making a million, but she is making a good living, and her grandmother is very proud of her.

Here is the lesson she learned: If your business relies on impulse buying, you had better know exactly how many people will go by your door and how many will enter and make a purchase—*before you open your doors.*

By the way, it took more than two years for the owners to fully lease the new mall that Lucy first looked at.

Specific primary research techniques worked for Ben and Lucy. The key to their success was knowing who their customers were and what they wanted. Their businesses were driven by the amount of traffic passing by their doors—in one case it was cars and in the other, people. Now let's return to Elizabeth Wood (remember Crazy's Roadhouse in Chapters 4 and 5?) and see how she helped Max, the owner, determine whether he had a good location.

"That's a stupid question," quipped Max. "Of course I have a great location—just look at my sales."

"Just a minute," cautioned Elizabeth. "Because you are fortunate enough to have customers, this does not mean you have the perfect location." Elizabeth knew what she was talking about because she was standing in front of Max, a little smugly, with the results of her customer survey. "Let me ask you: Where do your customers live?"

That's easy," said Max. "They live in the neighbourhood. That's why I chose this location." Not wanting to burst Max's balloon, Elizabeth agreed he was partly right. "The fact is, your lunch trade lives at the workplace. That is, 'place of work' is the most important location criterion at lunch. As a matter of fact, the perfect luncheon location would be within walking distance of 'white-collar' industry."

Then Elizabeth explained to Max that most of his lunch customers were forced to drive to his restaurant, and that's why there were always a few empty seats at lunch during the first part of the week. "Now, as for your night and weekend trade," she continued, "most live at least 15 km from your restaurant. Your TCs are 'grazers' who say that their household income is $50,000 plus per year and who come from all over the city. The most important thing to them is that they can get here within 20 minutes and there is adequate parking. Yes, parking is very important to them. You should begin thinking about the potholes in your parking lot before you start losing business."

Now that Elizabeth knew where Max's customers lived and worked, there was a lot more they could talk about. For the next few hours, they brainstormed new ideas and approaches to making the location more accessible to the customer. For example, how could Max speed up the food service at lunch?

Now let's consider the importance of primary research for the home-based business. Remember Mina Cohen from Chapter 4? She was in the travel and learning business. She worked out of her home, but her location was at the dig site. There is no doubt the archaeologists at the site demand that she and her customers "dig" with care. Much of her location analysis would concern itself with finding prime dig sites for her customers to visit.

For Ron Taylor (Chapter 5) and the business of cocooning for teens (basement recreation rooms), what is his location? His customer's house, of course. His location strategy is all about finding homes where teens live.

We can't stress it enough. If you operate a service business from home, your location analysis is just as important as if you are renting. After all, your location is at your *customer's* home or place of work. All of these cases point to the need for primary research before you decide your location. If you can support primary analysis with secondary data, so much the better.

Many of you will choose not to operate your business out of the home, although we encourage you to give serious thought to this strategy. For those who plan to rent a location, we'll enter the complex world of leases.

SOME THINGS YOU MUST KNOW ABOUT LEASES

A lease document is drawn up by the property owner's lawyer. Although its language is very specific, the terms spelled out are provisional—that is, the terms are proposed as a starting point for negotiation. Nothing you see in the contract is cast in stone...unless you agree to it. Obviously, the terms proposed will probably favour the property owner. Consider the proposed lease seriously. Discuss it with your own lawyer and with others who have experience with leases, and determine how best to begin the negotiation. The following pages will guide you through this process.

ENTREPRENEUR, READ YOUR LEASE

Entrepreneur Mick Beatty failed to read the terms of his lease. He thought he had a "gentlemen's agreement" with his landlady, but he was wrong. His story points out the importance of *assuming nothing* when it comes to leases.

"I was on vacation from the East when I discovered the perfect location. It was in the sleepy tourist town of White Rock, on the edge of the world in a fabulous part of British Columbia.

"It was late summer, I remember, and I'd just spent a week driving through the mountains from Calgary. When I reached White Rock, I thought I was home.

"I discovered Eddie's Pub my first evening in town. It faced the beach, and sitting there sipping a cool one, I could watch the sun reflect off the water. From time to time, people would drift in for a casual drink, and while sitting there, feeling like a million, I must have talked to 20 different folks.

"They loved the place, too. And most of them looked upscale.

"Vacations don't last forever, and when I got back home, I kept thinking about Eddie's in White Rock. I was working then for one of the giant mega corporations, making good money in a pressure cooker of a job, and even though I was enough of a culture freak to appreciate Toronto, I wanted more out of life. After one particularly hectic day at the office, I sat and stared out the window, thinking about those three days I'd spent in White Rock, on the beach.

"A business trip took me to Vancouver that next spring, and I managed to haggle for an extra day so that I could stay overnight in White Rock and stop in for a drink at Eddie's.

"Double surprise.

"The sun was shining—and Eddie's Pub was for sale.

"I called my banker back East. He said I was crazy. I phoned two buddies, one from college, one from the squash club. They thought it would be fun to be part of a new venture and were ready to invest. I talked to Eddie, the owner, made a deal to pay him so much down and the rest out of profits, and suddenly I owned a small business.

"When I phoned my boss in Toronto, he said I was crazy, too. 'Living somewhere on a beach is just a dream,' he said. But what he said next saved my life. 'Tell you what, Mick. Don't pull the plug until you're absolutely sure. We'll give you six months. If you're still out there dreaming, send in your resignation. Meanwhile, have fun. Every man needs a fling before he settles down.'

"I said okay, and thanks. And that was that.

"The location at Eddie's is only 200 square metres. The layout is long and narrow, and we used mirrors from the Gay Nineties to give the place atmosphere. The traffic is mostly walk-in—beach people, stray tourists—and the only promotion I had to do was to put up a sign that said "Happy Hour 4–6:30." I shook hands with my customers, passed out complimentary drinks, served the best espresso in the Vancouver area, and started making money my first day.

"Then trouble showed up.

"I hadn't been open a week when I got a call from my landlady. She was a crusty-voiced lady I'd barely talked to, and she said over the phone that there had been some complaints about the music.

"'Hey,' I said. 'I'm sorry. Who's complaining?'

"'Your neighbours,' she said. 'They have rights, too, you know.'

"'Is it too loud?'

"'No,' she said. 'It's not the volume. It's that rock stuff that's causing the trouble. It irritates the other customers.'

"'Rock?' I said. 'It's not rock, it's more like—'

"'I don't know what you call it,' my landlady said. 'But it's got to stop. And right now.'

"'My customers like it,' I argued. 'The music is part of my atmosphere.'

"'Young man,' she said, 'what your customers like is neither here nor there. I own that property, and I have other tenants to think about. And if you have any questions, I'd advise you to read your lease.' She hung up.

"Well, I read the lease, carefully. And then I saw a lawyer. He confirmed what I'd read—according to the terms of the lease, my landlady had the power to tell me what kind of music I could play in my own small business.

"Incredible, but true.

"I tried turning off the music. Right away, my customers missed it. Drink orders fell off. I surveyed my neighbours and made a list of songs they didn't find offensive, but when I played that junk in the bar, my steady customers (who were becoming less steady) asked me to turn it off. As a last resort, I even visited my landlady and tried to **renegotiate the lease**. But she wouldn't budge.

"There was only one thing to do. I sold the business. I went back to my job in Toronto. I still owe some money to my partners, and when the tension builds at work, I always think of the sun on the water at White Rock. I'll go back sometime. But right now I'm a little soured on the place. It's too bad. They've got a great beach. And a great little bar where you can sit and watch the sun go down.

"My advice? Have a plan, get some experience before you start, and last of all, read the small print in your lease."

RENEGOTIATE THE LEASE

Obtain a new or modified contract for occupancy

ANTICIPATE THE UNEXPECTED

Bette Lindsay has always had a soft spot for books, and when she finally chose a business, it was a bookstore in a shopping centre. She had researched everything—trends, census data, newspapers, reports from real estate firms, and suppliers—but she failed to anticipate an important potential pitfall: dependency on an anchor tenant (a business in a commercial area that attracts customers).

Few small businesses are themselves "destination locations." They must count on anchor tenants to draw traffic. Bette made an assumption that the anchor tenant in her centre would be there forever. This case study shows the importance of having Plan B ready.

"My husband and I researched the small business field for almost two years, and my heart kept bringing me back to books. I've read voraciously since I was 7 years old, and I love a well-written story. So when a new shopping centre was opening 10 kilometres from our home, I told my husband, 'This is it.'

"Everything looked perfect. They had a great anchor tenant coming in—a supermarket that would draw lots of traffic. The real estate agent we'd been working with during most of our search showed us the demographics of the area, which documented that we were smack in the middle of a well-educated market. According to statistics put out by the federal government, a bookstore needs a population of

27,000 people to support it. Our area had 62,000 people, and the closest bookstore was more than eight kilometres away.

"Everything else looked good, too. We had lots of parking. The neighbours (three hardy pioneers like ourselves) were serious about their business and pleasant to work with.

"We wanted to be in for the Christmas season, because December is the peak season for bookstores. So we set a target date of mid-October. The contractor was still working when we opened a month later.

"We started off with an autograph party and we ran some bestseller specials. And even though construction work from our anchor tenant blocked our access, we had a very good Christmas that year. We started the New Year feeling very optimistic.

"One day in mid-January, construction work stopped on our anchor tenant's new building. The next day we read in the paper that the company had gone bankrupt.

"Well, the first thing I did was call the landlord. He was out of town, and his answering service referred me to a property management company. They said they knew nothing about what was happening and that all they did was collect the rent. January was slow. So was February, and March. In April, two of our neighbours closed up. The construction debris still blocked customer access. It was a mess.

"In May, I finally succeeded in getting in touch with the owner and tried to renegotiate the lease, but his story was sadder than mine.

"Fourteen months after we moved in, we finally got our anchor tenant. If I'd suspected it would take anything like that long, I could have built some provision for it into our lease."

Bette and her husband learned the hard way.

HOW TO REWRITE A LEASE

You live with a lease (and a landlord) for a long time. If you're successful in a retail business, your landlord might want a percentage of your gross sales receipts. If you're not successful or if problems develop, you're going to want several Plan B's and a **location escape hatch**—a way to cancel or modify your lease if your landlord fails to meet the specified terms. For example, your lease should protect your interest

- if the furnace or air conditioning system breaks down,
- if the parking lot needs sweeping or resurfacing,
- if the anchor tenant goes under,
- if the building is sold, or
- if half of the other tenants move out.

The possibility of such grief-producing eventualities needs to be dealt with—with precise words and precise numbers in the lease.

Read the lease slowly and carefully (Boxes 7.5 and 7.6 will help you). When you see something you don't understand or don't like, draw a line through it. Feel free to rewrite the lease if you need to. It's *your* lease, too, you see. If you need help from a lawyer, get it. And make sure that the owner (or the leasing agent) indicates his or her agreement with your changes by initialling each one.

Here's a checklist to start you on your rewrite.

1. **Escape clause.** If the building doesn't shape up or the area goes into eclipse, you will want to get out fast. Be specific. Write something like this into your lease: "If three or more vacancies occur in the centre, tenant may terminate lease."

LOCATION ESCAPE HATCH

A way to cancel or modify your lease if the landlord fails to meet the specified terms

2. **Option to renew.** Most businesses need at least six months to a year to get going. If your business does well, you will want to stay put. If it doesn't, you don't want to be saddled with a heavy lease payment every month. Get a lease for one year, with an option to renew for the next two or three.

3. **Right to transfer.** Circumstances might force you to sublet. In the trade, this is called "assigning." Make sure the lease allows you to transfer your lease without a heap of hassle if such circumstances arise.

4. **Cost-of-living cap.** Most leases allow the owner to increase rents along with inflation according to the consumer price index (CPI). To protect yourself, insist on a cost-of-living cap so that your base rate won't increase faster than your landlord's costs. Try for half of the amount of the CPI increase, a standard measure. Thus, if the CPI rises 10 percent, your rate will go up only 5 percent. It's fair, because the owner's costs won't change much. Major tenants in your centre will insist on a cap, so you should be able to negotiate one also. Proceed with confidence.

5. **Percentage lease. Percentage leases** are common in larger retail centres. They specify that the tenant pay a base rate plus a percentage of the gross sales. An example: $XX per square foot per month plus 5 percent of gross sales over $500,000 per year.

PERCENTAGE LEASE

Lease that specifies that the tenant will pay a base rate plus a percentage of the gross sales

6. **Floating rent scale.** If you're a pioneer tenant of a shopping centre, negotiate a payment scale based on occupancy. For example, you might specify that you'll pay 50 percent of your lease payment when the centre is 50 percent occupied, 70 percent when it's 70 percent occupied, and 100 percent when it's full. You can't build traffic to the centre all by yourself, and motivation is healthy for everyone, including landlords.

7. **Start-up buffer.** There's a good chance you'll be on location fixing up, remodelling, and so on, long before you open your doors and make your first sale. Make your landlord aware of this problem and negotiate a long period of free rent. The argument: If your business is successful, the landlord—who's taking a percentage—will make more money. If your business doesn't do well or if it fails, the landlord will have to find a new tenant. You need breathing space. You've signed on for the long haul. By not squeezing you to death for cash, the landlord allows you to put more money into inventory, equipment, service, atmosphere—the things that make a business go.

8. **Improvement.** Unless you're a super fixer-upper, you don't want to lease a place equipped with nothing but a dirt floor and a capped-off cold water pipe. You need a proper atmosphere for your business, but you don't want to use all your cash to pay for it before you open. Negotiate with the landlord to make the needed improvements and spread the cost of them over the total time of the lease. Otherwise, find a space that doesn't require heavy remodelling.

9. **Restrictive covenants.** If you're running a camera store, and part of your income derives from developing film, you don't want a Fotomat booth to move into your centre. If you're selling hearing aids, you don't want a stereo store next door. Build **restrictive covenants** (things that your landlord cannot do) into your lease to protect yourself.

RESTRICTIVE COVENANTS

Things that your landlord cannot do that are written into your lease to protect you

10. **Maintenance.** When the parking lot needs sweeping, who pays for it? If the air conditioner goes out, who pays? If the sewer stops up, who's responsible for the repairs? Get all of this written down in simple language. Your diligence with words and numbers will pay off.

Box 7.5 provides two online examples of leases and information on the language of leasing.

Box 7.5 The Language of Leases

Learn More About Commercial Leases—

- Lease Tips and Checklist

Link on to Toronto Commercial Real Estate: http://www.the-real-estate-lease-advisor.com/. Click the tips and tricks, and the lease checklist buttons.

- Office Lease

Link on to: https://www.legaldocs.com/htsgif.d/xolease.mv.
Here you will find an example of an office lease.

Before Signing on the Dotted Line

Before signing on the dotted line, be certain you understand the language of the lease. These terms will get you started.

- **Building gross area.** The total square-foot area of the building when the enclosing walls are measured from outside wall to outside wall.
- **Usable building area.** The square-foot area within the building actually occupied by tenants, measured from centre partition to centre partition.
- **Common area.** The square-foot area of the building servicing all tenants in common, such as lobby, corridors, lavatories, elevators, stairs, and mechanical equipment rooms. The building common area is usually between 10 and 12 percent of the gross building area.
- **Rentable area.** A combination of the tenants' usable building area plus each tenant's pro rata share of the common area.
- **Gross rent.** A rental per square foot, multiplied by the rentable area, to determine the annual rent due on a lease, where the landlord provides all services and utilities, including tenant janitorial services.
- **Net rent.** A rent per square metre (or foot) multiplied by the rentable area to determine the annual rent due under a lease, whereby the tenant also pays, in addition to the rent, its pro rata of all utilities and services and real estate taxes.
- **Loss factor.** The proportion of usable building area to total rentable area. The usable area is that in which you may put furniture and equipment for actual office use. The rentable area often includes a proportionate share of ancillary building services. The lower the loss factor, the more usable space there is. Loss factors can vary from floor to floor in the same building. Rentable area may be calculated in a different manner for one building than it is for another, and this will affect your comparison of rental proposals.

GROSS RENT

A rental where the landlord provides all services and utilities, including tenant janitorial services

NET RENT

A rental whereby the tenant also pays, in addition to the rent, its pro rata of all utilities, services, and real estate taxes

Box 7.6 Ask These Questions...

Before you sign a lease, ask these questions.

- Does the lease contain an escape clause?
- Does it have an option to renew?
- Can you "assign" the lease if you need to sublet?
- Do you have a ceiling on rent increases?
- Do you have a floating lease scale, according to how much of the centre is occupied?
- Have you tried to negotiate a period of free rent while you are preparing to open the doors?
- Have you negotiated to have the landlord make the needed improvements and charge you for them over the total time of the lease?

In a Nutshell

The main purpose of this chapter was to help guide you through the process of finding a location that is right for you, your business, and your customer. We have encouraged you to think about a multiple distribution strategy, to use your primary and new-eyes research as well as secondary sources, and to keep asking, "What is the best location according to my target customer?"

If you are planning to retail or manufacture your product or service, your choice of location is probably the most important decision you will make. You'll have to live with your selection for a long time. We encourage you to complete the location filter checklist and begin to understand the language and consequences of leases. Many of you will plan to start your business from your home. This is fine, but don't think that your location analysis is not important. A location checklist for your home-based business was also presented. We wanted you to make sure that your home office will satisfy the needs of your customer and won't destroy your personal life. Finally, we discussed the need to understand the language and consequences of leases.

Key Terms

business location	percentage lease
distribution channel	renegotiate a lease
franchising	restrictive covenants
gross rent	retailing
net rent	wholesaling
location escape hatch	

Think Points for Success

✓ The irony of the search for a start-up location is that you need the best site when you can least afford it.

✓ Think about your distribution strategy and your customer's needs before searching for a location.

✓ Take your time selecting a location. If you lose out on a hot site, don't worry; another one will eventually turn up.

✓ Even if you start up your business at home, you will need a location analysis.

✓ A site analysis for a street-side location should include everything that is unique to a specific building or space. Many successful centres have some dead traffic areas.

✓ Who are your business neighbours? Are they attracting your type of customers or clients? What will happen if they move or go out of business?

✓ Know the terms and buzzwords—net, gross, triple net, industrial gross, and so on—and be aware that they might mean slightly different things in each contract or lease agreement.

✓ Everything is negotiable: free rent, signage, improvement allowances, rates, maintenance, and so on. Don't be afraid to ask; a dollar saved in rental expenses can be worth more than $10 in sales.

✓ Talk to former tenants; you might be amazed at what you learn.

Business Plan Building Block

This section of your business plan explains why you have selected your location and how it satisfies the needs of your target customers and your business.

Your description should include the following key considerations.

• What is your distribution strategy?

• How close or accessible is your location to the target market?

- What distribution channels do you intend to use to reach the target customer if you do not have a storefront location?
- How does the location satisfy the exterior and interior requirements for the business? (If possible, include a floor plan or photos in an appendix.)
- How close is the competition to your location?
- What is the possibility of expansion?
- Is the building leased or owned? Has the lease been reviewed by a lawyer? (Include proof of ownership or a copy of the lease in an appendix.)
- Does the location conform to municipal bylaws and environmental regulations?
- Do you have a store layout plan?

    Now it's your turn. Using materials from this chapter, describe your distribution strategy and why you have chosen your location.

Checklist Questions and Actions to Develop Your Business Plan

Location

☐ What is your distribution strategy?

☐ What criteria are important to your location?

☐ What secondary research do you need to make a decision about location?

☐ If you plan to operate a home-based business, be sure to answer all the questions in Box 7.3.

☐ Define the importance of location for your target customer.

☐ Do you have a plan for your store layout?

☐ If you are operating a home-based business, how have you separated work from home?

☐ Why have you chosen the site that you have selected?

☐ If you have a home-based business, identify any zoning issues you face.

Case Study

QuestVest

Case Background

Revisit the QuestVest case study in the opening vignette. Gloria Brookstone was in the "safety for travellers business." She established QuestVest—a business operating out of the home that designed and sold vests for women. These stylish vests came with secret inside pockets to place money and valuables safely.

Case Study Questions

1. Entrepreneurial skills

    In the first seven chapters, we have talked about and provided numerous examples of the "E" personality traits and "E" skills of successful entrepreneurs.

    a. List at least five "E" personality traits displayed by Gloria Brookstone.

    b. List five "E" skills that helped Gloria start and grow her QuestVest business.

2. Trends create opportunities

    In Chapter 3, we learned that trends create market opportunities. Briefly describe four market trends that helped Gloria Brookstone grow her business.

3. Distribution channels

    a. What is a distribution channel?

    b. Briefly explain the difference between direct and indirect distribution.

c. Within the two broad direct and indirect distribution channels, list five possible types of subdistribution channels or ways in which you could distribute your product or service.

d. Gloria Brookstone's major distribution channel was wholesaling. She sold her QuestVests directly to high-end boutiques, but she also had three subdistribution channels and had come up with five more possible subdistribution channels. List these eight different subdistribution channels.

e. What four distribution channels did Adrienne Armstrong, owner of Arbour Environmental Shoppe use?

4. Home-based business

Gloria Brookstone chose to operate her business out of her home. She also chose to contract out her sewing to home-based seamstresses. What were the five advantages of this home-based strategy?

5. Store layout

a. Complete the "Store Layout Quiz" provided in Box 7.1, page 159. (http://crimeprevention.rutgers.edu/crime/shoplifting/layoutquiz.htm). How many store layout problems do you see? How would you correct these problems?

b. Familiarize yourself with techniques to protect you and your business against the common business crimes, such as break-ins, fraud, employee theft, shoplifting, and vandalism. Link onto http://crimeprevention.rutgers.edu/crimes.htm. List 10 ways you plan to protect your business.

6. Business plan location description

In your business plan, you will be required to write a section about your store location. We provide you with a "Sample Location Description" in Chapter 15, Box 15.9. On the book's support Web site, we also provide you with a sample Store Overview for Annie's Business Plan Proposal. Using these examples as templates, briefly describe the location for your business.

Notes

1. Adapted from Jeffrey Simpson, "Quite the Little Spot," *The Halifax Herald*, January 24, 1998; and the Ceilidh Connection Web site (http://www.ceilidhconnect.ns.ca).
2. See ProfitGuide.com, "Managing your Next Best Thing: Survey Says" http://www.profitguide.com/managing/article.jsp?content=20051122_171102_16392&page=1 (accessed April 2006).
3. Ron Knowles, *Writing a Small Business Plan: Course Guide* (Toronto, ON: Dryden, an imprint of Harcourt Brace, 1995), p. 44.

SUGGESTED READING

Bygrave, William D., and Andrew Zacharakis, eds. *The Portable MBA in Entrepreneurship*, 3rd ed. Mississauga, ON: John Wiley & Sons, 2003.

Edwards, Paul, and Sarah Edwards. *Best Home Businesses for People 50?+: Opportunities for People Who Believe the Best Is Yet to Be*. New York: Tarcher/Penguin Books, 2004.

Falk, Edgar A. *1001 Ideas to Create Retail Excitement*, revised ed. New York: Prentice Hall Press, 2003.

Levinson, Jay Conrad. *Guerrilla Retailing*. CITY: The Guerrilla Group Press, 2004.

McMyne, Michael, compiler, and Nicole Amare, ed. *Student Entrepreneurs: Fourteen Undergraduate All-Stars Tell Their Stories*. Nashville, TN: Premium Press America, 2003.

Norins, Patricia. *Ultimate Guide to Specialty Retail: How to Start a Cart, Kiosk, or Store*. Hanover, MA: Pinnacle Publishing Group, 2002.

Pink, Daniel H. *Free Agent Nation*. New York: Time Warner Book Group, 2001.

Pottruck, David S., and Terry Pearce. *Clicks and Mortar*. New York: John Wiley & Sons, 2001.

Segel, Rick. *Retail Business Kit for Dummies*. New York: For Dummies, 2001.

Seybold, Patricia, with Ronnie T. Marshak and Jeffrey Lewis. The *Customer Revolution: How to Thrive When Customers Are in Control*. New York: Crown, 2001.

chapter 8

Legal Concerns

This chapter will help you complete parts F and G of your Business Plan, Management and Personnel.

Henry Bemis was doing really well with his coffee service until one of his onsite coffee dispensers spewed boiling water all over the hands of Jody Dawn, a professional model. Jody's hands earned her just over $200,000 a year. The day her hands were burned, she was at a branch of a major bank, doing a De Beers–sponsored commercial for diamond rings and safety deposit boxes.

The model's hands were her living and her future. On the advice of her lawyer, Jody sued Henry and his Easy-Cup Coffee Service.

Henry had insurance, and the courts ended up awarding Jody $1 million.

Here's the way the court figured it:

She made $200,000 a year.

She could expect an active career of at least five years.

Five years × $200 000 = $1,000,000.

Luckily, Henry had had the good sense to incorporate and carried a lot of liability insurance. His personal assets were protected, and his business insurance paid the bill.

Although Henry Bemis's story is fictitious, the situation is possible and could happen to you. You might run your small business as a sole proprietorship or in partnership with another entrepreneur and be confident that it is in the best possible legal form. But are you sure? Or maybe you're in the planning stages of your new business, and you don't know what legal form (sole proprietorship, partnership, or corporation) is best. In this chapter, we will look at what kind of corporate structure might be best for you and your business. We'll also prepare you for some of the government red tape, help direct you toward legal advice, encourage you to have a will, and get you to think about bankruptcy.

LEGAL FORMS FOR SMALL BUSINESS

Generally, your small business can exist in one of three basic legal forms: a sole proprietorship, a partnership, or a corporation. For each of these standard forms of ownership (summarized in Table 8.1), we describe here some of the important business realities—and paperwork—you should be aware of.

LEARNING OPPORTUNITIES

After reading this chapter, you should be able to

- decide which legal form (sole proprietorship, partnership, corporation, or cooperative) is best for your business;
- anticipate potential surprises if you are going into business with someone else;
- explore the pros and cons of incorporating;
- conduct secondary research into corporations and incorporating;
- explore the various municipal, provincial, and federal legal regulations that might affect your business;
- develop tactics for finding the right lawyer and accountant;
- develop questions for probing the mind of a lawyer or accountant;
- understand the importance of having a will and succession planning; and
- describe and understand the bankruptcy process.

ACTION STEP
PREVIEW

39. Do some secondary research on corporations.
40. Take a lawyer and an accountant to lunch.

The cooperative is a fourth type of legal form to consider. Technically, it's a particular type or variant of the corporate structure. Highlights of this lesser known form of ownership are presented in the final part of this section.[1] It is also important to note that other business agreements, such as joint ventures, exist.

Table 8.1 Characteristics of the Four Main Legal Forms

Legal Form	Control	Need for Written Agreements	Raising Money	Taxes	Liability	Continuity
Sole proprietorship	absolute	may be needed for registration if own name not used	one-person show; save, save, save	profit or loss go with personal income	personally liable for everything	restricted—business ceases to exist when owner gets tired of business or dies
Partnership (limited)	total control by general partner	overwhelming	lots of laws	profit or loss passed onto ltd. partners	ltd. partners are liable only for $ invested	can be provided for in partnership agreement
Partnership (general)	divided	locate super lawyer	easier if more parties sign	profit or loss passed onto partners	personal liability for debts or misdeeds of partners	depends on buy-sell agreement
Corporation	shared (could be absolute)	locate super lawyer	market your "professional" appeal	some tax advantages to Canadian-controlled private corporations	limited to assets of incorporated entity; share-holders are usually not liable	perpetual existence

SOLE PROPRIETORSHIP

SOLE PROPRIETORSHIP

A business that is owned by one person

Most small businesses start out as a **sole proprietorship**. If you start a business on your own—without partners—you are a sole proprietor. A sole proprietorship, in the eyes of the law, is not a separate entity from the person: The business and the individual are the same. For example, the assets of the business are owned by the individual, and therefore the revenue and expenses are included in his or her personal income tax return.

The primary advantages of the sole proprietorship are that:

- it is relatively easy and inexpensive to set up,
- it is directly controlled by the owner/operator,
- it is flexible and subject to little regulation,
- business losses can be deducted from other income,
- wages paid for work performed by a spouse are deductible from the income of the business,
- other investors may be added by written agreement, and
- it offers some tax advantages in certain situations (see Box 8.1).

The major disadvantages of a sole proprietorship are as follows.

- The owner can be held personally liable for all debts of the business. Personal assets, such as the house and automobile, can be seized for nonpayment of bills, provided the necessary legal steps have been taken to do so. To avoid such an unfortunate occurrence, some entrepreneurs register certain personal assets in the name of their spouse. This is allowed as long as it is done at least one year before financial problems are encountered; otherwise, the court may construe the action as a deliberate attempt to outmanoeuvre creditors and will not allow it.

- Opportunity for continuity is restricted. The sole proprietorship ceases to exist when the sole proprietor goes out of business or dies.
- To some extent, the owner's ability to raise capital is limited. Many small businesses encounter financial problems, as their owners are reluctant to share ownership with others who are able to contribute the needed funds.
- The sole proprietor might be required to pay taxes at a higher tax rate in certain situations. Depending on the income level of the owners, tax rates for a sole proprietorship can be higher than those for a corporation. The sole proprietor includes the revenues and expenses from the business on his or her personal tax return, and the income is taxed at whatever his or her personal rate happens to be either in the three previous years and for the following seven years.

Sole proprietorships are regulated by the provincial/territorial governments and legal requirements vary from jurisdiction to jurisdiction; for more information, visit the Provincial Registrars Web page listed in Box 8.2.

Box 8.1   Did You Know?

Suppose you are a sole proprietor and your business suffers a loss. If you have income from other sources (a part-time job, for example), this business loss can be used to offset the other income. You can deduct your business losses as an expense on your personal income statement.

   If your business loss exceeds your other income in a particular year, the unused portion of that loss can be carried forward to offset income in future years. In this way, a sole proprietorship can offer its owner a "tax shelter." In contrast, losses sustained by a corporation can be used only to offset income earned by the corporation, not the owner, so there could be a decided tax advantage to a sole proprietorship—especially during the formative years of operation. We caution you, however, to get professional accounting advice. It is important to note that you will require solid financial records. You must be able to justify your income and expenses accurately. For example, if you needed this book to start your business, you must keep the receipt to use it as a legitimate business expense.

PARTNERSHIP

Many small businesses start as a partnership, and it works out well. A **partnership** is an association of two or more individuals carrying on a business to earn income. Legal requirements for forming a partnership vary from province to province, but generally a partnership can come into existence either through a written or oral agreement or, in some cases, even by implication. If you are considering a partnership, you must check out the specific regulations for the province in which you operate your business. (Visit the Provincial Registrars Web page listed in Box 8.2.)

PARTNERSHIP

An association of two or more individuals carrying on a business to earn income

Box 8.2 Bookmark This

Legal Forms for Small Business

- **Provincial Registrars:** http://bsa.cbsc.org/gol/bsa/site.nsf/en/su04910.html—Click on the province or territory where you want to register.
- **Partnerships:** http://bsa.cbsc.org/gol/bsa/site.nsf/en/su04911.html—Click on the province or territory where you want to register.
- **Federal Business Corporations, Incorporation Kit:** http://strategis.gc.ca/epic/internet/incd-dgc.nsf/en/cs02717e.html; and *Online Federal Incorporation:* http://www.cbsc.org/servlet/ContentServer?pagename=CBSC_FE/display&c=Services&cid=1081944215189&lang=en—Find out how to incorporate federally and how to complete and file documents online.
- **Provincial Business Corporations:** http://bsa.cbsc.org/gol/bsa/site.nsf/en/su04912.html—Click on the province or territory where you want to register.
- **Not-for-Profit Incorporation:** http://strategis.gc.ca/epic/internet/incd-dgc.nsf/en/h_cs02145e.html (federal) or http://bsa.cbsc.org/gol/bsa/site.nsf/en/su06561.html (provincial).
- **Cooperatives:** http://strategis.gc.ca/epic/internet/incd-dgc.nsf/en/h_cs01402e.html (federal incorporation) or http://bsa.cbsc.org/gol/bsa/site.nsf/en/su04913.html (provincial incorporation);
- **Canadian Co-Operative Association:** http://www.coopscanada.coop; Coopzone: http://www.coopzone.coop.
- **Doing Business in British Columbia?** Go to OneStop Business Registration: http://www.governmentagents.gov.bc.ca/progdesc/onestop.htm—If you thinking about starting a business in British Columbia, the OneStop Business Registration site is a great place to start. It will simplify your legal requirements and save you time.

Note: All Web sites accessed July 2006.

GENERAL PARTNERSHIP

A partnership in which each partner has a hand in managing the business and assuming unlimited personal liability for any debts

LIMITED PARTNERSHIP

A partnership composed of at least one or more limited partners and at least one general partner

There are two types of partnerships: general and limited. In a **general partnership**, each partner has a hand in managing the business and assumes unlimited personal liability for any debts. In a **limited partnership**—composed of one or more limited partners and at least one general partner—the general partner assumes both management duties and the downside risk. A limited partner's liability is limited to the amount of his or her original investment as long as he or she has had no role in management decisions.

Note that all partnerships must have at least one general partner.

There are some advantages to a partnership.

- It is easy to set up.
- New partners can be added (some claim that this structure is more flexible and has a greater chance of continuity than a sole proprietorship).
- It involves few legal requirements. You can form a partnership with a handshake and dissolve it without one (though this is not a wise endeavour).
- Risk is generally shared equally among partners—except in the case of a limited partnership.
- Partners can provide mutual support and different skills. One of the best things about a partnership is psychological: It offers the moral support and contribution of teammates.
- It offers more potential sources of capital.
- Partners are taxed as individuals, and in some cases (as is with proprietorships), this can be advantageous (see Box 8.1).

There are some disadvantages, however.

- Tax and estate-planning options are more limited than for a corporate structure (as discussed below).
- Partners and all their assets—personal and business—are, to some extent, at risk for any losses suffered.
- The reality is that sometimes business and personal liabilities of a particular partner aren't kept entirely separate. This can have potentially disastrous consequences to other partners whose shared business liability could result in unexpected personal losses.
- Decision making might be difficult if each partner wants to have equal rights.
- One partner can make decisions that bind all others.
- Dissolution can be ugly, sometimes resulting in the closing of the business or damaged feelings.

On the surface, partnerships can make a lot of sense. Two or more entrepreneurs face the unknown together and pool their skills. They might be able to raise more capital than one person could alone. But forming a good partnership can be as challenging as forming a good marriage. We strongly suggest that you get everything in writing before you start the business. Write out a partnership agreement with legal advice. Each partner should get his or her own lawyer.

At the very least, your written partnership agreement should include the following:

- rights and responsibilities of the partners;
- capital contributions of each partner;
- role and time that each partner will devote to the business;
- provisions for retirement, death, termination, and/or reorganization;
- how net income from business will be divided;
- means for settling disputes; and
- a mechanism for dissolving the partnership or winding up the business.

While a partnership agreement might not be legally required, it is highly recommended. Furthermore, professional advice is strongly recommended. For example, any partner can enter into a contract on behalf of the partnership. By doing so, a partner can bind all partners in an unfavourable contract, as all partners are jointly and severally liable for the obligations of the partnership. An example of a partnership agreement is shown in Box 8.3.

Box 8.3 A Sample Partnership Agreement

PARTNERSHIP AGREEMENT

This partnership agreement is made in _____ original copies between (the "Partners").   (*number*)

(1) _____
                          (*partner name*)

(2) _____
                          (*partner name*)

(3) _____
                          (*partner name*)

PARTNERSHIP NAME AND BUSINESS

1.01 The Partners agree to carry on a business of _____ as partners under the name _____.   (*type of business*)

        (the "Partnership")

No person may be introduced as a Partner and no other business may be carried on by the Partnership without the consent in writing of all the Partners.

1.02 The principal place of business of the Partnership for the time being is
_____.

(address)

TERM

2.01 The Partnership begins on _____ and continues until terminated in accordance with this agreement.   *(date)*

PARTNERSHIP SHARES AND CAPITAL

3.01 The Partners shall participate in the assets, liabilities, profits, and losses of the Partnership in the percentages beside their respective names (their "Partnership Shares"):

_____   -   _____ %

_____   -   _____ %

_____   -   _____ %

                                                    100 %

3.02 The Partners shall contribute a total of $_____ in cash, in proportion to their respective Partnership Shares, to the start-up capital of the Partnership by no later than _____ .

(date)

3.03 If further capital is required to carry on the Partnership business, the Partners shall contribute it as required in proportion to their respective Partnership Shares.

3.04 No interest accrues on a Partners' capital contributions to the Partnership in proportion to his Partnership Share. However, if a Partner makes an actual payment or advance for the purpose of the Partnership beyond his Partnership Share (an "Additional Advance"), he is entitled to _____% per annum interest from the Partnership on the Additional Advance until refunded by the Partnership.

BANKING ARRANGEMENTS AND FINANCIAL RECORDS

4.01 The Partners shall maintain a bank account in the name of the Partnership business on which cheques may be drawn only on the signature of at least _____ of the Partners.

(number)

4.02 The Partners shall at all times maintain full and proper accounts of the Partnership business accessible to each of the Partners at any time on reasonable notice.

PARTNERS' ACCOUNTS AND SALARIES

5.01 The financial records of the Partnership shall include separate income and capital accounts for each Partner.

5.02 No Partner may receive a salary for services rendered to the partnership but the profit or loss of the Partnership business shall be periodically allocated among the Partners' separate income accounts and each of the Partners may, from time to time, withdraw against a credit balance in his income account.

5.03 The capital accounts of the Partners shall be maintained in proportion to their respective Partnership Shares.

5.04 No Partner shall draw down his capital account without the previous consent in writing of the other Partners. If a Partner draws down his capital account below his Partnership Share, he shall bring it up to his Partnership Share on the demand of any of the Partners.

MANAGEMENT OF PARTNERSHIP BUSINESS

6.01 Each partner may take part in the management of the Partnership business.

6.02 Any difference arising in the ordinary course of carrying on the Partnership business shall be decided by the Partners having a majority of the Partnership Shares.

PARTNERS' DUTIES AND RESTRICTIONS

7.01 Each Partner shall devote substantially all of his ordinary working time to carrying on the business of the Partnership.

7.02 Each Partner shall at all times duly and punctually pay and discharge his separate debts and liabilities and shall save harmless the property of the Partnership and the other Partners from those separate debts and liabilities and, if necessary, shall promptly indemnify the other Partners for their share of any actual payment or discharge of his separate debt and liabilities by the Partnership.

7.03 No Partner shall assign or encumber his share or interest in the Partnership without the previous consent in writing of the other Partners.

7.04 No Partner shall bind the Partnership or the other Partners for anything outside the ordinary course of carrying on the Partnership business.

FISCAL YEAR-END

8.01 The fiscal year-end of the Partnership shall be _____ in each year. *(month and day)*

TERMINATION OF PARTNERSHIP

9.01 The Partnership may be dissolved at any time during the joint lives of the Partners by a Partner giving notice in writing to the other Partners of his intention to dissolve the Partnership, in which case the partnership is dissolved as from the date mentioned in the notice as the date of dissolution, or, if no date of dissolution is mentioned, as from the date of communication of the notice.

9.02 The Partnership is dissolved on the death or insolvency of any of the Partners or on any of the Partners becoming a mental incompetent so found by a court of law.

9.03 On dissolution of the partnership, subject to any contrary agreement binding the former Partners and their estates and after making any necessary adjustments in accordance with generally accepted accounting principles to allow for any debit balances in the Partners' separate capital accounts, the Partnership business shall be promptly liquidated and applied in the following order:

   a. to pay the debts and liabilities of the Partnership;
   b. to refund any outstanding additional advances, together with accrued interest;
   c. to distribution of the credit balances of the Partners' separate income accounts:
   d. to distribution of the credit balances of the Partners' capital accounts;
   e. to distribution of any residue to the Partners in proportion to their respective Partnership Shares.

ARBITRATION OF DISPUTES

10.01 Any dispute between the Partners arising out of or related to this agreement and any amendments to it, whether before or after dissolution of the Partnership, shall be referred to and settled by a single arbitrator agreed upon by the Partners or, in default of such agreement, to a single arbitrator appointed pursuant to the legislation governing submissions to arbitration in the jurisdiction whose laws govern this agreement. The decision of the arbitrator is final and binding on the Partners with no right of appeal.

MISCELLANEOUS

11.01 In this agreement, the singular includes the plural and the masculine includes the feminine and neuter and vice versa unless the context otherwise requires.

11.02 The capitalized headings in this agreement are only for convenience of reference and do not form part of or affect the interpretation of this agreement.

11.03 If any provision or part of any provision in this agreement is void for any reason, it shall be severed without affecting the validity of the balance of the agreement.

11.04 Time is of the essence of this agreement.

11.05 The terms of this agreement may only be amended in writing dated and signed by all the Partners.

11.06 This agreement binds and benefits the Partners and their respective heirs, executors, administrators, personal representatives, successors, and assigns.

11.07 This agreement is governed by the laws of the Province of _____.
Executed under seal on _____.
(date)

Signed, sealed and
Delivered in the presence of:

_____ (witness)	_____ (Partner signature(s))
_____ (witness)	_____ (Partner signature(s))
_____ (witness)	_____ (Partner signature(s))

Source: http://www.wecm.ca/docs/partnership.doc

The Shotgun

Partnerships, like marriages, do not always last. When a business partnership (or marriage for that matter) breaks up and the partners seek a divorce, one of the most disputed areas of contention is usually money or the value of the business. The sale price of a business, especially during an impending emotional breakup, is generally quite subjective. Often, it becomes extremely difficult to determine a fair price or market value for the business.

For this reason, a partnership agreement (and a shareholders agreement as discussed below) must contain a clear process in which the partnership can be disbanded equitably. There are numerous methods of dispute resolution. Some partnership agreements, for example, might contain an arbitration clause in which all partners would have to accept an arbitrator's decision.

In the case of an irreconcilable ownership dispute, many small businesses choose a "shotgun" method of resolution. The partnership agreement (or shareholders agreement) will contain a **shotgun clause** stating that one partner can make a buyout offer to the other partner for his/her share of the business. The receiving partner has the option (within a set period of time) of either accepting this offer or buying out the partner who proposed the offer under the exact same terms.

Some experts—such as Robert Berman, a business author, columnist, and expert specializing in strategic planning—claim that a shotgun clause is fair and efficient for most small businesses because it removes subjectivity. According to Berman, "If the partner who made the original offer to buy the business undervalues the business in the view of the partner that received the offer, the partner who received the offer can buy the business at that price, hence that partner should believe he received a very good deal. On the other hand if the partner who received the offer believes that the partner who made the offer overvalued the business, he can accept the offer and should be pleased that he received more than he believed the business was worth. Either way, both parties should be very satisfied with the outcome of the transaction."

A shotgun clause does not work in every case, for example if the partner receiving the buyout offer does not have the available cash to purchase the business. But according to experts like Berman, this clause solves the majority of problems associated with the dissolution of a business partnership on a fair and equitable basis. If you decide to go the partnership route, it is strongly advisable that you get professional help on the issue of partnership dissolution and conflict.[2]

SHOTGUN CLAUSE

A provision stating that one partner or shareholder can make a buyout offer to the other partner for his/her share of the business. The receiving partner has the option (within a set period of time) of either accepting this offer or buying out the partner who proposed the offer under the exact same terms.

CORPORATION

A **corporation** is a legal entity that exists under authority granted by provincial or federal law. It stands legally separate from the owners, and it does business in the name of the corporation. It can sue and be sued.

Because a corporation is an artificial entity, a creation on paper, it needs more paperwork to justify its existence. There are fees required, as well as meetings of the board of directors. The secretary of the corporation must keep accurate, complete records of what transpires at meetings.

Nonetheless, for many businesses, it's worth forming a corporation, because it creates a shield between the creditors and the owner's personal wealth. To keep the shield in place, active owners can become *employees* of the corporation; their business cards have the corporate name and logo and specify their job title. At the same time, owners sign contracts as *officers* of the corporations.

Following are some of the reasons why you should think about incorporating, or not incorporating, your business. In the end, your decision will depend on two key factors: your tax situation and your desire to limit your liability. However, we want to emphasize that becoming a corporation won't solve all your problems. In most cases, it won't immunize you against your creditors. The banks, for example, will still want a personal guarantee, which could mean your house. Taxes won't be eliminated either. In fact, in the early years, the bank will treat a newly incorporated business as if it were a sole proprietorship. If you have losses, you are better off as a sole proprietor. Let's start with the major reasons for thinking about incorporating.

> **CORPORATION**
>
> A legal entity with the authority to act and have liability separate and apart from its owners

Reasons for Incorporating

Liability

A corporation acts as a shield between you and the world. If your business fails, your creditors may not come after your house, your beach condo, your Porsche, your first-born, or your hard-won collections—provided you've done it right.

To keep your corporate shield up, make sure you: (1) hold scheduled meetings; (2) keep up the minute book; and (3) act as if you are an employee of the corporation. Here's an everyday example of the corporate shield at work: One of your employees gets into a fender-bender while driving on company business. If you're a corporation, the injured parties will come after your corporation and not you. Reducing your liability or risk of being sued is a major reason for incorporating. We should stress, however, if your employees use *their own* cars on company business, make sure they're insured for an absolute minimum of $1 million.

See how limited liability helped Henry Bemis in the opening vignette. Again, remember that banks and other creditors will want personal guarantees as well as business guarantees; thus, the limited liability advantage of the corporation may be somewhat reduced.

You Might Enjoy Some Tax Advantages

Taxation laws are complex, and a good accountant can dream up several ways to minimize taxes, regardless of what legal form you choose. However, a concept called "integration" attempts to ensure that income is taxed to the same degree whether it is held by an individual or channeled through a corporation. You won't get rich on your tax savings. Tax laws and rates vary slightly from province to province in Canada. We therefore strongly recommend that you see an accountant to help you determine the best organization form from a tax standpoint.

However, there are some tax advantages to being incorporated—the major ones of which are listed below.

1. In general, a special small business tax rate applies to income under **$400,000 (2007)**. The general corporate income tax rate varies from approximately 31 percent to **38 percent**, depending on the province. The reduced rate for Canadian companies on the first $250,000 varies from approximately 16 percent to 22 percent, depending on province (see, for example, Taxtips.ca: http://www.taxtips.ca/glossary.htm#SBD).

2. Only incorporated companies are eligible for manufacturing and processing tax credits.

3. Certain tax-free benefits, such as some insurance premiums, are available only to employees of incorporated companies.

4. With regard to pensions, there are still greater options for tax deferral under the corporate form.

5. Owners of corporations can potentially enjoy personal tax savings. For example, once the income of a business reaches a certain level, the total tax paid by the corporation and the owner will be less than that which the owner of a sole proprietorship would pay. The exact level depends on the individual situation. As a ballpark figure, once you start earning $25,000 to $30,000 (income after expenses), it would be time to consider incorporating to save you some personal tax.

6. Benefits can be paid to employees in different forms by a corporation, which could yield a tax saving. These forms include salaries, dividends, and profit-sharing plans. In the case of a deferred profit-sharing plan, for example, a corporation can make contributions on behalf of employees. The contributions are allowed as a current business tax deduction, but the employee pays no tax until withdrawals are made. This type of plan is not available to the sole proprietorship. Careful analysis needs to be made in each situation to determine the optimal structuring of an owner/manager's earnings. You should be aware of the different forms of compensation and, if necessary, consult an accountant for advice on those your business should use.

If you want to learn more about the tax benefits of incorporating, a good starting point is the Canada Revenue Agency (CRA) Web site (http://www.cra-arc.gc.ca). Obviously, the whole issue of corporate tax benefits is complicated. You should always seek the advice of a corporate tax accountant in these matters.

You Upgrade Your Image

What does the word *corporation* imply to you? IBM? Bell? GM? Heavy hitters, right? Let's look at the word with new eyes.

Corporation comes from the Latin, *corpus*, which means "body." To incorporate means to make or form a shape into a body. Looked at from that angle, incorporating starts to sound creative.

It will sound that way to lots of your TCs, too. As a corporation, you might be perceived to:

• have more longevity and solidity in the world,
• attract better employees, and
• enjoy more prestige.

You Have the Opportunity of Channelling Some Heavy Expenses

For example, with some legal help, you can write a medical assistance clause into your bylaws. Here's the way it works:

1. Your corporation pays the insurance premium on your health insurance.
2. Your corporation reimburses you for the deductible.

3. Your corporation writes off the money paid to you as a business expense.

4. You aren't liable to pay taxes on the reimbursement.

You Simplify the Division of Multiple Ownership

For example, say you're going into the printing and graphic business with two very good friends.

The business needs $110,000 to get started.
You can contribute $60,000.
Friend A delivers $25,000.
Friend B delivers $15,000.
You borrow the remaining $10,000 from your friendly banker.
The way to handle the ownership is with stock. You get 60 percent, Friend A gets 25 percent, and Friend B gets 15 percent.

You Guarantee Continuity

If one of your shareholders or founders dies (or departs by motor-sailor or other means), the corporation will likely keep chugging along. That's because you've gone through a lot of red tape and planning to set it up that way.

It's one of the few justifications for red tape we know. However, if you are an individual incorporated and you die, the business will likely die with you anyway.

You Can Offer Internal Incentives

When you want to reward a special employee, you can offer stock options or a promotion (for example, a vice presidential title) in addition to (and sometimes in place of) pay raises. Becoming a corporation officer might carry its own special excitement, which gives you flexibility. An ownership position (shares) can also motivate an employee to keep the company's best interest in mind.

You Are in a Good Position for Estate Planning

As your company grows, you might want to set up other companies and include members of your family in your organization. At this point, you can engage in complicated share exchange and asset transfers. If you find yourself in this situation, you should consult a knowledgeable corporate estate lawyer.

There are also some potential disadvantages of incorporating. These are listed below.

Potential Disadvantages of Incorporating

Potentially Fewer Tax Write-Offs at the Beginning

Business losses incurred by a corporation can be used for taxation purposes only to offset income of the preceding three years and the seven successive years. If your business suffers losses in its first few years of operation, the losses of the early years could conceivably never be used to reduce tax liability. In the case of a sole proprietorship, however, losses from the business can be used to offset income from other sources in the year in which they are incurred. Thus, if losses are projected in the beginning years of the business and you have income from other sources, it may well be advantageous not to incorporate your business.

Higher Start-up Costs

Start-up costs are higher if you choose to incorporate rather than carry on business as a sole proprietorship or partnership. For example, federal incorporation costs $200 if done electronically (no lawyer). Provincial incorporation varies from province to province. For example, in Ontario, the cost of provincial incorporation is $300 by mail and $400 to $495 if done electronically (through OnCorp Direct: http://www.oncorp.com/home/index.asp). Although it is not necessary to obtain legal and accounting advice to incorporate, we strongly advise you to do so, particularly if you are considering setting up with a complex share structure. If you decide to use a lawyer and professional accounting services, the cost could easily be $2,000 to $3,000. Of course, legal advice means legal fees.

Increased Paperwork

Carrying on business as a corporation might increase the number of tax filings you are required to make. For instance, the Canada Business Corporations Act requires that you file an annual return (Form 22) each year and inform the Corporations Directorate of any changes in your board of directors or the location of your registered head office. You have to file separate income tax returns for yourself, which might lead to an increase in your ongoing professional costs. Your company is also required to maintain certain corporate records. Furthermore, you will likely be asked to register your company in any province or territory where you carry on business. Registration is different from incorporation. Although a company may be incorporated only once, it may be registered in any number of jurisdictions to carry on business. You should contact the local corporate law administration office in each province or territory in which you plan to carry on business to determine what filing requirements you will have to fulfill.

The Process of Incorporation

Obviously, the issue of incorporation is somewhat complicated. Some of the most frequently asked questions, and their answers, are summarized below.

Who Can Form a Corporation?

Under most circumstances, one or more individuals who are 18 years of age or older can form a corporation. Similarly, one or more companies or "bodies corporate" may incorporate an additional company. These persons or companies are called incorporators. An incorporator may form a corporation whose shareholders, officers, and directors are other persons, or may serve as the sole director, officer, and shareholder of the company. An incorporator is also responsible for organizational procedures, such as filing the articles of incorporation and designating the first directors.

Do I Incorporate Federally or Provincially?

A company can incorporate either federally (under the Canada Business Corporations Act) or provincially, under the laws of a province or territory. Whether you incorporate federally or provincially, you will be required to register your business in the province or territory where you carry on business.

A major advantage of incorporating federally is that the head office can be located in any Canadian province, and it can be relocated if circumstances dictate. If you have the intention (either now or sometime in the future) of operating in more than one jurisdiction, you should probably choose to incorporate federally in order to simplify your business relations later. Still, the federal corporation must register in each province in which it is doing business.

Another reason given for choosing federal incorporation is the heightened name protection provided to federal corporations. While every incorporating jurisdiction in Canada screens potential corporations, the level of scrutiny varies. At the federal level, stringent tests are applied before the right to use a particular name is granted.

A final major advantage of federal incorporation is limited liability. A federally incorporated company is considered a legal entity anywhere in Canada. Therefore, its shareholders are protected by limited liability anywhere in the country. In contrast, a provincially incorporated company is a legal entity only in the province or territory in which it is incorporated. Thus, its shareholders are not protected by limited liability if it does business outside of its own jurisdiction.

What Kinds of Businesses Can Incorporate?

Almost any type of business may incorporate. However, banking, insurance, loan and trust companies, and nonprofit corporations are incorporated under different statutes. There are no restrictions such as minimum company size on the businesses.

Do I Need to Hire a Lawyer to Incorporate?

No, though we recommend you do. A lawyer can provide valuable advice, but that is not required for incorporation. If you want to incorporate without a lawyer, get ready for a lot of paperwork.

Do I Need a Board of Directors?

Yes. Your company must have at least one director. In your articles of incorporation, you are required to specify the number of directors. At each annual general meeting, shareholders elect directors (depending on the length or term of office the shareholders choose).

Shareholders may decide that, for various reasons, they want to remove a director they had previously elected. This is a simple procedure. It generally needs the approval of a majority of the votes represented at a meeting of shareholders called for the purpose of removing the director.

Who Can Be a Director?

A director must

- be at least 18 years old,
- be of sound mind (mentally competent), and
- be an individual (a corporation cannot be a director).

He or she must also not be an undischarged bankrupt.

In addition, a majority of the directors of a corporation must be individuals who are ordinarily resident in Canada. You should keep this in mind when electing directors and filling vacancies. There is no requirement for directors to hold shares in the corporation, nor is there any restriction against their holding shares.

What Are the Responsibilities of the Board of Directors?

The company's directors are responsible for the overall supervision of the affairs of the corporation. They approve the company's financial statements; make, amend, and repeal bylaws; authorize the issuance of shares; and call and conduct directors' and shareholders' meetings. The directors, in turn, usually appoint officers, who are responsible for day-to-day operations. In a small, private corporation, one individual may act as sole shareholder, director, and officer.[3]

Must a Company Have Shareholders?

Yes. An active company must have at least one class of shares (ownership) and at least one shareholder (owner). A person or company who owns shares in a corporation is called a shareholder. Generally speaking and unless the articles of incorporation provide otherwise, each share in the corporation entitles the holder to one vote. A person becomes a shareholder by acquiring shares from the company (buying shares from the treasury) or from an existing shareholder. The larger the number of shares held, the larger the number of votes (and, in most cases, control) a shareholder can generally exercise.

Shareholders have limited liability in the corporation, and usually are not liable for the company's debts unless, as noted earlier, the bank requires the owner/shareholders to pledge personal and company assets. On the other hand, shareholders generally do not actively run the corporation. Shareholders also have legal access to certain information about the corporation. For example, shareholders are entitled to inspect (and copy) the corporate records, and are entitled to receive the company's financial statements. Shareholders also elect directors, approve bylaws and bylaw changes, appoint the auditor of the corporation (or waive the audit requirement), and approve certain major or fundamental changes to the corporation. These changes could include matters such as a sale of assets of the business, a change of name, and articles of amendment altering share rights or creating new classes of shares.

Do I Need a Shareholders Agreement?

SHAREHOLDERS AGREEMENT

A legal document that establishes the rights of shareholders (owners) and the duties and powers of the board of directors and management

A **shareholders agreement** establishes the rights of shareholders (owners) and the duties and powers of the board of directors and management. A shareholders agreement is not necessary, but we strongly advise that you have one, except, of course, if you are a one-person corporation. It is an agreement entered into usually by all shareholders. The written agreement must be signed by the shareholders who are party to it. While shareholders agreements are specific to each company and its shareholders, most of these documents deal with the same basic issues. An example of a shareholders agreement can be found by linking onto Mike Volker's, "The Shareholders Agreement—a Sample Agreement" (http://www.sfu.ca/~mvolker/biz/agreesmp.htm).

A typical shareholders agreement includes the following clauses.

Article 1: Definitions
Article 2: Conduct of Affairs of the Corporation
Article 3: Transfers of Shares
Article 4: Real Property
Article 5: Death of a Shareholder
Article 6: Bankruptcy, etc.
Article 7: Powers of Attorney
Article 8: General Sale Provisions
Article 9: Arbitration
Article 10: General Provisions

The relationship among shareholders in a small company tends to be very much like a partnership agreement, with each person having a say in the significant business decisions the company will be making.

Here are some of the major provisions of a shareholders agreement.

- **Who sits on the board of directors.** A very common shareholders agreement provision for a small company gives all the shareholders the right to sit on the board of directors or to nominate a representative for that purpose.
- **How the future obligations of the company will be shared or divided.** The shareholders may agree, for example, that when other means of raising funds are not available, each shareholder will contribute more funds to the company on a pro rata basis.
- **How future shares are purchased.** For example, three equal partners could agree that no shares in the corporation will be issued without the consent of all shareholders/directors. In the absence of such a provision, two shareholders/directors could issue shares by an ordinary or special resolution (because they control two-thirds of the votes) to themselves without including or requiring the permission of the third shareholder/director.
- **The right of first refusal.** This provision states that any shareholder who wants to sell his or her shares must first offer them to the other shareholders of the company before selling them to an outside party.

- **Rules for the transfer of shares.** This provision is often termed the **buy-sell option**—a statement in a shareholders agreement that spells out how the shares will be transferred in such an event as the death, resignation, dismissal, personal bankruptcy, or divorce of a shareholder. More information on this important clause is provided in a separate section below.
- **Other shareholders agreement provisions.** These may include non-competition clauses, confidentiality agreements, dispute-resolution mechanisms, and details about how the shareholders agreement is to be amended or terminated.

Shareholders agreements are voluntary. If you choose to have one—and, as you now know, we recommend you do—it should reflect the particular needs of your company and its shareholders. While undoubtedly the best advice is to keep your agreement as simple as possible, we strongly suggest that you consult your professional advisors before signing any shareholders agreement.

Will I Need a Buy-Sell Option?

As we noted above, a shareholders agreement should (although not legally required) include a **buy-sell option** that clearly states what happens if one partner should die, become disabled, or want to sell his or her interest in the business. Restrictions can be detailed in plans governing, for instance, when a shareholder can or must sell his or her shares, or what happens to those shares after the individual shareholder has left.

When business owners split up, and most eventually do for one reason or another, a shareholders agreement—and partnership agreement, for that matter—with a buy-sell formula will very likely save the business and keep you out of court. Think of it as a prenuptial agreement.

Often, these buy-sell agreements are funded by joint life insurance on the owners (partners), so that if you die, the business or the other owners will collect the life insurance proceeds and use those funds to buy out the interest in the business. Otherwise, your surviving family members might find it very difficult to sell the interest in the business they inherit from you, except at a giveaway price. In many instances, financial institutions will make a "buy-sell" agreement a condition of the loan. As with partnership agreements, many small businesses shareholder agreements will contain a "shotgun" provision in case of irreconcilable shareholder disputes.

Do I Have to Get a Corporate Seal?

Not necessarily. A corporation under the federal Canada Business Corporations Act, for example, is not required to have a seal. If you wish to have a corporate seal for your corporation, you may purchase one from a legal stationery store or commercial supplier.

If I Decide to Incorporate, What Next?

Our advice: See a lawyer—despite the cost savings of doing it yourself. For example, if proper legal formalities are not followed, the shareholders can actually be liable for the corporation's debts. However, should you want to do it yourself, contact your provincial authority if you want to incorporate locally or the Corporations Directorate of Industry Canada should you decide to incorporate federally. And, if you are going to do it on your own, get ready for lots of paperwork. You might also want to check out the "Federal Business Incorporation" Web page listed in Box 8.2.

COOPERATIVE [4]

A **cooperative** is an organization owned by the members who use its services. Cooperatives can provide virtually any product or service, and can be either a nonprofit or for-profit enterprise. Cooperatives exist in every sector of our

BUY-SELL OPTION

A statement in a shareholders agreement that spells out how the shares will be transferred in such an event as the death, resignation, dismissal, personal bankruptcy, or divorce of a shareholder

COOPERATIVE

An organization owned by the members who use its services

Disadvantages of Cooperatives

A few disadvantages of cooperatives are as follows.

- With large member groups, it is sometimes difficult to get agreement. Conflict resolution becomes an issue.
- Management is supposed to be a cooperative (shared) responsibility. In some cases, management becomes unwieldy because of differing goals and objectives or, in other cases, lack of experience.
- Some members find it difficult to work cooperatively or in teams.
- Some major institutions are not familiar or comfortable with how cooperatives work, making financing relatively more difficult to obtain.

Establishing a cooperative is tricky. We strongly advise you to consult with provincial or federal authorities and a lawyer. We also encourage you to network with co-ops in your area to understand how they are managed, and to learn first-hand the advantages and disadvantages of the co-op form of business. You might also want to visit the Web pages listed under "Cooperatives" in Box 8.2.

Box 8.4 Everybody Is an Owner

A good example of a successful Canadian cooperative is Mountain Equipment Co-op (MEC)—a collectively owned retail cooperative selling quality outdoor gear and clothing.

Founded in Vancouver, MEC has 11 retail outlets (as of 2006) across Canada and more than two million members. Members can shop at any of 11 retail stores, online, or by mail order from their catalogue. All stores are distinguished by their environmentally conscious design. For example, the interiors are open to take advantage of natural light and often feature climbing walls and full product demonstrations.

Everyone who shops at MEC is an owner. Customers are part owners who pay a $5 lifetime share in the cooperative—a value that has not changed since 1971. There is even a special category of membership for those who are 15 or under.

As a cooperative, MEC is governed democratically by its members. In cooperatives, there is only one vote per member, not per share, as in a corporate structure. MEC shares are not public: They do not trade on a stock exchange. The members of MEC do not buy shares to earn a financial return on their investment. A share entitles the member to the purchasing benefits of the cooperative. All members are free to vote annually for the Board of Directors.

The MEC goal is to provide its members with quality products at reasonable prices. Its aim is to stay financially healthy, but it does not seek to earn a profit. When MEC does earn a surplus, it is allocated to its members in the form of additional patronage shares in MEC (as stated in their "rules," which reflect their members' wishes). The portion allocated to each member is based on the amount the member purchased at MEC during that year. Pooling members' shares for mutual benefit in this manner helps maintain a solid capital base and a financially healthy organization.

We encourage you to learn what it is like to be an owner of a socially responsible company. Click onto MEC home page. If you are so inclined, pay the $5 and become a member and a part owner. This will give you an opportunity to get involved and be a member of a very successful company.

Sources: Reprinted by permission of Mountain Equipment Co-op. Mountain Equipment Co-op Home page, "About Membership", http://www.mec.ca

---

ACTION STEP 39

Do some secondary research on corporations

Before you take any action with legal forms, you need a lot of information and professional advice.

We suggest you begin by logging onto the Internet. A good place to start is with the Web pages listed in Box 8.2. If you prefer hard copy, go to the library or the resource centre of a college or university. You can also check out the bookstores; handbooks on incorporation through various self-counsel series are helpful.

Once you get familiar with the broad concepts, you might want to do some specific research of companies in your industry. Write to the companies, or get on the Net and visit their sites. Remember that a cooperative is an option. You might also want to talk to a few small business owners you know. Get their opinion. What kind of structure would they suggest, and why?

While you are doing this research, remember to keep looking around with new eyes.

Now it's time to do a little research on your own. Complete Action Step 39.

YOUR BUSINESS NAME

So you now have a business idea you think will fly. You've spent a lot of time on your business plan and are beginning to think that it just might work. You've come up with a name for your business that you are proud of. Where do you go from here?

We suggest you next think about some legal protection for your name. After all, you don't want someone else to go out and start a business using your name. The process of protecting your business name will depend, in part, on the province where you want to conduct business and your legal form (which is one of the reasons we wanted you to consider your legal framework in the first part of this chapter). What follows is this whole procedure, simplified, but again we advise you to get some professional help.

According to provincial authority, a sole proprietorship or partnership does not necessarily have to register its name. Normally, if your business name is exactly the same as your own name, registration is not needed. For example, Mary Smith could operate a business as Mary Smith without registration. However, she would have to register the name of her business if the business name differed—even slightly—from her name. If she called her business Mary Smith *Consulting*, then she must register that name with the province where she is conducting her business.

Provincial registration does not require the business name to be unique. Thus, in some cases, you can register your business name without a search, but we advise that you do one, as you might later find out that there are other businesses with similar names. If your registered name causes confusion with another business, you might be subject to penalties and might even have to change the name of your business. In other words, provincial registration does not necessarily protect your business name.

In searching a name you have two choices: doing a provincial search or doing a federal search. All incorporated businesses must register their corporate name with any province in which they do business. Although provinces will do a name search for you, your best bet is to ask for a federal name search report. If you incorporate federally, and we suggest you do, you will need a NUANS (Newly Upgraded Automated Name Search) report. A NUANS report is a five-page document that includes a list of business names and trademarks that sound similar to the name you are proposing. The list is drawn from the national data bank of existing and reserved business names, as well as trademarks applied for and registered in Canada.

A NUANS will make you aware of any existing businesses that could prevent you from using your business name. It also lets you know whether your proposed trademark is already in use by another business. This saves you from having to change the name of your business later when you find out that you have been infringing on a trademark.

A NUANS report is obtained from private businesses known as Search Houses, which are listed under Incorporating Companies, Incorporation: Name Search, Searchers of Records, or Trademark Agents in the Yellow Pages.

Generally, when you register a name in federal incorporation, you must submit the NUANS report along with your proposed business name. The request for a numbered company is the same with one exception. You may request the federal government to grant your corporation a designating number, followed by the word "Canada" and a legal element, to serve as your corporate name. For this specific case, a NUANS report is not required. Any other kind of proposed name must be supported by a NUANS report. If there is another name that is similar to your name, you will be asked to make a new choice for your incorporated company.[4]

MORE RED TAPE

When you start your business, you will become subject to all kinds of federal, provincial, and municipal red tape. Box 8.5 provides a checklist of some of the requirements your business may be confronted with. One thing is for certain: You will have to deal with the CRA. Thus, we focus here on the major CRA start-up requirements because these will be common for everyone. We will also get you started on finding out your responsibilities regarding retail sales taxes—which, of course differ, according to which province you do business in.

THE BUSINESS NUMBER (BN)

Your first step in doing business with the Canada Revenue Agency is your business number (BN). The BN is the federal government's numbering system that helps to streamline the way it deals with businesses. It is based on the idea of "one business, one number."

Box 8.5 Checklist of Requirements That Might Affect Your Business

Have you considered the following?

Municipal

- Building permits. (Failure to obtain proper municipal permits is one of the most common and costly mistakes by new business owners. **Remember**, do not lease a new location until these permits have been approved.)
- Regulations regarding home-based or home-occupation business
- Zoning, rezoning, and obtaining a minor variance
- Subdivision approval and consent to severance
- Demolition control and permits
- Site plan control approval
- Licensing of business and trades
- Compliance with municipal bylaws such as signage regulations and non-smoking regulations
- Hours of operation
- Inspections—such as fire, health, traffic, and building inspections
- Municipal tax (e.g., realty tax, business tax)
- Any more?

Provincial

- Health and safety regulations (Strict adherence to health and safety regulations is an important legal issue—one to which we will return in Chapter 9.)
- Workers' Compensation Board or Workplace Safety Insurance Board (WSIB)
- Provincial/territorial employment standards (e.g., hours of work, minimum wage, vacation pay, overtime pay, equal pay for equal work)
- Health insurance
- Environmental control regulations
- Provincial tax (e.g., corporate, retail sales, tobacco, gasoline, land transfer tax)
- Any more?

Federal

- Business Number (BN)
- GST/HST
- Payroll deductions (e.g., Canada Pension Plan, insurance, income tax)

- Food and drug regulations and inspection
- Patents, trademarks, copyrights, and industrial designs
- Federal corporation tax
- Any more?

You will need a BN if you require one of the four CRA business accounts: corporate income tax, import/export, payroll deductions, or the Goods and Services Tax (GST) or Harmonized Sales Tax (HST). According to government, businesses will eventually be able to use their BN for other CRA accounts and other government programs. For instance, you will be asked to state the name of the business, its location, and its legal structure. You will also be required to outline what your business's sales will be. Without this type of information, you won't be able to complete the BN registration form.

If you decide you need a BN, you will have to complete Form RC1, Request for a Business Number. For more information, contact your local CRA office. A good source of information is the CRA Publication RC2, *The Business Number and Your Canada Revenue Agency Accounts* (available at http://www.cra-arc.gc.ca).

PAYROLL DEDUCTIONS

According to the CRA, you are an employer if you pay salaries, wages, bonuses, vacation pay, or tips to people working for you; or if you provide benefits such as lodging or room and board to the people working for you. If you are an employer, you will be responsible for deducting the following from your employees' paycheques:

- income tax,
- Canada Pension Plan (CPP) contributions, and
- Employment Insurance (EI) premiums.

You might also be required to make payments and be subject to certain regulations under the workers' compensation legislation.

Payroll deductions can be complicated. So before you start your business, we strongly advise you to visit or call your local CRA office. An advisor might even come to your business and help you get started with all the forms you need. If you have a computer (and you should), the CRA will give you a disk, *Tables on Diskette* (TOD) (T4143). It contains all the information you need to calculate deductions from your employees' pay for all pay periods. This disk is even available on the Internet on CRA's Electronic Distribution System. Another good source of information on payroll deductions is the CRA publication *Employers' Guide to Payroll Deductions*. You might want to consider outsourcing your payroll functions to a payroll service provider. For many business owners, the "small cost" of using a payroll service provider can be a wise investment, not only creating time for concentrating on other matters, but getting expert advice when dealing with any disputes with CRA or provincial regulators.

FEDERAL INCOME TAXES

Generally, business income includes any money you earn with the reasonable expectation of making a profit.

If you are not incorporated, that is, you are a sole proprietor, business income (or loss) forms part of your overall personal income for the year. You will be taxed on your net earnings from the business, which you will include on your personal tax return as self-employment income. As a sole proprietor, you must file financial statements with your personal income tax return. It is most likely (if you are not in farming and fishing) that you will be required to submit one of the following two forms along with your T1:

- Form T2124, *Statement of Business Activities*, and
- Form T2032, *Statement of Professional Activities*.

As a sole proprietor, you are not eligible to be covered by Employment Insurance, but you will have to pay income tax and Canada Pension Plan (CPP) premiums on the self-employment income reported on your personal tax return. Depending on the province in which you operate, Workers' Compensation premiums may be payable. Self-employed people and their spouses or common-law partners have until June 15th each year to file their tax returns. However, any tax owing must still be paid by April 30th.

A partnership by itself does not file an annual income tax return. Each partner must include a share of the partnership income or loss on a personal, corporate, or trust income tax return. As such, partners must file either financial statements or one of the two proprietorship forms referred to above along with their personal tax forms. Partnership taxes can get a little complicated, so you should get some accounting advice or, at the very least, consult with the Canada Revenue Agency.

A corporation must file a corporation income tax return (T2) within six months of the end of every taxation year, even if it doesn't owe taxes. Corporations report on an annual basis and are normally free to choose their year-end date. Corporations are also required to attach completed financial statements and the necessary schedules to the T2 return and you must also complete a separate personal (T1) tax return.

DIVIDEND

An amount distributed out of a corporation's retained earnings (accumulated profits) to shareholders

If your small business is incorporated, whether or not you pay yourself a salary is a tax planning decision. Another option is to pay yourself (and other shareholders, depending on share structure) a **dividend**—an amount distributed out of a corporation's retained earnings (accumulated profits) to shareholders—which is not deductible for the corporation. There are many factors to consider, and professional advice in this area is recommended. If you decide to pay yourself a salary, you will be required to deduct income tax and CPP premiums from your salary, but as owner of the business you will not be eligible to be covered by Employment Insurance. Depending on the province in which you operate, Workers' Compensation premiums may be payable, even if you do not pay yourself a salary. See, for example Taxtips.ca (http://www.taxtips.ca/contact.htm#repro).

Corporate tax is complicated, and you definitely should get professional help. But if you really do want to try it yourself, the best place to start is the "Setting Up Your Business" page on the CRA Web site and Taxtips.ca (see Box 8.6).

GST/HST

The Federal GST (Goods and Services Tax) is a tax that applies at a rate of 6 percent to the supply of most goods and services in Canada. The HST (Harmonized Sales Tax) includes a sales tax that applies at a single rate of 14 percent to taxable sales made in the 3 participating provinces of Newfoundland and Labrador, Nova Scotia, and New Brunswick. Rather than charging a provincial retail sales tax as well as GST, only the HST is charged, at a rate of 14 percent. The HST has the same basic operating rules as the GST. The federal component of HST is 6 percent, and the provincial component is 8 percent.

If your taxable revenues do not exceed $30,000, you do not have to register for the GST or HST. However, you can register voluntarily, and in general, we suggest you do, for three major reasons.

1. **Business image.** Charging GST (which will require you to file for a Business Number) gives you a professional image. It gives the customer appearance that you are financially respectable (earn more than $30,000) and intend to stay in business for the "long haul."

2. **Customer relations.** At the point when you begin making in excess of $30,000 (say two years down the road), you will have to begin charging an additional 6 percent. Your returning customers might not be pleased with this, and might very likely see it as a price increase.

3. **Financial.** As we describe below, businesses that sell GST-taxable goods and services and are "small suppliers" are able to recover the GST that they have paid on their purchases. If you are not GST registered, you cannot collect the GST you pay on your purchases. See, for example, Taxtips.ca (http://www.taxtips.ca/gst.htm#WhatIsGST).

Although the consumer ultimately pays the GST/HST, businesses are normally responsible for collecting and remitting it to the government. Businesses that must register or that register voluntarily for the GST/HST are called registrants. Registrants can claim a credit, called an input tax credit, to recover the GST/HST they paid or owe on their business purchases. If they pay more than they collect, they can claim a refund. Since there are goods and services that are tax exempt (most medical and dental services and daycare services provided for less than 24 hours a day, for example), it is important that you check with the CRA before you start your business.

To register for the GST or HST, contact your nearest tax services office. You will be asked to fill out Form RC1, *Request for a Business Number*, as we discussed earlier. You can get more information from the CRA publication *General Information for GST/HST Registrants* or from the CRA's Web site (http://www.cra-arc.gc.ca). The CRA has a very useful guide, RC4022, *General Information for GST/HST Registrants* (http://www.cra-arc.gc.ca/E/pub/gp/rc4022/README.html).

PROVINCIAL SALES TAXES

Provincial sales taxes (PST) are charged in many provinces on retail sales of many goods and services. Businesses that sell taxable goods and/or services in each province are required to register as a vendor to collect the provincial retail sales tax.

In all provinces except Quebec and Prince Edward Island, GST is charged on the selling price of the item before PST is applied, thus avoiding GST being charged on PST. In Quebec and PEI, the reverse is the case. Each province has its own regulations and rates—in Ontario, the PST is 8 percent, whereas it is 7 percent in B.C., Saskatchewan, and Manitoba, for example. As we have noted above, Newfoundland and Labrador, Nova Scotia, and New Brunswick charge a Harmonized Sales Tax, or HST—a 14 percent tax rate that includes both PST and GST.

If you want to learn more about the rules and regulations for your province, link onto the two PST sites provided in Box 8.6—especially the Taxtips.ca site.

Box 8.6   Bookmark This Tax and Legal Information

Guide for Canadian Small Business (Canada Revenue Agency): http://www.cra-arc. gc.ca/E/pub/tg/rc4070/README.html—"Setting up Your Business" is the first chapter of the CRA's *Guide for Canadian Small Businesses*. Topics include

- How does a sole proprietorship pay taxes?
- How does a partnership pay taxes?
- How does a corporation pay taxes?
- Legal requirements for keeping records,
- Retaining and destroying records, and
- Bringing assets into a business.

Canadian Tax and Financial Information: http://www.taxtips.ca—This is a great site to answer many of your tax and legal questions. Taxtips.ca is owned by a small private company located in Nanaimo, British Columbia. It is prepared by a husband and wife team who are retired from owning and operating a small business, with one being a retired professional accountant. The goal is to be a reference site for easy to understand tax, financial, and related information. Their information is updated and timely.

Here is just a limited selection of questions you can get answered:

1. What books and records must be kept for a business?
2. How does a self-employed person choose a year end when starting a business?
3. What is the deadline for filing a tax return for a self-employed person?
4. Where can I get the forms to file a corporate tax return?
5. If I have a small business, do I have to file both a personal and a business tax return?
6. Do my small business financial statements have to be audited?
7. As the owner of a small business, should I pay myself a salary? What deductions would apply?
8. Can I write off my business losses against my other income?
9. Should you incorporate your small business?

Provincial sales tax (PST): Taxtips.ca "Provincial Sales Taxes": http://www.taxtips.ca/provincial_sales_tax.htm—Here you will find the **general rates** of provincial sales taxes for most purchases and links to the provincial (or federal) Web sites regarding provincial sales taxes.

Another good site to help you get started is Canada Business, Taxation (Provincial and Federal) http://www.cbsc.org/servlet/ContentServer?cid=1102940239020& pagename=OSBW%2FCBSC_WebPage%2FCBSC_WebPage_Temp&c=CBSC_WebPage

GET A LAWYER AND AN ACCOUNTANT

The business world has become something of a legal jungle. As an entrepreneur, you can't possibly be expected to know and understand all the laws and their tax implications. So take the time to find a lawyer and an accountant who can help you with your specific needs.

A good small business lawyer and an accountant can help you create the right business and tax structure for a partnership or a corporation—a structure that gives you the flexibility and tax advantages you'll need. Some small business owners we know have invited their lawyer and accountant to sit on their board of directors or board of advisors. If you're incorporated, you might even want to think about inviting your lawyer and/or accountant to sit on your board of directors and provide "no-cost" advice in exchange for shares in the business. Remember, however, you might have to pay for directors' liability insurance.

Now let's learn from the experience of Paul Webber. If he had had sound professional advice, his story might have turned out differently.

A PARTNER'S UNFORESEEN DEATH

Paul Webber was a software game developer when he met MaryAnn Dominic. MaryAnn, a likable woman, had four years' experience designing game software and was a dynamite salesperson. They got together and formed Gamestar.

Their first year was okay—they netted more than $50,000 apiece—and their second year was looking even better. By May of their second year, their projections told them they could make $75,000 each before the end of the summer. They thought it felt great to have cash, and to celebrate, they went out to dinner.

At dinner, MaryAnn passed out and was pronounced dead by the paramedics on their arrival. At 32 years of age, MaryAnn Dominic was dead of a heart attack. Two weeks after the funeral, Paul was on the phone with a customer when MaryAnn's widower, Jason, walked in. Jason had inherited MaryAnn's half of the business.

Paul didn't like Jason's being his partner, but there was nothing he could do. He and MaryAnn had no succession plan for their business. They were young. What were the chances of either one dying? Paul knew he would have to break his back to teach Jason the business. Game software was a competitive field—it changed before you could take a breath—and Jason would have to learn an awful lot in a short time.

Paul was a good guy, so he tried. The first month, he was extra tired because he was handling his own customers while also spending long hours trying to teach Jason the business. The second month, two clients who were ignored defected to a competitor. Paul heard about it through the grapevine. The third month, the company almost ran out of cash, and Paul had to dump in $5,000 from his personal account to keep suppliers happy.

And Jason wasn't learning the business. Instead, he was getting in Paul's hair, and was spending money. Jason wasn't able to hold up his end, and there was no improvement in sight.

Paul hung on for another week. Then he did the only thing he could do for his own survival. He took what customers he had left and rented an office six blocks away in an attempt to keep going. He figured he had paid his dues to MaryAnn.

It wasn't long before Jason's lawyer came calling, though, making Paul nervous and unsure of the consequences and the future.

As we learn from Paul Webber, you will also need professional advice to help you draft a will, and a succession plan to handle unforeseen events that take you by surprise and may cost you dearly.

GET A WILL

The importance of an up-to-date will cannot be overstated. Contrary to what most people believe, if you die without a will, things will not automatically work out as you would have wished. Disaster can result.

—David Chilton, author of *The Wealthy Barber*[6]

If you die without a will, all your assets will be frozen. The courts will then pay off all debts and divide up your business assets according to a set of rigid rules. If you want your property, business, or shares transferred a certain way after your death, you must say so in a will. If you have partners or other owners, make sure they have a will and that you all understand what is going to happen if someone dies. Here are a few rules, drawn from *The Wealthy Barber*.[7]

1. Get a lawyer. Don't do it yourself. There are many issues to consider, both from a business and from a personal perspective.
2. Make your lawyer aware of your business arrangements.
3. Before you see a lawyer, decide exactly what you want to happen with your business should you die. Make sure that you discuss this with your business partners or other owners. Remember also that you have the right to know what is going to happen to the business if one of your key shareholders or partners dies.
4. Choose an executor. This is a person who will handle your affairs and carry out the will's instruction.
5. Make sure your business in insured in the event of your death.
6. Make sure that you have a succession plan in the event of your death.
7. Don't procrastinate. Do it now!

SUCCESSION PLANNING—ESPECIALLY FOR THE FAMILY-OWNED BUSINESS[8]

John R. Beever doesn't know how his business would function if he fell out of an airplane today—but he's prodding his family and key managers to discuss it.

Mr. Beever, 59, runs a family-owned custom woodwork manufacturing business that his great-grandfather started in 1876. But discussing the future ownership and management of the business raises thorny questions. Mr. Beever's two sons, Geoffrey and John C., are in their 30s and vice presidents of the firm. Both are enthusiastic about the business, and both are bright. Both want to succeed their father. Which son, if any, does the senior Mr. Beever choose as successor? Will that son be able to steer the company through a new era? And will Mr. Beever be able to let go and watch others toil without him?

SUCCESSION PLANNING

The process of establishing the procedures to change or transfer ownership or control of a business

In small business, **succession planning** refers to the process through which an owner establishes the procedures to change or transfer ownership or control of the business. The succession process—especially with family-owned business—requires owner/managers like Mr. Beever to deal proactively with a slew of sticky questions: How can they choose among several capable successors? What happens if no one in the family is really interested in taking over?

As an owner here are some key succession issues that you must prepare to confront:

- Is continuing the business into the next generation in the best interest of family members?
- Can family members handle the stress that continuity planning will cause?
- Who should be included in the decision making?
- What is the vision for the family business?
- What qualities should the next company leader have?
- How can important contacts be transferred, along with the title of owner?
- How can the owner make a graceful exit? Once owners decide to go, they should go quickly—and not look back.
- On the unexpected death of the owner, how should control and ownership be transferred?

If you want to learn more about succession issues and potential problems in family-owned business: Click onto Canada Business (http://www.cbsc.org/servlet/ ContentServer?pagename=CBSC_FE/display&c=GuideFactSheet&cid= 1081945276597&lang=en) and "Succession Planning" (http://www.fambiz.com/ template.cfm?Article=Succession/loyola-591.html&Keywords=succession% 20planning&Button=fambiz).

Now you're ready to do Action Step 40.

BANKRUPTCY

Entrepreneurs are optimists by nature. As you prepare to open your doors, the last thing you want to think about is the prospect of being forced to close them. But business failures do happen, and it's not too early to learn about some of the legal concerns arising from them.

If nothing else, an understanding of the bankruptcy process should encourage you to be proactive and avoid debt problems in the first place. Box 8.7 will also help you do this. In Chapter 11, page 283, we will encourage you to seek out and get a copy of your credit rating. But, for many young entrepreneurs, an important issue is not only the maintenance of a good credit rate but also the creation of a credit rating. So in Chapter 11, we will also help you develop a positive credit history.

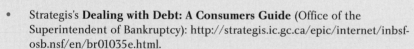

Box 8.7	**Bookmark This**

- Strategis's **Dealing with Debt: A Consumers Guide** (Office of the Superintendent of Bankruptcy): http://strategis.ic.gc.ca/epic/internet/inbsf-osb.nsf/en/br01035e.html.

Many Canadians and Canadian companies will face a financial crisis at some time. Some debt problems are easy to solve, but others need professional assistance. The best way to deal with your financial problems is to get control before they get out of hand. This booklet might help you decide whether or not you have a serious debt problem. It also gives some suggestions for solving your difficulties and avoiding them in the future.

TEN THINGS YOU SHOULD KNOW ABOUT BANKRUPTCY[9]

1. WHAT IS BANKRUPTCY, AND WHAT ARE THE BENEFITS TO THE DEBTOR?

Bankruptcy is a legal process, regulated by the Bankruptcy and Insolvency Act, by which you may be discharged from most of your debts. The purpose of the Act is to permit an honest, but unfortunate, debtor to obtain a discharge from his or her debts, subject to reasonable conditions. Once you are legally bankrupt, you are required to perform specific duties as outlined in the Act.

ACTION STEP 40

Take a lawyer and an accountant to lunch

Canvass your business contacts for the names of three to five lawyers and accountants with experience in forming small business corporations and partnerships. If possible, concentrate on those who have worked in your industry.

Talk to them by phone first, and then take the most promising candidates to lunch. (Lunch is optional, but your inquiries are vital.) Many lawyers and accountants offer a free first visit. If you are a business student, how about inviting a lawyer or accountant into your classroom? Have a list of questions ready.

The first thing you're looking for are professional advisors you can get along with. Then look for experience in the world of small business. For example, a hot trial lawyer might have a lot of charisma, and your personal lawyer might know a lot about buying a house or drafting wills, but you want a nuts-and-bolts small business specialist who can save you time, pain, and money.

Prepare a list of questions. Find out about fees and costs. Compare the cost, for example, of having your lawyer write up a complex partnership buyout agreement with the cost of setting up a corporation. In the event of your death, what will happen to your estate? Can they help you think about your succession plans? Use some questions presented in this chapter to start you off in your discussion.

A good lawyer and accountant will offer you perspectives that will be helpful in the formation of your business. You may have to look awhile, and it may cost you some dollars up front, but there's no substitute for sound professional help.

BANKRUPTCY

A legal process, regulated by the Bankruptcy and Insolvency Act, by which you may be discharged from most of your debts

2. HOW DOES ONE BECOME BANKRUPT?

First, you meet with a trustee in bankruptcy, who will assess your financial situation and explain other options available to you. If you decide to become bankrupt, the trustee will help you complete several forms, which you will have to sign. You are considered a bankrupt only when the trustee files these forms with the Official Receiver.

3. WHAT HAPPENS TO MY PROPERTY?

When you declare bankruptcy, your property is given to a trustee in bankruptcy, who then sells it and distributes the money among your creditors. Your unsecured creditors will not be able to take legal steps to recover their debts from you (such as seizing property or garnisheeing wages).

You do not have to assign to the trustee exempt property such as basic furniture, tools-of-trade, and, under certain circumstances, the GST credit payments. Exempt properties will vary from province to province. Your trustee can tell you what these are.

4. WHAT KIND OF FORMS WILL I HAVE TO SIGN?

You will have to sign at least two forms. One is an *Assignment*, and the other is your *Statement of Affairs*. In the assignment, you state that you are handing over all of your property to the trustee for the benefit of your creditors. In the statement of affairs, you list your assets, liabilities, income, and expenses. In addition, you will have to answer several questions about your family, employment, and disposition of assets.

5. DOES THE BANKRUPTCY AFFECT MY CO-SIGNERS?

Your bankruptcy does not cancel the responsibility of anyone who has guaranteed or co-signed a loan on your behalf. For example, if your parent co-signed a loan for you, that parent would be liable to pay the loan in full, even if you decide to file for bankruptcy.

6. WHEN IS A BANKRUPT DISCHARGED?

There will be an automatic discharge for first-time bankrupts nine months after they became bankrupt unless the trustee recommends a discharge with conditions or the discharge is opposed by a creditor, the trustee, or the Superintendent of Bankruptcy.

7. WHAT IS THE EFFECT OF A BANKRUPTCY DISCHARGE?

The bankrupt is released of most debts. However, some debts are not released, such as an award for damages in respect of an assault, a claim for alimony, spousal or child support, a debt arising out of fraud, any court fine, or debts or obligations for student loans when the bankruptcy occurs while the debtor is still a student or within 10 years after the bankrupt has ceased to be a student.

8. HOW DOES BANKRUPTCY AFFECT EMPLOYMENT?

For the most part, bankruptcy should not affect your employment. However, there are some special cases. For example, you might have difficulty being bonded. Your trustee will be able to give you more information on other possible restrictions or prohibitions.

9. IS THERE ANYTHING I CAN DO TO IMPROVE MY CREDIT RECORD?

Should you wish to improve your credit record after obtaining your discharge from bankruptcy, you could, for instance, contact your banker and request a meeting. For this meeting, you could bring your paycheque stubs, your budget, and your discharge papers. You could explain that you have obtained your discharge and ask the banker how you can earn your way back to a good credit record.

10. DOES IT COST ANYTHING TO GO BANKRUPT?

Yes. There is a filing fee to be paid to the Superintendent of Bankruptcy. In addition, the trustee is entitled to be paid. These fees are prescribed by the *Bankruptcy and Insolvency Rules*.

In a Nutshell

There are three basic legal forms for your small business: sole proprietorship, partnership, and corporation (limited company). You can run a business as a sole proprietorship with a minimum of difficulty. You might need only a city licence, a resale licence, and a business name. If you use a business name other than your own, you will probably need to register the name with your provincial government. Be careful, however—this might not give you exclusive rights to use the name.

The legal paperwork for a partnership is a little more involved. It might be possible to form a partnership with a handshake, but we wouldn't advise it. Get a lawyer, and have a partnership agreement drawn up before you start. There are good skill-related reasons for forming a partnership. Let's say you're an inventor; you need a partner who can manage and sell. Let's say you're good at marketing; you need a partner who can run the office and keep the books. You might also form a partnership because you need the financial capital. Remember, however, these are the only two good reasons for forming a partnership—to provide skills and money. At least one of these needs must be met, or you're asking for trouble. For example, friendship is not a good enough reason for a partnership arrangement.

Forming a limited company or corporation takes the most paperwork and costs the most money. However, it gives you the most flexibility, as well as a shield in case your business hurts someone.

In this chapter, we also discussed the government red tape that will confront you when you start your business. We recommended that you seek some legal protection for your business name. We also emphasized the importance of using a lawyer and accountant to help structure your business, prepare your will, and begin drafting a succession plan. Finally, we asked you to start thinking about some of the legal concerns arising from bankruptcy.

Key Terms

bankruptcy

buy-sell option

cooperative

corporation

dividend

general partnership

limited partnership

partnership

shareholders agreement

shotgun clause

social entrepreneurship

sole proprietorship

succession planning

Think Points for Success

✓ Know the advantages and disadvantages of the basic legal forms when you establish your business.

✓ Get a lawyer and a partnership agreement drawn up before you form a partnership.

✓ Incorporation can help limit your liability.

✓ Protect your business name, and do a NUANS search to make sure you have not infringed on another business's name or trademark.

✓ Get a will, and start thinking about a succession plan.

Business Plan Building Block

LEGAL STRUCTURE

State the type of legal structure—proprietorship, partnership, corporation, or cooperative—you intend to institute for your business. List the reasons why you chose this structure.

_____

_____

_____

_____

_____

RED TAPE FILE

Set up a red tape file. Make a list of all the municipal, provincial, and federal regulations with which you are going to have to comply. Beside each regulation, write the contact telephone number, address, and other pertinent information.

Checklist Questions and Actions to Develop Your Business Plan

Legal Concerns

❑ Explain why you selected your legal form of ownership.

❑ What professionals have you referenced in your business plan, and did you allow for the appropriate cost?

❑ What are the major legal risks for your industry, and how will you address them?

❑ Are you prepared for the legal red tape?

❑ Do you have a will and a succession plan?

Case Study

YOUR PAL STEVE

I have to admit, the motor-sailor was my idea. I persuaded my partner, Steve Savitch, to buy a boat—actually it was a fancy, 14-metre rig called *The Ninja*—for the partnership. We could write off some of the payments as an expense, and it would do our company image a world of good.

Steve and I had been friends for a dozen years and partners in Savitch and Johnson, Business Consultants, for the past three. We'd done quite well, and each of us was going to clear more than $50,000 this year. I persuaded him we could afford this perk. Besides, my marketing instinct told me it could really help close a few deals.

About two months after we bought the boat—and had a lot of fun—a fellow who sells radar equipment called me. Seems Steve had bought $2,000 worth of goods, and this chap was wondering when he'd get paid. After I hung up the phone, my secretary buzzed me with Mary, Steve's wife, on the line wanting to know where Steve was.

I thought he was on a business trip with a few of our best clients. As it turned out, Steve had disappeared with *The Ninja*, and no one knew where. In the end, I got stung for all his business debts, including the payments on *The Ninja*.

The problem was that Steve and I never saw the need for having anything in writing. We were both men of good faith (or so I had thought). We had each pulled our weight in business, and we had balanced each other's skills. For the first time in 12 years, I made an appointment to talk to a lawyer. He just shook his head. "You should have come to me a lot sooner, Phil," he said. "A *lot* sooner. And while I am at it, Phil, you should also have been in close touch with a professional accountant. These 'business write-offs' you're talking about might not be acceptable according to the CRA."

Last week, when I was closing the place down and getting ready to go back to work for my old boss, I got a postcard from Tahiti. "Sorry partner," Steve wrote. "Didn't mean to run out on you, but it was the only way I could handle the home front. These things happen.... Your pal, Steve."

Case Study Questions

1. Partnership agreements
   a. What is a partnership agreement?
   b. Briefly explain the two basic types of partnership agreements. Would a partnership agreement necessarily have protected Phil from Steve's actions?
   c. What are the advantages and disadvantages of a partnership agreement? What was Phil's major reason for wanting to establish an unwritten partnership agreement as opposed to a corporation?
   d. Suppose that Phil had approached his lawyer to draft a written partnership agreement. List the major items that should be included in this agreement that might have protected Phil.

2. Corporate structures
   a. What would be the major advantages and disadvantages for Phil to have established a corporate structure?
   b. If Phil had established a corporate structure, would a shareholders agreement have been required by law?
   c. Would you have advised Phil to have a shareholders agreement? Why? Why not?
   d. List five key issues a shareholders agreement should address. (Here, in addition to the text, you might want to link onto "Understanding the Shareholder Agreement": http://strategis.ic.gc.ca/sc_mangb/stepstogrowth/engdoc/step8/ssg-8-7.php).
   e. Briefly explain the type of legal structure—a partnership or corporation—that would have provided Phil with the most protection against Steve's actions.

3. Cooperatives
   a. What are the major reasons for considering a cooperative legal structure? Would this legal form have been of benefit to Phil?
   b. In Box 8.4 (page 192) we captioned the successful Mountain Equipment Co-op (MEC). What are the major reasons why MEC established a cooperative form of ownership? How do these MEC objectives differ from Phil's businesses objectives?
   c. As an owner of MEC, you would be entitled to receive subscription shares and patronage shares. Briefly explain these two types of share options. (Hint: Click onto "About MEC Shares":). http://www.mec.ca/Main/content_text.jsp?CONTENT%3C%3Ecnt_id=10134198673220431&FOLDER%3C%3Efolder_id=2534374302881978&bmUID=1155224224741

Notes

1. Much of the research for this section was conducted on the Industry Canada, Strategis Web site (http://strategis.ic.gc.ca/engdoc/main.html).
2. Ezine article "The Value of Shotgun Clauses in Partnership Agreements!". (http://ezinearticles.com/?The-Value-of-Shotgun-Clauses-in-Partnership-Agreements!&id=202069.)
3. Industry Canada, Corporations Canada, *Guide to Federal Incorporation*: http://strategis.ic.gc.ca/epic/internet/incd-dgc.nsf/en/h_cs01914e.html (accessed July 2006).
4. Canadian Co-operative Association (http://www.coopscanada.coop/aboutcoop/statistics/) and Co-ops Canada (http://www.coopscanada.coop/aboutcoop/statistics/, both sites accessed July 2006).
5. Industry Canada: http://strategis.ic.gc.ca/epic/internet/incd-dgc.nsf/en/h_cs01914e.html (accessed July 2006).
6. David Chilton, *The Wealthy Barber* (Toronto: Stoddart Publishing, 1989), p. 67.
7. Chilton, *The Wealthy Barber*. Pages 69–71
8. Fambiz.com, "Succession Planning," by Adriane B. Miller: http://www.fambiz.com/template.cfm?Article=Succession/loyola-591.html&Keywords=succession%20planning&Button=fambiz (accessed July 2006).
9. Industry Canada, Office of the Superintendent of Bankruptcy, *Dealing with Debt: A Consumer's Guide*: http://strategis.ic.gc.ca/epic/internet/inbsf-osb.nsf/en/br01035e.html (accessed July 2006).

SUGGESTED READING

Canada Revenue Agency. *Employer's Guide: Remitting Payroll Deductions.* Form xxx.

Canada Revenue Agency. *General Information for GST/HST Registrants.* Form RC4022(E) Rev. 03.

Canada Revenue Agency. *The Business Number and Your Canada Revenue Agency Accounts.* Form RC2.

Carter, Tom. *Write Your Will in Three Easy Steps.* Vancouver, BC: Self-Counsel Press, 2004

Chilton, David. *The Wealthy Barber.* Toronto: Stoddart Publishing, 1989.

Eberhart, Frank. *Plan Ahead: Protect Your Estate and Investments.* Bellingham, WA: Self-Counsel Press, 2004.

Fletcher, Denise E. *Understanding the Small, Family Business.* London: Taylor & Francis, 2002.

Industry Canada, Corporations Directorate. *Name Granting Guidelines.* Form xxx.

Industry Canada, Corporations Directorate. *Small Business Guide to Federal Incorporation.* Form xxx

Kamoroff, Bernard B. *Small Time Operator: How to Start Your Own Business, Keep Your Books, Pay Your Taxes, and Stay Out of Trouble (Small Time Operator).* Willits, CA: Bell Springs Publishing, 2004.

Ward, John. *Perpetuating the Family Business: 50 Lessons Learned from Long Lasting, Successful Families in Business.* New York: Palgrave Macmillan, 2004.

Warner, Ralph. *How to Run a Thriving Business: Strategies for Success & Satisfaction.* Berkeley, CA: Nolo Press, 2004.

Warner, Ralph, and Denis Clifford. *The Partnership Book: How to Write a Partnership Agreement.* Berkeley CA: Nolo, 2001.

Risk Management Issues

Chapter 9 will help you manage risk and prepare parts H, I, and J of your Business Plan, the Financial Section

Patty Fisher really liked kids, so she joined forces with her husband and made plans to open a daycare centre. They secured a bank loan and bought a property in a neighbourhood of young families with an average of 2.5 children. They spent weekends painting and fixing up the place. They worked hard, but it was fun, and it made them feel a part of something warm and cozy.

About three weeks before their opening, they called the light and power people to ask them to turn on the lights. "Sure thing," said sales manager Don Farthington. "Just send us a cheque for $700, and the lights will be on in a jiffy."

"What?" Patty asked. "Did you say $700?" They had around $800 in the kitty, but that was earmarked for emergencies.

"That's right. You're a new commercial customer with a good credit rating. That's the reason the figure's so low."

"You think $700 is low?" Patty asked in disbelief.

"For your tonnage," he said, "it's right on the money."

"Tonnage? What tonnage?"

"Your air conditioner," Don said. "You have a five-ton unit on your roof."

"But we're not planning to run it!" Patty said. "The breeze here is terrific. We don't need the air conditioner."

"Sorry, ma'am. Our policy is pretty clear. Sometimes we get three months' deposit, but for your business we'll only require the two. Is there anything else I can help you with today?"

"No," Patty said. "Absolutely nothing." As she hung up, she made a vow to take a good hard look at the daycare budget. They simply could not afford any more surprises like this.

Although a business plan is designed to demonstrate how the business will prosper, there is a need to demonstrate flexibility when things do not go exactly as planned. What can go wrong and what can be done to eliminate downside risk? When you interview successful entrepreneurs and ask them what surprises they had not anticipated when they started, they usually have quite a few. Almost always, you hear that it cost more and took longer than they had planned.

In the opening vignette, aspiring daycare operator Patty Fisher was badly shaken by an unexpected electricity charge. To protect yourself from such unpleasant surprises, you need at least one Plan B; we begin this chapter by showing you how to create one.

LEARNING OPPORTUNITIES

After reading this chapter, you should be able to

- develop a Plan B to minimize the ill effects of unfortunate surprises;
- determine your insurance needs and costs;
- draft a health and safety policy and action plan;
- develop a list of precautions that will help minimize the opportunities for employee dishonesty;
- understand the main characteristics of patents, copyrights, and trademarks;
- prepare a 12-month start-up checklist.

ACTION STEP
PREVIEW

41. Prepare your Plan B checklist.
42. Calculate your insurance needs and costs.
43. Draft a health and safety policy and action plan.
44. Navigate an online tutorial on patent applications.

ACTION STEP 41

Prepare your Plan B checklist

Now that you've got your business well in mind, take a few minutes to brainstorm a list of surprises that could cost you money or time, and, if possible, how you can turn these problems into opportunities. Use the checklist in Box 9.1 to help you get started.

Next, conduct some primary research. Talk to businesspeople in your industry. If you are intending a street-side location, ask the neighbours what has happened to them and how they're doing in this location. Talk to vendors, suppliers, customers, and insurance brokers. If you are going to operate out of the home, ask the opinion of other home entrepreneurs.

When you finish your list, put a checkmark beside each item that will cost money.

PLAN B

An alternative strategy for bailing the business out of a tight spot created by some unforeseen or unfortunate situation

DEVELOPING A PLAN B

Reading the opening vignette, you might have wondered how Patty could have overlooked such an important detail. Remember that a budding entrepreneur is confronted with a formidable to-do list. That's why having at least one **Plan B**— an alternative strategy for bailing the business out of a tight spot created by some unforeseen or unfortunate situation—is a must before you open your doors. Box 9.1 presents a Plan B checklist that could help eliminate surprises, and Box 9.2, on page 210, provides some useful online resources.

Of course, we understand that there is a certain amount of risk in every decision that the owner of a small business makes. Risk is a fact of life. We are encouraging you to acknowledge risk and find ways to minimize its consequences. Here, we want you to be proactive and think about alternative strategies if your decisions don't pan out. For example, what happens if your computer crashes? What is your Plan B to back up important information? Too many small businesses suffer because they did not back up their data regularly. We might also add here that some entrepreneurs we know have benefited from the availability of "prepaid" legal services. They pay a certain monthly fee for legal advice and a select number of services (see, for example, Prepaid Legal Service Inc.: http://wserver0.prepaidlegal.com/index.html).

If you get into the habit of making lists, doing mind maps, and writing everything down in your 24/7 Adventure Notebook, you'll improve your chances of surviving in small business. Action Step 41 will also help you anticipate potential surprises.

Box 9.1 Plan B Checklist

Here's a checklist of some obvious start-up concerns. Add to this list as you think of things.

1. Advisors
- ❏ Lawyer
- ❏ Banker
- ❏ Accountant/bookkeeper
- ❏ Insurance agent
- ❏ Commercial real estate agent
- ❏ Mentor (advisory board)
- ❏ Consultants
- ❏ Suppliers
- ❏ Chamber of commerce
- ❏ Professional association
- ❏ Other organizations

2. Organization
- ❏ GST registration (if necessary)
- ❏ PST registration
- ❏ DBA ("Doing business as" = business name)
- ❏ Partnership agreement
- ❏ Corporation
- ❏ Other

3. Licences and Permits
- ❏ Business licence
- ❏ Resale permit
- ❏ Department of Health requirements
- ❏ Liquor licence

❏ Fire inspection permit
❏ Local building inspection
❏ Other

4. Location

❏ Lease review (lawyer)
❏ First and last months' rent (Rent might have to be paid while you are making improvements. Estimate time needed to do improvements.)
❏ Security deposit
❏ Leasehold improvements
❏ Insurance
❏ Security system
❏ Utilities, deposits, estimated monthly costs
    ❏ Electric
    ❏ Gas
    ❏ Water
    ❏ Phone installation
❏ Other

5. Auto (Consider new, used, leased)

❏ Autos
    ❏ New/used
    ❏ Lease/purchase
❏ Trucks
    ❏ New/used
    ❏ Lease/purchase
❏ Insurance
❏ Maintenance, repairs

6. Equipment

❏ Computer
❏ Office
❏ Retail space
❏ Warehouse
❏ Manufacturing area
❏ Kitchen
❏ Dining area
❏ Communication
❏ Other

7. Fixtures

❏ Tables
❏ Chairs
❏ Desks
❏ File cabinets
❏ Workbenches
❏ Storage cabinets
❏ Display cases
❏ Lighting

8. Supplies

❏ Pencils and pens
❏ Notepaper and letterheads
❏ Tape
❏ Dictionary
❏ Calendar
❏ Appointment book
❏ Coffee, tea, soft drinks, bottled water
❏ And so on. Have you prepared a checklist of suppliers? (See Box 9.3.)

9. Inventory

❏ What are the minimum and maximum average inventory requirements you need on hand to do business on your first day?

10. Advertising/Promotion

❏ Signs
❏ Business cards
❏ Fliers/brochures
❏ Displays
❏ Ad layouts and graphics
❏ Media (newspaper, radio, other) costs
❏ Trade show booths
❏ Other

11. Banking

❏ Chequing account
  ❏ Cheque charges
  ❏ Interest on account
❏ Chequing/bookkeeping system
❏ Deposit box
❏ Savings/chequing account
❏ Credit
  ❏ Credit cards
  ❏ Personal lines of credit or letter of credit
  ❏ Loans and interests
  ❏ Credit from suppliers/vendors

12. Employees

❏ Application/employment forms completed (e.g., employer registration number from Canada Revenue Agency)
❏ Training program

Box 9.2 Bookmark This

- **Checklists for Going into Business:** The Canada Business Service Centres provides questions and worksheets to help you think through what you'll need to know and do. Here are two examples:
  - **Feasibility Checklist for Starting a Small Business:** http://www.cbsc.org/servlet/ContentServer?pagename=CBSC_FE/display&c=GuideFactSheet&cid=1081945275631&lang=en
  - **Start up Checklist:** http://www.cbsc.org/servlet/ContentServer?cid=1102940239535&pagename=OSBW%2FCBSC_WebPage%2FCBSC_WebPage_Temp&c=CBSC_WebPage
- **Guide for Canadian Small Business, Canada Revenue Agency:** http://www.cra-arc.gc.ca/E/pub/tg/rc4070/rc4070-e.html—Start with this page to register your business at the federal level.
- **Meeting Place for Young Entrepreneurs:** http://www.youthbusiness.com/services/meeting/level2.cfm?id=0&nav= 1.0.0.0.0.0.0.0.0.0—This virtual meeting place is found on the Canadian Youth Business Foundation's YouthBusiness.com site. Use the discussion boards to get advice from other young entrepreneurs.
- **Canada Business Service Centres:** http://sbinfocanada.about.com/od/businessservicecentres/

Canada Business Service Centres provide business support ranging from business information through advice, counselling, and workshops. These listings will help find a Canada Business Service Centre near you.

- Do you think you have an invention? You might want to check it out with Canadian Innovation Centre: http://www.innovationcentre.ca/index.html— Ideas are evaluated and advice is provided on costs, engineering, and the steps required to launch, position, and market a product. The Centre makes clients aware of how to manage the risks involved in bringing ideas to market.

Box 9.3 Suppliers' Checklist

- Can you make a list of every item of inventory and all operating supplies needed?
- Do you know the quantity, quality, technical specifications, and price ranges desired?
- Do you know the name and location of each potential source of supply?
- Do you know the price ranges available for each product from each supplier?
- Do you know about the delivery schedules for each supplier?
- Do you know the sales terms of each supplier?
- Do you know the credit terms of each supplier?
- Do you know the financial condition of each supplier?
- Is there a risk of shortage for any critical materials or merchandise?
- Are you aware of which suppliers have an advantage relative to transportation costs?
- Will the price available allow you to achieve an adequate markup?

Source: Canada Business, "Feasibility Checklist for Starting a Small Business" (http://www.cbsc.org/servlet/ContentServer?pagename=CBSC_FE/display&c= GuideFactSheet&cid=1081945275631&lang=en). Another vendor/supplier checklist that serves as a reminder of the kinds of supplier and vendor information you should keep can be found on Entrepreneur.com (http://www.entrepreneur.com/Home/HM_Static/ 1,4472,formnet_inventory,00.html).

INSURANCE PLANNING

If you plan on going into business for yourself, you will likely need some sort of insurance. (Types of business insurance are shown in Box 9.4.) If you operate a home-based business, you will probably need extra insurance as well; in most cases, basic homeowners' insurance will not cover your business needs (see Box 9.5, on page 214). You must make sure that all vehicles are insured for business purposes. In calculating your insurance needs, you should first consider all the insurable risks faced by your business. We emphasize, however, you can never be insured for a bad management decision—and that's why you have to have your Plan B.

In general, the following risks can be covered by insurance if you have followed the law:

- Personal injury to employees and the general public. Some retail stores have become targets for "slip and fall" claims. Certain businesses have higher personal injury claims, and you need to protect accordingly.
- Employment practices such as hiring, firing, sexual discrimination, and libel.

- Loss to the business caused by the death or disability of key employees or the owner—an essential coverage needed to protect your business.
- Loss or damage of property—including merchandise, supplies, fixtures, and building. A standard fire insurance policy pays the policyholder only for those losses directly caused by fire. Make sure when dealing with your insurance agent that you understand your policy thoroughly. Keep asking until you do.
- Loss of income resulting from interruption of business caused by damage to the firm's operating assets (storms, natural disasters, electrical blackouts).

Other indirect losses, known as consequential losses, might be even more important to your company's welfare. They include

- extra expenses incurred when obtaining temporary quarters;
- loss of rental income on buildings damaged or destroyed by fire, if you are a landlord;
- loss of facility use;
- continuing expenses after a fire—salaries, rents paid in advance, interest obligations, and so on; and
- loss of customer base.

Box 9.4 Types of Business Insurance

As an entrepreneur, you can purchase insurance to cover almost any risk. Each of the following types of business insurance protects you from a different type of financial loss.

1. **Fire and general property insurance** protects against fire loss, vandalism, hail, and wind damage.
2. **Consequential loss insurance** covers loss of earnings or extra expenses when business is interrupted because of fire or other catastrophe.
3. **Public liability insurance** covers injury to the public, such as customer or pedestrian injury claims.
4. **Business interruption insurance** provides coverage in case the business is unable to continue as before.
5. **Crime insurance** protects against losses resulting from burglary, robbery, and so forth.
6. **Bonding.** Two important types of bonds for small business owners are **fidelity bonds**, which provide insurance coverage from employee theft, and **completion bonds**, which provide insurance coverage to ensure that work on a contract is competed as agreed.
7. **Malpractice insurance** covers against claims from clients who suffer damages as a result of services that you perform.
8. **Errors and omissions insurance** covers against claims from clients who suffer from injury or loss because of errors you made, things you should have done but failed to do, or warnings you failed to supply.
9. **Employment practices liability insurance (EPLI)** covers against claims from employees for employment practices: sexual harassment, wrongful discharge, discrimination, breach of contract, libel, and so on.
10. **Key man insurance** covers the life, death, dismemberment, or physical disability of owner(s) or key employee(s).
11. **Product liability insurance** covers injury to the public, such as customer use or misuse of products.
12. **Disability (long-term) and critical illness insurance** covers owners and employees against disability and serious illness and usually allows for payments to be continued during rehabilitation. Disability/critical illness for an owner is a much greater risk than death, and few owners insure themselves adequately.

FIDELITY BONDS

Insurance that protects an employer against employee dishonesty

COMPLETION BONDS

Insurance coverage to ensure that work on a contract is competed as agreed.

13. **Life and supplemental health insurance for employees.**
14. **Extra equipment insurance** covers specialized equipment not covered in standard policies.
15. **Directors' and officers' liability insurance.** If company stock is held by outside investors, directors and officers should be protected.
16. **Auto insurance.** A business can be liable for injuries and property damage caused by employees operating their own or someone else's vehicle while on company business. The company might have some protection under the employees' liability policy, but the limits are probably inadequate. If employees use their vehicles while on company business, you should purchase non-ownership liability insurance.
17. **Life insurance and disability.** In the event of a serious disability, or death, you will need "key man" insurance to cover the financial obligations of the business. Note that many financial institutions will require you to have life and disability insurance as a condition of your loan.

You can protect yourself against consequential losses by obtaining business interruption insurance (see Box 9.4).

What type or types of insurance should you carry, and how much coverage should you have? To answer these questions, you should consider

- the size of any potential loss,
- the probability of loss,
- the resources available to meet a loss if one occurs, and
- the probability of lawsuits (some industries and areas are heavily targeted).

If a particular loss would force you or your company into bankruptcy or cause serious financial damage, recognize the risk, and purchase insurance to help protect your assets. Losses that occur with predictable frequency, such as shoplifting and bad debts, can usually be absorbed by the business and are often budgeted as part of the normal cost of doing business; the cost of the loss should be incorporated into the price. Where probability of loss is high, a more effective method of controlling the loss is to adopt appropriate precautionary measures and purchase better-than-adequate insurance. The key to purchasing insurance (and all risk management issues) is simple: *Do not risk more than you can tolerate losing.*

The insurance planning worksheet in Table 9.1 and Action Step 42 will help you calculate your insurance needs and costs.

In addition to business insurance, you will likely need the advice of a business insurance professional, who will probably not be the same person who brokered your homeowner's or auto policies. We suggest you network your way to a good business insurance agent—the same way you select a lawyer. You will want someone who understands your business, product liability, errors and omissions, bonding, burglary coverage, and key employee insurance—health, fire, life, and so on.

Insurance companies frequently put together packages for particular types of businesses, such as retail, wholesale, and service. Also explore group rates through your trade association or your local chamber of commerce. Most chambers of commerce offer a small business insurance package. Joining a group insurance program can save you a lot of money.

Remember that insurance is only one of the options to reduce risk—and in some cases, it should be considered the last resort. Insurance can reimburse you only for unintentional, unforeseen, and uncontrollable losses, not for everyday business risks. Other options include eliminating the risk with a Plan B (as we discussed above), reducing it, assuming it, or transferring it to someone else.

ACTION STEP 42

Calculate your insurance needs and costs

Network your way to a business insurance salesperson. Discuss your business plan with him or her, and complete the insurance planning worksheet in Table 9.1. Calculate the cost of insuring your business for the first year (include in your estimate any up-front deposit). Remember, if you operate your business out of the home, you will need business insurance.

Keep your completed insurance worksheet on hand. It will help you estimate your cash flow in the next chapter.

Box 9.5 How Do I Insure My Home Business?

If you're running a business from your home, you might not have enough insurance to protect your business equipment. A typical homeowner's policy provides only $2,500 coverage for business equipment, which is usually not enough to cover all of your business property. You might also need coverage for liability and lost income. Insurance companies differ considerably in the types of business operations they will cover under the various options they offer. It's wise to shop around for coverage options as well as price.

When insuring your home business, you should consider

- business property (desks, computer, etc),
- theft,
- business continuation,
- liability (coverage for bodily injury arising from your home business),
- medical insurance, and
- auto insurance.

If you are using your car for business activities—transporting supplies or products, or visiting customers—you need to make certain that your automobile insurance will protect you from accidents that might occur while you're on business.

In addition to your auto insurance, you have three basic types of home protection policies to choose from—depending on the nature of your business and the insurance company you buy it from.

1. Homeowner's Policy Endorsement

You might be able to add a simple endorsement to your existing homeowner's policy to double your standard coverage for business equipment such as computers. For as little as $25, you can raise the policy limits from $2,500 to $5,000. Some insurance companies will allow you to increase your coverage up to $10,000 in increments of $2,500.

We also strongly advise that you buy homeowner's liability endorsement. You need liability coverage in case clients or delivery people get hurt on your premises. They might trip and fall down your front steps, for example, and sue you for failure to keep the steps in a safe condition.

The homeowner's liability endorsement is typically available only to businesses that have few business-related visitors, such as writers. But some insurers will provide this kind of endorsement to piano teachers, for example, depending on the number of students. These types of endorsements are available, but they vary, so you should shop around.

2. In-Home Business Policy/Program

An in-home business policy provides more comprehensive coverage for business equipment and liability than a homeowner's policy endorsement. These policies, which may also be called in-home business endorsements, vary significantly depending on the insurer.

In addition to protection for your business property, most policies will reimburse you for the loss of important papers and records, accounts receivable, and off-site business property. Some will pay for the income you lose (business interruption) in the event that your home is so badly damaged by a fire or other disaster that it can't be used for a while. They'll also pay for the extra expense of operating out of a temporary location.

Some in-home business policies allow a certain number of full-time employees, generally up to three. The policies also generally include broader liability insurance for higher amounts of coverage and may offer protection against lawsuits for injuries caused by the products or services you offer, for example.

In-home business policies are available from homeowners insurance companies and specialty insurers that sell stand-alone in-home business policies. This means that you don't have to purchase your homeowners insurance from them.

3. Business Owners Policy (BOP)

Created specifically for small-to-mid-size businesses, this policy is an excellent solution if your home-based business operates in more than one location. A BOP, like the in-home business policy, covers business property and equipment, loss of income, extra expense, and liability. However, these coverages are on a much broader scale than the in-home business policy.

A BOP doesn't include workers compensation, health or disability insurance, or auto insurance.

Source: Reprinted by permission of the Insurance Information Institute (http://www.iii.org).

Table 9.1 Insurance Planning Worksheet

Required Insurance Types	Yes	No	Annual Cost ($)
1. Personal liability	❑	❑	_____
2. General and public liability	❑	❑	_____
3. Product liability	❑	❑	_____
4. Vehicle	❑	❑	_____
5. Errors and omissions liability	❑	❑	_____
6. Malpractice liability	❑	❑	_____
7. Key man insurance	❑	❑	_____
8. Directors and officers	❑	❑	_____
9. Life insurance	❑	❑	_____
10. Health	❑	❑	_____
11. Crime insurance	❑	❑	_____
12. Business interruption	❑	❑	_____
13. Extra equipment	❑	❑	_____
14. Consequential loss	❑	❑	_____
15. Employment practices liability insurance (EPLI)	❑	❑	_____
16. Fire and theft	❑	❑	_____
17. Business loan	❑	❑	_____
18. Personal disability and critical illness	❑	❑	_____
19. Bonds (fidelity, surety)	❑	❑	_____
20. Home	❑	❑	_____
21. Other	❑	❑	_____
Total Annual Cost			_____

As a final note, we want to emphasize that many small business owners ignore the need for a shareholders or partnership agreement with a buy-sell option (as we discussed in Chapter 8), or they put off having a will drawn up. The few hundred dollars you might spend on professional fees to draw up these types of necessary protective legal agreement is probably one of the best investments you and your associates will ever make.

WORKPLACE HEALTH AND SAFETY

Why worry about safety? Simply because workplace accidents can destroy your business. According to the Canadian Centre for Occupational Health and Safety (CCOHS) and Human Resources and Social Development Canada, three people die from a work accident or occupational disease every working day in Canada. On average, a worker is injured on the job every nine seconds—amounting to some 800,000 injuries per year. Every year, about $5 billion is spent to compensate workers injured on the job—about $80,000 for each working minute. When you add to this all the indirect costs—replacement workers' wages and training costs, overtime, and so on—the real cost is in the $10 billion range.

Besides the incalculable cost of pain and grief, there are high monetary costs attached to workplace accidents. These costs can include the inability to meet your obligations to customers, wages paid to sick and disabled workers, wages paid to substitute employees, damaged equipment repair costs, insurance claims, workers' compensation, and administrative and record-keeping costs. Both humanitarian desires and economic good sense have encouraged employers to create and maintain safer and healthier working conditions.

Occupational health and safety (OHS) legislation in Canada outlines the general rights and responsibilities of the employer, the supervisor, and the worker. As a general rule, the legislation applies to all workers performing work for an employer. Exactly who is responsible for what varies by jurisdiction and by workplace. However, the basic guiding principle is that if a worker is injured in the course of performing work for the employer, the employer might be held liable.

There are two basic levels of OHS legislation—federal and provincial. The federal government and each of the 10 provinces and three territories have their own OHS legislation—which makes this issue a complicated and sometimes confusing one. Federal OHS legislation is governed by the Canada Labour Code, Part II. This legislation affects private- and public-sector workers in the federal jurisdiction, which includes the following businesses and enterprises:

- the public service;
- Crown corporations; and
- international and interprovincial industries, including air, rail, roads, pipelines, banking, broadcasting, shipping and ports, and telecommunications.

If you think your business might be governed by federal legislation, we suggest that you visit the Occupational Health and Safety Web site of the Department of Human Resources and Social Development (HRSDC http://www.hrsdc.gc.ca/asp/gateway.asp?hr=en/lp/lo/ohs/overview/index-ohs.shtml&hs=oxs).

For the vast majority of small and medium-size businesses, OHS is governed by provincial law. In each province or territory, there is an OHS Act that normally applies to all workplaces in that region except private homes or farming operations. Usually, a department of labour or ministry is responsible for OHS; in some jurisdictions, however, occupational health and safety is the responsibility of the workers' compensation board or commission. To find out exactly what your responsibilities are, you should consult the relevant legislation and government department or agency. Information on OHS legislative requirements for each province/territory, along with contact sources, is provided on the CCOHS Web site at http://www.ccohs.ca (see also Box 9.6). In this section, we will cover four basic elements of OHS legislative responsibilities: government, employee, and employer responsibilities; joint health and safety committees; workplace hazardous materials; and due diligence.

OHS GOVERNMENT, EMPLOYEE, AND EMPLOYER RESPONSIBILITIES

Workplace health and safety is everyone's responsibility. These basic responsibilities, rights, and conditions are well summarized on the following CCOHS Web page:

> OHS Legislation in Canada—Basic Responsibilities:
> http://www.ccohs.ca/oshanswers/legisl/responsi.html#_1_2

Here you will find basic answers to the following questions:

- What are the general responsibilities of governments?
- What are the employees' rights and responsibilities?
- What are the supervisor's responsibilities?
- What are the employer's responsibilities?
- What does legislation say about forming health and safety committees?
- What is the role of joint health and safety committees?
- What happens when there is a refusal for unsafe work?

Box 9.6 Bookmark This

Health and Safety Regulations

- **Department of Human Resources and Social Development (HRSDC):** http://www.hrsdc.gc.ca/asp/gateway.asp?hr=en/lp/lo/ohs/overview/index-ohs.shtml&hs=oxs—Learn about occupational health and safety requirements for businesses that are set forth in Part II of the Canada Labour Code.

- **Canadian Centre for Occupational Health and Safety (CCOHS):** http://www.ccohs.ca—Learn about provincial/territorial OHS legislative requirements, employer and employee responsibilities, joint health and safety committees, workplace hazardous materials, and due diligence.

- **Workers' Compensation.** Don't start your business until you have checked out your health and safety responsibilities. For small business, laws relating to safety are mainly a responsibility of the provinces or territories. Learn about your and your employees' safety rights. Go to the Canada Business services site, "Becoming an Employer": http://www.cbsc.org/servlet/ContentServer?pagename=OSBW/CBSC_WebPage/CBSC_WebPage_Temp&c=CBSC_WebPage&cid=1102940239275#workers, and click onto the Worker's Compensation and Workplace Safety site for your province or territory.

JOINT HEALTH AND SAFETY COMMITTEES

A **joint health and safety committee (JHSC)** is a group consisting of labour and management representatives who meet on a regular basis to deal with health and safety issues. In all Canadian jurisdictions, a JHSC is either mandatory or subject to ministerial decision. There are some exceptions, however, depending on the size of workforce, industry, accident record, or some combination of these factors.

JOINT HEALTH AND SAFETY COMMITTEE (JHSC)

A group consisting of labour and management representatives who meet on a regular basis to deal with health and safety issues

In smaller companies, for example, a health and safety representative is all that may be required. In some cases, a representative might not even be needed. The best way to proceed on this issue is to contact your OHS government authority and legislation to make sure you know your legal responsibilities. We also suggest that you visit the CCOHS's Health and Safety Committees Web page:

http://www.ccohs.ca/oshanswers/hsprograms/hscommittees/whatisa.html.

Here you will find answers to these questions:

* What is a joint health and safety committee?
* Who is responsible for establishing a joint health and safety committee?
* What does a joint health and safety committee do?
* Is a committee or a representative required?
* What are the sources of legislation regarding joint health and safety committees?
* When are health and safety committees required, how many people are on the committee, and who are committee members?

WORKPLACE HAZARDOUS MATERIALS

WORKPLACE HAZARDOUS MATERIALS INFORMATION SYSTEM (WHMIS)

A comprehensive national plan for providing information on the safe use of hazardous materials used in Canadian workplaces

An important part of complying with OHS workplace safety legislation is making sure that you deal appropriately with hazardous materials. The **Workplace Hazardous Materials Information System (WHMIS)** is a comprehensive national plan for providing information on the safe use of hazardous materials used in Canadian workplaces. By law, you must provide information on hazardous material via product labels, material safety data sheets (MSDS), and worker education programs. Information on WHIMS is provided on the CCOHS general Web page

http://www.ccohs.ca/oshanswers/legisl/intro_whmis.html.

Here you will find answers to these questions:

* What are the main parts of WHMIS?
* Why was WHMIS created?
* How was WHMIS developed?
* Is WHMIS a law?
* What are the duties under WHMIS?
* What are controlled products?
* Who enforces WHMIS?
* How do I get more information?

DUE DILIGENCE

DUE DILIGENCE

The level of care, judgment, and caution that an employer would reasonably be expected to provide in order to prevent injuries or accidents in the workplace

In the context of occupational health and safety, **due diligence** is the level of care, judgment, and caution that an employer would reasonably be expected to provide in order to prevent injuries or accidents in the workplace. As an employer, you might be legally responsible for situations that are not specifically addressed in the OHS legislation. Due diligence requires you to implement a plan to identify possible workplace hazards. Find out more about due diligence by visiting the CCOHS OHS Legislation in Canada—Due Diligence Web page:

http://www.ccohs.ca/oshanswers/legisl/diligence.html.

Here you will find answers to these questions:

* Why does due diligence have special significance?
* How does an employer establish a due diligence program?
* What is an example of a due diligence checklist?

It's time to apply your understanding of workplace health and safety to your own business. Complete Action Step 43.

THEFT AND FRAUD PREVENTION

One of the nastiest surprises for a budding entrepreneur is employee dishonesty. You might think that because you're small, employees won't steal from you, but you're wrong. Small firms get hit more often than big ones. Here are some examples of employee dishonesty:

- credit card fraud;
- cheque deception;
- shoplifting;
- cash register vulnerability (e.g., employees shortchanging customers);
- bookkeeping theft;
- fraudulent refunds;
- counterfeit money;
- fitting room theft;
- burglary;
- robbery;
- theft of items from stockroom, layaway, and displays;
- computer fraud;
- manipulation of timecard data;
- illegal use of company time;
- fraudulent trip expense reports; and
- "sweethearting" (discounts for family and friends).

You will not be able to eliminate theft and fraud, but there are a number of things you can do to reduce the risk. You can begin by establishing a code of conduct that clearly communicates the legal—among other—consequences of employee dishonesty. First, have your employees sign the code of conduct, and review it on a regular basis. Next, establish a set of anti-theft/fraud rules and procedures (Box 9.7 will help you get started). If you suspect employee dishonesty, take prompt action.

PATENTS, COPYRIGHTS, AND TRADEMARKS[1]

Patents, copyrights, and trademarks are the three major forms of intellectual property that can be protected through federal legislation. These are important elements of your business. If you fail to protect them, (1) you might lose your business, (2) your ideas might be stolen, or (3) your products might be copied. In Canada, intellectual property is largely the responsibility of the Canadian Intellectual Property Office (CIPO) (see Box 9.8). Because intellectual property laws are complex and subject to change, you should consult with a lawyer who has experience in this area.

ACTION STEP 43

Draft a health and safety policy and action plan

To complete this Action Step, you will need answers to these questions:

- How will you encourage a healthy and safe working environment?
- What will your responsibilities as an owner be?
- Who will be responsible for safety?
- What will be the responsibilities of your employees?
- Do you need a safety coordinator?
- What are the rules and regulations for your business regarding workers' compensation?
- Who is your government OHS inspector? What are his or her expectations?

For assistance in developing your occupational health and safety policy and action plan, visit the following Web pages:

- Guide to Writing an OHS Policy Statement: http://www.ccohs.ca/oshanswers/hsprograms/osh_policy.html; and
- The Worker's Compensation and Workplace Safety site for your province or territory: http://www.cbsc.org/servlet/ContentServer?pagename=OSBW/CBSC_WebPage/CBSC_WebPage_Temp&c=CBSC_WebPage&cid=1102940239275#workers.

Box 9.7 Anti-Theft/Fraud Measures

Here's a list of precautions that will help minimize the opportunities for employee theft and fraud.

- Sign all cheques yourself.
- Don't let any one employee handle all the aspects of bookkeeping.
- Insist that all bookkeeping be up-to-date and clear.
- Insist that your bookkeeper take scheduled vacations.
- Do regular physical inventories.
- Open all mail containing payments yourself.
- Track all cash transactions, and maintain a rolling annual cash flow on a monthly basis.

- Use numbered order forms, and don't tolerate missing slips.
- Insist on **fidelity bonds** for every employee who handles cash.
- Triple-check references on résumés and employment applications.
- If your business is a cash business, be there. Absentee owners, beware!
- Try to eliminate cash by accepting debit, credit, and "smart cards."
  Learn more about protecting your business against common business crimes such as break-ins, fraud, employee theft, shoplifting, and vandalism. Link onto "What Crime Concerns You?" (http://crimeprevention.rutgers.edu/crimes.htm).

Box 9.8 Bookmark This

Canadian Intellectual Property Office (CIPO): http://strategis.gc.ca/sc_mrksv/cipo/welcome/welcom-e.html

The Canadian Intellectual Property Office (CIPO), a Special Operating Agency associated with Industry Canada, is responsible for the administration and processing of the greater part of intellectual property in Canada. CIPO's areas of activity include patents, copyrights, and trademarks. To learn more about protecting your intellectual property, visit the CIPO Web site.

TEN THINGS YOU SHOULD KNOW ABOUT PATENTS

1. What is a patent?

PATENT

A federal government grant that gives an inventor exclusive rights to his or her invention

A **patent** is a federal government grant that gives an inventor exclusive rights to his or her invention. Patents cover new inventions (process, machine, manufacture, composition of matter) or any new and useful improvement of an existing invention. Patent protection applies in the country that issues the patent. In Canada, this protection extends for 20 years from the date of filing. Patents are granted for products or processes that are new, workable, and ingenious (novel, useful, and inventive). In this way, patents serve as a reward for ingenuity.

Patenting your invention can take several years. The process usually begins with an initial patent search to compare your invention with current patent and technical literature. Then you assemble a patent application, which includes a detailed description of your invention and the claims that are the basis for your patent protection. In Canada, a patent is given to the inventor who first files an application. It's therefore wise to file as soon as possible after completing your invention, because someone else might be on the same track.

2. Why obtain a patent?

Without a patent, you will be able to protect your invention only as a trade secret. Your secret will be out the moment you publish or begin to sell your invention, and anyone will be able to exploit your invention. Even if you can maintain your secret, if someone else independently makes the invention, that person might be able to obtain a patent and prevent you from exploiting the invention.

3. Is a patent application mandatory?

To have patent protection, you must apply for and receive a patent. Application fees range from about $350 to $500. Because patent laws are national, you must obtain patent protection in each country in which you want protection.

4. Who can apply for a patent?

The legal owner of an invention can obtain the patent. Typically, the owner is the inventor or inventors. However, if an inventor sells his or her rights, then a second party will own the invention and be able to obtain a patent. If the inventor makes the invention as part of an employment contract, the employer might own the invention and have the right to the patent.

5. How long is a patent effective?

The life of a patent in Canada is 20 years from the date the application was first filed. Payment of maintenance fees throughout the life of the patent is also required to keep it in force.

6. How do I obtain a patent?

You can obtain a patent in Canada by submitting a patent application, with the appropriate fee, to

The Commissioner of Patents
The Canadian Intellectual Property Office
Place du Portage Phase I
50 Victoria Street,
Hull, Quebec
K1A 0C9

The *Guide to Patents* gives additional information on the requirements for obtaining a patent. You can consult the tutorial on how to write a patent application.

7. Do I need to hire a patent agent?

You can do it yourself, but the Canadian Intellectual Property Office strongly advises that you employ the services of a patent agent. Patent agents are professionals with experience in drafting applications and navigating the patent process. They will be able to help you ensure that you get all of the rights to which you are entitled. A list of registered patent agents is available from the Patent Office.

8. Does a patent in Canada protect my rights in other countries?

No. Patent laws are national, so you must obtain a patent in each country in which you want protection.

10. Can libraries or educational institutions make multiple copies of parts of books or articles for student use?

No. The making of multiple copies requires the consent of the copyright owner. This consent may be obtained through a licensing agreement with a photo-copying collective. However, the Copyright Act does allow the copying by individuals of parts of works for private study or research. Such copying should be minimal. This exception falls within the "fair dealing" section of the Act.

TEN THINGS YOU SHOULD KNOW ABOUT TRADEMARKS

1. What is a trademark?

TRADEMARK

A word, symbol, or design, or a combination of these, used to distinguish the goods or services of one person or organization from those of others in the marketplace

A **trademark** is a word, symbol, or design, or a combination of these, used to distinguish the goods or services of one person or organization from those of others in the marketplace. There are three basic types. *Ordinary marks* are words and/or symbols that distinguish the goods or services of a specific firm. *Certification marks* identify goods or services that meet a standard set by a governing organization. *Distinguishing guise* identifies the unique shape of a product or its package.

Will the Trade-marks Office ensure that my trademark is not infringed?

The Trade-marks Office does not act as an enforcement agency. You are responsible for monitoring the marketplace for cases of infringement and taking legal action, if necessary.

Who can register a trademark?

Companies, individuals, partnerships, trade unions, or lawful associations, provided they meet the requirements of the Trade-marks Act, can register a trademark.

How long is registration effective?

A registration is valid for 15 years and is renewable every 15 years thereafter on payment of a fee.

2. What is the difference between a registered and an unregistered trademark?

A registered trademark has been approved and entered on the Trade-mark Register held by the Canadian Trade-marks Office. Registration is proof of ownership. An unregistered trademark might also be recognized through common law as the property of the owner, depending on the circumstances.

3. Why register a trademark?

Registration is direct (prima facie) evidence of exclusive ownership across Canada and helps ward off potential infringers. It enables you to protect your rights more easily should someone challenge them, as the onus is on the challenger to prove rights in any dispute. The process of registration, with its thorough checks for conflicting trademarks, will ensure that you are claiming a unique mark and help you avoid infringement of other parties' rights. A registered trademark is a prerequisite for franchising a business.

Is registration mandatory?

No, but it is advisable.

4. Do I need to hire a trademark agent?

You can do it yourself, but the Canadian Intellectual Property Office strongly advises that you employ the services of a trademark agent. Trademark registration can be a complex process; an experienced agent can save you time and money by avoiding pitfalls such as poorly prepared applications and incomplete research.

5. How do I register a trademark?

You must file an application with the Trade-marks Office in Hull, Quebec. The application undergoes stringent examination to ensure it meets the requirements of the Trade-marks Act.

6. Does registration in Canada protect my rights in other countries?

No. If your products are sold in other countries, you should consider applying for foreign registration. Contact a trademark agent or the embassy of the country in question to find out about procedures.

7. What is the difference between a trademark and a trade name?

A trade name is the name under which you conduct your business. It can be registered as a trademark, but only if it is used as such—that is, used to identify wares or services.

8. May I register my own name as a trademark?

Normally, you may not register a proper name—neither yours nor anyone else's—as a trademark. An exception might be made if you can demonstrate that the name has become identified in the public mind with certain wares or services.

9. What are the steps of trademark registration?

Trademark registration usually involves

- a preliminary search (done by you or your agent) of existing trademarks,
- an application,
- examination of your application by the Trade-marks Office,
- publishing of the application in the *Trade-marks Journal*,
- time for opposition (challenges) to the application, and
- allowance and registration (if there is no opposition).

10. May I allow other parties to use my registered trademark?

Yes. You may sell, bequeath, or otherwise transfer your rights to a trademark through a process called assignment. You may also license rights to your trademark.

GETTING ADVICE

Yes, you must be prepared because there's a boatload of surprises awaiting every entrepreneur who enters the marketplace.

We've talked about Plan B, formulating your strategy, thoroughly researching your market, and peering into the future to see what lies ahead. But there's another angle to planning: It's called seeking advice.

Think for a moment about where you are right now on your road to the marketplace. You're more than halfway through this book. You've analyzed your skills and needs. You've probed your past and surveyed your friends. You've discovered what success means to you, plotted trends, and found your industry segment. You've profiled your target customer, studied the demographics, and developed a marketing strategy, including your promotion campaign. You've examined the prime and indirect competition. You've used your new eyes to find a dynamite location. Now you need to find a small business guru or establish an advisory board and get some advice.

Where might you find a business guru or someone who should be on your advisory board? Well, what about your banker? Many people come to him or her for money—some of them carrying business plans, others not knowing a spreadsheet from a bed sheet. What about your accountant? What about the real estate broker who helped you with your search for a location? What about your business insurance specialist or a retired person who is very knowledgeable about your industry? An advisory board should be no more than three to five people. Have you contacted your local Canada Business Service Centre? You can even get advice over the Net.

You can use your network to find other people who can help you. Show them your goals, objectives, and list of potential surprises, and ask for their advice. Ask them for their ideas about what other surprises might be in store for you. If one of those persons gives you wonderful advice, consider putting him or her on your advisory board or, if you're incorporated, on your board of directors. Remember, you can make anyone part of your team—your lawyer, accountant, small business professor, even your customer.

PLANNING AHEAD: TWELVE-MONTH START-UP CHECKLIST

Think about the things you need to start action on 12 months before you open your door for business. For example, if you want to place an advertisement in the Yellow Pages, you might need to plan for it 10 months before the business opens or wait until the next edition comes out. Refer to Box 9.9 for an example of a 12-month checklist.

Box 9.9 Complete Your Own Start-up Appendix for Your Business Plan

1 year before launch

- Research the demand for your product or service from both primary and secondary sources.
- Read an environmental scan that addresses your project.
- Prepare a test market analysis, including an analysis of competition, price, and market share.
- Register your product or service.
- Write out your mission and goals, and start your business plan.
- Establish your form of ownership.
- Set up a system to record all costs (with invoices) relating to your start-up expenses. Travel costs, for example, should be documented. These are start-up costs that you will be able to deduct from your income when the business is in operation.

10 months

- Establish the strength of your equity base and need for venture capital.
- Identify your potential fixed and variable costs.
- Investigate all channels of distribution.
- Identify potential suppliers and establish prices.
- Investigate packaging, design, and potential promotion approach.
- Start search for site location to be established three months before opening.
- Establish a good relationship with a banker and a lawyer.

8 months

- Evaluate the results of the field test and establish prices and a promotion strategy.
- Confirm suppliers and prices.
- Start getting confirmed prices on promotion material.
- Prepare an overall capital and operating budget.
- Prepare position descriptions for staff.
- Complete competitive analysis.
- Establish an advisory board.
- Investigate all external funding sources.
- Complete your business name search.

6 months

- Start listing potential locations.
- Meet with board of advisors to assess progress and problems.
- Clearly identify target market for your promotion strategy.
- Order any fixed assets that require long delivery time.
- Establish leases where appropriate.
- Gain approval from the appropriate government bodies if producing a product that requires it.
- Place advertisement if necessary in the Yellow Pages (might need to be sooner depending on your start date and the new phone book release).

- Establish a bank line of credit.
- If a home business, verify the city/township bylaws.
- Establish your Web site

5 months

- Finalize location.
- Prepare a design and schedule for leasehold improvements.
- Order signs.
- Order inventory and supplies.
- Contact telephone company for information about home office service options.

4 months

- Contact the leasehold improvements.
- Finalize packaging (including design).
- Finalize your promotional approach.
- Complete details for GST with the Canada Revenue Agency.

3 months

- Sign for all utilities and hookups.
- Develop job descriptions, and place ads for staff.
- Take possession of location.
- Start renovations and install fixed assets.
- Meet with board of advisors.

2 months

- Select staff to start.
- Start marketing approach depending on nature of business, and finalize renovations.
- Start receiving fixed assets.

1 month

- Shelve and price inventory.
- Start staff as required.
- Train new staff.
- Get marketing campaign under way.
- Etc., etc., etc.—all you forgot about!

Launch

- Hold grand opening.
- Offer opening specials.

Note that *almost all* the work takes place before the official opening.

In a Nutshell

Start-up needs to go smoothly. What you don't need are expensive surprises that knock you and your business for a loop. Before you open your doors, you need to have anticipated as many potential unpleasant surprises as possible and have a plan of action for each one of them. For example, how would you turn the following unwanted surprises into opportunities?

- Your landlord decides to evict your business.
- Your Yellow Pages ad is terrible.
- The customer that accounts for 75 percent of your business declares bankruptcy.

Expecting and planning for the unexpected can make the difference between life and death in business. As you seek to manage risk by considering your insurance, health and safety, and other needs, just remember two things: No one can anticipate everything, and setting up will probably cost more and take longer than your planning indicates.

Key Terms

completion bonds

copyright

due diligence

fidelity bonds

joint health and safety committee (JHSC)

patent

Plan B

trademark

Workplace Hazardous Materials Information System (WHMIS)

Think Points for Success

✓ Listen to your competition so that you can change and improve.

✓ Create partnerships and outsource what you can.

✓ Be aware of closing dates for Yellow Pages advertising and other key media.

✓ Keep a time log that tells everyone (you, your founders, your key employees) how you are progressing on the plan.

✓ Make sure your partners are as committed to the business as you are, and have a shareholders or partnership agreement.

✓ Keep an ongoing list of unfortunate surprises that could hurt your business. Write down how you can turn these surprises into opportunities.

✓ Always have a Plan B. And a Plan C. And a Plan D.

✓ Let some key customers in on your planning; let them see it with their own eyes. Go one step further—create a customer board of directors.

Business Plan Building Block

Develop a list of issues that are unpredictable and difficult to control. Complete Table 9.2, or create your own list.

Problem   **Opportunity**

_____

_____

_____

_____

_____

_____

INSURANCE NEEDS AND COSTS

Make a list of your insurance needs and costs as recorded in your insurance planning worksheet. (See Action Step 42 and Table 9.1.)

_____

_____

_____

_____

_____

_____

_____

_____

BEGIN THE FIRST DRAFT OF YOUR START-UP APPENDIX

What things do you need to start action on before you open you door for business? Return to Box 9.9 for an example of a 12-month checklist.

Checklist Questions and Actions to Develop Your Business Plan

Protecting Your Business from Costly Surprises

- ❏ What operational goals and objectives do you want to achieve?
- ❏ What risks and challenges does your business face, and how will you address each one?
- ❏ Develop a start-up schedule beginning 12 months from the launch, indicating all the activities you must undertake (e.g., place Yellow Pages phone advertisement), along with costs related up to start-up. Note, this could be a two- or three-page schedule.
- ❏ What are the major cash drains in your business?
- ❏ What types of insurance and employee bonding will you have for your business?
- ❏ Do you have a health and safety policy in place?
- ❏ Do you plan to protect your idea, product, or service by obtaining a patent or copyright and/or by registering a trademark?

Case Studies

CASE 1: YOUR BUSINESS IDEA

Case Background

By now you should have a fairly good idea of the kind of business you want to start. This first case study is about you and your business. We want you to be proactive and begin thinking about possible risks and health safety issues for your business idea.

Case Study Questions

1. Plan B Solutions
   a. When survivors from any field or profession get together, they often like to share horror stories. In Table 9.2, we've collected a few of these small business "surprises" that we have encountered over the years. We want you to brainstorm with friends or classmates. Come up with some preventive measures to help avoid these costly surprises for your business—before you start your business. What are your Plan B solutions? Complete column 2 of Table 9.2.

Table 9.2 Your Plan B Solutions

Surprise	Plan B Solutions?
Your computer crashes	
Your landlord decides to evict you and your business	
The newspaper doesn't run the ad for your grand opening	
A staff member borrows your car and gets in an accident	
You're operating your business out of your house. While you are away, there is a robbery, and you lose your computer and $2,000 in cash	

Surprise	Plan B Solutions?
An hour after you sign your name to guarantee the lease, your best friend and partner gets cold feet and pulls out; you have nothing in writing to protect you against your partner's change of heart	
For eight weeks, during your peak season, the city has the sidewalk in front of your store torn up; the noise is deafening	
Your general contractor goes bankrupt	
Your bookkeeper disappears with $100,000, your books, two trade secrets from the company safe, and your spouse	
Your best salesperson is hired away by the competition	
Your largest customer declares bankruptcy; the money owed you in receivables is 50 percent of your gross annual sales	
The bank where you have your chequing account refuses to extend you a $20,000 line of credit to buy more inventory to supply a new customer	

b. After brainstorming your Plan B solutions in question 1a., we now want you to think about your business idea. Complete Table 9.3 by listing five costly surprises that might arise and provide your Plan B solutions. Be sure to put this in your 24/7 Adventure Notebook.

Table 9.3 Plan B Solutions

Possible Costly Surprises	Your Plan B Solutions
1.	
2.	
3.	
4.	
5.	

2. Health and Safety

As we note in the text, you should be thinking about workplace health and safety issues before your start your business.

a. In relation to occupational health and safety, what is meant by the term *due diligence*?

b. Draft a health and safety policy statement for your business. Action Step 43 will provide you with some guidance.

c. Before you start your business, you should familiarize yourself with the techniques to protect you and your business against the common business crimes, such as break-ins, fraud, employee theft, shoplifting, and vandalism. Review the list of precautions in Box 9.7 (page 219). Link onto "What Crime Concerns You?" (http://crimeprevention.rutgers.edu/crimes.htm). List 10 ways you plan to protect your business.

CASE STUDY 2: IT WAS A FATAL ACCIDENT

Case Background
George Lopez's best friend died unexpectedly. George was furious! His friend had been hospitalized for a minor surgical procedure, and a health care worker accidentally brushed against a poorly attached intravenous (IV) line, disconnecting it and subsequently causing George's friend's death.

When George heard the news by phone, he tried to throw the phone across the room, and it snapped back. Angrily, he inspected the cord and observed that a simple "click lock" attached it. If only his friend's IV tube had been attached by such a "click lock," his friend would still be alive. Within weeks, George designed a workable prototype of an "IV click lock."

Today his IV click lock has become the world standard for IV delivery, because George protected his idea.

More information on this invention and George's successful business can be found by clicking onto the ICU Medical Incorporated home page (http://www.icumed.com/about.asp).

Case Study Questions
1. Patents, copyrights, and trademarks are the three major forms of intellectual property that can be protected through federal legislation.
   a. Briefly explain each of these three legal forms of protection.
   b. If George Lopez wanted to sell his "IV click lock" in both Canada and the United States, which form of intellectual property would you advise George to use to help protect his inventive idea?
   c. Click onto the Canadian Intellectual Property Office (CIPO) Web site provided in Box 9.8. If you wanted to patent your idea, briefly describe the steps you would have to take to patent a new product or service.

Notes

1. Adapted from the Canadian Intellectual Property Office (CIPO) Web site (http://strategis.gc.ca/sc_mrksv/cipo/welcome/welcom-e.html).

SUGGESTED READING

Bareham, Steve. *Don't Get Caught in Risky Business*. Toronto: McGraw-Hill, 1999.
Canada Revenue Agency (CRA). *Guide for Canadian Small Business*: Ottawa: CRA, 2001.
Holloran, ed. *Credit and Collection: Letters Ready to Go!* New York: NTC Business Books, 1998.
Industry Canada, Canadian Intellectual Property Office. *Stand Out from Your Competitors*. Canadian Intellectual Property Office, Publishing Centre, 2004.
Industry Canada, Canadian Intellectual Property Office. *A Guide to Copyrights*. Ottawa: Canadian Intellectual Property Office, Publishing Centre, 2005.
Industry Canada, Canadian Intellectual Property Office. *A Guide to Patents*. Ottawa: Canadian Intellectual Property Office, Publishing Centre, 2004.
Industry Canada, Canadian Intellectual Property Office. *A Guide to Trade-Marks*. Ottawa: Canadian Intellectual Property Office, Publishing Centre, 2002.
OHS Canada. *Stayin' Alive*. Toronto: OHS Canada Magazine. (http://www.businessinformationgroup.ca/oh&s/stayinalive.asp)
Tompkins, Chuck. *The Insurance Wars*. Minot, ND: Western Agency, 2005 (http://www.theinsurancewars.com).

10

The Power of Numbers

Chapter 10 will help you prepare parts H, I, and J of your Business Plan, the Financial Section. Financial statements and ratios are important measures of the financial health of your start-up business. Cash is the lifeblood of your business, and cash flow is a key financial statement.

Ray and Joan Stewart were worried about their financial future. It seemed that every time the Canadian economy hiccupped, large corporations would respond with massive layoff notices. Ever since the early 2000s, fortysomething Ray had known that his job with a large technology company was no longer secure. Some of his coworkers had already received their walking papers, and Ray was expecting his own golden handshake any day now. His cash-starved employer would be sorely tempted to replace him and his $75,000 salary with an eager twentysomething content to earn $35,000 a year.

The Stewarts' financial worries did not end there. They were supporting two teenagers, both of whom planned to attend college or university in a few short years. Would they be able to afford the ever-rising tuition fees? As well, a couple of disastrous investments in the stock market had left them wondering if there would be anything besides the Canada Pension Plan to support them in their golden years.

Ray and Joan resolved to take control of their financial future by starting their own business. It was a formidable challenge, and they knew they needed help. Fortunately, Joan had done some networking in her small business class, which had led her to Patrick, a part-time college professor and small business consultant specializing in start-ups.

"No more procrastinating," Joan said to Ray one evening. "We'll call Patrick and get our thoughts and fears out in the open. Let's see what he has to say."

They met with Patrick the following week. He listened carefully as they explained their financial situation and voiced their concerns. At the end of the meeting, he said, "If you feel comfortable with me, I will help you. But remember, there'll be a few road bumps—especially when it comes to finance. And by the way, you have just travelled smoothly over the first money hurdle. This first session is free.

"The major source of funding for any new business almost always comes from the owner(s). So the two of you must begin by getting your personal financial house in order. To begin your journey, I want both of you to begin a review of your financial fitness and to draft your personal financial vision. Here are some online sites to help get your started..."

LEARNING OPPORTUNITIES

After reading this chapter, you should be able to

- formulate a personal financial vision;
- test your financial fitness;
- assemble a team of financial advisors;
- estimate your start-up costs;
- create your own balance sheet;
- project monthly sales and propose a sales forecast;
- understand that cash is the lifeblood of your business;
- understand that bills are paid with cash, not profit;
- create a cash flow projection and a pro forma income statement; and
- use ratios to measure the financial health of your business.

ACTION STEP PREVIEW

45. Put your personal financial vision in writing.
46. Assemble a team of financial advisors.
47. Estimate your start-up costs.
48. Draft a projected cash flow.
49. Draft a projected income statement—a moving picture of your business.

In this chapter and the next, we will encourage you to move out into the world of finance. These financial chapters will help you understand the fundamentals of small business financing and get you ready to complete your financial plan. We'll help you get your personal finances in order, set financial goals, get your financial plan together, and find out how much money you'll need for your first year of operation and beyond.

Once you are ready with the knowledge and information to create your financial plan, we will encourage you to visit the sites provided in Box 10.3. Before you create your financial plan, however, you should familiarize yourself with the financial basics contained in this chapter and in Chapter 11—unless, of course, you have a strong financial background.

As we learned from Patrick in the opening vignette, and as you will again find out in Chapter 11, odds are that you will be the major banker for your start-up business. This means that your financial plan will begin with you and your financial fitness and vision. We encourage you to review your financial fitness and formulate a clear financial vision. We will introduce you to the basic financial statements and the financial indicators a business needs to survive and grow.

YOUR FINANCIAL FITNESS

We want you to begin your journey to finance your business by reviewing your personal financial situation. After all, if your personal finances are not in order, how can you expect to ask other people to invest in you and your business? The first step is to check out your financial fitness. The E-Exercises and sources provided in Box 10.1 will help you do that. These are the Internet sites that Patrick gave to Ray and Joan in the opening vignette to help them get started. We will ask you to come back and review this information in Chapter 11 when it comes time for you to create your financial statements.

FORMULATING A PERSONAL FINANCIAL VISION

For many budding entrepreneurs, the world of finance is daunting. Ray and Joan Stewart are typical, in that they did not have a clear picture of their financial future. They lacked the guidance and direction of a personal financial vision.

We can't tell you what your financial vision should be. That's up to you. Some examples of a personal financial vision might be to

- be financially independent,
- be able to afford to travel to other countries,
- be able to afford a new home and the furniture to fill it, or
- have the financial ability to retire and smell the roses before the big 5-0.

Having a financial vision will not, of course, guarantee the success of your business venture—but it will provide you with some all-important guidance and direction. Some entrepreneurs want to strike it rich. Others, like the Stewarts, seek financial security. Still others set for themselves the goal of earning enough money to support an early retirement.

We want you to begin thinking about your financial future. What is your financial vision? We encourage you to complete Action Step 45 and put your financial vision in writing.

ACTION STEP 45

Put your personal financial vision in writing

Sit back, close your eyes, and take a moment to dream. Where, financially speaking, do you want to see your business one year from now? How about five years from now? Ten years from now?

In the space provided below, write down your personal financial vision. Express it in terms of an objective—"to be financially independent," for example.

My personal financial vision is

_____
_____
_____
_____
_____
_____
_____

Get in the habit of asking yourself every morning, "What am I going to do today that will bring my financial vision one step closer to reality?"

Box 10.1 E-Exercises

Check Out Your Financial Fitness

How Do You Manage Your Money?

Do you think you're doing a good job of managing your money? Or do you feel your spending is out of sync with your income? To see what kind of shape you're in, take a few minutes to fill out the Canadian Bankers Association's financial fitness test (http://www.cba.ca/en/viewPub.asp?fl=6&sl=23&docid=27&pg=2). You can also find this text in pdf format at http://www.cba.ca/en/content/publications/Man_Mony.pdf, on page 6.

Test Your Financial IQ

What is your aptitude for and interest in personal financial planning? Take the MSN Money Financial IQ Test (http://moneycentral.msn.com/investor/calcs/n_finq/main.asp).

Is Financial Planning Important to You?

Take the one-minute test from the Canadian Financial Planners Standards Council (http://www.cfp-ca.org/public/public_testyourfinancialiq.asp).

Take the Debt Quiz

If you think that you might have a debt problem, take a few moments to answer the questions on this site (http://www.creditcounsellingcanada.ca/debt_quiz.html).

Getting Help

If after taking these online tests, you discover that you need help with personal financial planning, we suggest you **get help now**. Here are some sources to get your started.

- Credit Counseling Canada: http://www.creditcounsellingcanada.ca/creditor_info.html—Here you will get help to solve your debt problems and learn to manage money and credit wisely.

- Canadian Bankers Association: http://www.cba.ca/en/viewPub.asp?fl=6&sl=23&docid=27&pg=18—Provided is a list of not-for-profit organizations. Find the nearest credit counselling service nearest you.

- The YourMoney Network (YMN): http://www.yourmoney.cba.ca—A one-stop online resource that offers non-commercial financial information for youth. YMN hosts 54 partners that provide information from all walks of the financial world on more than 800 resource areas.

- Managing Money: http://www.cba.ca/en/viewPub.asp?fl=6&sl=23&docid=27&pg=1—Managing Money offers a step-by-step approach to budgeting, which is the first step in assessing and managing the flow of your money. The site also looks at borrowing and credit use.

GETTING FINANCIAL ADVICE

The first step for the Stewarts was to bring Patrick onboard. His job would be to guide them through the maze of small business financing. In the Chapter 9, we stressed the importance of making a small business guru or an **advisory board** part of your risk management strategy. Your business guru could be anyone from a banker to a real estate broker to a knowledgeable retired person. To help you with the financial section of your business plan—and perhaps with the formulation of your personal financial vision as well—you will need to find advisors with expertise

ADVISORY BOARD

A group of individuals with expertise in various areas who provide advice but are not normally associated with the day-to-day operations of your business

Assemble a team of financial advisors

Use your networking skills to find people who can assist you in managing your financial affairs. Record the name of each person, along with other relevant information, in a chart like the one shown in Table 10.1.

Consider making one of your chosen financial advisors part of your **advisory board**. In many cases, this person will be your financial mentor. Don't be afraid to ask your mentor, or other financial advisors, to review your personal financial plan. This will help keep you grounded in the financial realities of your business.

in a wide range of financial matters (forecasting, taxes, retirement planning, bookkeeping, etc.). Action Step 46 and Table 10.1 will assist you with the task of assembling an advisory financial team. Good advice in finding a financial advisor can be found by linking onto the Financial Planners Standards Council, "Finding a Planner" link (http://www.cfp-ca.org/public/public_ouradvertising.asp#).

ESTIMATING YOUR START-UP COSTS

In small business, you don't just rent a location, throw open the doors, and begin to show a profit. The reality is, it takes time and planning for a start-up to make money. In fact, you're likely to discover that you need a good deal more start-up capital than you ever expected.

To find out how much start-up money you'll need, you will have to complete an application of funds table. You're going to have to estimate all your expenses you pay before starting your business. Then you will have to organize this information into an application of funds table. To begin, we suggest that you divide your **application of funds**, or start-up expenses, into four categories:

1. **general start-up costs**—including organizational costs, prepaid expenses, and inventory and office supplies;
2. **leasehold improvements**—carpeting mirrors, light fixtures, etc.;
3. **equipment**—tables, chairs, computer, etc.; and
4. **cash reserve fund**—cash on hand before you start your business (a pool of uncommitted cash).

Your cash reserve fund is your cash and bank account balances immediately before you start your business. There is no set formula for estimating how big this cash reserve should be. This will depend on your financial needs, tolerance for risk, and type of business, among other things. However, one rule of thumb for calculating cash reserve is to estimate your major operating disbursements for three months. These would be expenses such as rent, salaries, and utility bills, as shown in our cash flow in Table 10.6. You can refine your estimate for cash reserve using a method such as that shown in Table 10.2.

Table 10.3 provides further examples of the types of start-up expenses in the first three categories. Now we want you to complete Action Step 47.

APPLICATION OF FUNDS

Expenses you pay before starting your business

THE OPENING BALANCE SHEET

A **balance sheet** is a snapshot of the financial health of your business—what it owns and what it owes—at a given point in time. Not only is this key financial statement required by all bankers, you will need a balance sheet even if you decide to finance your own business. There are two common types of balance sheets: the opening balance sheet and the closing balance sheet. We will discuss the closing balance sheet later in the chapter. Here we focus on the opening balance sheet.

BALANCE SHEET

A financial snapshot of what the business owns and what it owes at a given point in time

An opening balance sheet is a snapshot of the financial position of your business in the period immediately before you open your doors. Table 10.4 provides an example of a typical opening balance sheet. The upper section of the balance sheet shows **assets**—the dollar value of what the business owns (equipment or inventory, for example). The lower section shows what the business owes, in the form of liabilities and equity. **Liabilities** are the dollar value of what the business owes to parties other than the owner. **Equity** is the dollar value of what the business owes the owner. Sometimes a balance sheet is arranged with assets shown on the left-hand side of the page and liabilities plus equity provided on the right.

ASSETS

The dollar value of what the business owns

LIABILITIES

The dollar value of what the business owes to parties other than the owner

EQUITY

The dollar value of what the business owes the owner

Table 10.1 List of Financial and Business Advisors

1. Mentor
2. Banker
3. Accountant/bookkeeper
4. Investment advisor/broker
5. Insurance agent(s)
6. Lawyer
7. Tax consultant
8. Personal/entrepreneurial coach
9. Realtor (if you have a business for a high potential for multiple locations)
10. Business broker (if buying a business, this option should be considered)
11. Franchise consultant/broker (if considering a franchise)

For each type of advisor, you should include contact information such as the individual's name, address, telephone number, and e-mail address.

ACTION STEP 47

Estimate your start-up costs

Now that you've got your business well in mind, take a few minutes to brainstorm a list of items you'll need to complete Table 10.2— your cash reserve fund. Then move on to Table 10.3 and begin listing and costing all your general start-up items, leasehold improvements, and equipment needs. Helpful worksheets can be found on the book's support Web site.

Don't rush this Action Step. Getting accurate numbers is critical to the survival of your business. Keep trying to uncover potential surprises and, if necessary, consult with vendors, suppliers, and other entrepreneurs. Write down your estimates in your 24/7 Adventure Notebook.

Table 10.2 Estimating Cash Reserve (Cash and Bank Account Balances at Start-up)

Item	Your estimate or monthly expenses based on sales of: $ _____ Column 1 ($)	Your estimate of how much cash you need to start your business. (see Column 3). Column 2 ($)	What to put in Column 2 (These figures are typical for one kind of business. You will have to decide how many months to allow for your business.) Column 3 ($)
Salary of owner-manager			2 × column 1
All other salaries and wages			3 × column 1
Rent			3 × column 1
Advertising			2 × column 1
Auto/truck/delivery expenses			3 × column 1
Supplies			3 × column 1
Phone/fax/Internet			3 × column 1
Other utilities (heat/electricity)			3 × column 1
Insurance			2 × column 1
Business taxes			2 × column 1
Bank payments			3 × column 1
Maintenance			3 × column 1
Legal/other professional fees			2 × column 1
Miscellaneous/unexpected expenses			2 × column 1
Total cash required to cover start-up operations—your cash reserve funds			Add rows 1–14. This amount will be recorded in the current assets of your opening balance sheet (see Table 10.4)

Why does a balance sheet balance? The answer is quite simple. By definition,

Assets (what the business owns) = **Liabilities** (what the business owes others) + **Equity** (what the business owes the owner)

Now let's examine each of these balance sheet components more closely.

ASSETS—WHAT THE BUSINESS OWNS

Assets are generally divided into three major categories: current assets, fixed assets, and other assets.

Current Assets

CURRENT ASSETS

Assets or holdings of a business that can be converted into cash or consumed in the production of income in a short period of time (usually one year)

Current assets are assets or holdings of a business that can be converted into cash or consumed in the production of income in a short period of time. Under accounting rules, the period of time is almost always within one year. Current assets are recorded in order of liquidity. As Table 10.4 shows, they include the following.

- **Cash.** This is your cash reserve from your application of funds table (Table 10.3). It is the cash the business has available in the business account or on hand immediately before you start your business. This definition of cash could also include marketable securities, such as Canada Savings Bonds.
- **Accounts receivable.** This is the total amount of money owed to the business by its customers who have purchased goods and services on credit. On an opening balance sheet, the dollar value of accounts receivable would normally be zero, because you have yet to start your business.
- **Inventory/office supplies.** Inventory is recorded as the dollar value of all the physical items you have for sale in the course of doing business or as the dollar value of the items you use in the course of making your product. Office supplies are items such as paper, pencils, and computer supplies. They are things you will use up over the current (one-year) period in the course of selling your products or services. Depending on your type of business, you might want to categorize your inventory and supplies separately. If you have difficulty deciding if an item is a piece of equipment or an inventory/supply item, think of the former as lasting more than a year (and thus retaining some sort of value) and inventory/office supplies as lasting one year or less (and thus having no appreciable value after that point).
- **Prepaid expenses.** Before you open your business, you'll likely have to prepay your insurance and your first month's rent. Prepaid expenses are classified as current assets because they are considered as being consumed in the production of income. Some banks do not classify prepaid expenses as current assets, however. Obviously, it would be difficult for them to "cash in" your prepaid insurance if your business were to fail.
- **Other current assets.** This category includes any remaining current assets you might have that can be translated into cash within a year. This might include, for example, a note payable or a security you don't want to cash in just yet.

Fixed Assets

FIXED ASSETS

Longer term (more than one year) holdings or assets of a business that are used to earn revenue or produce products or services

Fixed assets are the longer term (more than one year) holdings of a business that are used to earn revenue or produce products or services. Fixed assets are not for sale in the normal course of doing business. As Table 10.4 shows, fixed assets include such items as

- equipment,
- furniture and fixtures,

Table 10.3 Application of Funds

1. General Start-up Costs	Subtotal	Total
• Organizational Costs		
— Legal		
— Accounting		
— Government registration		
— Franchise fees	$_____	
• Prepaid Expenses		
— Insurance		
— Licences and permits		
— First and last months' rent		
— Security deposits		
— Utility deposits		
— Opening advertising and promotion	$_____	
• Opening Inventory		
— Total inventory on hand in order to do business the first day	$_____	
• Office Supplies		
— Office supplies on hand to do business the first day	$_____	
Total General Start-up		$_____
2. Leasehold Improvements		
— Carpeting		
— Mirrors, light fixtures		
— Electrical, plumbing		
— Signage		
— Washrooms		
— Air conditioning		
— Wallpaper and painting		
Total Leasehold and Improvements		$_____
3. Equipment Costs		
— Tables, chairs, desk, work benches		
— Filing cabinets		
— Storage cabinets		
— Cell phone		
— Computer		
— Copier		
— Fax machine		
— Auto		
Total Equipment Costs		$_____
4. Cash Reserve Fund		
— Total cash on hand immediately before the business opens. This estimate must be justified (see, for example, Table 10.2).		$_____
Total Application of Funds		$_____

- leasehold improvements,
- land and buildings, and
- autos and trucks.

Other Assets

These are intangible assets that cannot be assigned a fixed value. Items in this category include franchise fees; organizational fees, such as government registrations; consultant fees; and pre–start-up legal and accounting fees.

LIABILITIES—WHAT THE BUSINESS OWES OTHERS

Liabilities are normally divided into two major categories: current liabilities and long-term liabilities. In some cases, the liability section of the balance sheet includes a category called "other long-term debt."

Current Liabilities

CURRENT LIABILITIES

Outstanding debts or obligations that are expected to come due within one year of the date of the balance sheet

Current liabilities are outstanding debts or obligations that are expected to come due within one year of the date of the balance sheet. They include

- **accounts payable**—total money that the business owes to suppliers;
- **contracts or notes payable**—total money owed within the next year on such items as equipment, leasehold improvements, or a personal loan;
- **line of credit**—if you have dipped into it;
- **demand loan**—a loan that is due on demand and thus is recorded as owing within the next 12 months; and
- **long-term loans**—current portion.

Let's say that you have negotiated with your bank manager a long-term loan of $35,000. Let's also assume that you have agreed to repay the loan by paying $5,000 per year. Part of this yearly payment—let's say $3,000 for the purposes of this example—will go to repay the amount you borrowed—that is, the $35,000. This is called the principal portion of a loan. The other part of your loan repayment, in this case $2,000, will be used to pay interest charges. The current portion of your long-term debt is the principal payment on your loan for the 12 months following the date of your opening balance sheet. This is the amount due on your long-term debt within the next year. Remember, the current portion *does not* include your interest payments.

Long-Term Liabilities

LONG-TERM LIABILITIES (DEFERRED LIABILITIES)

Debts or financial obligations that are due after one year

Long-Term liabilities (deferred liabilities) are debts or financial obligations that are due after one year. They include bank loans, loans to shareholders (if you are incorporated), and long-term liens or notes payable. They should not be confused with the current portion of the long-term debt. In the previous example of the $35,000 loan, we calculated the current principal portion (due over the next year) of this long-term loan to be $3,000. If we subtract the current portion ($3,000) from the total loan ($35,000), we arrive at a long-term portion of $32,000. This is the amount due after the first year.

During negotiations for a long-term loan, a financial institution might ask you to sign a demand note that gives the lender permission to "demand on notice" the full amount of your loan. Technically, a demand note should be recorded as short-term loan (current liability), because your lender can ask you to pay the full amount of the loan at any time. Thus, if our $35,000 loan were a demand loan, it would be recorded as a current liability.

Table 10.4 Opening Balance Sheet (Date of Opening _____)

ASSETS			
Current assets	$	$	$
1. Cash and marketable securities			
2. Accounts receivable			
3. Inventory/office supplies			
4. Prepaid expenses			
5. Other current assets			
6. **Total current assets**			
Fixed assets			
7. Equipment/furniture/fixtures			
8. Leasehold improvements			
9. Land/buildings			
10. Auto/truck			
11. Other fixed assets			
12. **Total fixed assets**			
Other assets			
13. Organizational fees (legal, accounting, etc.)			
14. **Total other assets**			
15. **(6 + 12 + 14) TOTAL ASSETS**			
LIABILITIES			
Current liabilities (due within the next 12 months)			
16. Long-term loans (current portion)			
17. Short-term loans			
18. Accounts payable			
19. Other current liabilities			
20. **Total current liabilities**			
Long-term liabilities			
21. Long-term loans (minus current portion)			
22. Mortgages and liens payable			
23. Loans from shareholders (if applicable)			
24. Other long-term debt obligations			
25. **Total long-term liabilities**			
26. **(20 + 25) TOTAL LIABILITIES**			
EQUITY			
27. Cash—Owner's capital (if a proprietorship or partnership)—shares outstanding (if a corporation)			
28. General start-up (organizational costs, etc.)			
29. Equipment/material/labour (provide details)			
30. **TOTAL EQUITY**			
31. **(26 + 30) TOTAL LIABILITIES AND EQUITY**			

Other Long-Term Debt

This optional category includes any other long-term obligations, such as an equipment loan, a note payable, or a long-term loan to a relative.

Once you get a handle on yearly revenue estimates—and this might take some time—you're going to have to think about your monthly revenue. It is not sufficient to simply divide by 12 and forecast the same level of sales in each month; rather, you must base the monthly forecast on some sort of monthly growth factor and especially the seasonal nature of the business. Most businesses experience peaks and valleys. For example, if you're in the ice cream business, sales will "heat" up in the summer and drop off in the fall. The same is true of hardware (especially home improvement supplies) and auto parts, when everyone is getting the travel bug. If you run a ski shop, you might have to order your skis at a summer trade show, pay for them when they arrive in September, and wait until late February to make the final sale. For example, the owners of DISCovery Books and Magazines (see Table 10.6) knew from their market research that 50 percent of their sales would be made during the September-to-December period. Their understanding of the seasonality of their industry helped them determine how much inventory they would need to support sales over the peak period. (Service Sector Statistics at http://www.census.gov/mrts/www/data/html/nsal03.html provides monthly sales for a number of different types of businesses. It also provides a very good indicator, albeit for U.S. businesses, of seasonal trends for various industries.)

STEP 3: FORECASTING RECEIPTS

Receipts from Operations or Sales (Lines 5 and 6)

In your cash flow projection, you're going to have to figure out when you will actually collect your money. Cash receipts from the operations of your business can come from either cash sales (line 5) or receivables collected (line 6), if you offer credit. For example, if you're in the bed-and-breakfast business, you probably collect your money ahead of time (i.e., when the customer books the accommodation). A retailer normally gets paid when the product is sold. DISCovery Books and Magazines is a retail business whose monthly sales forecast (line 1) is the same as the revenue forecast (line 5). Other businesses must wait to be paid. They offer credit. There is a time delay between when the sale is made and when the actual cash is collected. For example, in a service trade, you might complete your work and bill for your service in July but not be paid for 30, 60, or even 90 days. On the cash flow, you would record this as a sale for July (lines 1 and 3). If you expect to be paid for this sale 30 days later (in August), then you would record it as cash in, receivables collected for August (line 6). Should your business fall into this category, you must have a policy in place for dealing with late payments; it will help you avoid a situation in which you are required to pay bills when there is no cash coming in. Box 10.2 shows the typical payment and collection time lines for an electrical service company.

Other Cash in Receipts

When you are forecasting any cash that comes into the business, you will also have to think about any receipts (or cash in) from loans (line 7), investments (line 8), or the sale of fixed assets (line 9). Note that the initial investments or receipts of term loans (recorded in the opening balance sheet) will appear in the opening balance column. Any subsequent loan, investment, or asset sale will be recorded in the month it is received. For example, If DISCovery Books and Magazines planned on selling some of its fixed assets in February, then the expected cash received would be recorded on line 9 for February.

STEP 4: FORECASTING DISBURSEMENTS

Variable Disbursements

You must forecast your variable costs or purchases on a monthly basis (line 15). You will start with a certain amount of inventory, but as you begin to sell your product, you will have to replace that inventory. Purchases of supplies and material are called variable costs, because they depend on the expected sales. This involves pre-planning your purchases of inventory. Sometimes you simply replace the inventory you have during the previous month. Sometimes you will plan to build up your inventory prior to busy sales periods. Once this forecast has been made, forecast your cash disbursements in this area. If you pay cash for these purchases, the disbursement is equal to the purchase. If you have credit terms from the suppliers, then the purchase in one month becomes a disbursement from accounts payable the following month. (For example, a purchase in January becomes a disbursement in February.)[3]

Fixed Disbursements

You must project your fixed disbursements on a monthly basis. Fixed disbursements are called fixed because they don't change as sales go up or down. For example, your rent payments do not normally vary according to your sales. For DISCovery Books and Magazines, these fixed expenses are listed in lines 16 to 31. Normally, these expenses are projected evenly throughout the year. Note, for example, that rent for DISCovery Books and Magazines is fixed at $1,200 per month (line 21). In some cases, expenses such as advertising might change if the owner sees a need to increase (decrease) advertising expenses for certain months. For example, in the case of DISCovery Books and Magazines, the advertising budget (line 16) was increased in anticipation of the December increase in sales. In forecasting these expenses there are a few key points you should be aware of.

Loan Payments (Lines 18 and 27)

The principal payments (line 27) and interest payments (line 18) from any loan must be recorded as separate entries on the cash flow. Suppose, for example, that you borrow $5,000 for one year and pay an interest rate of, say, 6 percent. The total cost of the loan will be $5,164. Your total monthly loan payments ($430) will be blended to include both the payments on the principal you borrowed ($5,000) and the interest ($164). Your cash flow must show your monthly interest payments ($164 ÷ 12) and principal payments ($5,000 ÷ 12) separately. How do you separate principal and interest payments on a loan? The best way is to go to a loan calculator on the Internet (for example, Bankrate.ca, http://www.bankrate.com/can/popcalc2.asp, or CIBC loan calculator, http://www.cibc.com/ca/loans/personal-loan.html). In addition, there are financial tables that provide this information.

Many entrepreneurs want to pay off their loans quickly to save on the interest charges. Here, the cash flow is an important determinant of how much a business can afford to pay off. For example, suppose that the owners of DISCovery wanted to pay off their $35,000 loan (line 11) in one year. Suppose, as well, the interest rate was 6 percent. The total cost of the loan, including principal and interest, would be about $36,150. DISCovery's original loan payments were $6,600 (line 18 + line 27). Payment for this new loan arrangement would increase cash disbursements by about $29,550 ($36,150 – $6,600). It would thus wipe out its original positive cash balance of $27,395. DISCovery Books and Magazines could find itself in a serious cash flow crunch. This shows how your cash flow can tell you how much your business can afford to pay off in loans each month.

Table 10.6 Monthly Cash Flow—DISCovery Books and Magazines Inc.

	Opening Balance	6% July	7% August	9% September	10% October	12% November	19% December	6.5% January	4.5% February	5% March	5% April	8% May	8% June	Total
Step 1														
Step 2														
1. SALES		9,000	10,500	13,500	15,000	18,000	28,500	9,750	6,750	7,500	7,500	12,000	12,000	150,000
2. —														
3. TOTAL SALES		9,000	10,500	13,500	15,000	18,000	28,500	9,750	6,750	7,500	7,500	12,000	12,000	150,000
Step 3														
Receipts														
4. Cash In														
5. —Cash Sales		9,000	10,500	13,500	15,000	18,000	28,500	9,750	6,750	7,500	7,500	12,000	12,000	150,000
6. —Receivables Collected														
7. —Loan Proceeds														
8. —Personal Investment														
9. —Sale of Fixed Assets														
10. —Equity	80,000													80,000
11. —Loans	35,000													35,000
12. —														
13. Total Cash In (lines 5 through 12)	115,000	9,000	10,500	13,500	15,000	18,000	28,500	9,750	6,750	7,500	7,500	12,000	12,000	265,000
Step 4														
Disbursements														
14. Cash Out														
15. —Purchases		5,255	9,880	9,305	8,030	8,720	6,575	5,080	3,760	3,045	6,545	7,440	8,420	82,055
16. —Advertising		200	200	200	200	400	400	100	100	200	100	100	200	2,400
17. —Auto and Truck														
18. —Bank Charges and Interest		300	300	300	300	300	300	300	300	300	300	300	300	3,600
19. —Insurance		450												450
20. —Professional Fees														
21. —Rent		1,200	1,200	1,200	1,200	1,200	1,200	1,200	1,200	1,200	1,200	1,200	1,200	14,400

	Opening Balance	July	August	September	October	November	December	January	February	March	April	May	June	Total
		6%	7%	9%	10%	12%	19%	6.5%	4.5%	5%	5%	8%	8%	
22. —Business Taxes and Licences														
23. —Telephone		50	50	50	50	50	50	50	50	50	50	50	50	600
24. —Utilities (Heat, Light, Water)		150	150	150	150	150	150	150	150	150	150	150	150	1,800
25. —Wages—Employees														
26. —Principal Draw or Management Salaries		1,600	1,600	1,600	1,600	1,600	1,600	1,600	1,600	1,600	1,600	1,600	1,600	19,200
27. —Term Debt (Principal Portion Only)		250	250	250	250	250	250	250	250	250	250	250	250	3,000
28. —Purchase of Fixed Assets (during operating period)														
29. —Taxes														
30. —Materials and Supplies (1%)		100	100	100	100	100	100	100	100	100	100	100	1,200	
31. —Miscellaneous (3%)		325	325	325	325	325	325	325	325	325	325	325	3,900	
32. —Start-up (Application of funds excluding cash reserve)	105,000												62,790	44,210
33. —														
34. Total Cash Out (lines 15 through 33)	105,000	9,880	14,055	13,480	12,205	13,095	10,950	9,155	7,835	7,220	10,620	11,515	12,595	237,605

Step 5

Summary

	Opening Balance	July	August	September	October	November	December	January	February	March	April	May	June	Total
35. Total Cash In (line 13)	115,000	9,000	10,500	13,500	15,000	18,000	28,500	9,750	6,750	7,500	7,500	12,000	12,000	265,000
36. Plus: Cash Forward (Prev. Mon.—line 39)	10,000	10,000	9,120	5,565	15,585	8,380	13,285	30,835	31,430	30,345	30,625	27,505	27,990	
37. Equals: Total Cash Available	115,000	19,000	19,620	19,065	20,585	26,380	41,785	40,585	38,180	37,845	38,125	39,505	39,990	265,000
38. Less: Total Cash Out (line 34)	105,000	9,880	14,055	13,480	12,205	13,095	10,950	9,155	7,835	7,220	10,620	11,515	12,595	237,605
39. Equals: Closing Bank Balance	10,000	9,120	5,565	15,585	8,380	13,285	30,835	31,430	30,345	30,625	27,505	27,990	27,395	27,395

Draft a projected cash flow

Begin projecting your cash across the first year of your business. If you don't have an electronic spreadsheet program such as Microsoft Excel, you can download the cash flow budget worksheets from either of the two sites provided in Box 10.3. If you don't have access to a computer, use the blank cash flow worksheet provided in Table 10.7. Alternatively, major banks and most large accounting firms can supply you with worksheets for preparing your cash flow.

1. Calculate the cash you'll start the year with. In the case of DISCovery Books and Magazines, this was $10,000 (see Table 10.6, line 39).

2. For each month, enter the amount of cash you'll receive from sales or accounts receivable.

3. Enter any loans in the month you receive the cash from the lender.

4. Total the above, which will give you the cash available for each month.

5. Now list all disbursements (cash going out). Spread these out, too.

6. Then subtract disbursements from cash available, which gives you a monthly cash flow.

7. Examine your work. Have you explored the quirks of seasonality? Have you discovered the minimum and maximum time lags between when you make a sale and when the business gets paid in cash for the sale? Does the picture look accurate? Have you checked with an expert?

If your cash flow picture looks good, test your money management skills by dropping in a couple of "what ifs." What surprise expenses could throw a monkey wrench into your new business?

In Chapter 15, Action Step 72, we will ask you to refine these numbers.

Purchases of Fixed Assets (Line 28)

In your monthly cash flow, you record only the cash outlays for those fixed assets you plan to buy throughout the year. If you purchase fixed assets to start your business, these purchases will already be accounted for in your opening balance column, line 32. Therefore, if DISCovery Books and Magazines planned to purchase more shelving in November, it would record a cash disbursement (line 28) only when it paid the invoice for this planned expense.

Principal Draw or Management Salaries (Lines 25 and 26)

If the business is not incorporated, the cash flow will record any money transferred to the owner operator (wages to owner) as a principal draw. On the income statement, these amounts will not show up as wages because, technically, they are not wages. They will be recorded as a reduction in equity on the ending or year-end balance sheet. If the company is incorporated, the owner can receive a wage, which is normally recorded as a management salary on the cash flow and ending balance sheet.

Dividends or Shareholder Loans

These should be recorded separately when the cash is withdrawn or injected.

Depreciation

Depreciation is not a cash item and as such is not recorded in a cash flow.

STEP 5: SUMMARY OF CASH FLOW (LINES 35 TO 39)

This is the final step in creating your cash flow. It tells you how much cash you have available at the end of each month (line 39). For example, DISCovery's opening balance was $10,000 (line 39). This is the cash available at the beginning of July for operations during this month (line 36). During July, its receipts (or cash in) were projected to be $9,000 (line 35). Thus, the total cash available for July was $19,000 (Line 37). DISCovery's cash expenses (disbursements) in July were projected to be $9,880. We now subtract these July disbursements (line 38) from the cash available (line 37) to find out how much cash is available at the end of July, as shown in line 39 ($9,120). The owners of DISCovery make these summary calculations for each month. At the end of the year, they have a positive cash position of $27,395. DISCovery started out with $10,000 and ended up with $27,395. This means that the business generated $17,395 in cash over the period, so this company had a so-called positive cash flow over the period.

Please Note. You should have no negative numbers for line 39. If you do, it means that you have run out of cash—and this is not good. A negative cash flow means that you will be unable to pay your bills. If you do have a projected negative cash position, you are going to have to go back and rethink your projections and plans. You can't run a business without cash. When there is cash shortfall, it will normally require new equity, debt, or a bank line of credit.

Now it's your turn. Action Step 48 leads you through the mechanics of a monthly cash flow projection. Box 10.4 provides you with a reminder on some important points to consider. After you have completed Action Step 48, show the results to an expert. Does the picture look accurate? Does your business have a positive cash balance or a negative one? It's better to know the truth now, while you're working on paper. Paper truth is a lot easier on the pocketbook than real truth.

Table 10.7 Projected Cash Flow Statement—Worksheet

STEP 1						Month							Total
	1	2	3	4	5	6	7	8	9	10	11	12	
Opening Balance													
STEP 2													
1. Sales													
2.													
3. Total sales													
STEP 3: Receipts													
4. Cash in													
5. Cash sales													
6. Receivables collected													
7. Loan proceeds													
8. Personal investment													
9. Sales of assets													
10. Equity													
11. Loans													
12.													
13. Total cash in (lines 5 through 12)													
STEP 4: Disbursements													
14. Cash out													
15. Purchases													
16. Advertising/promotion													
17. Auto and truck													
18. Bank charges and interest													
19. Insurance													
20. Professional fees													
21. Rent													
22. Taxes and licences													
23. Telephone													
24. Utilities (heat/light/water)													
25. Wages: employees													
26. Principal draw or management salaries													
27. Term debt (principal portion only)													
28. Fixed assets purchase													
29. Taxes													
30. Materials and supplies													
31. Miscellaneous													
32. Start-up application of funds (excluding cash reserve)													
33.													
34. Total cash out (lines 15–33)													

	Month												Total
Opening Balance	1	2	3	4	5	6	7	8	9	10	11	12	
STEP 5: Summary													
35. Total cash in (line 13)													
36. Plus: cash forward (previous month, line 39)													
37. Equals: total cash available													
38. Less: Total cash out (line 34)													
39. Equals: Closing bank balance													

Box 10.2 Electric Works—Payment and Collection Time Lines

Payments

Wages: weekly
CPP deductions: monthly
Income tax payments: quarterly
Raw materials: 30 days
Electricity inspector: 10 days

Collections (even though the terms might be net 30 days)

Three or five contractors: 45 days
One contractor: 60–90 days
One contractor: 90–120 days

Box 10.3 Bookmark This

Financial Planning Sites

- **E-Module 3, Your Financial Plan—A Step-by-Step Guide to Financing Your Start-up Business:** Detailed, step-by-step instructions for completing a financial plan to open and operate a business. The site includes a discussion of the importance of keeping financial records, financial templates, and worksheets to help you create and evaluate five basic financial statements:
  - sources and application of funds,
  - opening balance sheet,
  - cash flow,
  - income statement, and
  - ending balance sheet.
- **Business Planning and Financial Forecasting: A Start-up Guide:** http://www.sbed.gov.bc.ca/ReportsPublications/BUSINESS_PLANNING.pdf—This online financial resource provides detailed instructions on how to create your own financial plan. It is designed for the start-up business and contains a template with seven MS/Excel worksheets. This information is then assembled into the required financial statements. The model is interactive. Information can be changed, and the results of the change are immediately calculated for each of the financial statements. This site will guide you through a reasonable first draft of your financials. However, you will have to make some adjustments for your particular situation.

- **Business Owner's Toolkit (CCH):** http://www.toolkit.cch.com/tools/tools.asp—Contains links to a downloadable balance sheet template, a cash flow budget worksheet, and an income statement template. The worksheets are easy to use and can be modified to suit your needs.
- **Performance Plus** (Industry Canada): http://strategis.ic.gc.ca/epic/internet/inpp-pp.nsf/en/Home—Use this online performance-benchmarking tool to find out where your business stands as compared to a relevant industry average.
- **Attacking Business Decision Problems with Break-Even Analysis:** http://www.cbsc.org/servlet/ContentServer?pagename=CBSC_SK%2Fdisplay&lang=en&cid=1083346949372&c=GuideFactSheet—This article on the Business Infosource Web site illustrates ways in which break-even analyses can be applied to sales, profits, and costs.
- **Zacks:** http://www.zacks.com—This is primarily an American Web site. However, it has been recommended to us as a site providing valuable industry benchmarks and North American competitor financial information.

Box 10.4 Cash Flow—Important Points to Consider

The three most important ingredients in managing and operating a business? CA$H, CA$H, and more CA$H. And yet more than 80 percent of small businesses do not use a cash flow forecast.

- Two factors ensure that you have sufficient cash to operate comfortably:
    1. a 12-month forecast of sales and expenses and
    2. a workable and realistic policy stating when you pay your bills and when you can turn sales into cash.
- Cash flow includes principal, bank payments, and interest—separately.
- Cash flow includes only cash in and cash out, not depreciation.
- Your year-end cash flow provides many of the estimates you'll need for your projected income statement.
- Before offering credit, do a cash flow.

PRO FORMA INCOME STATEMENT

A **pro forma (or projected) income statement** is an itemized statement of sales (or revenues) and corresponding expenses. Like cash flow, it is an indicator of the financial health of your business. The major difference is that the income statement is not about cash; for example, as we explain below, an income statement records a sale even if you have not yet received the money. Normally an income statement is for a one-year period (sometimes on a quarterly basis). In a business plan, you might have to provide projected income statements for the first five years, depending on the size and complexity of your business.

For those of you who are not familiar with an income statement, we have constructed a typical projected year-end income statement for DISCovery Books and Magazines Inc. (see Table 10.8). Action Step 49 will help you project your own income statement. The major elements of an income statement are discussed next.

PRO FORMA (OR PROJECTED) INCOME STATEMENT

An itemized statement of sales (or revenues) and corresponding expenses

SALES

On the income statement, all revenues (sales) are recorded, even though you might not yet have received the actual cash. For example, in the case of DISCovery Books and Magazines Inc. (Table 10.8), the yearly sales or revenue is $150,000. This figure

ACTION STEP 49

Draft a projected income statement—a moving picture of your business

You can download income statement worksheets from any of the "Business Planning Tools" sites provided in see Box 10.3. If you don't have access to a computer, use the blank income statement worksheet provided in Table 10.9 on page 258. Also, all major banks and most major accounting firms can supply you with worksheets for preparing your income statement.

Generate the numbers for the projected period as follows:

1. Using sales data from your cash flow, record the sales forecast for the year.
2. Calculate your cost of goods sold; subtract that from sales, and you have gross profit.
3. Add up all expenses, and subtract those from gross profit. That gives you the net before taxes.
4. Subtract taxes. (Governments will tax you on paper profit, so you have to build this figure in.)

The figure at the bottom is net profit after taxes for the year.

In Chapter 15, Action Step 73, we will ask you to refine these numbers.

Table 10.8 Pro Forma Income Statement—DISCovery Books and Magazines Inc.

Sales (revenue)	$150,000
Cost of goods sold	
Opening inventory	50,000
(plus) purchases	82,055
Subtotal	132,055
(minus) closing inventory	42,055
(equals) cost of materials	90,000
Total cost of goods sold	90,000
Gross profit	60,000
Operating expenses	
Rent	14,400
Utilities	1,800
Salaries—Employees	
Salaries—Principal draw (manager's salary)[1]	19,200
Advertising	2,400
Office supplies	1,200
Insurance	450
Maintenance and cleaning	
Legal and accounting	
Delivery expense	
Licences	
Boxes, paper, etc.	
Telephone	600
Depreciation	4,000
Miscellaneous	3,900
Total operating expenses	47,950
Other expenses	
Interest	3,600
Total: Other expenses	3,600
Total expenses	51,550
Net profit (loss) (pre-tax)[2]	8,450

[1] As we have said in the text, if a business is incorporated, then owner(s) salary will be recorded on the income statement. However, if this is a sole proprietorship then the owner's salary will not be recorded on the income statement. In the case of a sole proprietorship, the owner's salary will be recorded as an owners draw on the ending balance sheet.

[2] If DISCovery Books and Magazines were not incorporated, you would use the term *net income* rather than *profit*. The amount of this net income would then be recorded on the owners personal tax form (T1) as self-employed income.

is the same as the yearly cash sales figure in the cash flow statement (Table 10.6, line 5), for the simple reason that DISCovery is a cash business—when it sells a book, it gets the money right away. However, many businesses operate differently. As we noted in our discussion of cash flow, many businesses, such as those in the service trades, can make a sale and not be paid until at least 30 days later.

COST OF GOODS SOLD (CGS)

Cost of goods sold is the cost of materials or the variable costs (those costs that depend on sales) that you use up over a specified period ($90,000, in the case of DISCovery Books and Magazines Inc.). CGS is calculated as follows:

- Take the value of your opening inventory/office supplies from your opening balance sheet.
- Add the value of your purchases over the income statement period.
- Subtract the value of your closing inventory/office supplies. This will be the value of the inventory/office supplies from your closing inventory (usually after one year). If you were actually running a business, you would normally get this number by doing a physical inventory.

In the case the case of DISCovery, its cost of good sold was calculated as follows: CGS ($90,000) = opening inventory ($50,000) + purchases ($82,055) – closing inventory ($42,055).

GROSS PROFIT

Gross profit is your total sales minus your cost of goods sold. In the retail business, some refer to this as the contributions margin. As Table 10.8 shows, DISCovery's gross profit is $60,000 ($150,000 – $90,000).

OPERATING EXPENSES

These are the expenses you incur in the day-to-day operations of your business. Many of these items can be taken from the total disbursements column of your cash flow. These costs do not normally depend on the sales and as such are sometimes called fixed costs. For example, the yearly rent recorded in DISCovery's income statement (Table 10.8) is $14,400, the same number that appears in the company's cash flow statement (see Table 10.6, line 21). Rent is a so-called fixed cost, because you have to pay rent irrespective of your level of sales. When calculating your operating expenses, there are some important considerations to include.

- **Expenses**. Expenses are recorded in the income statement, even though you might not have paid for them yet. For example, if DISCovery had not paid for its rent in the past month, the total rent disbursements in the cash flow would have been reduced by $1,200, to $13,200. On the income statement, however, the rent costs would have remained unchanged at $14,400.
- **Principal payments and interest**. Principal payments on a bank loan are not an operating expense and thus are not recorded as an expense in the income statement. Interest payments on a loan are recorded in the income statement as an interest expense ($3,600 in the case of DISCovery). Please note that interest on a loan is not recorded as an operating expense.
- **Owner's draw**. If you are not incorporated and you pay yourself a salary, you should record this expense as an owner's draw in the closing balance sheet. You do not record this disbursement on your income statement. However, if your business is incorporated and you pay yourself a wage, you should record this expense as a management salary in your income statement.

OTHER EXPENSES

These are expenses to the business that do not relate to the operations. In the case of DISCovery, its other expense would be interest ($3,600) on its bank loan. This is because interest on a bank loan has nothing to with the operations costs of the business.

Table 10.9 Projected Income Statement (Period Ending _____)

Sales (revenue)			_____
Cost of goods sold			
Opening inventory	_____		
(plus) purchases	_____		
Subtotal		_____	
(minus) closing inventory	_____		
(equals) cost of materials	_____		
Total cost of goods sold		_____	
Gross profit			_____
Operating expenses			_____
Rent	_____		
Utilities	_____		
Salaries—employees	_____		
Salaries—principal draw (manager's salary)	_____		
Advertising	_____		
Office supplies	_____		
Insurance	_____		
Maintenance and cleaning	_____		
Legal and accounting	_____		
Delivery expense	_____		
Licences	_____		
Boxes, paper, etc.	_____		
Telephone	_____		
Depreciation	_____		
Miscellaneous	_____		
Total operating expenses			_____
Other expenses	_____		
Interest	_____		
Total: Other expenses			_____
Total expenses			_____
Net profit (loss) (pre-tax)			

NET PROFIT (BEFORE TAXES)

Net profit before taxes is defined as gross profit minus total operating and other expenses. In the case of DISCovery, its net profit is

$$\$ 60,000 - 51,550 = \$8,450$$

PROFIT IS NOT CASH

A quick glance at DISCovery Books and Magazines's monthly cash flow (Table 10.6) and income statement (Table 10.8) makes it obvious that profit and cash are not the same thing. DISCovery's profit was $8,450, but its cash increase was $17,395 ($27,395 − $10,000). The cash increase might have given the book-store's owners the illusion that they were doing better than they actually were. However, their cash flow did not reflect the fact that they were using up their equipment (depreciation). In addition, the cash flow did not take into account that DISCovery had a little more cash available because it used up some of its opening inventory and didn't replace it. (As the income statement shows, the opening inventory was $50,000, and the closing inventory $42,055.) By adjusting for changing inventory in the cost of goods sold entry, the income statement provides a dose of reality.

KEY INCOME STATEMENT RATIOS

Calculating income statement ratios will help you to determine how healthy your business is and how it compares to other businesses in your selected industry. You can learn more about your industry ratios at Industry Canada's *Performance Plus* (http://strategis.ic.gc.ca/epic/internet/inpp-pp.nsf/en/Home) site and your local resource centre, and check out the Dun & Bradstreet *Industry Norms and Key Business Ratios*, or you can contact your industry association directly. If you have the numbers for your business, you can calculate your income statement ratios using the online calculators provided in Box 10.5, page 267.

Four key income statement ratios are listed next.

GROSS PROFIT MARGIN

Gross profit margin equals gross profit (or contribution margin) divided by total sales. Sometimes, this ratio is multiplied by 100 to yield a percentage value. The higher this ratio or percentage is, the better. For example the DISCovery Bookstore (Table 10.8, p. 256) has a gross profit margin of $60,000/$150,000 × 100 = 40 percent. Is this good? It's hard to know unless we can compare it to industry averages. One source might be Industry Canada, *Performance Plus* (http://strategis.ic.gc.ca/epic/internet/inpp-pp.nsf/vwGeneratedInterE/Home). When we check out the financials for Book Stores and News Dealers (NAICS Number 45121), the gross profit margin for the industry as a whole (for 2002) was about 34 percent (incorporated businesses). But note that DISCovery had projected sales of $150,000. *Performance Plus* provides income statement data for businesses with different sales volumes. For businesses with average sales of $147,000 (lower half of all incorporated businesses), the gross profit margin is 40 percent, which is the same as DISCovery's ratio. DISCovery's gross profit margin is in line with industry averages—according to this one source.

What would happen if the gross profit margin were 45 percent? This would mean that DISCovery would be earning 5 percent more in gross profit for every dollar it sells. Its gross profit would now be $67,500 ($150,000 × .45), and its total profit would be increased by $7,500, from $8,450 to $15,950, so DISCovery—and all businesses—should always be looking at ways to improve the gross profit margin. DISCovery, for example, might want to try to reduce its cost of goods sold (through better buying). Another way might be to add or promote products of services with a higher gross profit margin. For example, if magazines had a 70 per-cent gross profit margin, then it would be in DISCovery's financial interest to pro-mote its magazine business. Or, how about having a little lounge that sells hot coffee and tea? Coffee and tea have a very high gross profit margin—as most restaurant owners know. DISCovery customers would be able to browse books and magazines while sipping a tasty cup of coffee or tea. DISCovery would not only improve its service but also raise its average gross profit margin and net profit.

GROSS PROFIT MARGIN (CONTRIBUTION MARGIN)

gross profit divided by total sales

PROFIT MARGIN

Profit margin equals net profit (before taxes) divided by total sales. In most cases, this ratio is multiplied by 100 to yield a percentage value. Again, the higher this ratio or percentage is, the better off is the business. In the case of DISCovery (Table 10.8), the profit margin would be 5.6 percent ([$8,450 ÷ $150,000] × 100). DISCovery produces $.056 (5.6 cents) in profit for every loonie of sales. The owners of this business would want to check this ratio out with the average profit margin for their particular industry. When we check out the *Performance Plus* financials for Bookstores and News Dealers (NAICS Number: 45121, for the year 2002), the profit margin for the industry as a whole was only about 1 percent. In addition, according to *Performance Plus*, incorporated businesses with average sales of about $150,000 showed a −5 percent profit margin. Bookstores with average sales of about $150,000 lost money. This means that DISCovery had better double-check all its operating costs and make sure they are right. According to *Performance Plus*, the industry is showing a loss. What would happen if DISCovery owners went to the bank to get a loan to start their business? If the bank knew that the average industry profit was negative, they would be very careful about providing any financing to the owners.

INVENTORY TURNOVER

If your inventory sits unsold on the shelf, you can't make money. You want to sell your stock on hand or inventory as quickly as possible. One indicator of how fast you are *turning over* or selling and replacing your inventory is called the inventory turnover ratio. **Inventory turnover** normally refers to the number of times each year a company turns over or replaces its inventory. The higher this ratio is, the better. There are two standard ways of calculating this ratio. The simplest method is

INVENTORY TURNOVER

The number of times each year a company turns over or replaces its inventory

$$\text{Inventory turnover} = \frac{\text{Cost of goods sold}}{\text{Average inventory*}}$$

*Note: Average inventory is usually calculated by taking inventory at the beginning of the year and adding inventory at the end of the year and then dividing by 2. If you know what the monthly inventory is, you would simply add the inventory for each month and divide by 12. If you know what your monthly turnover is, you would simply add the turnover rate for each month to get your yearly rate.

Let's return to the DISCovery example in Table 10.8, page 256.

Cost of sales = $90,000

$$\text{Average inventory} = \frac{\$50,000 + \$42,055}{2} = \$46,028$$

$$\text{Inventory turnover} = \frac{\$90,000}{\$46,028}$$
$$= 2$$

Of course, not all items in the bookstore will turn over at this rate. Magazines will turn over much more quickly than, say, history books, but on average, all the items in the store will turn over twice in a year.

Is this ratio of 2 efficient? Is DISCovery Bookstore turning over its inventory fast enough? Are too many of its books just "sitting on the shelf"? One common way to find out how well you are doing is to compare this with industry ratios. There are commercial data banks, such as Dun & Bradstreet, that can provide this information. As well, industry associations or suppliers might have the numbers. If we go to Industry Canada's *Performance Plus* for incorporated businesses (NAICS Number: 45121, Bookstores and News Dealers) we find that the inventory turnover ratio for the book selling industry is 4 (368/94), and about 3 (87.7/31.6) for bookstores with average yearly sales of $147,000 (lower half of all businesses). So it seems that DISCovery's turnover rate is a little low relative to industry standards.

We must be careful when comparing ratios, however. Not all industries have similar inventory turnover ratios. For example, according to *Performance Plus*, grocery stores (NAICS: 4451, incorporated businesses, 2002) have an inventory turnover ratio of 16 and jewellery stores (NAICS: 44831) have an inventory turnover of only about 2. This makes sense, as grocery stores have a lot of perishable items such as milk and bread, which cannot sit on the shelf very long. They must turn over quickly. On the other hand, jewellery stores might have to wait a while to sell some of their more expensive items. DISCovery should know the industry standards and always be on the lookout for ways to improve its inventory turnover ratio. What would happen, for example, if DISCovery were able to operate effectively with an inventory turnover of, say, 3? How much inventory would it have to keep on hand? Here is the answer:

$$\text{Inventory turnover} = \frac{\text{Cost of goods sold}}{\text{Average inventory at cost}}$$

$$\text{Average inventory} = \frac{\text{Cost of goods sold}}{\text{Inventory turnover}}$$

$$= \frac{\$90,000}{3}$$

$$= \$30,000$$

With a new, more efficient turnover of 3, DISCovery would be able to reduce its yearly average inventory on hand by $16,028 ($46,028 − $30,000 = $16,028). It would have $16,028 more cash. This extra cash can be invested or used to buy more products.

GROSS MARGIN RETURN ON INVENTORY INVESTMENT

If you are in the manufacturing or retail business, you can increase your turnover but still not make more profit. A high turnover does not necessarily lead to higher profits. You could be selling more of a particular product and not be making any profit because your profit margin is so low. The idea in retail and manufacturing is to find products that have both a high profit margin and a high turnover.

There is an income statement ratio that helps us determine which products have the best chance of making the most profit given the turnover and gross profit or contributions margin. It is called the **gross margin return on inventory investment (GMROI)**. It measures the gross margin earned on the invested inventory. This ratio takes into consideration both gross profit and inventory turnover and is calculated as follows:

$$\text{GMROI} = \text{Gross profit margin (\%)} \times \text{Sales-to-stock ratio}^*$$

$$^*\text{The sales-to-stock ratio} = \frac{\text{Total sales (revenue)}}{\text{Average cost of inventory}}$$

The main point here is that you should always be on the lookout for products that have a high GMROI. These are the products you will want to promote. If you are planning a business and want to check your GMROI, you are going to

GROSS MARGIN RETURN ON INVENTORY INVESTMENT (GMROI)

An income statement ratio (gross profit margin × sales-to-stock ratio) that takes into consideration both gross profit and inventory turnover

have to rely on industry averages. For example, according to Industry Canada's *Performance Plus*, the GMROI for Incorporated Book Stores and News Dealers (NAICS Number: 45121, 2002) with sales averaging about $147,000 is about 185 (40.2 × 4.6). The GMROI for DISCovery is 130 (40 × 3.26), so DISCovery has a lower-than-average GMROI. It might now want to check out which products have the highest GMROI and promote these products.[4]

THE CLOSING BALANCE SHEET

The closing balance sheet will give you a final indicator of the financial health of your business. A typical closing balance sheet is shown in Table 10.10, and its main elements are described next.

ASSETS

- **Cash**—your cash position, the final number in your projected cash flow statement.
- **Accounts receivable**—money owed to your business at the end of the financial period.
- **Inventory/office supplies**—the closing inventory taken from your projected income statement.
- **Equipment**—the equipment estimate taken from your opening balance sheet.
- **Leasehold improvements**—the leasehold improvements estimate taken from your opening balance sheet.
- **Depreciation**—your estimate of depreciation taken from your projected income statement.
- **Other assets**—your estimate of "other assets" taken from your opening balance sheet.

LIABILITIES

- **Current debt**—your estimate of the principal due over the next year.
- **Accounts payable**—money for such things as rent and inventory that your business owes to others.
- **Long-term debt or liabilities**—your total principal due for all long-term loans minus the current portion.

OWNER'S EQUITY

Owner's equity—what the business owes the owner—is calculated as follows.

Equity at start of period (total equity from your opening balance sheet)
+
Profit over the period (net profit from income statement)
−
Owner's draw
=
Total equity at the end of the period.

As we noted earlier, the owner's draw is recorded in the closing balance sheet only if the business is unincorporated. If you pay yourself a wage and your business is incorporated, you record this expense as a management salary in your income statement.

Table 10.10 Closing Balance Sheet (Period Ending _____)

Assets			
Current assets			
Cash	_____		
Accounts receivable	_____		
Inventory/office supplies	_____		
Prepaid expenses	_____		
Other current assets	_____		
Total current assets		_____	
Fixed assets			
Equipment, furniture, fixtures	_____		
Leasehold improvements	_____		
—Depreciation/amortization	_____		
Land/buildings	_____		
Auto/truck	_____		
Other fixed assets	_____		
Total fixed assets		_____	
Other assets			
Organizational costs	_____		
Total other assets		_____	
Total assets			_____
Liabilities and equity			
Liabilities			
Current debt (due within the next 12 months)			
Bank loans—current portion	_____		
Loans—other	_____		
Accounts payable	_____		
Other current liabilities	_____		
Total current liabilities		_____	
Long-term debt			
Long-term (minus current portion)	_____		
Mortgage and liens payable	_____		
Loans from shareholders	_____		
Other long-term debts	_____		
Total long-term liabilities		_____	
Total liabilities			_____
Owner's equity			
Equity at start of period	_____		
(plus) profit over period	_____		
(minus) owner's draw	_____		
Total equity			_____
Total liabilities and owner's equity			_____

KEY RATIOS BASED ON THE BALANCE SHEET AND THE INCOME STATEMENT

Given that you have an income statement and an ending balance sheet, there are a number of important ratios you could calculate based on both of these two statements. Two of the most important ratios are the return on investment and the return on owner investment.

1. **Return on investment (ROI)** equals the net profit (before taxes) divided by total assets. This is usually multiplied by 100 to give a percentage. It is a measure of effectiveness. How well are your assets generating profit? Let's say your total assets were $100,000 and your net profit was $10,000. Then your ROI would be (10,000 ÷ 100,000) × 100 = 10 percent. Now let's assume that you have some assets that are not contributing to profit—say a car that you are not using very much for business. You could reduce your assets by selling the car for $20,000. Your ROI would then be 12.5 percent. This means you are making more effective use of your assets. The higher the ROI, the better.

2. **Return on owner investment** equals net profit (before taxes) divided by the owners' equity (investment). This is usually multiplied by 100 to give a percentage. This ratio helps the owner decide if their investment is effective. The higher the ratio, the better. Suppose profit was $10,000 and the owners' equity was $50,000. The return on owner investment (equity) would be (10,000 ÷ 50,000) × 100 = 20 percent. The owner is getting a 20 percent rate of return from the business. In this case, it seems as though the owner has made a good business investment. On the other hand, if the return on owner investment was 2 percent, the owner would not be getting a "good" return and should consider getting out of the business. Owner's equity could be invested somewhere else and make a "better" return. Online calculators for these ratios are provided in Box 10.4.

BREAK-EVEN ANALYSIS

The break-even point is the point at which your sales revenue equals your total expenses (costs). At this point, you neither make money nor lose any. The break-even lets you know what it is going to take to survive and thus provides a good indication of the financial viability of a business idea. The break-even can also be used to evaluate a business expansion or any other business expenditure. You are simply asking how much additional revenue will be required to cover the additional costs. Many new business owners use the break-even level of sales as a starting point for forecasting their yearly cash flow and income.

To calculate break-even you will need to know the value of your fixed costs and the value of your variable costs and your output capacity. [5]

Total costs equal fixed costs plus variable costs.

Fixed costs (sometimes referred to as indirect expenses) are those expenses that do not depend on sales—rent, heat hydro, etc. Generally, these are your operating expenses based on your income statement. It is common practice (for planning purposes) to include bank interest and principal payments. Remember, the income statement does not include principal bank payments. You will have to get this number from your cash flow.

Variable costs (cost of goods) are those costs that depend on the level of sales—materials and shipping costs, for example. Sometimes these are referred to as indirect expenses. In some cases these indirect expenses may also include costs such as contract labour hired during peak sales periods.

Capacity governs your output. It can be measured in units of production, billable hours, or sales volume.

There are two basic ways to calculate your break-even—the unit method and the revenue method.

1. Unit Method

To calculate the break-even in units we use the following formula

$$\text{Break-even in units} = \frac{\text{Fixed costs}}{(\text{Unit price} - \text{unit cost})}$$

The example below shows your how to calculate break-even using the unit method.

Jan is a home-based potter who makes custom mugs by the case. Her maximum capacity is 15 cases of mugs per week. She has calculated the variable cost (cost of materials) for each case, including clay, glaze, and packaging, to be $50 per case. It cost Jan $3,000 per week in fixed costs to run her business. This would include her wages and bank payments (both principal and interest).

Jan can now calculate her break-even sales level and corresponding price per case depending on the number of units she can produce as shown in Table 10.11. For example, if she produces 5 cases, her total costs would be her fixed costs plus her variable costs [($3,000) + (5 × $50)] = $3,250. She knows that her break-even level of sales occurs where total costs = total revenue = $3,250. If she is producing 5 cases, the price she must charge to break even is her total revenue ($3,250) divided by the number of units or cases (5), which equals $650 per case. If she sells 5 cases at $650 per case, her total revenue will equal her total costs and she will break even. She now prepares a break-even table showing the number of cases produced and the corresponding price/per case that she would have to charge (See Table 10.11 and Figure 10.1). Her capacity is 15 cases so that is where it will end. Note that Jan's break-even is not a point but varies for each different price point ranging from $650 to $250.

For many start-ups, the projected break-even is the first step in establishing the viability of the business idea. For example, suppose that after Jan does her competitive and market research, she estimates that she could sell 12 cases of her custom mugs at $425. This would generate revenue of $5,100 ($425 × 12). Her total cost would be $3,600 ($3,000 + [$12 × 50]). Her weekly profit would be $1,500. She is projecting sales of 12 cases per week, and she now knows that as long as she can sell at least 8 cases, she will turn a profit.

Table 10.11 Jan's Pottery: Break-Even per Week Based on the Number of Units Produced

Units Produced	Fixed Costs	Variable Costs	Price per Unit
5	$3,000	$250	$650
6	$3,000	$300	$550
7	$3,000	$350	$479
8	$3,000	$400	$425
9	$3,000	$450	$383
10	$3,000	$500	$350
11	$3,000	$550	$323
12	$3,000	$600	$300
13	$3,000	$650	$281
14	$3,000	$700	$264
15	$3,000	$750	$250

Now suppose that her market research told her that she could get only $200 per case. She would have to produce 20 cases per week to break even, but her capacity is only 15. This means that given her cost structure and market research, her business would not be financially viable.

2. Break-Even Using Gross Profit Margin (Revenue Method)

Sometimes a company doesn't sell products, or it sells so many different products that doing a break-even for each unit doesn't make sense. In this case, such as in retail businesses, we calculate the break-even in revenue rather than in units. Break-even is normally calculated by the following formula.

$$\text{Break-even} = \frac{\text{Fixed costs}}{\text{Gross profit margin}}$$

Fixed costs will normally include both operating expenses and other expenses. These numbers will come from your income statement. In most cases, you will want to add in your principal payment on your loan. Remember, principal payments are not recorded on your income statement. You will get this number from your cash flow.

Let's return to DISCovery Books and Magazines. Based on its income statement (Table 10.8), its fixed costs are $51,550 (total operating expenses [$47,950] + other expenses [$3,600]). Based on the cash flow (Table 10.6, line 27), we add in the principal payments for its loan ($3,000). The total adjusted fixed costs are $54,550 ($51,550 + 3,000). Its gross profit margin is .4 (60,000 ÷ 150,000). DISCovery's break-even is $136,375 ($54,550 ÷ 4). The projected sales of $150,000 are only about 10 percent higher than its break-even level. With projected sales of only $150,000, it's unlikely that many lenders would lend DISCovery any money, unless the owners could provide a convincing argument that the $150,000 sales estimate was their worst-case scenario. And in many cases, the break-even forecast provides owners and lenders with this so-called worse-case sales estimate.

A break-even analysis is also useful when considering the financial implications of launching a new product or service, as we show in the example below.

A small manufacturing company was completing a plan for its second year of operation. Its first-year sales were $177,000. Its fiscal year ended in December. A sales breakdown for the last three months of the first year looked like this:

October	$24,000
November	$29,000
December	$15,000
Total	$68,000

The owners took a look at the numbers and called in a consultant to help. The consultant gathered information from sales reps, owners, and customers, and projected sales for the second year at a whopping $562,000. The owners reacted with disbelief.

"You're crazy," they said. "That's over three times what we did last year."

The consultant smiled. "Didn't you tell me you were going to add three new products?"

"Yes."

"And new reps in March, June, and September?"

"Yes, but—"

"And what about those big promotions you've got planned?"

"Well, sure. We've planned some promotion. But that doesn't get us anywhere near three times last year."

"All right," the accountant said. "Can you do $275,000?"

The owners got into a huddle. Recalling the fourth quarter, they were sure they could stay even, and 4 × $68,000 (fourth-quarter sales) was $272,000. They knew they had to do better than last year.

"Sure. No problem. We can do $272,000."

"All right," said the consultant, rolling out his break-even chart. "I've just projected $562,000 in sales for the year. To break even, you need only $275,000."

"Hey," the owners said. "We're projecting $90,000 in the first quarter."

"I'm glad you're thinking my way," the consultant said. "Because if you don't believe you can reach a goal, you'll never get there." He paused, and then he said, "By the way, that $90,000 is three times what you did in your first quarter last year!"

"Just tell us what to do," the owners said.

Following a careful cash flow analysis, the consultant determined that the company would need to borrow money. The owners knew their business—industry trends, product line, competitors, sales, and promotion plans—but there was no way the bankers would believe a tripling of growth. The key to getting the loan was to convince the bankers the company could do better than the break-even, at $275,000. The break-even chart (see Figure 10.1) was built on the $562,000 sales figure. Note on the chart that after $280,000 in sales, the firm has passed its break-even point and is making a profit.

The banker granted the loan, realizing that the company could pass the break-even point with room to spare. The key was a combination of numbers and confidence. And that is the final piece of advice we want to give you in this chapter. Whatever numbers you forecast for your new business, make sure you can back them up with solid research. This will give you the confidence to find the money you'll need. Now you are ready to move on to Chapter 11 and learn how to Shake the Money Tree.

Box 10.5 Bookmark This

Ratio and Break-Even Calculators

- **BDC, Ratio Calculators:** http://www.bdc.ca/en/business_tools/calculators/overview.htm?cookie%5Ftest=1
- **Bankrate.com, Small Business Ratio Calculators:** http://www.bankrate.com/brm/news/biz/bizcalcs/ratiocalcs.asp
- **CreditGuru.com, Ratio Calculators:** http://www.creditguru.com/ratios/calculate.html.
- **Dinkytown.net, Financial Calculators:** http://www.dinkytown.net/business.html
- **Bplans.com, Break Even Calculator:** http://www.bplans.com/common/calculators/breakeven.cfm
- **Weatherhead School of Management, Break-Even Analysis:** http://connection.cwru.edu/mbac424/breakeven/BreakEven.html
- **Steiner Marketing, Break-Even Calculator:** http://www.steinermarketing.com/calc_break_even.htm
- **ANZ, Breakeven Calculator:** http://www.anz.com.au/australia/business/calculator/businessbenchmark/break_even.asp

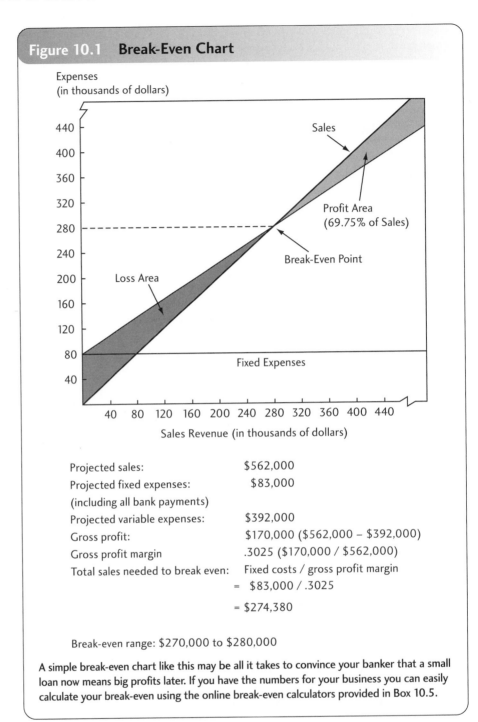

Figure 10.1   Break-Even Chart

Projected sales:	$562,000
Projected fixed expenses: (including all bank payments)	$83,000
Projected variable expenses:	$392,000
Gross profit:	$170,000 ($562,000 – $392,000)
Gross profit margin	.3025 ($170,000 / $562,000)
Total sales needed to break even:	Fixed costs / gross profit margin
	= $83,000 / .3025
	= $274,380

Break-even range: $270,000 to $280,000

A simple break-even chart like this may be all it takes to convince your banker that a small loan now means big profits later. If you have the numbers for your business you can easily calculate your break-even using the online break-even calculators provided in Box 10.5.

In a Nutshell

Not surprisingly, many entrepreneurs find it difficult to project numbers for their business. There are several explanations for this:

- They're action people who are in a hurry; they don't think they have time to sit down and *think*.
- They're creative; their strengths are greater in the innovation area than in the justification area.
- They tend to think in visual terms rather than in numbers or words.

- They don't know enough about the power of numbers.
- They think if they do what they love, money will follow—and money doesn't necessarily follow love.

Business is a numbers game, and you have to know the rules. In spite of the entrepreneur's feelings about numbers and projections, survival in the marketplace depends on having the right numbers in the right colour of ink. This chapter helps you formulate a financial vision, estimate your start-up costs, create a balance sheet, project your cash flow and pro forma income statement, use ratios to plan your business, and understand the value of break-even analysis.

The idea in projecting numbers is to make them as realistic as possible. That is the key. Your numbers might seem reasonable to you, but you must make them seem reasonable to others as well. You make them believable by keeping them realistic and documenting them properly. You need to relate each projection to your specific business and to industry standards, and then to *document* them (tell where they came from) in your business plan. This chapter will help you make your projections believable to your banker as well as to yourself.

Key Terms

advisory board

application of funds

assets

balance sheet

cost of goods sold (CGS)

current asset conversion cycle

current assets

current liabilities

fixed assets

equity

gross profit

gross profit margin (contribution margin)

gross margin return on inventory investment (GMROI)

inventory turnover

liabilities

long-term (deferred) liabilities

net profit (before taxes)

pro forma (or projected) income statement

projected (pro forma) cash flow

Think Points for Success

✓ Financial statements such as balance sheets, cash flows, and income statements bring the words of the business to life, and there must be a direct link between what is stated in the business plan and what appears in the financial statements.

✓ It's cheaper to make mistakes on a spreadsheet, before you go into business.

✓ When you work out numbers for a business plan, spend time completing your cash flow. Many business people feel that cash flow is the most important statement, and we agree.

✓ If you have a negative cash position in any one period, be proactive and plan how you will pay your bills.

✓ When you visit your banker to ask for money, make sure you know how much you're going to need for the long run.

✓ Use balance sheet and income statement ratios to test the financial health of your business.

✓ Projecting will help you control the variables of your business: numbers, employees, promotion mix, product mix, and the peaks and valleys of seasonality.

✓ Do lots of "what if" scenarios. Be cautious. Most entrepreneurs tend to be overly optimistic on sales and underestimate expenses.

Business Plan Building Block

NOW IT'S YOUR TURN

Explain how you developed your sales projections. Use hard data wherever you can. Summarize your research, and list people and firms that have influenced your conclusions. Include cost of goods sold, expenses, capital needs, and best- and worst-case scenarios. If you are using computer software or online templates to develop your plan, enter the information that you have developed in the text to fill in the cash flow and income statement.

Checklist Questions and Actions to Develop Your Business Plan

The Power of Numbers

❑ Do you have a financial vision?

❑ What are your estimated start-up costs?

❑ Validate your sales forecast based on your primary and secondary market research.

❑ Identify all your cost and pricing assumptions.

❑ Prepare an opening balance sheet.

❑ Prepare a monthly cash flow the first year and a quarterly cash flow for the next two years. Wherever there is a cash shortfall, it will require new equity, debt, or a bank line of credit.

❑ What is your fallback position if your sales forecast and cash flow don't reach expectations?

❑ Prepare an annual income statement for the first year.

❑ Prepare a closing balance sheet.

❑ What concerns might the banker have about your pro forma cash flow, income and expense statement, and balance sheet, and what is your response?

❑ Is your break-even within range of your minimum sales forecast?

❑ How do your financial ratios compare to industry averages obtained from sources such as *Performance Plus*?

Case Studies

CASE STUDY 1: FINANCING YOUR BUSINESS—GETTING STARTED

As we learned in this chapter, a financial plan to open a business should contain at least four basic financial statements for the first year of operation:
- an opening balance sheet based on your application and sources of funds,
- a projected monthly cash flow for the first year of operation,
- a projected income statement for the first year, and
- an ending balance sheet after the first year of operation.

If you're now ready with the financial information for your business idea, we encourage you to "take a stab at it" and create a first draft of your financial plan. Remember, even once it is completed, it is not written in stone. This plan, especially if you use the financial templates provided in Box 10.3, can be used to answer plenty of "what if" statements, such as "What if I want to pay off my business loan over a shorter period of time?"

CASE STUDY 2: DISCOVERY BOOKS AND MAGAZINES INC.—FINANCIAL STATEMENTS

If you're not ready to do a financial plan for your business idea, answer the following case study questions based on the DISCovery example we have referred to throughout this chapter.

Case Study Questions

1. Application of Funds

   Complete the following application of funds table for DISCovery using the cash flow statement (Table 10.6, page 250) and the income statement (Table 10.8, page 256) provided in the text.

2. Opening Balance Sheet

   a. Complete Table 10.13—Opening Balance Sheet for DISCovery—using the completed application of funds table (question 1 above), cash flow statement (Table 10.6, page 250), and the income statement (Table 10.8, page 256) provided in the text.

   b. Evaluate this opening balance sheet for DISCovery using the current ratio, quick ratio, and debt-to-equity ratio. Compare the current ratio and the debt-to-equity ratio with the Industry averages based on those provided by Industry Canada's *Performance Plus* (http://strategis.ic.gc.ca/epic/internet/inpp-pp.nsf/en/h_pm00059e.html) for incorporated businesses (NAICS 45121), lower half category (average sales of $147,000).

3. Cash Flow

   a. Review the DISCovery cash flow in the text (Table 10.6). Suppose the owners wanted to "save on interest costs" and decided that they wanted to pay off their loan of $35,000 in the first year. Calculate the revised total cash balance at the end of the first year. Would you advise the owners to pay off their loan over this one-year period?

Table 10.12	Application of Funds, DISCovery Books and Magazines	
General start-up costs		
Organizational costs	$????	
Prepaid expenses	$9,575	
Opening inventory/office supplies	$????	
Total general start-up costs		$62,375
Leasehold improvements		$19,800
Equipment costs		$????
Cash reserve fund		$????
Total Application of Funds		$????

b. If the owners of DISCovery decided they wanted to pay off their entire loan in the first year, how would this decision affect the opening balance sheet and the first-year income statement?

c. Suppose that DISCovery offered very liberal credit terms and received cash payments two months after they made a sale. Show how this would affect the closing bank balance. How would this decision affect the opening balance sheet?

4. Income Statement

a. Up until this point, the financials of DISCovery look fairly healthy. Evaluate DISCovery's projected income statement (Table 10.8) based on its gross profit margin, profit margin, turnover, and gross margin return on inventory investment (GMROI). One set of industry averages is provided by Industry Canada, *Performance Plus*: (http://strategis.ic.gc.ca/epic/internet/inpp-pp.nsf/en/h_pm00059e.html) for incorporated businesses (NAICS 45121), lower half category (average sales of $147,000).

b. After doing your analysis in 4(a), what advice would you give to the owners of DISCovery?

5. Ending Balance Sheet

a. Given the opening balance sheet (Question 2), the cash flow (Table 10.6, page 250), and the income statement (Table 10.8, page 256), create an ending balance sheet for DISCovery. Remember, if you have made no arithmetic or accounting errors, your total assets will equal total liabilities plus equity—CONGRATULATIONS!

b. Suppose that at the end of the year, DISCovery decides to pay an extra $10,000 toward the principal payment (for its loan). How would this transaction affect the projected cash flow, income statement, and ending balance sheet?

c. DISCovery was an incorporated business. On the income statement and cash flow, the owners of DISCovery paid themselves a wage ($19,200). Suppose DISCovery was not incorporated, and the owners paid themselves in terms of an owner's draw. How would this affect the projected cash flow, income statement, and ending balance sheet?

d. Calculate DISCovery's return on investment (ROI) and return on owner investment.

e. If you were advising the owners of DISCovery on the basis of the financial statements, would you advise them to go ahead and start their business? Why? Why not?

Table 10.13 Opening Balance Sheet, DISCovery Books and Magazines (Date of Opening _____)

ASSETS			
Current assets	$	$	$
1. Cash	?????		
2. Accounts receivable	0		
3. Inventory/office supplies	?????		
4. Prepaid expenses	?????		
5. Other current assets	0		
6. **Total current assets**		?????	

ASSETS			
Fixed assets	**$**	**$**	**$**
7. Equipment/furniture/fixtures	?????		
8. Leasehold improvements	?????		
9. Land/buildings	0		
10. Auto/truck	0		
11. Other fixed assets	0		
12. **Total fixed assets**		?????	
Other assets			
13. Organizational fees (legal, accounting, etc.)	?????		
14. **Total other assets**		?????	
15. **TOTAL ASSETS (6 + 12 + 14)**			?????
LIABILITIES			
Current liabilities (due within the next 12 months)			
16. Long-term loans (current portion)	?????		
17. Short-term loans	0		
18. Accounts payable	0		
19. Other current liabilities	0		
20. **Total current liabilities**		?????	
Long-term liabilities			
21. Long-term loans (minus current portion)	?????		
22. Mortgages and liens payable	0		
23. Loans from shareholders (if applicable)	0		
24. Other long-term debt obligations	0		
25. **Total long-term liabilities**		?????	
26. **TOTAL LIABILITIES (20 + 25)**			?????
EQUITY			
27. Cash—owners capital (if a proprietorship or partnership) —shares outstanding (if a corporation)	?????		
28. General start-up (organizational costs, etc.)	0		
29. Equipment/material/labour (provide details)	20,000		
30. **TOTAL EQUITY**			?????
31. **TOTAL LIABILITIES AND EQUITY (26 + 30)**			?????

Notes

1. Western Economic Diversification Canada and Small Business BC, *Business Planning and Financial Forecasting: a Start-up Guide* (http://www.sbed.gov.bc.ca/ReportsPublications/BUSINESS_PLANNING.pdf), p.25.
2. *Business Planning and Financial Forecasting*, p. 21.
3. *Business Planning and Financial Forecasting*, p. 28.
4. A good discussion on the gross margin return on inventory (GMROI) can be found in Michael Levy, Barton A. Weitz, and Sheryn Beattie, *Retailing Management*, Canadian edition (Toronto: McGraw-Hill Ryerson, 2005), pp. 238–240.
5. *Business Planning and Financial Forecasting: a Start-up*, pp. 17–19.

money and who doesn't," says Earle. "I guess they saw something in me, and they decided to give me the money." The $50,000 was enough to purchase the franchise, and the franchisers worked out an arrangement whereby she could cover the additional costs over time.

Within a couple of years, Earle expanded the store by nearly 50 percent, to 3,200 square feet. The store has been so successful that she was able to cover the cost of the last expansion without additional loans, and in the meantime, she's paid off the original loan ahead of time.

And now the banks come to her. "I don't even need to go and ask," she says. "Now, they come and ask me if I want some money."

Oh, and she still works with the same lawyer; he sees her just about every day, as his office is in the same mall as her store. "It's quite funny," Kelly says.[1]

Every business, regardless of its size or stage of development, will need some sort of financing. Where do successful entrepreneurs find money to start their businesses? The answer seems to be "almost everywhere," and persistence seems to be a key ingredient. Kelly Earle, in the opening vignette, received a loan from a local business development centre and "love" money from her mom, and even the franchiser helped out by deferring some payments. Persistent entrepreneurs like Susan Squires-Hutchings, owner of The Potter's Wheel Incorporated in St. John's, Newfoundland, have even been able to get some start-up money from their landlords.[2] But the key to success for many entrepreneurs like Susan and Kelly is perseverance. They believed in what they were doing, and eventually they found the money. So, if you don't succeed in getting financing the first time, we want you to keep trying. After all, most entrepreneurs don't get what they want the first time.

A number of possible sources of financing are listed in Box 11.1. For start-up business, it should come as no surprise, however, that the major source of financing will be you, the owner. As shown in Table 11.1, most start-ups rely heavily on informal or owner-based financing, such as personal savings and loans, personal lines of credit, and **love money** from family and friends. Start-ups are less likely to use formal types of financing, such as commercial loans and commercial credit cards, and leasing.

LOVE MONEY

Investment from friends, relatives, and business associates

> ### Box 11.1 Sources of Financing—Where Does the Money Come From?
>
> Research shows that at least 50 percent of the small- and medium-sized businesses in Canada rely on banks and other financial institutions to provide them with some sort of financing (whether for start-up, expansion, or ongoing funding). A personal guarantee on business loans is almost always requested—especially for start-ups. Other sources of financing include
>
> - personal lines of credit (37%),
> - personal credit cards (33%),
> - personal savings (35%),
> - personal loans (14%),
> - retained earnings (31%),
> - supplier credit (39%),

3. **Length of credit history** (15 percent). The third factor is th
credit history. The longer you've had credit—particularly if i
credit issuers—the more points you get.
4. **Mix of credit** (10 percent). The best scores will have a mix
credit, such as credit cards, and installment credit, such as m
loans. Consumers with a wide range of experiences are p
credit risks.
5. **New credit applications** (10 percent). The final category i
new credit—how many credit applications you're filling c
compensates for people who are rate shopping for the best
loan rates.

How do you find out what your credit rating is? Unde
Reporting Act, the three credit reporting agencies are require
with a copy of your credit report on request. Getting this inforn
difficult. Action Step 50 will help you work through the process

Now we want you to think about how much **unsecured cr**
draw on.

HOW MUCH UNSECURED CREDIT DO YOU HAVE?

Credit usually refers to money loaned or the ability of an indiv
to borrow money. **Collateral** is something of value—such as prc
that is pledged as a guarantee to support the repayment of 1
Unsecured credit is credit extended to a borrower on the pro
debt with no collateral required.

We encourage you to find out how much unsecured credit y
give you a very general picture of how the financial world rates yc
the business side, once you've done this you can determine whe
untapped sources of funds for your start-up, or fallbacks and eme
your business or personal expenses. Use Table 11.2 or a blank
learn your credit limits on your charge accounts, look at your
ments. If your credit cards have low limits, now might be the time t
before you open your business or quit your job. You might need
several businesses for limit information if it is not clearly stated c

When you've filled in the amounts for each account you h
Surprised? Few people are aware of how much credit they have
you tell your boss what to do with your job, you might want to a
tional issues or concerns.

1. **Order complete medical checkups for your entire fami**
ask to read through your medical files to make sure there
that might preclude you from obtaining extended health
future. Examples might include "possible problems with d
In addition, pre-existing conditions, such as uncontrolled
sure, can be a major roadblock to securing extended healt
2. **Check out the costs and possibility of extended or addi
dental insurance.** Two frequently overlooked types of health
long-term disability and critical illness. If you are unable to c
insurance plan, a group plan might be available through a b
ciation or possibly through a provincial program. Look in
plans. Many entrepreneurs find they need one member of t
tinue working for a company that provides family coverage.
go back and review the insurance planning section in Chap

- leasing (16%),
- business credit cards (26%),
- government lending agencies/grants (7%),
- loans from employees, friends, and relatives (10%),
- non-related private loans (5%),
- public equity (2%),
- venture capital (2%),* and
- angle investment (4%).**

*Venture Capital = 1% according to Statistics Canada, *Survey of Suppliers of Business Financing*, 2002.
*Angle Investment = 4% according to Statistics Canada Survey 2000.

Source: Statistics Canada, *Survey of Financing of Small- and Medium-sized Enterprises*, 2002.

Table 11.1 Financing by Stage of Business Development

Type of Startup Financing	Usage Rate by Start-ups (%)	Usage Rate by SMEs (%)
Informal Types		
Personal savings of owner(s)	66	35
Personal credit lines of owner(s)	23	21
Personal loans of owner(s)	19	14
Loans from owner's friends/family	12	10
Formal Types		
Commercial loans and credit lines	29	49
Leasing	12	16
Commercial credit cards	8	26
Government grants or loans	5	7

SME = Small- or medium-sized enterprise.
Source: Industry Canada, *Small and Medium-Sized Enterprise Financing in Canada—Part II: Financial Structure of Canadian SMEs* (http://strategis.ic.gc.ca/epic/internet/insbrp-rppe.nsf/en/rd01046e.html#note37).

Chances are that, you, the owner, will be the major source of financing. Thus, before you begin to shake the money tree, we encourage you to check out your credit rating, calculate your available credit, come to grips with your personal financial situation, budget for your future financial needs, and think about your risk tolerance. We'll also warn you to be very careful about asking for money from your friends and family.

Next we will help you understand and prepare to meet your banker. You will also be introduced to some of the other major sources of external capital, including the government. We also want you to be aware of the pros and cons of debt versus equity financing. In case you want to do a detailed financial plan for your business, we have provided financial templates and instructions in the Student Resources section of the book's support Web site.

Throughout the chapter, we encourage you to have faith and persist in your search for money. In Rick Spence's insightful analysis of Canada's PROFIT 100 companies,

one of the important lessons he s
companies was, "If your story truly
somewhere."[3]

BEFORE YOU SHAKE

As we have seen, most new ventures
can usually be borrowed if you hav
sufficient equity in a home. So be
financing for your business, you ar
ation. We begin by asking you to c

WHAT IS YOUR CREDIT HISTO

Lenders, such as retailers and fina
agencies with factual informatio
you want to borrow money to buy
officer at your bank or financial i
and will probably request a cre
important issue when you apply
lenders often request credit inf
obtaining a copy of your credit r

In Canada, there are three
Canada Incorporated, Trans Unio
that keep track of all your finan
loans, liens, legal judgments, a
assemble financial information i
time the information is kept on
Most of your credit information

Each lender has its own pol
customers, so your credit file wi
you as a potential customer. Th
credit are provided below.

1. **How you pay your bills** (35
   is how you've paid your bills
   activity. Paying all your bills
   basis is bad. Having account
   bankruptcy is worst.
2. **The amount of money y**
   (30 percent). The second r
   how much money you owe c
   lines, and so on. Also consid
   able. If you have 10 credit
   that's $100,000 of availab
   credit available tend to use
   "Carrying a lot of debt do
   Watts says. "It doesn't hurt a
   who consistently max out t
   never use their credit don
   scores use credit sparingly

ACTION STEP 50

Find out what your credit rating is *(continued)*

pay for your FICO. The cost is about $20, and you can get the information online. See, for example, Equifax (https://www.econsumer.equifax.ca/ca/main?forward=/view/common/template.jsp&body=/view/product_info/sp_detail.jsp#).

Your Credit Rating—Address Information

- Equifax Canada Inc., Consumer Relations Department: Box 190, Jean Talon Station, Montreal, QC H1S 2Z2.Tel: (514) 493-23141, 1-800-465-7166. Fax: (514) 355-8502 (http://www.eqifax.ca).
- Trans Union Consumer Relations: 709 Main Street W, Suite 3201, Hamilton, ON L8S 1A2. Tel: 1-800-663-9980. Fax: (905) 527-0401 (http://www.tuc.ca/).
- Northern Credit Bureaus Inc.: 336 Rideau Boulevard Rouyn–Noranda, QC J9X 1P2. Fax: 1-800-646-5876 (http://www.creditbureau.ca).

NET WORTH (PERSONAL EQUITY)

The market value of your personal assets minus your total personal liabilities

PERSONAL BALANCE SHEET

A list of the market value of assets (what you own) and liabilities (what you owe) that will show your net worth or personal equity

DEVELOP A PERSONAL BALANCE SHEET

In Chapter 10, you estimated your start-up costs. Do you have enough start-up money to be your own banker? Begin by getting a total for your personal assets. Personal assets are things you own that have a monetary value. The value of your assets would be the market value. Market value means the selling price of a possession, not how much you paid for it. Next, you tally up your personal liabilities. Liabilities are the debts you owe to other people or institutions. You are now ready to calculate your **net worth**, or personal equity. Find out your net worth by subtracting the market value of your assets (what you own) from the total value of what you owe. It will look something like the one in Table 11.2.

Pulling together a **personal balance sheet** or net worth statement is important because it tells you where you are with money now, and it will indicate your borrowing capability. The higher your net worth, the more you will be able to borrow. We encourage you to complete Action Step 51 and find out what your net worth is.

Now we want you to move on and chart your money future. How much do you need to live on? Can the business pay for your current lifestyle?

Table 11.3   Personal Balance Sheet (or Statement of Net Worth)

Assets (what you own)	Current Market Value ($)	Current Market Value ($)
1. Liquid assets		
Cash (chequing, savings, etc.)	$_____	
Stocks, bonds, etc.	$_____	
Cash surrender value of life insurance	$_____	
Other liquid assets	$_____	
Total liquid assets		$_____
2. Investment assets		
Mutual funds, real estate investments, etc.	$_____	
RRSPs/pension fund	$_____	
Other investments	$_____	
Total investment assets		$_____
3. Personal (fixed) assets		
Furniture	$_____	
Residence	$_____	
Auto/boat	$_____	
Jewellery/art	$_____	
Other	$_____	
Total personal (fixed) assets		$_____
4. Total assets (1 + 2 + 3)		$_____

Liabilities (what you owe)	Current Market Value ($)	Current Market Value ($)
5. Short-term debt (liabilities)		
Credit cards owing	$_____	
Personal loans (amount outstanding)	$_____	
Income tax owed	$_____	
Other loans outstanding	$_____	
Total short-term debt		$_____
6. Long-term debt (liabilities)		
Mortgages (amount owing)	$_____	
Loans to purchase investment and other personal assets	$_____	
Other long-term debt	$_____	
Total long-term debt		$_____
7. Total debt (5 + 6)		$_____
8. Personal equity (4 − 7, i.e., Total assets − Total liabilities)		$_____

CHART YOUR PERSONAL MONEY FUTURE

Will you new business be able to support your current lifestyle? You won't know until you chart your personal money future. Look ahead into the next year. List your expenses, such as those for shelter, food, medical bills, transportation, insurance, phone, school, clothes, and utilities. If you need a worksheet, the sites provided in Box 11.3 will help.

Box 11.3   Personal and Family Budgets and Worksheets

- Royal Bank, personal budget calculator: http://www.rbcroyalbank.com/RBC: RF0VCo71A8cAAg2ObJw/tools.html
- CBA's *Managing Money* Web site: http://www.cba.ca/en/viewPub.asp?fl=6&sl= 23&docid=27&pg=6
- Brock University's personal budget worksheet: http://www.brocku.ca/gradstudies/ financial/Personal_Budget_Worksheet.xls
- Concordia University: http://web2.concordia.ca/financialaid/planning/
- CCH's *Business Owner's Toolkit*: http://www.toolkit.cch.com/text/P01_2150.asp
- About.com's "Budget Worksheet": http://financialplan.about.com/library/ n_budget.htm

Review your personal budget. How much extra in your budget can you commit to the venture? How much do you need to live on each month? Go back to the business cash flow and income statements that you created in Chapter 10.

ACTION STEP 51

Prepare your personal balance sheet (net worth)

Sit down with a pencil and paper and do some figuring. You might want to use Table 11.3 as a template.

1. List everything you own that has cash value, and estimate its worth. Include cash, securities, life insurance, accounts receivable, notes receivable, rebates/refunds, autos and other vehicles, real estate, pension, and so on.

Don't stop now. Go on to list the market values of your home furnishings, household goods, major appliances, sports equipment, collectibles, jewellery, tools, computer, livestock, trusts, patents, memberships, interests, investment clubs, and so on.

Add up the amounts you've written down. The total represents your assets.

2. List every dime you owe to someone or something: accounts payable, contracts payable, notes payable (such as car loans), taxes, insurance (life, health, car, liability, etc.), mortgage or real estate loans, and anything else you owe. These are your liabilities.

3. Subtract your liabilities from your assets to find your net worth. It's that simple.

Now you know how much you have. You need these figures to determine your financial needs and also to assess the financial contribution you will be able to make to your business.

Have you budgeted enough to live on? Are you willing to change your lifestyle? Are you willing to rent? Share an apartment? Live in your parents' home? If you're planning on living at home, is your family prepared to support you? Are they willing to make sacrifices to help you realize your dream? These are the types of questions you are going to have to think about.

You've thought about your credit, reviewed your personal financial situation, and mapped out your financial needs. It's now time to go back and think again about your risk tolerance.

ASSESS YOUR RISK TOLERANCE

Ask yourself, "How much am I willing to risk? $10,000? $20,000? $200,000?" Are you willing to go deeply in debt for your venture? A sushi vendor we once knew worked for more than seven years and spent thousands of dollars before he hit on a successful way to flash-freeze his product. If additional capital is needed down the road, will you and your partner(s) be able to provide equal shares? If not, will that be a problem, as the proportions of the amounts invested change? Go back to Action Step 51 and do a reality check. Are you willing to give up a successful career with benefits for the unknown? If you lose your house, will you be devastated, or will you pick yourself back up and start again, like a true entrepreneur?

You must also consider the risk tolerance level of your family members and partners. It might be time now for you to go back to Chapter 3 and revisit your values. What are your family values? Talk with your family about the time and money sacrifices that might be involved in developing your new venture. Is your family onboard? Are your loved ones ready to take the financial risk? For many, short-term financial pain is worth long-term gain; for others, it's not worth it! Before leaping into the new venture, decide what you and your family are willing to sacrifice. Above all, try to truly listen to them. Sometimes, what with the adrenalin of entrepreneurship, you can miss the message.

Now that you have reviewed your personal finances, you are a lot closer to finding out how much of your money you can put in the business. It's time to shake each branch of the money tree and look at your possible sources of financing. As we've already explained, the most fruitful money branches for start-ups will be informal—you, your family, and your friends—so that is where we'll begin.

INFORMAL SOURCES OF FINANCING

SELF-FINANCING

For start-ups, self-financing will be the most important source, and it might be your only one. New businesses have to rely on savings, personal loans, personal lines of credit, and credit cards. Review your personal balance sheet (Table 11.3). How much money can you draw on from your savings? Can you get a personal loan based on your equity? Go back to your current financial credit sources (Table 11.2). How much can you get from your personal line of credit? Can you finance your business from the judicious use of credit cards? Think about your monthly budget. How much do you need to live on?

Now we want you to look at look at other sources of informal financing— your family and friends—the second most popular source, as shown in Table 11.1.

FAMILY AND FRIENDS

For many entrepreneurs, heading to Mom and Pop is the second branch to shake after they've looked at their own financial contributions. If you plan on making it your next stop, think again! Having a banking relationship with your parents is fraught with potential problems. Before continuing further, ask yourself, "Is money for this venture worth damaging or losing my relationship with my parents?" At the moment, you might just be thinking about speeding ahead with your venture, and all you can see is success; the reality is, however, you could fail. You might not be able to pay back your parents in a timely fashion—or ever!

Consider your parents' emotional tie to money. Especially if your parents or grandparents are past their prime and lived through the Depression, for many money means security. If you borrow money, they might not truly feel secure until you have completely paid it back. Also, if you take a needed vacation while you still owe them money, will you feel guilty? Will you feel guilty if you purchase a new car? Will you truly be secure in expanding your business if you are not secure in your lending relationship? If you are borrowing money from friends or family, be sure that the loss of that money will not affect the lenders' future or lifestyle.

In addition to borrowing money directly from parents, you might consider asking them to co-sign loans. Remember, that legally obligates them to the debt and will affect their financial transactions and borrowing capabilities. Also, your parents, friends, or relatives might be more willing to lend you money if you put up your house, car, or jewellery as collateral.

Remain at your job, or get another job and save for another year before striking out on your own rather than risking the capital of those you love. Mixing money and personal relationships is never easy, and with family it tends to be even more emotional and volatile. Long-running family issues come into play, and sibling relationships might also be harmed. There are unseen and unknown issues for both parties. How will you deal with them? If your folks get sick, will you be able to pay back the loan? If your dad and mom want to be part of the business to oversee their investment, how will you feel? Do you want your parents only as lenders, or will you consider taking them on as partners and investors?

As with all lending transactions, the lender wants to know what the money is going to be used for, the chance of default, what the interest rate will be, and how soon the loan will be repaid. If you are still willing to borrow from friends and family after reviewing potential issues and problems, here are a few things you can do to alleviate some of the difficulties.

* **Don't accept more money than your lender can afford to lose.** Borrowing Grandma's last $20,000 is not fair to you or to Grandma.
* **Put everything in writing.** Establish a partnership or shareholders agreement (discussed in Chapter 8) detailing the roles of all concerned.
* **Make it a business loan, not a personal loan.** Have loan papers drawn up. State the time period of the loan, interest rate, payment date, collateral, and late payment penalties.
* **Include in the loan a provision for repayment in case of emergencies.** This will alleviate a lot of stress and concern for both parties.
* **Discuss thoroughly with the lenders the company's goals and any potential problems.** Make sure they understand that the loan will be for a certain length of time. If the business starts to be profitable, it might still require their cash infusion. Cash is not profit—as we now know.
* **Get outside advice.** Don't finalize the deal until the lender has discussed it with an independent advisor.

One family we know lends to all their adult children in a bank-like fashion. To purchase a home, one son might receive a $50,000 loan at 7 percent interest. A daughter purchasing a franchise might receive a loan of $50,000 with an 11 percent

credit, banks will want to know the status of your accounts payable and receivable. We suggest you plan to send your banker regular updates, even if he or she doesn't request them.

Invite Your Banker to Your Business

On your own turf, you won't feel so intimidated, and the banker will better understand your business. Communications will flow more easily, and your enthusiasm might just become contagious.

Have a Backup Banker

Shop around as you would for any major purpose. Make your banker aware—in a non-threatening way—that you do have other options, but don't bluff. Seek out other options even after you get the loan. Bankers respect healthy competition for good clients.

Respect the Banker's Rules

Understand the banker's rules to have paperwork completed correctly and on time. Most account managers are overworked. Try to make their job easy.

Have an Up-to-Date Plan

You must have a properly prepared financial plan, and you must be able to justify every number.

Get Professional Advice

Make sure your banker is aware you are receiving professional advice. Have your loan agreement reviewed by an accountant, lawyer, and, most important, an experienced businessperson—your financial mentor.

Be in Sync

Make sure that you and your banker see eye to eye before you apply for the money. If you foresee a personality conflict, start looking for another banker.

Ask for Enough

Show your banker that you can forecast and understand your situation. It helps the banker sleep at night, too.

Get Ready for Personal Guarantees

Many entrepreneurs say, "I incorporated so I won't have to sign my life away." From a banker's perspective, if you have a new corporation, few assets, and no track record, you'll probably have to personally guarantee your loan. It is very important to understand that the amount of a guarantee *might be negotiable*—and the amount of this guarantee should be one of your major concerns as you, the owner, "shop around" for the banker that is right for you.

If you do have to sign personally for a loan, make a decision right away to begin finding a way to get rid of personal guarantees. If your business is running smoothly after the first few years, be ready to switch your account to another bank if your bank doesn't want to lift or reduce the guarantees.

Negotiate the Best Deal You Can

The bank will respect you for being a good negotiator. If you still have a job, negotiate for a line of credit or loan while you are still employed. Personal lines of credit are reviewed each year, and chances are you can maintain this line if you keep up a good credit rating.

Understand the Banker's Discretionary Limits

Different managers have different maximum amounts they can lend, depending on their position and bank policy. Try to find out what the lending limit is for your prospective banker. If it is below the amount you are asking, he or she will need to get approval from a supervisor.

If you are planning to take out a loan for your business, remember that banks and financial institutions are in the business of making money for their shareholders. Before you get a loan and "sign on the dotted line," *read the fine print* of your loan agreement. Remember the "buyer beware" rule, and be prepared for the following.

Spousal Guarantee

In certain provinces, laws governing matrimonial assets might mean that your spouse's guarantee would be required. Needless to say, you should try to avoid spousal guarantees, but if you do get your spouse to sign on the dotted line, your relationship had better be rock solid.

Premium Rates

Be prepared to pay a premium interest rate. Banks consider small business high risk and charge accordingly. For the privilege of controlling your destiny, you can expect to pay as much as the prime rate plus 3 percent on unsecured loans, and usually prime plus 1 percent on secured loans.

Demand Loans

Most loans to small businesses, both operating and term, are demand loans. This means that there is a footnote on your financial agreement that says your financial institution can "demand" full payment at any time for virtually any reason. If, for example, your bank manager gets cold feet because of a faltering economy, he or she can call your loan and go after you personally if you have signed a guarantee. Try to avoid this type of demand loan arrangement, or, at the very least, try to limit the demand portion of the loan. Always have a backup plan in place in case the bank calls your loan.

Collateral

If you have no assets or security, you won't get a loan—period. Banks are not in the business of risking their shareholders' money. All banks will ask for business and personal (if they can get it) security or collateral for your loan. It is common practice to request a collateral amount that far exceeds the value of the loan. One Canadian study, for example, estimated that the average bank collateral requested by banks for start-ups was four times the value of the loan. Collateral for established business was at least double the amount of the loan. In effect, banks will ask you to guarantee personally an amount far in excess of what you are asking for—even if you are an existing business. The more collateral the banks have, the more secure they feel. We reiterate: You should negotiate to limit your collateral, especially if it is personal.

Insurance

Most banks and financial intuitions will require you to have the standard personal and business insurance (fire, theft, etc.) to protect them should you have an unexpected problem. In many cases, a bank or financial institution will even require you to sign over your life insurance and disability policies to them. You should make absolutely sure that those close to you are also protected should you die or become incapacitated.

Covenants

There are literally dozens of covenants or legal conditions that could be built into your loan agreement to protect the lender. Some of these are likely to include

- an environmental assessment;
- maintaining a minimum level of cash;
- restrictions on certain financial activities, such as the payment of bonuses and dividends, without the lender's approval;
- a mandated time period (for example, 90 days after year-end) for providing financial statements to the bank (if this covenant is in your agreement, try not to agree to provide an audited statement—it could cost you thousands of dollars);
- a shareholders or partnership agreement; or
- a maximum on the size of capital purchases you can make without bank approval.

Fees

Banks might require you to pay a range of user and service fees for setting up your line of credit, requesting your loan balance, writing cheques, and using credit card facilities. Some of these fees are negotiable, and some are not. Here are the two major user fees that you should try to avoid or at least negotiate.

- **Application fee.** You might be asked to pay a loan application fee (usually ranging from $100 to $200), which is the bank's cost (including the cost associated with preparing a credit application form) for evaluating its opportunity to deal with you.
- **Loan management fees.** You might very well be subjected to additional fees if your bank is required to spend time on activities such as monitoring your accounts receivable or inventory, meeting with clients, and preparing statements.

Many owners of small businesses don't become aware of these extra charges until after the fact. Find out what your obligations are before you sign anything.

We also encourage you to keep a running list of questions to ask prospective bankers. These will get you started:

- What are your lending limits?
- Who makes the decisions on loans?
- What are your views on my industry?
- What experience do you have in working with businesses like mine?
- Could you recommend a qualified lawyer? A bookkeeper? An accountant? A computer consultant?
- Are you interested in writing equipment leases?
- What kind of terms do you give on accounts receivable financing?
- What is the bank rate on Visa or MasterCard accounts? What credit limit could I expect for my business credit cards?
- What interest can I earn on my business chequing account?
- Do you have a merchants' or commercial window?
- Do you have a night depository?
- If you can't lend me money, can you direct me to people who might be interested in doing it?
- Do you make Canada Small Business Financing (CSBF) loans? (We'll discuss CSBF loans later in the chapter.)
- If I open up a business chequing account here, what else can you do for me?

OTHER SOURCES OF START-UP CAPITAL

James Brown knows the benefits of looking around. After his doctors told him he would never work again as a fisherman in Nova Scotia, he was able to secure a small loan of $500 from Calmeadow Nova Scotia. He found a loan that was based on his character, "not on collateral." As the business grew, he borrowed a total of $16,000, including supplier credit. He now has two employees and operates year-round.[7]

By now, you should have improved your money savvy and developed a firm grasp on your personal finances. And ideally, you've also befriended a banker. Now it's time to zero in on some other sources of start-up capital—as James Brown and Kelly Earle, featured in the opening vignette, did. For more information on other sources of financing, see Box 11.5.

Box 11.4   Sources of Financing

- **Government and Community-Based Financing Programs** (Industry Canada): http://www.cbsc.org/servlet/ContentServer?bistopic=Financing&pagename= CBSC_FE/CBSC_WebPage/CBSC_WebPage_Temp&lang=eng&cid=1091019988523& =CBSC_WebPage—Here you will find a long list of government and community-based financing programs, such as the Community Business Development Corporation (CBDC), Women Entrepreneurs' Fund, and the Canada/Alberta Western Economic Partnership Agreement funding.

- **Small Business Funding Centre:** http://www.grants-loans.org/grantsloans/ index.php—This is a great site that can lead you to all kinds of loan and granting programs. Depending on the size and nature of your business, you might be eligible for anywhere from $100 to $100,000.

- **Private Sector Assistance** (Industry Canada): http://strategis.ic.gc.ca/epic/internet/ insof-sdf.nsf/en/h_so03324e.html—Search this comprehensive database for financial providers that can meet your specific business needs. Browse a list of banks, credit unions, leasing companies, venture capital companies, and much more.

- **Micro-Credit** (Industry Canada): http://strategis.gc.ca/epic/internet/insof-sdf.nsf/en/h_so03327e.html—Search through a wide array of micro credit providers to find financing of less than $25,000 to suit your particular business needs.
- **Government Assistance** (Industry Canada): http://strategis.gc.ca/epic/internet/insof-sdf.nsf/en/h_so03325e.html—Access a wealth of information about government programs and services relevant to your business situation.
- **Venture Capital**
  a. Canadian Venture Capital Association: http://www.cvca.ca—Learn more about venture capital. You can even find a list of Canadian venture capitalists.
  b. National Angel Organization (NAO): http://www.angelinvestor.ca—The NAO does not make angel investments, but the links section (http://www.angelinvestor.ca/s_5.asp) contains the names and Web sites of angel investors whose members have participated in NAO initiatives.

Angels

ANGELS

Wealthy individuals from the informal venture capital market who are willing to risk their money in someone else's business

We want you to return for a moment to our Crazy Plates case study in Chapter 3, pages 72–75. The first product launch "bombed," but the team didn't give up. They found the money they needed to begin again from an angel investor, William Holland, the chief executive of CI Investments. **Angels** refer to wealthy individuals from the informal venture capital market (e.g., retired small-business people) that are willing to risk their own money in someone else's business. In Canada, angels have financed approximately twice as many firms as have institutional venture capitalists. They tend to finance the early stages of the business with investments in the order of $100,000.[8] (Angel investor links are available on the NAO site, Box 11.4.) Angels often require an active management or operations role. They are most active in smaller firms, where they might even get involved in the "hands-on," day-to-day operations. In larger firms, the role of the angel is more distant and usually takes the form of management advice and counsel through the board of directors.

Angel investors can be hard to find, but you can start with professional advisors (accountants, lawyers, etc.), your local chamber of commerce, and the local office of the Business Development Bank of Canada (http://www.bdc.ca); or visit the "Private-Sector Assistance" page on the Industry Canada Web site (see Box 11.4).

Suppliers

Most suppliers will offer your small business at least 30 days to pay for their product once you are established. Suppliers might also allow you to defer your payments over a longer period if you pay some sort of interest charges on the deferred payment. You might even want to negotiate a consignment arrangement with some hungry suppliers. In this case, the supplier owns the goods until you sell them. In Box 11.5, we describe one strategy that can help you negotiate more favourable terms with your suppliers.

Customers

Customers, especially for home-based and service businesses, are a potential source of credit. Don't be shy about asking for a deposit before you provide a service or go out and purchase supplies and materials. For example, if you are in the "fix it" business, get your customers to pay for your materials before you start the job by asking them for a deposit. That way, you can be a little more confident you will get full payment, and you don't have to tie up your own money.

Box 11.5   The Vendor Statement Form

An often overlooked technique for reducing your capital requirement is to probe your vendors (major suppliers) for the best prices and terms available. Professional buyers and purchasing agents ask their vendors to fill out an information sheet, writing down the terms and conditions of their sales plans. This is a good idea for you as well.

As the owner of a small business, you must buy professionally, and a **vendor statement** will help you do just that. With this form, your vendors' verbal promises become written promises. How well you buy is as important as how well you sell, because every dollar you save by "buying right" drops directly to the bottom line. To compete in your arena, you need the best terms and prices you can get. The statement will help you get the best.

Personalize your form by putting your business name at the top. Then list the information you need, leaving blanks to be written in. Some of the basics include

- the vendor's name;
- the vendor's address, phone number, fax number, e-mail, and Web site, if applicable;
- the sales rep's name;
- the vendor's business phone number (Will the vendor accept collect calls?);
- the vendor's home phone number (for emergencies);
- the minimum purchase required;
- quantity discount size (How much?) and conditions (What must you do to earn?);
- whether dating or extended payments terms are available;
- advertising/promotion allowances;
- policies on returns for defective goods (Who pays the freight?);
- delivery times;
- assistance (technical, sales, and so on);
- product literature available;
- point-of-purchase material provided;
- support for grand opening (Will the supplier donate prize or other support?);
- the nearest other dealer handing this particular line;
- special services the sales rep can provide; and
- the vendor's signature, the date, and some kind of agreement that you will be notified of any changes.

Remember, the information the vendor writes on this statement is the starting point for negotiations. You should be able to negotiate more favourable terms with some vendors because these people want your business. Revise your application form as you learn from experience how vendors can help you.

VENDOR STATEMENT

A personally designed form that allows you to negotiate with each vendor from a position of informed strength

Leasing

About one-third of all small businesses use leasing as a source of debt financing, amounting to about $3 billion in contracts annually. Commercial banks are now getting more involved in the leasing business.

A leasing company (lessor) will purchase an asset such as equipment, computers, automobiles, or land. The small business (lessee) will then sign a legal agreement to pay the lessor a fixed amount over a specific period of time. There are several types of leasing arrangement, including a "walk-away lease," or "net lease," which entitles the lessee simply to return the asset at the end of the term.

A "capital," or "open-end," lease requires the lessee to buy back the asset at the end of the term. Most leases can be tailored to the lessee requirements, and the lease type will depend on the situational needs.

The obvious advantage is that a small business does not have to tie up its start-up or operating funds. Unlike loans, leases normally cover the total asset costs, including installation and transportation charges. Lease charges are usually fixed and are likely higher than a bank loan rate. They provide small businesses with a reliable payment schedule. A lease might be one of the few options in hard economic times, when loans from financial institutions might not be available. As well, lease payments are a business expense.

Leasing also has its disadvantages, however. For example, chances are that the lease will cost you more over the long run. Leasing companies are in the business of making money, and they have to meet their profit margins. Unless you have a specific kind of lease, you will have no assets to show for after the lease is over. In other words, leases do not improve the asset base of the business. A lease payment also commits the owner over a specific period of time and thus limits the flexibility the owner might otherwise have to sell the equipment for a more efficient factor of production. One other note of caution: Lease rates normally carry a high interest rate.

Employees and Employers

If you have a good idea, a current or past employer might well be a possible source of start-up capital. When you hire employees, don't be afraid to offer them a part of the action in return for a small investment.

Micro Lending Programs

Several non-government and community-based agencies have initiated innovative start-up programs to aid very small businesses, or micro businesses (see Box 11.6). According to the Department of Finance, "micro-credit refers to small loans made to low-income individuals to sustain self-employment or to start up very small businesses. Although there is no standard definition of micro credit, in practice such loans are quite small, amounting to a few thousand dollars."[9]

One well-known micro-lending organization is the Canadian Youth Business Foundation (CYBF). PropertyGuys.com—a company that we highlight in Chapter 14—is a good example of a highly successful Canadian franchise organization that relied on the start-up and micro-lending assistance of the CYBF. According to Ken LeBlanc, a founding partner and president of PropertyGuys.com, "Without the injection of capital from the CYBF loan, I would dare say we would not exist as we are today."[10] More information on this innovative program can be found in Box 11.7. Another good example of a micro-lending initiative is the Calmeadow program used by James Brown to start his business in Nova Scotia (profiled at the start of this section). Calmeadow (http://www.calmeadow.com) also operates in other centres across Canada. There are basically two types of community-based models: the lending circle (also known as peer lending), and very small loans with no group affiliation but which require some sort of security. Because there is no central clearinghouse for these types of micro-borrowing opportunities, you are going to have to start by getting in touch with local economic development departments and chambers of commerce.

> ### Box 11.6   Canadian Youth Business Foundation: Community-Based Funding Program
>
> Look into the Canadian Youth Business Foundation's (CYBF) community-based funding program. This business loan program provides essential start-up credit to youth (ages 18–34) who have good business ideas but not the resources to get up and running.
>
> Loans are available only in locations where CYBF has set up a program in partnership with a local community organization. The pool of funds available in each community is limited. Therefore, loans (up to $15,000) are granted on a merit and need basis, similar to a scholarship, to young people most likely to succeed and where the money will make a critical difference to the individual's ability to begin the enterprise.
>
> At the very least, you're going to need a business plan to qualify. For more information, visit the CYBF Web site (http://www.cybf.ca/).

Government Programs

A number of local, provincial, and federal programs are designed to assist small businesses. These plans change from time to time, however, so it is important to obtain the most recent information from the respective government. Governments know a growth market when they see one, and they do make an effort to help. In recent years, they have been moving away from helping finance small business to merely providing information and advice. However, a number of financial support programs for small business still exist—the sources of which are far too numerous to detail here. We encourage you to visit a government information office even before you begin putting the final touches on your plan. A good starting point would be a visit or call to the Canada Business Service Centre for a location nearest you (http://canadabusiness.gc.ca/gol/cbec/site.nsf/en/bg00341.html). You can also find a lot of information on government support programs via the Internet (see Box 11.4).

Venture Capitalists

With venture capital firms, we enter the world of high rollers and high fliers. Unlike banks, which lend money that is secured usually by real estate or other "hard" assets, venture capitalists don't lend money. They are equity investors who buy a piece of the business with private or publicly sponsored pools of capital. Venture capitalists gamble on the business's rapid growth, hoping to reap a 300 to 500 percent return on their investment. They often expect at least 35 percent annual return on their investment.

According to Canada's Venture Capital & Private Equity Association (http://www.cvca.ca), venture capital people prefer to enter the financial picture at the second stage of a firm's development, when the business has proven its potential and needs a large infusion of cash to support growth. In the late 1990s, the hungriest consumers of venture capital were technology companies with high-growth potential. For example, high-tech firms secured about 66 percent of the $2 billion invested from venture capital in 1998.[11] Not surprisingly, the venture capital dried up after the technology bubble burst early in 2000.

ACTION STEP 52

Prepare to meet your lenders

Know who your potential lenders are and why they should want to help you.

Part A

List potential lenders and investors. Begin with yourself, your family, and your friends, and then move on to business acquaintances and colleagues. Don't forget institutional leaders.

Part B

Now list some reasons why lenders should want to invest in your business. What inducements are you offering potential investors? If you're offering them a very small return on investment (ROI), what are you offering that will offset that?

Think about the legal form of your business. Would you attract more investors if you incorporated?

Part C

Test your tactics by talking to a few friends. Tell them, "This is just a test, and I'd like your reactions to my new business venture." Watch their reactions, and make a list of the objections they give you—the reasons why they cannot lend you money.

Using your list of your friends' objections, write down your answers to those objections. Are there any you cannot answer? What does this mean for your business?

Cooperative Partnership

More and more small businesses are beginning to recognize the financial benefits of combining resources in some kind of cooperative arrangements. These types of arrangements go under many names: joint venture, strategic partnering, strategic alliance, corporate partnering, and so on. No matter what business you are in or what business you want to start, you can benefit from establishing strong collaborative alliances. For example, if you are establishing a home office, why not consider entering into an agreement with major customers or clients who need your services? They will supply you with an office, and in return, you provide them with the services they require for a set number of hours per week. If you have a product you want to sell and need the distribution channel, why not enter into a marketing agreement with a larger, more experienced firm? It will market and sell the product that you supply. If you have a new idea and have built a prototype, you don't have to manufacture the product yourself: Strike up an arrangement with a manufacturing plant to build the product, and you simply sell it. The number of options available is limited only by your imagination.

In Action Step 52, we ask you to list potential lenders and investors and to develop your persuasive arguments. Without persuasive inducements to lenders, they have no reason to invest in your business. If you need help in listing your reasons, you might begin by profiling your target customer. List industry trends, and dovetail them with a scenario of where your product or service fits. Move from there to marketing strategy, selling, the profit picture, and return on investment.

In the final part of Action Step 52, you will test your tactics on friends. Ask your friends to respond as though they were potential investors. You want to hear objections so that you can address them. When you have completed this Action Step, you will be truly prepared to meet your lenders.

WILL THAT BE DEBT OR EQUITY?

DEBT FINANCING

An obligation of a business to repay a lender the full amount of a debt (loan) in addition to interest charges

If you or others invest money in a business and expect, in return, a portion of ownership, this is called an equity, or ownership, investment. Equity investors, as owners, usually expect a say in the day-to-day operations of the business and how the profit or net income is to be distributed to the owners. When others, or even you, lend money to a business, this is called **debt financing**—an obligation of a business to repay a lender the full amount of a debt (loan) in addition to interest charges.

If a business is financed through debt (a loan), it is obliged to repay the lender the full amount of the debt in addition to interest charges on the debt. A lender does not usually get any ownership rights or say in the operations of the business. The type of debt instrument will depend on the particular business need. For example, you would obtain a mortgage for buying a building and use a credit card or operating loan for purchasing inventory.

How should you finance your business: debt or equity, or some combination of the two? The trick is to find the right balance between debt and equity—one that will satisfy the needs of you, the owner; the business; and the market. However, in looking for money to finance your business, remember that any "external" source of capital will always consider the extent of your financial commitment to the business. Normally, an investor will require at least a 50 percent investment by the owner. In terms of the solvency ratios discussed in Chapter 10, lenders like to see a debt-to-equity ratio that is less than 1.

If personal funds (equity) are not sufficient, you must decide on debt or selling a piece of the ownership (also equity), or some combination of the two.

Generally, Canadian independent businesses rely far more on debt than on equity, with the banks playing a predominant role as sources of financing.

Listed below are some of the pros and cons of debt versus equity financing.

ADVANTAGES OF DEBT

Financing through debt, mainly by line of credit, is useful in meeting a short-term deficit in the cash flow or in financing lower risk projects. For example, it would be appropriate where money is needed to fund inventory before it's sold. Some of the advantages of debt are

- the entrepreneur does not have to give up or share control of the company,
- the term of the debt (loan) is generally limited,
- debt may be acquired from a variety of lenders, and
- the kind of information needed to obtain the loan is generally straightforward and would normally be incorporated into the business plan.

DISADVANTAGES OF DEBT

Taking on debt can become problematic when a project is risky and the return is uncertain. For example, new product development is no guarantee of success in the marketplace. It would be more appropriate to find an investor to share the risk in this activity rather than going into debt. Debt can also become a problem if it isn't managed properly. The most frequent errors include

- taking on more debt than the company needs to fund expansion,
- adopting too restrictive a policy toward debt and thus not accessing funds that might be readily available,
- misapplying funds in ways that yield inadequate returns and make it difficult for the company to repay its loans, and
- making mistakes in servicing the debt (accepting inappropriate repayment terms, encountering cash flow difficulties, or taking on too large a debt-service burden).

ADVANTAGES OF EQUITY

Many entrepreneurs associate finding an investor with giving up control of their company. An appropriate investor, however, can contribute expertise, contacts, and new business as well as money. If the result is substantial growth in profitability, the original owner's overall wealth will increase, even if his or her share in the company is somewhat smaller. Equity investment is especially appropriate for

- larger projects with longer time frames or additional skill requirements,
- high-risk ventures where the costs of debt would be prohibitive,
- rapidly growing ventures that might quickly exhaust available bank financing as they expand, and
- situations in which debt financing is not available.

DISADVANTAGES OF EQUITY

Finding an investor brings another viewpoint to a company, and there is always the danger of incompatibility and disagreement. Because an equity owner is an integral part of the company, however, it becomes much more difficult to terminate the relationship if disagreements occur. With a partner, it is important to have a share-holders agreement.

There is another point to consider when deciding between debt and equity. Canada is a country with significant regional differences, and these might become apparent to entrepreneurs attempting to secure equity financing. In some parts of the country, businesses might not have the same access to equity capital as do their counterparts established closer to larger financial centres. Access will also be influenced by the availability of government funding through provincial programs and federal regional economic development agencies, such as the Atlantic Canada Opportunities Agency and Western Economic Diversification Canada. On the other hand, regionalism plays less of a role in securing business loans. For example, each of Canada's major chartered banks operates a nationwide system of branches, all of which offer the same access to loans on the same terms in any member branch.

Finally, equity investment should not normally be used for short-term obligations. For example, it would not make much sense to get a new partner to finance inventory fluctuations. Equity is usually thought of as a long-term financial instrument.

PRIMARY TYPES OF DEBT FINANCING

The major types of debt financing for start-up business are spelled out below. Other "secondary" types of financing are shown in Table 11.4.

Shareholder Loans

SHAREHOLDER LOAN

Owner investment in the form of a loan

Should you decide to incorporate your business—and there are a number of good reasons for doing so, as we will learn in the next chapter—you have the option of investing by means of a **shareholder loan**. Although many banks will not lend money to a business per se, they will provide a personal loan to the owner, who, in turn, lends the money to the business. There are a number of advantages to an owner in investing in the form of a loan as opposed to equity (through purchasing shares). First, you can deduct the interest payments as a company expense. If you buy shares (equity investment), however, you will receive payment in the form of dividends, and these dividend payments are not tax deductible by the company. Second, in most cases, it is easier to withdraw your money when it is in the form of a loan. And third, if your loan is properly secured, your investment will be safer in the event of a business failure. The main point here is that there are advantages to lending the company money, but you really should make sure that you get sound professional advice.

Canada Small Business Financing (CSBF) Loans

CANADA SMALL BUSINESS FINANCING (CSBF) LOAN

A loan guaranteed by the federal government under the Canada Small Business Financing Act

Under the Canada Small Business Financing Act, the federal government guarantees loans to small businesses through Canadian chartered banks and a few other Canadian financial institutions, such as Alberta Treasury Branches, and credit unions/caisses populaires.

The CSBF program has become a major funding source for start-up business. Historically, of the total CSBF loans granted, about one-third has gone to firms less than a year old. These loans can be used to finance up to 90 percent of the cost of the purchase and improvement of three categories of fixed assets:

- the purchase of land required to operate the business;
- the renovation, improvement, modernization, extension, and/or purchase of premises; and
- the purchase, installation, renovation, improvement, and/or modernization of new or used equipment.

Table 11.4 Secondary Types of Loans and Credit Arrangements

Type of Loan	Explanation
Floor plan loan	These loans are provided mainly by manufacturers to stock up goods in the retailers' or distributors' premises. The retailer reimburses the manufacturer for the loan amount when the product is sold.
Bridge financing	This type of interim financing provides short-term funding to cover the cost of a start-up project until long-term funds become available.
Mezzanine financing	Mezzanine financing combines long-term lending with an equity position.
Factoring	This form of financing is available from specialized firms (and banks, to a limited extent). A business sells its accounts receivable to a factoring company at a discounted rate (as much as 85 percent of a "high-quality" account). This will reduce the risk of not receiving a payment and frees up needed cash.
Letter of credit	Letters of credit are widely used in exporting and importing businesses. One of the most common exporting problems, for example, is collecting the accounts receivable. A popular method—and the most secure one—is a letter of credit issued by the purchaser's bank. This is the purchaser's guarantee that the money has been set aside and will be paid to the supplier on satisfactory delivery. Most banks and major financial institutions can provide this letter, given proper security, of course.
Inventory financing	In some cases, banks and financial institutions will allow small businesses to borrow against a percentage value of their inventory. The business must have inventory that can be readily sold. Depending on the salability of the inventory, the owner could receive financing as high as 70 percent or as little as 30 percent of the market value.
Accounts receivable	In this type of financing, the money owed by customers of a business (accounts receivable) becomes the collateral for a loan. Banks and financial institutions have been known to provide as much as 75 percent of the value of the accounts receivable that are not more than 60 days old. Again, adequate security is an important consideration in determining the percentage value of the receivables.
Conditional sale	Some manufacturers will provide financing to small businesses for a particular product on a conditional basis. They will require a substantial down payment and then allow the business to pay for the remaining portion on an installment basis over a period of time. This is termed a conditional sale because the business will own the product only on the condition that all the payments are made.

CSBF loans are available to all businesses operating for profit in Canada—excluding farms and charitable or religious enterprises—that have annual gross revenues of less than $5 million. These loans cannot be used to acquire shares or provide working capital and may not exceed $250,000. Borrowers must pay the federal government a one-time, up-front loan registration fee of 2 percent of the amount of each loan. This amount may be added to the loan. The maximum rate of interest charged by the lending institution cannot exceed the prime rate plus 3 percent for floating-rate loans or the residential mortgage rate plus 3 percent for fixed-rate loans. This interest rate includes an administration fee of 1.25 percent, which is paid back annually to the government. Personal guarantees may not exceed 25 percent of the amount of the original loan. The maximum period over which a loan may be repaid is 10 years.

It is important to note that some of the terms and conditions, including the interest rates, are negotiable. In the past, at least one major bank has eliminated the requirement for personal guarantees under the CSBF program. Other banks have reduced the interest rate to prime and added automatic overdraft protection of up to 10 percent of the CSBF loan. Our advice: CSBF loans are a great opportunity, but shop around for the best deal. For more information, visit the "Canada Small Business Financing Program link on Industry Canada's Strategis Web site (http://strategis.ic.gc.ca/epic/internet/incsbfp-pfpec.nsf/en/la00049e.html).

Operating Loans (Line of Credit)

OPERATING LOAN (LINE OF CREDIT)

Money lent to help finance short-term business needs, such as inventory and accounts receivables

Operating loans (sometimes called revolving loans) are used by more than 75 percent of small-business borrowers to finance their short-term business needs. Normally, these loans help finance inventory and accounts receivable—that is, money that has yet to be received from customers to whom a product has been sold. It is important to note that a line of credit or operating loan should not be used to finance the purchase of fixed assets. Generally, the line of credit is the largest part of the loans outstanding of a small businesses' debt obligations.

How much can you borrow? In the normal course of business, the amount will be determined by whichever is lower, your authorized borrowing limit or your margin requirement.

1. Your authorized borrowing limit is established by determining your projected maximum (peak) cash needs in any one month of the year. This is one of the main reasons why accurate projected cash flows are so important.
2. Your margin requirements are based on the fact that you can borrow only up to a specific percentage of accounts receivable outstanding and inventory on your books in any one month. Although you might have a predetermined operating line of, say, $50,000, this doesn't mean that you can go out and use all of it when the need arises. These margins, or limits, will vary depending on the policies of the bank or financial institution. For example, in the past, banks have been known to finance up to 66 percent (sometimes as high as 75 percent) of accounts receivable that are less than 60 days old. But this margin, or percentage, will vary depending on the quality of the receivable and the type of industry. As for inventory, the margin might be as high as 50 percent of the market value but is often lower, depending on how easy it is to sell your inventory. The bottom line here is that if you need an extra $50,000 in a given period to finance inventory and receivables, you will get only a portion of this, and the rest will come from your resources.

PRIME RATE

The lowest rate of interest charged by banks on commercial loans to their most preferred customers

What interest rate will you pay? Depending on the financial institution and the business circumstances, you can normally expect to pay 1 to 3 percent above the **prime rate** for an operating loan. The so-called prime rate, set by each financial institution, is the interest rate the institution charges to its most creditworthy clients. Expect to pay higher interest rates for smaller operating loans. For example, you might pay as much as 3 percent above prime for a $25,000 loan and only 1 percent above prime for a $2 million operating loan. The main point is that interest rates for operating loans can differ from financial institution to financial institution, so we encourage you to shop around. You can negotiate a rate closer to prime if you have good security.

What security is required? An operating line of credit will be secured by the accounts receivable or inventory as well as a personal guarantee. Personal guarantees are required because financial institutions will never recover the full value of an asset should your business fail. Remember, the amount of your personal guarantee is negotiable. At the very least, you should try to limit your personal guarantee to the amount of the unsecured portion of the loan. So if you have an operating loan of, say, $25,000 that is secured by inventory for $12,000, then you should try to keep your personal guarantee below $13,000.

Term Loans

Term loans are used by close to one-half of small businesses and are the major source of medium-term (two to five years) and long-term (greater than five years) financing. In most cases, businesses use term loans to finance the purchase of fixed assets, such as equipment, a truck, or furniture. They may also be used to finance expansion or renovation.

How much can you borrow? Under normal circumstances, you will be able to borrow up to 75 percent of the value of buildings or property. In the case of equipment, you should expect to get about 50 percent of the asset value. Normally, you will repay the loan through a fixed schedule of payments, which corresponds to the life of the asset. If you expect a piece of equipment to last five years, then the payments would be spread over five years.

What interest rate will you pay? Term loans can be repaid at either a fixed or a floating interest rate. A **fixed rate** is one that remains the same over the period of a loan. A **floating rate** changes according to fluctuations in the prime rate. Many small businesses prefer a fixed interest rate because they know how much they have to pay and can budget accordingly. However, fixed rates are generally not available for loans of less than $25,000, and banks will normally charge higher interest for a fixed term. The reason is that a term loan usually commits the bank for several years, increasing the risk that a business might deteriorate. It should be noted that when short-term rates are low, financial institutions will be even more inclined to ask for a higher interest premium for a fixed term loan. Why? Because of the increased risk of rising interest rates. As with operating loans, the terms and conditions for term loans differ from bank to bank.

What security is required? Financial institutions will require you to secure a term loan with the asset being purchased and, in most cases, a guarantee backed by personal assets. If you default on the term loan, the institution will be able to liquidate the asset and hold you personally responsible for any outstanding balance. Again, you should always try to limit your personal guarantees to a specific amount.

PRIMARY TYPES OF EQUITY FINANCING

At some point, you are going to have to decide whether to incorporate your business. We covered the pros and cons of incorporating in Chapter 8. At this point, we want you just to understand that the type or form of equity that your business will require will depend, to some degree, on the legal structure of your business.

If you plan to run your business as a sole proprietorship or partnership, your investment in the business will simply be recorded as an owner's personal investment. You are the owner, and your equity is what you personally put into the business. The main point here is that if other partners are involved in your business, a handshake is not enough. You must have some sort of agreement outlining the terms and conditions of each equity investor's contribution. You will need a partnership shareholders agreement that details such issues as Who is investing what? How will the investment

TERM LOAN

Loan used for medium- to long-term financing of fixed assets, such as equipment, furniture, expansion, or renovation

FIXED RATE

Interest rate that remains the same over the period of a loan

FLOATING RATE

Interest rate that changes with changes in the prime rate

be paid back, and under what conditions? What happens if someone dies? What is the procedure for selling out? What happens if the business fails? You should draw up a formalized legal agreement, with each equity investor consulting his or her own legal and financial advisors beforehand. The legal cost of a shareholders agreement is approximately $300 to $500 for a straightforward agreement.

Should you decide to incorporate, we strongly recommend that you have a lawyer draw up a shareholders agreement to detail the rights and responsibilities of each equity investor. In the case of incorporation, you can structure an equity investment in a number of ways to benefit and protect both you and your potential shareholders. For small businesses, the three principal forms of equity financing are common shares, preferred shares, and convertible debentures. As any formalized equity arrangement can become quite complex, we strongly suggest that you get some expert advice before you sign any agreements.

Common Shares

COMMON SHARES

Equity investments that confer part-ownership of the company but are not as safe as preferred shares should the company fail

Common shares confer part-ownership of the company and are frequently issued in exchange for a company's initial capital. As the company grows, the shares increase in value and provide dividend income. If the company fails, however, common shareholders risk losing their investment. As an incentive to investors to place capital in small businesses, some provinces have set up development corporations that will repay as much as 25 to 30 percent of a shareholder's investment in such enterprises.

Preferred Shares

PREFERRED SHARES

Equity investments that confer part-ownership of the company, earn investors dividends at a fixed rate, and are safer than common shares

Preferred shares may also be offered to investors. Such shares also represent partial ownership of the company. Preferred shares, however, usually earn a dividend at a fixed rate and in the event of business failure, they are better protected than common shares, although their claim is still junior to that of debt holders. A company derives several advantages from issuing preferred shares. Unlike debts, preferred shares have no maturity date, and dividend payments are not as binding as interest payments on debt.

Convertible Debentures

CONVERTIBLE DEBENTURES

Loans that can be exchanged for common shares at a stated price and are better protected than common and preferred shares

Convertible debentures are loans that can be exchanged for common shares in a company at a predetermined price. Like other debentures and bonds, they carry a fixed interest rate and a specified date by which they must be paid. As do shareholders, the holders of convertible debentures have the opportunity to benefit if the company grows. They are also better protected than are holders of common or preferred shares in the event of a failure. And because the debenture is a type of loan, interest is tax deductible. As a result, larger companies might find it easier to sell convertible debentures than other types of equity. Issuing convertible debentures is therefore a way to raise equity more cheaply than by selling common shares.

In a Nutshell

Money creates its own world. It has its own customs, rituals, and rules. Before you start asking people for money for your business, spend the needed time researching the world of money. Here are some things you can do to streamline your research.

1. Get your personal finances in order.
2. Take some time, prepare, and study the world of finance.

3. Find someone who knows more about money than you do, and keep asking questions.
4. Know that loans are made on the basis of the four Cs: cash, character, capacity (to repay), and collateral.
5. Start to develop the financial section for your business plan. You need to show your plan to bankers, vendors, and lenders. If you feel overwhelmed, start with an outline. (See Chapter 15 for a model plan.)
6. Begin thinking of a banker as your gateway to the world of money.
7. Search out potential lenders.
8. Establish your balance between equity and debt.

Key Terms

angels

Canada Small Business Financing (CSBF) loan

collateral

common shares

convertible debentures

credit

debt financing

fixed rate

floating rate

four Cs of credit

love money

net worth (personal equity)

operating loan (line of credit)

personal balance sheet

preferred shares

prime rate

shareholder loan

term loan

unsecured credit

vendor statement

Think Points for Success

✓ Your banker can provide a wealth of information. Maintain a good relationship with him or her. If your banker ever turns you down, there is usually a very good reason. Correct it.
✓ How well you buy is as important as how well you sell.
✓ Partner with your vendors or customers. It's often the best way to get the best deals.
✓ In dealing with bankers, vendors, and lenders, use lots of open-ended questions, such as "What else can you do for me?"

Business Plan Building Block

POTENTIAL SOURCES AND EQUITY AMOUNT

List your potential sources and amount of equity for your start-up business. Complete the table below.

Potential Sources of Equity	Potential Amount ($) (Market Value*)
Personal equity	_____
Savings	_____
Borrow on your life insurance	_____
Mortgage your property	_____
Obtain a line of unsecured personal credit from your bank, credit union, or other financial institution	_____

3

12

Building and Managing a Winning Team

Chapter 12 will help you prepare parts F and G of your business plan, Management and Personnel.

Charlene Webb loved food. Baking was her first passion. She began her career as a hotel assistant chef—armed with a two-year course in hotel management at a local college and a part-time course in management at a local university. But Charlene had always had a streak of independence in her, and it wasn't long before she decided to open her own business—a gourmet cookware shop in a major mall.

She hired two assistant managers and three shift supervisors, thinking that good management would be the key to her success. She made one of her mangers responsible for basic bookkeeping.

But just six months after opening day, Charlene knew she was in trouble. Three cheques had been returned "NSF," and she was not clear why this had happened. Charlene learned too late that her manager-bookkeeper had no skills in accounting. Apparently, Charlene had been losing money every month, and because her books were a mess, she had no idea why. Sales seemed to be on target, so she assumed that the costs were too high.

Charlene found an accountant and learned that high labour costs were, indeed, the main problem. She had too many managers and not enough workers. But by this time, it was too late. Creditors were knocking at the door. She scrambled for a buyer, took her losses in a "fire" sale, and found herself back in the kitchen working part-time at a local restaurant. She also worked two nights a week as a waitress at a local bar. This extra work helped pay off her outstanding business accounts.

After two years of hard work, she finally got herself out of debt and wanted her independence back. By this time, she had become very interested in the fashion industry, so she decided to open a women's specialty store. The shop was small—about 1,500 square feet—and was located in a neighbourhood centre in an upscale rural community of about 20,000 people.

This time she had a different management strategy. First, she hired Jill, a local accountant, on a contract basis. Jill would do the books and provide her with monthly income and cash flow statements. At the first meeting, Jill told Charlene that full-time employees would increase her labour costs by as much as 40 percent, so

LEARNING OPPORTUNITIES

After reading this chapter, you should be able to

- understand the basic management functions of leading and organizing;
- chart your organizational structure;
- consider the benefits of a virtual or network organization;
- evaluate the skills that you and the members of your founding team possess;
- understand the value of an advisory board and external advisors;
- take another look at yourself and identify your strengths, weaknesses, and business needs;
- use the idea of balance to brainstorm your ideal team and scout potential team members;
- develop an action plan with your new team before you open the doors;
- consider the merits of the just-in-time team, partnerships, leased employees, and the independent contractor or associate;
- recognize the need for a mentor; and
- learn how to hire your first employee.

ACTION STEP PREVIEW

53. Understand your personal strengths and weaknesses.
54. Consider a just-in-time team.
55. Find a mentor.
56. Decide who's in charge of what.

4. Communicate. Bring your vision to others effectively and with confidence.

5. Check progress and results. Know where you are, so you can get where you want to go.[3]

To learn more about what this type leadership is all about, see Box 12.1. A brief summary of other leadership styles can be obtained by linking onto Legacee, "Different Types of Leadership Styles" (http://www.legacee.com/Info/Leadership/LeadershipStyles.html).

What is your leadership strategy? How will you empower—give power to—your business? Be prepared to include a statement about how you are going to motivate your team to achieve the goals and objectives that will make you—and them—successful. Don't be afraid to show emotion. Emotion is a driving force, and, in fact, some experts say that leadership is the emotional part of managing.

Box 12.1   Leadership from Within

Leadership is no longer about being in front of the pack, scoring the most goals, being first in sales, or having the highest position. Peter Urs Bender, "Canada's presentation guru," in his book *Leadership from Within*, helps us understand a new kind of leadership that must "come from within."

According to Bender, leadership is about these things.

1. **People.** The other things—sales, profit, equipment, numbers, and systems—are important, but they are just tools and measures to help us make progress.
2. **Being the leader of you.** Find a vision, put it into action, and you will automatically become the leader of others.
3. **Internal motivation.** Command-and-control, "shape up or ship out" behaviour is quickly being replaced by an approach that involves coaching, empowering, and inspiring.
4. **Striving for perfection while accepting our imperfections.** Being a leader means accepting that we are human.
5. **Change.** It's about making conscious choices to bring about positive change.
6. **Confidence.** You must truly believe that things can be better.
7. **Growth.** Going beyond what we have done before.
8. **Energy.** Energy comes from your belief that something good is about to happen—a belief in a positive future. Energy is contagious.
9. **Creating a positive experience.** Leaders can motivate and make people feel excited and positive about work and life.
10. **Creating results.** True leadership is the ability to turn vision into results.
11. **Reducing fear and increasing hope.** Leaders are able to make changes and increase people's confidence and sense of hope.

Source: Peter Urs Bender, *Leadership from Within* (Toronto: Stoddart Publishing, 1997), pp. 7–11. Reprinted by permission of Stoddart Publishing Co. Limited, Toronto, Ontario.

ORGANIZING

In Chapter 8, we discussed ways in which you might want to organize your business—sole proprietorship, partnership, corporation, or cooperative. But you are also going to have to come to grips with such organizing questions as What tasks are there to be done? Who does them? How are the tasks to be grouped? Who reports to whom? and Where are decisions made? This means you are going to have to think about a structure or organizational framework that will help you accomplish these types of tasks.

The key to developing an organizational structure or framework for your business is to remember that we are deeply entrenched in a business environment that demands innovation, proactivity, and risk taking. Businesses can no longer form bureaucratic structures that inhibit the transfer of information. Table 12.1 shows the basic differences between the new "organic" structures and the old mechanistic ones. Bureaucracies inhibit the flow of information. In the management section of your plan, you will have to explain how you will organize your activities and structure your business to focus on your target customer and respond to a changing environment.

Traditionally, most small businesses have been organized on the basis of function, geography, or type of customer. Examples of these traditional types of structures are shown in Figure 12.1.

Table 12.1 Organic versus Mechanistic Organizational Structure

Organic	Mechanistic
1. Channels of communication open with free flow of information throughout the organization	1. Channels of communication highly structured with restricted information flow
2. Operating styles allowed to vary freely	2. Operating styles must be uniform and restricted
3. Authority for decisions based on expertise of the individual	3. Authority decisions based on formal line management position
4. Free adaptation by the organization to changing circumstances	4. Reluctant adaptation, with insistence on holding fast to tried and true management principles
5. Emphasis on getting things done unconstrained by formally laid-out procedures	5. Emphasis on formally laid-down procedures, with reliance on tried and true management principles
6. Loose, informal control with emphasis on norm of cooperation	6. Tight control through sophisticated control systems
7. Flexible on-job behaviour permitted to be shaped by the requirements of the situation and personality of the individual doing the job	7. Constrained on-job behaviour required to conform to job description
8. Participation and group consensus used frequently	8. Superiors make decisions, with minimum consultation and involvement of subordinates

Source: Dr. Pradip N. Khandwalla, *The Design of Organization* (New York: Harcourt Brace Jovanovich, 1977), p. 411. Reprinted by permission of the author.

At this point, we want you to consider the benefits of the **virtual** or **network organization**. In this type of organizational structure, the core business functions (such as sales, accounting, retail, and manufacturing) are separated from the main business by small businesses or independent teams, often called **strategic business units**. What this means is that a business no longer has to compete under one roof. Activities such as human resources, advertising, maintenance, and sales can be contracted out to small businesses on an as-needed basis or handled by remote employees.

Here's how the concept might work for an advertising agency. The entire agency might consist of only one person who presents the client with an idea. Once the idea is approved, the single person assembles "associates": graphic designers, copywriters, photographers, models, performers, and media experts to produce the package. The team is virtual—it is not housed in one central location—and might even have a "shamrock" structure, as shown in Figure 12.2. This virtual ad agency has little staffing overhead but can bring together the best talent to provide the client with a

VIRTUAL ORGANIZATION (OR NETWORK ORGANIZATION)

Organizational structure in which the major functions are broken up into strategic business units

STRATEGIC BUSINESS UNITS

Independent teams or small businesses that support the functional needs of the main organization

> ### Figure 12.1 Charting Your Organizational Structure: Three Traditional Approaches
>
> **FUNCTIONAL**
> The functional approach to an organizational structure is one of the most widely used forms in small business. Teams are formed according to the duties or functions they perform, such as accounting, service, or sales. Shown below is a simple functional organizational chart for a restaurant.
>
>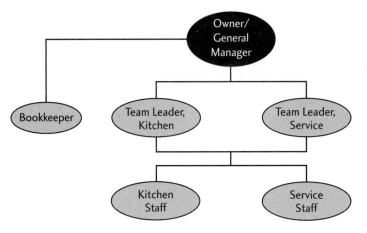
>
> **GEOGRAPHIC**
> Some types of independent business might decide to organize on the basis of geography. Provided below is an example of a "flat" service type of organization chart that has a structure based on territory or geography.
>
>
>
> **CUSTOMER DRIVEN**
> Some independent businesses are starting to organize their company on the basis of type of customer. After all, it's the customer who drives the business. Here is one simple example of a small research and development organization that has a "customer-driven" organizational structure.
>
>
>
> Source: Ron Knowles, *Writing a Small Business Plan: TVO Course Guide* (Toronto: Dryden, an imprint of Harcourt Brace & Company, Canada, 1995), pp. 49, 50. Reprinted by permission.

high-quality campaign at a reasonable cost. Once the project is completed, the team of associates disbands, with each member moving on to other projects.

For independent businesses, the virtual organization can allow the little guy to compete with the larger firm without sacrificing scale, speed, or agility. It is much like forming an all-star team to exploit a market opportunity. Here are some key characteristics of the virtual organization structure.

- **It is customer driven.** It is created to take advantage of a specific, customer-driven, time-based opportunity.
- **It is flexible.** It is disbanded when the opportunity ceases to exist.
- **It relies on mutual trust and teamwork.**
- **It is based on outsourcing.** Requirements are met with outside resources, not those from inside the organization.
- **It promotes supplier competition.**
- **It delegates selling duties to selling agents, not staff.**
- **It offers a web of associates or partners.** The corporate structure is linked by a web of alliances such as partnerships, joint ventures, and associates. This web replaces the traditional core functions such as manufacturing, warehousing, and supply.
- **It relies on outside expertise.** Emphasis is shifted from in-house knowledge to outside expertise.[4]

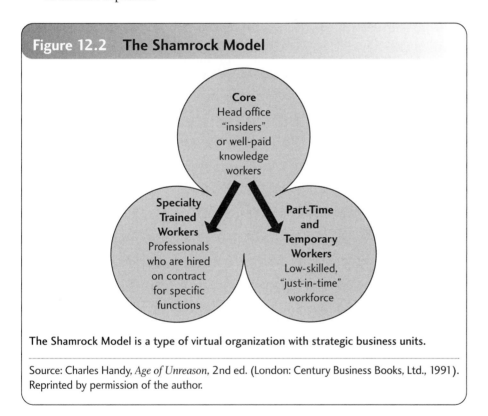

Figure 12.2   The Shamrock Model

Core
Head office
"insiders"
or well-paid
knowledge
workers

Specialty Trained Workers
Professionals who are hired on contract for specific functions

Part-Time and Temporary Workers
Low-skilled, "just-in-time" workforce

The Shamrock Model is a type of virtual organization with strategic business units.

Source: Charles Handy, *Age of Unreason*, 2nd ed. (London: Century Business Books, Ltd., 1991). Reprinted by permission of the author.

TEAMWORK

THE FOUNDING TEAM

A business is only as strong as the people who breathe life into it.[5] Therefore, it is important to think about the skills that you and the members of your founding team possess and how these skills will help bring your product or service to market. Three areas you should focus on are management team profiles and ownership structure, the board of directors or advisory board, and human resources requirements.

MANAGEMENT TEAM PROFILES AND OWNERSHIP STRUCTURE

No matter how large or small your business is, good management is central to its success. It is important to think through and identify all management categories, necessary skill sets, and possible job titles. It isn't necessary to fill each position with a different person. You should, however, be able to identify the people who are capable of assuming roles when necessary, whether it be you or someone else. You should have a current copy of everyone's résumé in addition to profiles of each member of your management team (even if the team is just you) that demonstrates his or her unique skills. You should be able to describe how each person will add to the team's success. And you should be able to answer these questions:

- What are the major categories of business management in your company (marketing, sales, research, administration, etc.)? Explain your function and the functions of the key team members.
- Who are the people who have agreed to work with your business? What are their job descriptions?
- What positions are still unfilled at your company?
- What skills and job experience will the people who fill these positions have?
- What skills do you personally have (including any skills from last job or business)? How do these skills correlate with your business?
- What is the compensation package for you and the management team (salary, benefits, profit-sharing schemes, etc.)?
- What work contracts, non-competition agreements, and other contractual agreements have you put in place for your management team?
- What is the ownership structure of your business (including percentages controlled by the management team, if applicable)?

BOARD OF DIRECTORS OR ADVISORY TEAM

In the case study at the end of this chapter, we highlight MSM—a recognized leader in the Canadian transportation industry. The company's success is largely due to its two founding partners—Mike McCarron and Robert Murray—who constantly seek out advice. They rely on a broad-based team of advisors ranging from lawyers and accountants to transportation specialists, and they even make a point of treating some of their senior managers as advisors.[6]

Creating a board or team of advisors for your company is an excellent way to benefit from the skills and expertise of people you might not yet be able to afford to employ. If you have decided to incorporate, now is the time to give some serious thought to your board of directors. In Chapter 8, you found out that, by law, you must have a board of directors. Many small companies take the easy route and simply elect key shareholders to the board. We want you to think now about forming a board that will provide true guidance and advice to your company. It is your chance to make a lawyer or accountant part of your team. If you need marketing help, elect a marketer. As we learned, your company's board of directors can make some very important decisions in the guidance and direction of your company. You don't want to lose this important opportunity to get outside expertise and advice.

But what happens if you have decided not to incorporate? You can also draw on the power of teamwork and advisors. Forward-looking entrepreneurs, like Charlene in the opening story, have created what is termed an "advisory board" with a rather formalized structure. Mike McCarron and Robert Murray of MSM (end-of-chapter case study) created a less formalized advisory team approach. You can include professionals such as bankers, lawyers, and accountants—even your business professor. It is important to make sure you look for board/advisory members who can supplement skills your business might be lacking; for example, if your business is technology based, try to include people with marketing and finance backgrounds. Colleagues, associates, and friends can also take on a semi-official responsibility for the company's welfare and meet with you four or five times a year to review your updated business plan or new objectives, or to discuss difficult problems. Some enterprising entrepreneurs we know have even created a customer board of advisors. Sounds a little unusual? Not at all. Since customers drive a business, it only makes sense to set up a formal mechanism like a focus group to listen to their concerns. Even if you are incorporated, an advisory board can be a big advantage. You will need as much help as you can get.

HUMAN RESOURCES REQUIREMENTS

Once you have defined your management and advisory team, you need to think about the other employees or independent associates your business might or might not need and what their function(s) will be. In the beginning, it might be just you and a selection of freelance, contract, or part-time help. You will need to think ahead and consider all the options you might be faced with. Many small business owners make the mistake of hiring only for their immediate needs. If the administrative assistant you hire in year two, for example, is chosen for future potential, then a workable "hire/train from within" policy could be a company strength. This type of hiring foresight is major strength of successful companies like MSM. You will need to give some thought to our human resources checklist, shown in Box 12.2. These are the types of issues we are going to work through in the latter part of the chapter.

Box 12.2   Human Resources Checklist

- ❏ How long do you plan to own this business?
- ❏ What jobs need to be done? Who is the best person to clean the bathroom, do the books, and prepare tax forms?
- ❏ What are your staffing options (e.g., part-time, full-time, leasing, contracting out)?
- ❏ How many people do you require for your business?
- ❏ What are the real costs (both money and time) of recruitment, selection, orientation, training, evaluating, and so on?
- ❏ What specific skills do employees and associates need to possess?
- ❏ Will your new employees fit in with the culture of your organization? Do they share your vision and mission?
- ❏ Are your employees protected by workers' compensation coverage? Is your business registered with your provincial workers' compensation board/commission? Most businesses—by law—need to be.
- ❏ Is there sufficient local labour? How will you recruit people if there is not?
- ❏ How will you train your team?
- ❏ What is your policy for ongoing training for your team?
- ❏ Are you hiring for the future? What is you policy on hiring and promoting from within?

BUILDING BALANCE INTO YOUR TEAM

As we will learn in the MSM case study, balance, not sameness, is essential in a winning team. For many entrepreneurs who have taken personal ownership of their ideas, finding this new freedom to let go and share their vision can be

involve the establishment of a separate new organization. The objective is to improve the competitiveness and capabilities of the individual members by using the strengths of the team. Depending on the need, the network may be organized in a variety of forms with regard to function, structure, and organization.

THE INDEPENDENT CONTRACTOR OR ASSOCIATE

Although it is wise to build a web of complementary business associates to ensure success of your start-up, the reality is that you might need an employee, or several. Should this be the case, you should first consider the benefits of the "near employee," or the independent contractor.

Many people misunderstand government rules on independent contractors. If you tell the worker when to start and stop work, and if you supply the tools or office equipment, you have an employee. On the other hand, if the work assignment is task or project driven, if the worker sets his or her own hours, if you pay by the job and not by the hour, and if most of the work takes place away from your office using the worker's resources, then you may have an independent contractor or associate relationship. Many real estate agents, for example, who work on straight commission would qualify as independent contractors.

Think about using independent contractors or associates. If you pay by the job, on contract, you can save a lot of administrative costs. To start with, you pay only for work performed. You don't pay for coffee breaks. If the job isn't done, you don't pay. Additional employee benefits that you, as an employer, pay take up a big chunk of your payroll. According to a KPMG survey, the wages and salaries that employers pay represent only about 58 percent of payroll costs. The remaining 42 percent are in benefits such as sick leave, employer's contribution to CPP, Employment Insurance, health insurance, and workers' compensation. What this means is that if you are paying an employee $172, you will be paying about $100 in wages, and $72 for benefits.[7]

A strong word of caution is in order, however. You need to be careful about the legal ins and outs of hiring on contract. We strongly recommend you check with both provincial/territorial and federal employment bodies, especially the Canada Revenue Agency (CRA), before you contract work out. Make sure, in writing if you can, that they will accept the conditions you set out for your associates or independent contractors. You can find a good discussion on the CRA regulations by linking onto the "Contractor vs. Employee—Canada Revenue Agency Regulations" site in Box 12.5.

EMPLOYEE LEASING

We also want you to consider employee leasing as a way of reducing administrative costs, paperwork hassles, legal issues, and costly benefits. Not unlike leasing physical property, you will be leasing people (employees) whose leasing organization handles payroll and most, if not all, of the human resources functions.

The leasing firm will help you keep in compliance with the myriad of federal, provincial, and local employment laws. Labour codes and employment standards codes are quite complicated! Keeping in compliance, in some cases, can become full-time job. For your protection, we suggest you use only a firm that has a strong track record and a sound financial background. Many new ventures are unable to offer employees health insurance benefits and retirement programs and thus lose out on top employees. Because of economies of scale, large leasing firms are able to provide these benefits to your "leased employees."

Employee leasing might appear to cost more initially, but it allows for additional benefits; for example,

- background screening checks are completed by the leasing organization;
- termination issues are eliminated—if the person doesn't fit the position, you can send him or her back to the leasing organization;
- turnover is reduced; and
- hiring costs (advertising, interviewing time, reference checks, turnover, etc.) are eliminated.

A list of employee leasing agencies can by found by linking onto Canadian Business Directory (http://www.canadianbusinessdirectory.ca/category.php?cat=1017).

GET A MENTOR

James and Brenda found their business mentor when they took a two-day "Look before You Leap" small business seminar. In time, they were able to bounce ideas back and forth and get valuable feedback from a guest speaker at the seminar who had 25 years of experience in the school of hard knocks. "We couldn't have done it without her," says Brenda. "She gave us strength, direction, and confidence. She agreed to be our mentor on the condition that we become a mentor for a new business owner once we became successful. That made us feel good. For her, it was not a question of if we were going to be successful, it was a question of when. She believed in us—unconditionally."

For independent business, **mentoring** is a mutually beneficial partnership between a more experienced entrepreneur or businessperson, and an entrepreneur who is in the infant, or start-up, phase of a venture. The experienced partner is one who is reflective about his or her venture and is able to communicate and share his or her understanding and knowledge about what has made the venture grow. The inexperienced entrepreneur, or protégé(e), is receptive to the suggestions of the mentor and is also willing to try to implement some of them in the new business.

Mentoring is an ongoing partnership that might last for a number of months before any benefits are realized by either partner. The partners need to commit themselves to regular meetings with a focused agenda. Usually, the mentor has more frequent and in-depth involvement than the advisory board.

Much of what is learned in small business comes from experience, as business, to a large extent, is an art. To be successful, we need to know how successful entrepreneurs think. We need help and direction, and in many cases we will not be able to get what we need from a book. That's why we need a mentor, someone who can give us start-up advice and encouragement.

Essential qualities of an effective small business mentor you should look for include

- **a desire to help**—individuals who are interested in, and willing to help, others;
- **past positive experiences as entrepreneur**—individuals who have had positive formal or informal experiences with a mentor;
- **a good reputation for developing others**—individuals who have a good reputation for helping others develop their skill;
- **time and energy**—individuals who have the time and mental energy to devote to the relationship;
- **up-to-date knowledge in the related field**—individuals who have maintained current, up-to-date technological knowledge or skills;

MENTORING

A mutually beneficial partnership between a more experienced entrepreneur or businessperson, and an entrepreneur who is in the infant, or start-up, phase of a venture

ACTION STEP 55

Find a mentor

First develop a list of attributes you are looking for in a mentor and areas where you need help. Network with your friends, coworkers, and business associates. Tell them what you're looking for—that is, a successful business owner with a good track record. The perfect mentor would be one with experience in your particular segment. You can also contact your local chamber of commerce, alumni association, Rotary club, or one or more of your local business clubs/associations, such as the Red Deer Business Advisory Network (BAN). You might want to see if your local small business centre can help, or you might want to return to the various networking sites provided in Chapter 6, Box 6.5 (page 142). You might also want to consider getting advice from a business coach (see, for example, the "My Story" link of Clive Prout: http://www.thesabbaticalcoach. com). You can even look for a virtual mentor on the Internet. Visit, for example, the "Mentor Programs" page on the Canadian Youth Business Foundation (http://www. cybf.ca/mentors.html) or the Young Entrepreneurs Association (http://www.yea.ca).

- **a learning attitude**—individuals who are still willing and able to learn and who see the potential benefits of a mentoring relationship; and
- **demonstrated effective managerial and mentoring skills**—individuals who have demonstrated effective coaching, counselling, facilitating, and networking skills.

Although we strongly suggest that you get a mentor, we think that you should be aware that mentoring relationships don't always succeed the first time. Here are four of the most frequent problems with mentoring relationships.[8]

- **Personality mismatch.** One or both members of the relationship might feel uneasy with the other, or they might not be able to achieve the level of friendship necessary for rich communication.
- **Unrealistic expectations.** It is important that expectations be defined clearly from the beginning.
- **Breaches of confidentiality.** To develop the type of relationship in which the mentor can be effective, he or she must first be perceived as trustworthy and able to keep confidences, and vice versa.
- **Lack of commitment.** Both parties must do what they say and say what they do.

Table 12.2 provides some guidelines for choosing your mentor. Now it's your turn. Start looking for your mentor. Complete Action Step 55.

Once you have located some candidates, develop a set of questions, and set up a meeting to pick their brains. Here are some things to consider in selecting a mentor:

- Do you feel comfortable with this person?
- Can you trust him or her?
- Is he or she easy to communicate with?
- Does he or she have experience and contacts that can help your new business?
- Is he or she willing to devote the time to help you?

After you have made your choice and the person has agreed to help you, keep in close contact. See the person at least once a month. Set up regular meetings with an agenda, and use the phone or e-mail to smooth out rough spots.

Table 12.2 Characteristics of Mentors

Mentors Are...	Your Mentor Must...
...winners	...have extensive business experience
...humble	...have at least one admitted failure
...caring	...truly care about you as a person
...believers	...truly believe you can move mountains
...guides	...be able to guide and direct without preaching
...encouragers	...be able to encourage the answer from within you
...honest	...have the strength and knowledge to be honest with you
...empathizers	...be able to empathize, not sympathize
...listeners	...want to spend time listening to you
...excited	...be excited about your ideas

Source: Ronald A. Knowles and Debbie White, *Issues in Canadian Small Business* (Toronto: Dryden, an imprint of Harcourt Brace & Company, Canada, 1995), p. 78. Reprinted by permission.

HIRING YOUR FIRST EMPLOYEE

You have considered all your options and the kinds of questions provided in Box 12.2. Before you hire your first employee, we want you to take another look at your personal skills, values, and passion. We again encourage you to do some self-analysis. Complete the online self-evaluation tests (Box 12.3). Revisit Action Step 16 (Chapter 3, page 56). Is the decision to hire staff consistent with your values? Do you have the demonstrated skills to manage people effectively? If you hire new employees, you are going to have to rely on new skills, such as administrating, delegating, organizing, communicating, and developing teamwork. As we learned in the opening story, this was a major downfall for Charlene's first business. Many entrepreneurs discover that after they bring staff onboard, they end up spending more time managing the staff than doing the business. They begin to lose their passion for the business. In fact, some business owners end up deciding not to grow their businesses, because they prefer not to manage staff and be responsible for all the administrative red tape.

If you decide that you need to hire employees and take on more of a managing role, then you are going to have to consider the following basic steps.

STEP 1: JOB ANALYSIS

First you will have to determine the jobs or functions that need to be done to achieve your businesses goals. Many entrepreneurs—especially those operating out of the home—suffer from loneliness and boredom. They hire staff to satisfy their social needs, not the requirements of the business. This can't be your reason. You will need to determine what jobs are required and how new employees will contribute to the objectives of your business. Revisit your cash flow and income statements (Chapter 10). How will these new functions improve output and contribute to the cash flow and profit? How much can the business afford to pay?

STEP 2: JOB QUALIFICATIONS

You will need to consider the skills/knowledge required to the job. What are the qualifications, traits, and characteristics considered to be essential for someone to carry out the job requirements successfully? These qualification issues include education level, relevant experience, skill level, or physical characteristics.

STEP 3: JOB REQUIREMENTS

Once you determine what the jobs are and the corresponding skills that are required, then you have to figure out who is going to do the work. First you should determine whether your current team is sufficient to fill future job requirements. Maybe you can solve the problem with overtime, for example. But, if you still anticipate a shortage, you are going to have to find new people or alternative ways to fill expected needs. Consider the pros and cons of the just-in-time team—strategic alliances, joint ventures, subcontractors, and employee leasing—as we discussed above.

If the just-in-time team is not an option, you will then have to consider the advantages and disadvantages of staffing—hiring employees on a part-time or full-time basis. Many small firms use part-time or temporary workers until the owners have a strong feel for what needs to be done and who is best suited to do the job.

Today, more than one in five workers is a part-timer (working less than 30 hours per week). There are a number of advantages for firms in hiring part-time employees. First, as part-time wage rates are typically 60 percent of regular full-time wages, you can reduce your labour costs significantly. Part-time workers also usually receive fewer benefits, which reduces yet another company expense. Part-time employment can also be an effective strategy for companies to benefit from the experience of the "retired" workforce, which, as we know, is a growth segment. You need to weigh these benefits against some of the negative long-term implications. For example, over-reliance on part-timers might leave your company without any experience or continuity. This could stifle your growth potential, as part-time workers normally have less commitment and loyalty to your company.

STEP 4: STAFFING DECISIONS AND RECRUITMENT

Should you decide to hire your staff, either part- or full-time, you have make four basic staffing decisions on

- recruitment,
- selection,
- training and development, and
- compensation.

Recruitment

In the process of finding the right staff, you will be confronted with two basic recruitment options: internal and external recruitment. Here are some pros and cons of each.

1. **Internal recruitment**—promotion from within the company

   Advantages include
   - knowledge of the organizational culture.
   - the performance history of the candidates is known, and
   - lower recruiting costs.

   Disadvantages include
   - internal rivalry and competition can ensue,
   - no "new blood" to enhance creativity and innovation, and
   - lower morale on the part of those that were passed over.

2. **External recruitment**—searching for employees from outside the company

   Advantages include
   - new blood,
   - new expertise, and
   - new energy.

   Disadvantages include
   - greater costs,
   - the new employee is not known to the organization,
   - it takes longer to "socialize" the employee, and
   - lower morale from those in the organization that were passed over.

   Some of the more common methods of finding new employees through external recruitment are
   - the Internet—one great source for job seekers and posting a job being the Human Resources and Skills Development Canada (HRSDC) site (http://www.jobbank.gc.ca/Intro_en.asp);
   - company Web sites;
   - employee referrals;

- word-of-mouth advertising;
- college/university placement offices;
- employment/temporary agencies;
- newspaper classified advertising; and
- ads in trade and professional journals.

In Box 12.4, we have provided you with the most common recruitment methods for small business.

Box 12.4   Did You Know?

1. Recruitment

A study by Duxbury and Higgins surveyed 103 Canadian small businesses and found the following: "Small businesses recruit employees by

- taking referrals (75 percent),
- placing ads in the newspaper (56 percent),
- asking friends and relatives if they know someone (40 percent),
- walk-ins (37 percent), and
- by going through private employment agencies (31 percent)."

Source: Monica Beauregard and Maureen Fitzgerald. *Hiring, Managing and Keeping the Best: The Complete Canadian Guide for Employers* (Toronto: McGraw-Hill Ryerson, 2000), p. 27; cited in Service Canada, "Exploring Recruitment Options" (http://www.hrmanagement.gc.ca/gol/recruitment/interface.nsf/engdocBasic/0.html).

2. Non-Financial Compensation

In a survey of 300 small businesses in Canada, the Centre for Families, Work, and Well-Being asked, "What are the work-life strategies that make small companies successful in concurrently meeting their business objectives and being a good place for employees to work?" The survey found that

- more than 80 percent of companies offer at least one flexible work arrangement for employees, and flextime is the most common arrangement;
- 83 percent provide time off to care for sick family members;
- 80 percent provide extended health care benefits;
- 70 percent offer time off for "eldercare"; and
- 21 percent offer an EAP.

Source: Canadian Plastics Sector Council, "Work-Life Balance" (http://www.cpsc-ccsp.ca/Employee Retention/Work-Life_Balance.htm).

Selection

Should you decide to recruit for the position, you will have to follow an **employee selection** process involving

- initial screening (application and interview),
- employment testing (aptitude, personality, or skills),
- selection interviews,
- background and reference checks,
- requests for and evaluations of physical examinations, and
- the decision to hire.

A critical stage in the selection process is the interview. About 86 percent of those hired by interview alone will not work out for the company, so you have to be very careful about hiring in this way. Should you decide to recruit a full-time

EMPLOYEE SELECTION

The process of determining which persons in the applicant pool possess the qualifications necessary to be successful on the job

employee, we want to emphasize that part-time employment is one of the least risky ways of "road testing" prospective employees. If you must select by the interview process, we suggest that you conduct at least two interviews in different venues or settings for your final candidates. Try to have existing employees, especially coworkers, involved in the hiring process. The attitude of prospective employees is a key factor. You must ensure that the new hire shares the values and beliefs of your company.

For more details on recruitment and selection, we suggest that you click onto the "Screening and Selection" or the "HR Filing Cabinet, The Hiring Process" sites of the Canadian Human Rights Commission, provided in Box 12.5.

Issues related to human rights, employment standards, and hiring are complicated, so the government has created brochures to help explain various regulations. About 90 percent of employee rights legislation comes under provincial jurisdiction, and provincial laws can vary extensively. Failure to follow legal requirements can result in stiff penalties or even lawsuits from disgruntled employees. So the best advice we can give you is to be very careful about what you say and check with your provincial labour departments if you have any doubts. You might find it beneficial to use an employment agency to hire your first few employees. For more information on hiring and other human resources planning issues, visit the Web pages listed in Box 12.5.

At the interview, ask the right questions. The trick is to prepare a list of questions that solicit responses to applicants' skills, experiences, or knowledge needed in the job. Similar questions should be asked of each applicant, so that you can evaluate their responses and suitability. You might want to look over a few books that employees use to prepare for job interviews. These could give you ideas on questions to ask. To start, here are some questions that you could use:

1. How did you prepare for this meeting?
2. Why do you want to work for us?
3. How do your skills match the job description?
4. What would you do in the following situation? (Explain a problem they might face on the job.)
5. What type of training will you need to perform this job?
6. What are some of the obstacles you have overcome?
7. What do you expect from a boss?
8. What gives you satisfaction in a job?
9. What do you think you will like most and least about this particular job?
10. What kinds of things disturb you on the job?
11. What have been your most pleasant work experiences?
12. What do you want to be doing in five years?
13. What would your references say about you?
14. What did you like or dislike about your last job?

In general, you can stay out of trouble if you avoid asking the following questions of job applicants:

1. age or birth date,
2. place of birth,
3. a woman's maiden name,
4. racial or ethnic background,
5. religious affiliation,
6. marital status and sexual orientation,
7. number of children and ages,
8. medical condition or non–job-related physical data, and
9. disabilities.

Training and Development

Once you decide to hire staff, you are going to have to put into place a program to train your new staff and then determine how much will this cost.

Compensation

There are two general types of financial compensation—direct and indirect. But we also want you to consider non-financial compensation.

Direct compensation is the wage or salary received by the employee. Examples include basic pay, which encompasses

- hourly wages and
- salaries; and

incentive (performance) pay, which takes in

- piecework,
- commissions,
- pay for knowledge,
- bonus pay, and
- profit sharing.

Indirect compensation (sometimes referred to as employee or fringe benefits) refers to the employee benefits and services that are given entirely or partly at the expense of the company. Many benefits are governed by federal and provincial laws. Examples include

- pensions,
- health insurance,
- vacation pay,
- sick leave, and
- child care.

Many small businesses informally offer some of these benefits—especially those related to time off and flexibility—to create a supportive work environment. Nonetheless, there are four major mandatory programs that require contributions by both employers and employees and which will increase your payroll by about 10 percent:

1. Canada and Quebec Pension Plans (CPP and QPP)—for retirement, disability, and survivors' and death benefits;
2. Workers' Compensation—for disability benefits and spouses' and dependents' pensions;
3. vacation and holiday pay; and
4. Employment Insurance.

Many small business owners have initiated non-financial compensation initiatives in their workplace, and have done so out of a conviction that providing such benefits can substantially improve productivity, revenues, and employee retention and commitment. Some of these non-financial forms of compensation include

- challenging jobs,
- recognition,
- flexible work hours,
- compressed workweek (working 10 hours a day for four days, for example).
- job sharing, and
- home-based work.

DIRECT COMPENSATION

The wage or salary received by the employee

INDIRECT COMPENSATION (FRINGE BENEFITS)

Employee benefits and services that are given entirely or partly at the expense of the company

WHAT DO EMPLOYEES REALLY COST?

If you plan on hiring, consider all the costs associated with hiring, training, and retaining employees, including

- ad placements (very expensive);
- recruiting and staffing;
- training;
- direct compensation (salary/wages);
- indirect compensation (especially Canada and Quebec pension plans, Workers' Compensation, vacation and holiday pay, and Employment Insurance);
- space, furniture, and equipment;
- additional management time; and
- any additional perks you might offer (car allowance, etc.).

Each employee can cost you his or her salary plus 60 percent of that salary or more. Employees in an entrepreneurial venture need to pull more than their own weight. So our best advice is—Select Wisely.

ACTION STEP 56

Decide who's in charge of what

It's time to impress your business plan reader. Investors or vendors are often more interested in the founders than in the Business Plan itself. Experience in the same type of business and former business experience and/or ownership are powerful positive components of the plan. You will need to focus on past responsibility and authority. Present the balance and diversity of your founding team.

Several paragraphs in the Business Plan might be sufficient for each key founder. If experience is lacking, discuss consultants or committed strategic partners who will bring balance to the management team and contribute experience and special skills. You might also want to include an organizational chart in your Business Plan's appendixes. Write short, strong bios for each member of your team. You will need to complete full résumés later for the appendix of your Business Plan.

Box 12.5 Bookmark This

- Canada Business, Becoming an Employer: http://www.cbsc.org/servlet/ContentServer?pagename=OSBW%2FCBSC_WebPage%2FCBSC_WebPage_Temp&submenu2=Becoming+an+Employer%3Cbr+%2F%3E&lang=eng&cid=1102940239275&c=CBSC_WebPage#payroll
- Canada Revenue Agency, Employee or Self-Employed? (RC 4110): http://www.cra-arc.gc.ca/E/pub/tg/rc4110/README.html
- Calgary Business Information Centre, "Contractor vs. Employee": http://www.calgary-smallbusiness.com/contractor.html
- Canadian Tax Foundation, "The Tax Cost of Hiring": http://www.ctf.ca/articles/News.asp?article_ID=177
- Government of Canada, Human Resources Management Centre, "The Hiring Process": http://campus.golservices.gc.ca/view_lesson.jsp?lang=en&courseId=21&lessonId=23
- Canadian Human Rights Commission, "Guide to Screening and Selection in Employment": http://www.chrc-ccdp.ca/publications/screening_employment-en.asp?lang_update=1
- CCH, Business Owner's Toolkit, "Recruiting and Hiring": http://www.toolkit.cch.com/text/P05_0001.asp
- Canadian Plastics Sector Council, "Work-Life Balance": http://www.cpsc-ccsp.ca/Employee%20Retention/Work-Life_Balance.htm

Now it's your turn again. Complete Action Step 56 once you have built your team. It's a great way to end this chapter on team building and a great way to start your new business.

In a Nutshell

Leading is a key management function, and you'll have to learn how to inspire and empower your team. In addition, you will have to be able to justify and chart your organizational structure. We want you to consider the benefits of a virtual or network organization. We also want you to understand that you won't be able do everything yourself. You will need a founding team with different skills and personalities, depending on your strengths and weaknesses and the needs of the business. We encourage you to think outside the box by considering less traditional team arrangements, such as subcontracting, joint ventures, strategic alliances, and mentoring. We also encourage you to take a proactive approach to human resources planning and recruitment. If you decide to hire employees either full- or part-time, we strongly suggest that you follow the recruitment and selection process we've set out.

Key Terms

direct compensation	leadership
employee selection	mentoring
indirect compensation	strategic alliance
joint venture	strategic business units
just-in-time team	virtual organization (or network organization)

Think Points for Success

✓ People tend to "hire themselves." How many more people like you can the business take?

✓ A winning team is lurking in your network.

✓ Look to your competitors and vendors for team members.

✓ Your company is people.

✓ Balance the people on your team.

✓ Have each team member write objectives for his or her responsibilities within the business.

✓ You can't grow until you have the right people.

✓ How much of your team can be built of part-timers and moonlighters?

✓ How "virtual" can you make your business structure?

✓ Can you form a joint venture or a strategic alliance?

✓ Do you know what your legal responsibilities are?

✓ What is your job selection process?

Business Plan Building Block

GENERAL MANAGEMENT

Who's in charge? Investors or vendors are often more interested in the founders than in the business plan itself. Experience in the same type of business and past business successes are powerful positive components of the plan. Focus on responsibility and authority.

A paragraph or two might be sufficient for each key founder. If retail experience is lacking, list consultants or committed strategic partners who can balance the management team. Consider including an organizational chart.

MANAGEMENT AND OWNERSHIP

Name the key players, and include their résumés, focusing on their contribution to your business and how they will give you a competitive edge. Save the full-blown résumés of the management team members for an appendix at the back of the plan.

The lender, vendor, or venture capital firm weighs the founding team as one of the most important factors. Present balance and diversity with a history of past achievement. It is here that you should explain your business form (incorporation, partnership, sole proprietorship, or cooperative). If you have more than two people on the team, include an organizational chart.

Your turn again. Who are the players in your business, and what role will each play?

_____
_____
_____
_____
_____

List consultants, advisory board members, or strategic partners who can contribute experience or special skills.

_____
_____
_____
_____
_____

HUMAN RESOURCE PLAN

1. Type of workers needed. Include just-in-time, seasonal, and part-time workers

_____
_____
_____

2. Compensation, commissions, bonuses, and/or profit sharing

_____
_____
_____

3. Provincial and federal compliance requirements

_____
_____
_____

4. Performance standards, training, and retraining

_____
_____
_____

5. Workers' compensation and insurance cost

_____
_____
_____

6. Employee handbook (look for professional help)

_____
_____
_____

7. Union contracts

_____
_____
_____

8. Professional certifications

_____
_____
_____

Checklist Questions and Actions to Develop Your Business Plan

BUILDING AND MANAGING A WINNING TEAM

❑ What major human resource issues does your business face, and how do you plan to address these issues?

❑ Have you included an employment schedule in your appendix and corresponding wage costs for your staff and yourself?

❑ Have you allowed for benefits? To comply with legal statutory requirements, you need to consider _at least_ 20 percent of your wage and salary costs for benefits.

❑ Do you have job descriptions in place and plans to conduct an annual performance appraisal?

❑ Do your wage rates fit within the industry norm? Are you prepared to pay more than the industry to be a "top draw" company?

❑ Outline your leadership style, and your strengths and weaknesses as an entrepreneur.

❑ How might a "virtual organization" work for you?

❑ If you are starting out just with yourself, at what point in sales or other volume indicator will you add a second or a third person?

Case Study

MANAGEMENT AND TEAMWORK AT MSM TRANSPORTATION

Case Background

Robert Murray and Mike McCarron are two of the founding partners of MSM Transportation Incorporated. When they started the company back in the late 1980s, they knew they were combining two different types of management expertise, plus two very different personalities. Mike, the company's managing partner and primary marketer, was enthusiastic, outgoing, passionate, and—as he admits—impulsive. Robert, Mike's partner and MSM's president, trained originally as a credit manager and came across as quiet, diplomatic, and thoughtful, and more of a long-term thinker. Oil and water? Of course.

Robert recalled that the duo's strength lay in the fact that they could disagree, argue feverishly, work it out, and move on. Their vision was to become a dominant player in the Canadian transportation industry. Because the two partners shared a similar vision for the company, if not the same temperament, debate became a positive force that generated new ideas and better decisions. In an industry notorious for its lack of marketing and financial skills, MSM benefited from both personalities, because they questioned each other's assumptions and strategies. Noted Robert, "My partner has made me much more effective and, I believe, much better at what I do."

Since its humble beginnings in the late 1980s, MSM has grown into a recognized leader in the Canadian transportation industry. In 2005, for example, MSM Transportation ranked highest in customer satisfaction among Canadian shippers—according to the readers of *Canadian Transportation & Logistics* magazine. It has become a multimillion-dollar Canadian success story. MSM Transportation is now a group of six interrelated companies—MSM Group of Companies Incorporated—that employs close to 200 people, owns and operates over 300 pieces of equipment, and handles more than 50,000 shipments per year. MSM even owns a Junior A Hockey team.

In 2006, MSM earned membership into the Platinum Club of Canada's 50 Best-Managed Companies (https://www.canadas50best.com). To become a member of this élite group, MSM had to sustain a consistent profitability and growth and maintain its designation as one of this countries best-managed companies for a minimum of six consecutive years. To a large extent, the day-in and day-out success of this company relates to the teamwork, leadership, and management skills of the two founding partners. At MSM, McCarron and Murray have established an enthusiastic workplace culture and have ensured that all employees believe in and strive toward the MSM mission:

> *Customer Satisfaction through On-Time-Delivery is our prime goal, and MSM customers are paramount in our daily decisions and successes.*

Case Resources
- MSM Group of Companies, home page: http://www.shipmsm.com/index.html
- Mike McCarron, *Street Smarts*, "Moving Targets": http://www.shipmsm.com/Articles/SS200211%20-%20Moving%20Targets.pdf
- Legacee,"Different Types of Leadership Styles": http://www.legacee.com/Info/Leadership/LeadershipStyles.html
- Ray Jutkins, "The Situational Leader": http://www.rayjutkins.com/ezine/20030812.html
- Mike McCarron, *Street Smarts*, "Why Partnerships Fail": http://www.shipmsm.com/Articles/SS200206%20-%20Why%20Partnerships%20Fail.pdf
- Mike McCarron, *Streets Smarts*, "Personnel Best": http://www.shipmsm.com/Articles/SS200201%20-%20Personnel%20Best.pdf

Case Study Questions
1. Personality Types
   a. In Appendix 12.1, we describe four personality types—analytical, driver, amiable, and expressive. What were the dominant personality types of Robert Murray and Mike McCarron? According to Robert Murray, how did these two different personality types contribute to the success of the company?
   b. What is your personality type? Take a few minutes and conduct the personality analysis provided in Appendix 12.1.
2. Transformational Leadership
   a. The primary focus of transformational leadership is to make change happen—or "transform," as the name implies. According to the text, people with this

leadership style exhibit five basic types of behaviour. Briefly describe these five behavioural traits.

b. Over the past several years, MSM has had a successful track record in managing a "remote" location in Los Angeles. McCarron's transformational leadership style has had a lot to do with this success. Link onto the *Street Smarts* article entitled "Moving Targets," written by McCarron (http://www.shipmsm.com/Articles/SS200211%20-%20Moving%20Targets.pdf). List four ways in which McCarron inspires and stimulates his team.

3. Other Leadership Styles

a. The transformational style of leadership is particularly appealing and effective for many entrepreneurs, as its major focus is to make change happen. However, there are other leadership styles. For example, three classical styles are laissez faire (free rein), autocratic, and participative.

Link onto the Legacee "Different Types of Leadership Styles" site (http://www.legacee.com/Info/Leadership/LeadershipStyles.html). Briefly explain these three classic leadership styles.

b. Situational leadership is another style that has gained a great deal of popularity over the past 40 years. It's a "different stokes for different folks" approach. Because people and tasks are different, the leadership approach will depend on the situation. This approach involves a combination of four styles. Link onto "The Situational Leader" (http://www.rayjutkins.com/ezine/20030812.html). What are the four "S" styles or options available to the situational leader?

c. Given these various leadership styles, what type of leadership do you plan to use when you open your business? How will this style help you to achieve your goals and objectives? You might want to begin by linking onto the leadership E-Exercises provided in Box 12.3.

4. Organizational Structures

a. In this chapter, we described three types of traditional organizational structures used by small business. Briefly describe each of these types of classical organizational structures.

b. In the early 2000s, MSM launched an aggressive expansion policy. It expanded its freight forwarding, logistics, and distribution services, and even bought a Junior A hockey team. What type of organization structure did it create to handle this expansion? What are the five major benefits of this type of structure? (Hint: You might want to link onto the MSM, "Our Services" link, http://www.shipmsm.com/corp_services1.html.)

5. Strategic Partnerships

Strategic partnerships with customers, suppliers, and even employees have been critical to the success of MSM. Link onto *Street Smarts*, "Why Partnerships Fail" (http://www.shipmsm.com/Articles/SS200206%20-%20Why%20Partnerships%20Fail.pdf). According to Mike McCarron, what are five ways in which you can improve your partnership relationships?

6. Human Resource Requirements

a. In this chapter, we encouraged you to consider the "just-in-time" team and three specific human resource options (pages 318–321) before deciding to go out and hire full-time staff for your new business. Briefly describe these three alternatives to hiring staff.

b. According to Mike McCarron at MSM, "the quality of service our people deliver is the only competitive advantage any of us has." What advice does he offer when it comes time to hire a new staff member? (See *Street Smarts*, "Personnel Best": http://www.shipmsm.com/Articles/SS200201%20-%20Personnel%20Best.pdf.)

c. After considering your alternatives, you decide to hire a new staff member on a full-time basis. According to the text, what are the basic steps you should follow to improve your chances of getting the "right" person for your business? (See page 320.)

Notes

1. See, for example, Legacee, "Different Types of Leadership Styles." Available at http://www.legacee.com/Info/Leadership/LeadershipStyles.html (accessed July 2006).
2. Excerpted from J. Howell and B. Avolio, "The Leverage of Leadership," *The Globe and Mail*, May 15, 1998, p. C1. © 1998 Ivey Management Services. Used with permission from Ivey Management Services.
3. Peter Urs Bender, *Leadership from Within* (Toronto: Stoddart Publishing, 1997), p. 23. Reprinted by permission of Stoddart Publishing Co. Limited, Toronto, Ontario.
4. Adapted from Steven L. Goldman, Roger N. Nagel, and Kenneth Preiss, *Agile Competitors and Virtual Organizations* (New York: Van Nostrand Reinholdt, 1995).
5. Information for much of this section is excerpted or adapted from Royal Bank, *Business Plans*, "The Team." Available at: http://www.royalbank.com/sme/bigidea/team.html (accessed July 2006).
6. See, for example, *Street Smarts*, "Moving Targets." Available at: http://www.shipmsm.com/Articles/SS200211%20-%20Moving%20Targets.pdf (accessed July 2006).
7. Cited in Bruce Little, "Statistics Belie Perception of Less Help for the Needy, Part II," *The Globe and Mail*, January 20, 1994, pp. A1, A6.
8. Canadian Youth Business Foundation. Available at: http://www.cybf.ca/en_mentor.html (accessed July 2006).

SUGGESTED READING

Drucker, Peter F., and Peter M. Senge. *Leading in a Time of Change: What It Will Take to Lead Tomorrow*. New York: John Wiley, 2001.

Ferrazzi, Keith, and Tahl Raz. *Never Eat Alone: And Other Secrets of Success, One Relationship at a Time*. New York: Currency, 2005.

Fisher, Kimball, and Maureen Duncan Fisher. *The Distance Manager: A Hands-on Guide to Managing Off-Site Employees and Virtual Teams*. New York: McGraw-Hill, 2000.

Maxwell, John C. *Developing the Leader within You Workbook*. Nashville, TN: Thomas Nelson, 2001.

Maxwell, John C. *The 17 Essential Qualities Of A Team Player: Becoming The Kind Of Person Every Team Wants*. Nashville, TN: Nelson Business, 2002.

Smith, Shawn A., and Rebecca A. Mazin. *The HR Answer Book: An Indispensable Guide for Manager and Human Resources Professionals*. New York: AMACOM , 2004.

Steingold, Fred S., Amy Delpo, and Lisa Guerin. *The Employer's Legal Handbook*. Berkeley, CA: Nolo Press, 2004.

Sutton, Walt. *Leap of Strength: A Personal Tour through the Months before and Years after You Start Your Own Business*. Los Angeles: Silver Lake Publishing, 2000.

VanGundy, Arthur B., and Linda Naiman. *Orchestrating Collaboration at Work: Using Music, Improv, Storytelling and Other Arts to Improve Teamwork*. Hoboken, NJ: Pfeiffer, 2003

Urs Bender, Peter. *Leadership from Within*. Toronto: Stoddart Publishing, 1997.

Appendix 12.1

The Personality Analysis

Take a few minutes to do the following simple self-assessment. You will learn some fascinating things about yourself in the process. You might also want to compare yourself to others you know—a significant other, your children, or your coworkers.

In the following lists, underline those words (or phrases) that describe you best in a *business* or *work situation*. Total your score for each group of words.

GROUP

A   Reserved, uncommunicative, cool, cautious, guarded, seems difficult to get to know, demanding of self, disciplined attitudes, formal speech, rational decision making, strict, impersonal, businesslike, disciplined about time, uses facts, formal dress, measured actions.

Total score: _____

B   Take-charge attitude, directive, tends to use power, fast actions, risk taker, competitive, aggressive, strong opinions, excitable, takes social initiative, makes statements, loud voice, quick pace, expressive voice, firm handshake, clear idea of needs, initiator.

Total score: _____

C   Communicative, open, warm, approachable, friendly, fluid attitudes, informal speech, undisciplined about time, easygoing with self, impulsive, informal dress, dramatic opinions, uses opinions, permissive, emotional decision making, seems easy to get to know, personal.

Total score: _____

D   Slow pace, flat voice, soft-spoken, helper, unclear about what is needed, moderate opinions, calm, asks questions, tends to avoid use of power, indifferent handshake, deliberate actions, lets others take social initiative, risk avoider, quiet, go-along attitude, supportive, cooperative.

Total score: _____

Write your total scores below:

A = _____   C = _____

B = _____   D = _____

Next, determine which groups are larger and by how much:

A vs. C: Which is larger?   _____

         By how many points?   _____

B vs. D: Which is larger?   _____

         By how many points?   _____

Filling in the Personality Grid

Now mark your results on the grid below:

To determine where you fit on the vertical axis, look at your A vs. C result. For example,

     If A is larger than C by 6 points, put a dot (•) at A-6.
     If C is larger than A by 5 points, put a dot (•) at C-5.
     If A and C are equal, put a dot (•) at "0," in the centre of the grid.

To find your place on the horizontal axis, use your B vs. D result. For example,

If B is larger than D by 4 points, put a dot (•) at B-4.

If D is larger than B by 7 points, put a dot (•) at D-7.

If B and D are equal, put a dot (•) at "0," in the centre of the grid.

In the grid below, draw an X where lines extending from your two points meet (as shown in the sample). The quadrant you're in indicates your personality type.*

This sample grid shows the results for two different people: One is called a driver; the other is amiable.

Sample Grid

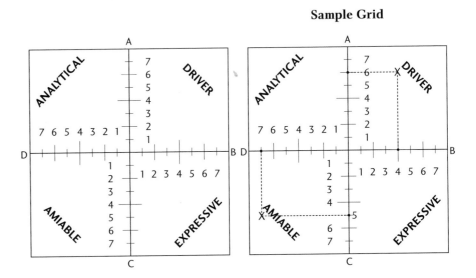

Interpreting Your Results

Now that you know where you fit, let's find out what it means!

The following words describe each of the personality types. Read those that apply to you, and see how these words fit your image of your own personality. Then ask others what they think. It helps to get different perspectives.

After considering your own personality, look at people around you. What personality types do they exhibit?

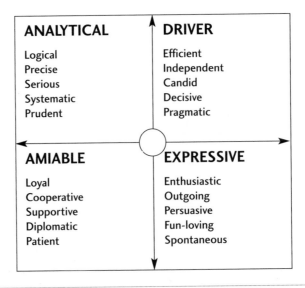

*These four personality types are adapted from *Personality Styles and Effective Performance*, by David W. Merrill and Roger H. Reid (American Management Association, 1996).

Remember that there is no right or wrong personality type. Different types simply think and act in different ways.

Understanding the Personality Types

Each personality has different needs, values, and motivations, and will exhibit different levels of assertiveness and responsiveness. Here are some general insights into each type—and some tips to help you get through life a little more easily.

THE ANALYTICAL

Also known as
> melancholic,
> thinker,
> thought person,
> processor, or
> cognitive.

The analytical person

- wants to know "how" things work;
- wants to be accurate, and to have accuracy from others;
- values numbers, statistics, and ideas; and
- loves details.

Analyticals fear being embarrassed or losing face. They also tend to be introverted and to hide their emotions from others.

THE AMIABLE

Also known as
> phlegmatic,
> feeler,
> people person,
> helper, or
> interpersonal.

The amiable person

- wants to know "why?" (e.g., Why am I doing this?),
- wants to build relationships,
- loves to give others support and attention, and
- values suggestions from others.

Amiables fear losing trust or having disagreements with others. Although somewhat introverted, they also tend to display their emotions.

THE DRIVER

Also known as
> choleric,
> director,
> action person,
> boss, or
> behavioural.

You should explore businesses for sale whether you're serious about buying or not. By now, you're far enough along in your quest to have a sense of the marketplace. Talking to sellers is just one more step in your education in entrepreneurship. Have fun, but leave your chequebook at home until you have done all your research.

Here are some tips to get you started on your exploration of the pros and cons of buying a business.

1. **Determine which type of entrepreneur you are before taking the plunge**. Some businesspeople are "serial entrepreneurs." They seek out and purchase a business with turnaround potential, work to restore it to financial health, and sell the revitalized business at a profit. Other entrepreneurs, on the other hand, thrive on the start-up phase of the entrepreneurial journey and are not so interested in the day-to-day operations. A review of the self-assessment Action Steps you completed in Chapter 1 will provide valuable clues as to your entrepreneurial strengths and weaknesses.

2. **Fall in love with the business, not the deal**. As you conduct your search, make finding the "right opportunity"—as opposed to getting the "right price"—a priority. Ask yourself such questions as Do I have what it takes to manage this business day in and day out? Will I enjoy interacting with the customers? With the employees? Can I see myself working each day to improve this business? Am I passionate about the business?

3. **Obtain legal representation and financial advice before you sign the contract**. The importance of due diligence cannot be overstated.

WHY PURCHASE AN ONGOING BUSINESS?

The overwhelming reason for buying an ongoing business is *money*, primarily the income stream, which can make it a good deal. If you do your research and strike a good deal, you can start making money the day you take over an ongoing business. Because many start-ups must plug along for months (maybe even years) before showing a profit, it's smart to consider the business purchase option. But remember: The uncertainties of a start-up business are reduced but not eliminated. When you buy a business, it is a financial investment. Make sure you are getting the "highest" rate of return on your time and investment dollars.

Other things to consider when buying an existing business might include the following.

1. If you find a "hungry seller," you should be able to negotiate good terms. You might be able to buy into a business for very little up-front cash and might also negotiate seller financing.

2. Fixtures and equipment will be negotiable. Be sure the equipment is in good working condition and has been well maintained. Ask to see service records. What equipment is being leased? Are there any liens on the equipment?

3. Training and support might be available through the seller and can sometimes be negotiated. If the seller is financing, he or she will have a stake in your success. Many banks like to see some seller financing, because they believe it secures the seller's interest and thus the bank's interest. Request that the owner continue to work in the business for a short time to help you adjust and to serve as a bridge with the customers.

4. An established customer base should be in place. You will need to determine how loyal the customers are and whether there is goodwill or ill will. If the customer base is not strong or loyal, consider this fact appropriately in your

There
owner you
use a repı
someone
cases, a r
Business b
tunities. A
your accoı
ness broke
or "Busine
also a gc
brokers_ca

Ask yo
the ones t
find a busi
with your l

You w
close to yo
you start.
Robbins is
the 30 bu
Hamilton-l
people lool
run. "Too n
"But they'ı
7/24 opera
you throug
advice, we
you're goin
do elsewhe
ment. This
about busil

DEALING

Reputable k
they often p
petency of l
food franch
so little abo
save you tin
Internation
tificate of c
are now mo
broker, we
numerous l
Business Br
business br
Players" link

A broke
or she sells
15 percent l

Some se
their custom

price negotiations. If business has recently been souring, goodwill might be difficult to quantify. Assess both the cost and the possibility of rebuilding customer loyalty.

5. Make sure that relationships with suppliers and distributors are in place. Spend time talking to suppliers and distributors to determine the status of the relationship. They should provide great insight.

6. The location might be excellent and not easily duplicated. Determine if the lease can be reassigned to you. Have your lawyer review the lease, and determine whether the owner of the building has other goals for the location.

7. Employees might possess specialized knowledge that can benefit your business immensely. In high-technology industries, purchasing businesses for brainpower is a common practice. You will have no guarantee, though, that the employees and their expertise will remain—you must consider the possibility that key employees will leave and compete.

8. Existing licenses and permits might be difficult to replicate. Check with your lawyer or licensing agencies to determine the availability and process of transferring licenses and permits before proceeding with any purchase.

9. Make sure that you will be able to see actual financial data and tax-reporting forms. Investigate!

10. An inside look into the business operation will determine whether using advanced technology could increase operational effectiveness and thus profits.

HOW TO BUY AND HOW NOT TO BUY

Smart buyers scrutinize everything about a business with a microscope, a Geiger counter, computer analysis, a clipboard, and sage advice from business gurus. They don't plunge into a business for emotional reasons. For example, you might have eaten lunch around the corner at Millie's Cafeteria with your pals for years, and when the place goes up for sale, nostalgia might make you want to write out a cheque for it on the spot. That would be a wrong reason to buy. Don't buy a business that way.

Every business in the country is for sale at some time. Deals are like planes. If you miss one, another will be along soon.

Good buys are always available to the informed and careful buyer, but they might be difficult to discover. Seeking the right business to buy is much like an employment search: The best deals are seldom advertised. In contrast, the worst business opportunities are advertised widely, usually in the classified sections of newspapers. When you see several ads for a particular type of business, you know where the unhappy businesspeople are.

Running your own ad can be a good idea, however. A man ran this ad in the business section (not the classifieds) of a large-circulation Toronto newspaper:

Sold out at 30. Now I'm tired of retirement and ready to start again.
Want to buy a business with over $1 million in annual sales. Write me
at Box XXXX. H.G.

H.G. received more than 100 replies, and he says that reading the proposals was one of the most educational and entertaining experiences he's ever had. Five of them looked like good deals, but only one fit his talents and interests. After three months of investigation, he decided he would rather start his next venture from scratch. (The firm he almost bought was a beer distributorship whose supplier went out of business the following year. Perhaps the seller knew something.)

ACTION S

**Study a busin
outside** *(cont*

5. **Check ou
competiti**
to be clos
or do you
kilometres
Could a c
next door
move in?

6. **Check wit
authoritie**
plans for t
is the local
ning to do
roads? Are
in order? A
for building
don't think
read about
ence in the

Most sellers who list with brokers, however, do so out of desperation, because they've already tried to sell their business to everyone they know. Probably 9 out of 10 fall into this category.

Spending time with a skilled broker can be a fascinating educational experience. If you want a particular type of business and are able to examine a half-dozen that are on the market, you will probably end up with a better grasp of the business than the owners have. Network with your business contacts to locate a competent broker, and ask brokers for referrals from former clients. And, as we've said so many times before, leave your chequebook at home. Don't let anyone rush you. More information on what business brokers do and what they can offer can be found by linking onto the Business Brokers sites provided in Box 13.1, page 342.

HOW TO LOOK AT THE INSIDE OF A BUSINESS

Once you have your foot in the door and have established yourself as a potential buyer, you will be able to study the inner workings of the business. Take full advantage of this opportunity. For general information on the business valuation process, visit the "Valuation of Small Businesses" Web page profiled in Box 13.2.

Study the Financial History

What you need to learn from the financial history is where the money comes from and where it goes. Ask to see all financial records (balance sheet, income statement, and bank statement for at least five years back, if they're available), and take your time studying them. If you don't understand financial records, hire someone who does. Your aim in buying an ongoing business is to step into an income stream. The financial records give a picture of that stream.

ACTION ST

**Study a busine
the inside**

Looking at a
inside enables y
real worth and t
be like to own it
ment (or have a
nity broker arr
serious inside l
you think you v
you go, review
explained in thi:
down a list of t
learn while yo
allow anyone t
the chequeboo
is free.

Box 13.2 Bookmark This

How Much Is a Business Worth?

1. **Valuation of Small Businesses** Link on to CCH Business Owner's Toolkit: http://www.toolkit.cch.com/text/P11_2240.asp. This page discusses the role of the business appraiser and how, in placing a price tag on a business, you need to consider the following.
   - **Key factors.** What factors are most important to buyers? What are secondary?
   - **Adding value.** How can the seller boost these important factors before the sale?
   - **Recasting financial statements.** How might the seller's accountant adjust the company's financial statements before showing them to potential buyers?
   - **Valuation methods.** What are some of the methods and formulas that are commonly used to put a price tag on a business?
   - **Partial interests.** If the owners are selling only part of the business, how does that affect the price?
2. **Valuing Your Business** Link on to Biz Help 24 http://www.bizhelp24.com/small-business-portal/selling-a-business-37.html. Here you will find plenty of discussion on valuation methods, such as the multiplier valuation, asset value, owner benefit valuation, and the comparison valuation.

Look at the history of cash flow, profit and loss, and accounts receivable. If the seller has a stack of accounts receivable a foot high, remember that

- after three months, the value of a current-accounts dollar will have shrunk to 90 cents;
- after six months, it will be worth 50 cents; and
- after a year, it will be worth 30 cents.

Like an auditor, review every receipt you can find. If a tavern owner tells you she sells 30 to 40 kegs of beer a week, ask to see the receipts from the suppliers. If none are offered, ask permission to contact the suppliers for records of shipment. Make her prove to you that she has bought from suppliers. You can then accurately measure sales. If the seller won't cooperate, walk away: She's hiding something.

Evaluate closely any personal expenses that are being charged to the business. (Your accountant can help you determine a course of action that will keep you out of trouble.) This allows you to get a clearer picture of the firm's true profits. Also, compare the financial results to industry standards.

It's also a good idea to look at cancelled cheques, income tax returns, and the salary the seller has been paying herself. If your seller was stingy with her own salary, decide whether you could live on that amount.

Tips

You can use the seller's accounts receivable as a point for negotiation, but don't take over the job of collecting them.

You might not have to pay GST/HST (see Box 13.3).

Compare What Your Money Could Do Elsewhere

How much money will you be putting into the business? How long will it take you to make it back? Have you figured in your time?

Let's say you would need to put $50,000 into this business and that the business will give you a 33.3 percent return, which is full payback in three years. Are there other investments you could make that would yield the same amount on your $50,000?

If you will be working in the business, you need to add in the cost of your time; say that's $25,000 per year (your present salary) over the three-year period, or $75,000 (assuming no raises). In three years, the business would need to return $125,000 after expenses and taxes to cover the risks involved with your $50,000 investment and to compensate you for the loss of $25,000 in annual salary.

Evaluate the Tangible Assets

Tangible assets are the things you can see and touch. If the numbers look good, move on to assess the value of everything you can touch, specifically the real estate, the equipment and fixtures, and the inventory.

- **Real estate**. Get an outside, professional appraisal of the building and the land. It might be worth more as vacant land than as a business.
- **Equipment and fixtures**. You can get a good idea of current values by asking equipment dealers and reading the want ads. Scour your area for the best deals, because you don't want to tie up too much capital in equipment that's outmoded or about to come apart. Suppliers have lots of leads on used equipment,

TANGIBLE ASSETS

Things your business owns that you can see and touch, such as real estate, equipment, and inventory

INVENTORY

Items carried in the normal course of doing business that are intended for sale

so check with them. If you're not an expert in the equipment field, get help from someone who is. Find out the maintenance costs in the past two years.

- **Inventory**. Count the **inventory** yourself, and make sure the boxes are packed with what you think they are. Make certain you specify the exact contents of shelves and cabinets in the purchase agreement. Don't get careless and write in something vague like "All shelves are to be filled." Specify what goes on the shelves. More important, find out if the inventory is salable, and if the styles and models of the stock are still valid. Don't accept old stock unless the discount is very low.

Once you've made your count, contact suppliers to learn the current prices.

If you find merchandise that is damaged, out of date, out of style, soiled, worn, or not ready to sell as is, don't pay full price for it. Negotiate. This is sacrifice merchandise, and it should have a sacrifice price tag.

In addition to all this, talk to insiders. There's no substitute for inside information. Every detective takes it seriously.

- **Bankers**. It is a must to discuss business with your banker and, ideally, with the current owner's banker. The latter will be limited with respect to what he or she can say, but your banker will be a good help in analyzing the financial statements.
- **Suppliers**. Will suppliers agree to keep supplying you? Are there past difficulties between seller and supplier that you would inherit as the new owner? Remember, you're dependent on your suppliers. How do suppliers evaluate the business?
- **Employees**. Talk to the key employees early. In small business, success can rest on the shoulders of one or two persons, and you don't want them to walk out the day you sign the papers.
- **Competitors**. Identify the major competitors, and interview them to learn what goes on from their perspective. You need to understand the industry fully. Expect some bias, but watch for a pattern to develop. (Chapter 5, you'll remember, tells how to identify the competitors.)

Get a Non-Competition Covenant

Once you buy a business, you don't want the seller to set up the same kind of business across the street. Customers are hard to come by, so you don't want to pay for them and have them spirited away by a cagey seller. Get an agreement, in writing, that the seller will not set up in competition with you—or work for a competitor, or help a friend or relative set up a competitive business—for the next five years. You will need a lawyer to prepare such an agreement. Be sure to specify the exact amount you're paying for the non-competition covenant. That way, the Canada Revenue Agency will allow you to deduct it against income over the life of the covenant.

Analyze the Seller's Motives

People have all kinds of reasons for selling their business. Some of these reasons favour the buyer, whereas others favour the seller.

Here are some reasons for selling that can favour the buyer:

1. retirement or ill health;
2. the seller is too busy to manage, as he or she has other investments;
3. divorce or other family problems;
4. disgruntled partners;

5. the seller expanded too fast and is out of cash;
6. poor management; or
7. the seller has burned out or for other reasons has lost interest.

These reasons for selling will favour the seller (Buyer, beware!):

1. decline in the local economy,
2. decline in this specific industry,
3. intense competition,
4. high insurance costs,
5. increasing litigation,
6. skyrocketing rents,
7. technological obsolescence,
8. problems with suppliers,
9. high-crime location,
10. nonrenewal of lease, or
11. the location is in a decline.

Examine the Asking Price

Many sellers view selling their firms as they would view selling their children; that is, they are emotionally attached to the business, and they overestimate its worth. Pride also plays a role; they might want to tell their friends that they started from scratch and sold out for a million. If you run into irrational and emotional obstacles, walk away or counter with reasonable terms—such as $100 down and 10 percent of the net profits for the next four years, up to $1 million.

Some industries have rule-of-thumb benchmarks for pricing. For example, a service firm might be priced at 6 to 12 months of its total revenue. Such pricing formulas are often unwise, however. The only formula that makes sense is the return on your investment minus the value of your management time, where

$$\text{Return on Investment (ROI)} = (\text{Hours spent} \times \text{Value of your time per hour}).$$

If you can earn 10 percent without sweating on high-grade bonds, you should earn at least a 30 percent return on a business that will make you sweat.

It can be useful to consult the newspaper financial pages to learn the **price/earnings (P/E) ratios** of publicly traded firms. Firms that have low P/E ratios (the stock price is less than 10 times its earnings) are not regarded as growth opportunities by sophisticated investors. Firms with above-average P/E ratios (price is more than 25 times its earnings) are regarded as having above-average growth potential. Thus, you should be willing to pay a higher price for a firm with above-average growth potential than for one that is declining. In fact, you should not buy a declining business unless you think you can either purchase it very inexpensively and turn it around or dispose of its assets at a profit.

PRICE/EARNINGS (P/E) RATIO
The market price of a common stock divided by its annual earnings per share for the latest 12-month period

Negotiate the Value of Goodwill

If the firm has a strong customer base with deeply ingrained purchasing habits, this has value. It takes a while for any start-up to build a client base, and the wait for profitability can be costly.

Some firms have built up a great deal of *ill* will—customers who have vowed never to trade with them again. A large proportion of the businesses on the market have this problem. If the amount of ill will is great, the business will have little value; it might be that *any* price would be too high.

6. "My staff has been robbing me blind. So the numbers are much lower than they really are. With good management, a lot more money can be made."
7. "We don't need lawyers and accountants here. It's not that much money."
8. "Slip me a few dollars 'under the table,' and I can drop the price."
9. "I want all cash for the business."
10. "It's not a lot to pay for this business. You're not risking much money, but the payoff can be massive."

Box 13.5   The Before-You-Buy Checklist

❑ How long do you plan to own this business?

❑ How old is this business? Can you sketch its history?

❑ Is this business in the embryonic stage, the growth stage, the mature stage, or the decline stage?

❑ Has your accountant reviewed the books and made a sales projection for you?

❑ How long will it take for this business to show a complete recovery on your investment?

❑ What reasons does the owner give for selling?

❑ Will the owner let you see bank deposit records? (If not, why not?)

❑ Have you calculated utility costs for the first three to five years?

❑ What does a review of tax records tell you?

❑ How complete is the insurance coverage?

❑ How old are the receivables? (Remember, age decreases their value.)

❑ What is the seller paying him- or herself? Is it low or high?

❑ Have you interviewed your prospective landlord?

❑ What happens when a new tenant takes over the lease?

❑ Has your lawyer checked for any potential problems in the transferral of licences and permits?

❑ Who are the major competitors?

 – Do you want to be close to competitors, or do you want to be kilometres away?
 – Could a competitor move in next door the day after you move in?
 – Have you checked out future competition?

❑ What do the neighbours know about the business?

❑ Will the neighbours help draw target customers (TCs) to your business?

❑ What is the life cycle stage of the community?

❑ Where is the traffic flow?

❑ What's the location?

 – How does the area fit into the city/regional planning for the future?
 – Is there good access?
 – Is parking adequate?
 – Is the parking lot a drop-off point for car-poolers?

❑ Is the building in good repair?

❑ Have you interviewed the seller's customers?

 – What do they like about the store? Is the service good?
 – How far will your TC have to walk?
 – What changes would they recommend?
 – What services or products would they like to see added?
 – Where else do they go for similar products or services?

❑ Have you checked that the customer lists are up to date?

❑ Who are the business's top 20 customers? Its top 50?

❑ Is the seller locked into one to three major customers who control the business?

❑ How well is the business using technology, computerized systems, and business management?

❑ Are you buying inventory? What is the seller asking?

❑ Have you checked the value of the equipment against the price of used equipment from another source?

❑ To whom does your seller owe money?

❑ Has your lawyer checked for liens on the seller's equipment?

❑ Do you have maintenance contracts on the equipment you're buying?

❑ Has your lawyer or escrow company gone through bulk sales escrow?

❑ Have you made certain that…

…you're getting all brand names, logos, trademarks, and so on that you need?
…the seller has signed a non-competition covenant?
…the key lines of supply will stay intact when you take over?
…the key employees will stay?
…the seller isn't leaving because of stiff competition?
…you aren't paying for goodwill but taking delivery on ill will?
…you are getting the best terms possible?
…you're buying an income stream?

PREPARE FOR THE NEGOTIATIONS

Let's say you know you're ready to buy. You've raised the money, and the numbers say you can't lose, so you're ready to start negotiating. (If you're an experienced entrepreneur, you already know how to negotiate. If not, some good books on the fine art of haggling are listed in the references section at the end of this chapter.)

We suggest two things about negotiations. First, when it comes time to talk meaningful numbers, the most important area to concentrate on is *terms,* not asking price. Favourable terms will give you the cash flow you need to survive the first year and then move from survival into success. Unfavourable terms can torpedo your chances for success, even when the total asking price is well below market value.

Second, when the seller brings up the subject of goodwill, be ready for it. Goodwill is a "slippery" commodity; it can make the asking price soar. It's only natural for the seller to attempt to get as much as possible for goodwill. Because you know this ahead of time, you can do your homework and go in primed to deal. Action Step 60 will help you with this. When the seller starts talking about goodwill, you can flip the coin over and discuss ill will—which hangs on longer, like a cloud above the business.

PROTECT YOURSELF

Evaluate each business opportunity by the criteria we present in this chapter. When you find one you think is right for you, start negotiating. Your goal is the lowest possible price with the best possible terms. Start low; you can then negotiate up if necessary.

If you are asked to put down a deposit, handle it in this way.

1. Deposit the money in an escrow account.
2. Include a stipulation in your offer that says the offer is *subject to your inspection and approval* of all financial records and all aspects of the business.

ACTION STEP 60

Probe the depths of ill will

How many products have you vowed never to use again? How many places of business have you vowed never to patronize again? Why?

Make a list of the products and services you won't buy or use again. Next to each item, write the reason. Does it make you sick? Does it offend your sensibilities? Was the service awful?

After you've completed your list, ask your friends what their negative feelings about particular businesses are. Take notes.

Study the two lists you've made. What are the common components of ill will? How long does ill will last? Is there a remedy for it, or is a business plagued by ill will doomed forever?

Now turn your attention to the business you want to buy. Survey your target customers. How do they feel about the business? You need to learn as much as you can about any ill will that exists toward the business.

Have fun with this step, but take it seriously—and think about the nature of ill will when your seller starts asking you to pay for goodwill.

Doing this gives you an escape hatch, so that you can get your deposit returned—and back out of the deal—if things don't look good. Also, consider working in the business for a few weeks with the option to back out if you have a change of heart.

NEGOTIATING THE PRICE

What is a fair price? Obviously, the seller and the buyer have arrived at their values from widely separated viewpoints.

The seller has committed considerable time and money to the business, often for less return than could have been earned elsewhere, and sees the sale as the opportunity to make up for the years of "doing without." The buyer, on the other hand, is concerned only with the present state and future potential of the business and cares little for the time and effort invested by the vendor.

Valuing a business is not an exact science. The valuation process involves comparing several approaches and selecting the best method, or a combination of methods, based on the analyst's knowledge and experience. Practitioners may use several methods to value businesses, such as asset-based pricing, market-based valuations, future earnings–based valuations (such as net present values), and so on. The particular method chosen can become quite complex and will depend on one or more of the following factors:

1. the nature of the business (retail, service, manufacturing, for example) and its operating history;
2. the industry and economic outlook;
3. the financial condition of the company;
4. the company's earnings and debt-paying capacity; and
5. the level of interest rates, which will affect both the cost of borrowing money to buy the business and your return on investment.

We provide three useful methods of valuing a small business below, but we caution you that these are only three of the many approaches and methods available. Should you find yourself wanting to buy a business, we strongly advise professional help in setting a fair price. You might also want to go back and check out the valuations methods suggested by CCH and Biz Help 24, provided in Box 13.2.

1. ASSET-BASED VALUATION

ASSET-BASED VALUATION

The purchase price of a business determined, in large part, by the assets of the business

In an **asset-based valuation**, the purchase price of a business is determined, in large part, by the assets of the business. If you are purchasing assets, the seller will usually have a spec sheet prepared, listing the assets and offering an estimate of their value. The asset value can be calculated using various formulas, including

- fair market value: the price of similar assets on the open market;
- replacement value: what it would cost to replace the asset (i.e., from the original supplier);
- liquidation value: what the asset would bring if the business were liquidated (as in a bankruptcy); or
- book value: a valuation based on the company's balance sheet.

In that list of assets, however, goodwill may be included, representing the value of intangibles, such as location, reputation, and the established customer base of the business. Goodwill is virtually impossible to value objectively; it depends more on instinct and gut feeling than on a strict accounting formula.

The most common method of asset valuation is the adjusted book value. The **book value** is the owner's equity, or total assets minus the total liabilities. The **adjusted book value** is the book value amended to reflect market values. For example, in the balance sheet shown for XYZ Company Limited on page 358, you would appraise the equipment. What is the real market value? What would it cost to replace this equipment? You would want to look at the inventory and ask: Can it actually be sold, or has it been sitting on the back shelf for 10 years? You would examine the accounts receivable. Are there any accounts there with no chance of collection?

An adjusted book value usually reflects a minimum valuation of a business. For example, suppose you wanted to buy XYZ Company. Examining the assets, you find $5,000 in assets that have no market value. Your adjusted book value, and thus the estimated value of the business, would be $33,890 ($38,890 – $5,000).

Furthermore, this valuation of individual assets tells only part of the story. The real value of the business depends to a large extent on the future income that it generates. This might not be directly related to the value of the assets, especially in service businesses. We therefore encourage you to look at the company's income history over a period of years (at least three is usual) to determine what its gross revenues, costs, cash flow, and profit were. You are really buying an income, and one way of looking at the purchase price is in terms of a return on your investment.

As a result, we are going to provide you with two other techniques for valuating a small business that take into consideration the revenue potential of the business.

2. ABILITY-TO-PAY VALUATION

Most new business owners cannot afford to buy a business without taking out a loan or getting some sort of earnout. So before buying a business, they want to make sure that the business can pay off the loan or earnout and, at the same time, have enough cash to pay all the other expenses—which include, of course, a salary to the new owner. A value of the business is thus determined by its ability to pay off the loan over a specified period and provide a reasonable return on the owner's investment.[2]

Provided below are the steps you would carry out this cash flow value.

Step 1: Estimate the Amount of Cash the Business Will Generate with No Debt and Reasonable Salary or Payment to the Owner

Start with the most recent cash flow of the business. Adjust this cash flow by adding back in any bank payments (both principal and interest) or payments to purchase fixed assets. Here you are making the assumption that the business is debt free and can pay a reasonable salary to you, the owner. At this point, you are looking at this cash flow only in terms of whether it can pay normal monthly operational costs.

Example

The end-of-the-year cash flow of DISCovery Books (Table 10.6, page 250) was $27,395. We know that it started with $10,000, so company operations generated $17,395 in excess cash over the first year. We will assume that these are actual and not projected numbers. To get the adjusted cash flow, we would *add*

BOOK VALUE

Owner's equity, or total assets minus total liabilities

ADJUSTED BOOK VALUE

The book value amended to reflect market values

ABILITY-TO-PAY VALUATION

A valuation approach based on the ability of a business to pay off its business loan and provide a reasonable return on the owner's investment over a specified period the bank payments—including both bank charges and interest ($3,600) and the principle portion of the term debt ($3000)—for an adjusted cash flow of $23,995 ($17,395 + $6600). Now you would check the salary paid to the owner DISCovery Books ($19,200). Suppose you felt that you needed to take home $3,600 more a year. Then the adjusted cash flow would be *reduced* by $3,600 and would be $20,395 ($23,995 – $3,600). You have now estimated the amount of yearly cash—$20,395—the business will generate with no debt and reasonable payment (salary) to you the owner.

Step 2: Calculate Your Return-to-Owners Investment

First you must determine how much you are prepared to invest in the business and what rate of return you expect. Then calculate the amount of cash the business will need to generate to give you a reasonable return on your investment.

You must subtract this amount from the available cash flow in Step 1. The cash remaining is the amount the business will generate that can support a rate of return on your investment. Note that this cash flow will still have to support loan payments—we'll get to that in Steps 3 and 4.

Example

In the case of DISCovery Books, suppose you were prepared to invest $30,000. First, you will have to determine what interest rate return you want for your business investment—10, 15, or 20 percent, for example. Suppose you decided that 15 percent was reasonable. This means that DISCovery would have to pay you, from its available cash, $4,500 each year ($30,000 × .15 = $4,500 per year). We know from Step 1 that DISCovery has $20,395 available in its first year. From this amount, you subtract the $4,500 to get $15,895. This is the amount the business has available to pay the interest on your investment in the first year. Most business owners want to see a rate of return of anywhere between 15 and 30 percent, so the expected rate of return used in this example (15 percent) is on the low side.

Step 3: Estimate the Number of Years You Reasonably Expect It Will Take to Pay Off the Loan to Buy the Business

Example

Let's suppose you were thinking about buying DISCovery Books and found that there were three years left on the lease. You know that financial institutions are reluctant to provide loans that extend beyond the term of the lease. In this case, a three-year loan might be reasonable. Note that with this valuation method, the longer the time period you choose, the higher the value of the business. So if you were selling DISCovery Books, you might want to think about getting the lease extended to raise your asking price.

Step 4: Estimate the Size of Loan Needed to Support the Available Cash Flow (Step 2) to Be Paid Off in the Period Specified in Step 3

Example

Assume that you want to buy DISCovery Books and decide to pay off the loan over three years. You do your research and decide that an estimated 8 percent interest rate would be reasonable. You know that you have $15,895 (Step 2) available in the first year. If you were to assume that this amount will also be generated in the next two years, then the total cash available to pay off a three-year loan will be $47,685 (3 × $15,895). So, over three years, the business will have $47,685 to pay for principal and interest on a loan.

But how do you find out the amount of the loan? You can get this estimate in a number of ways: financial calculators, special financial tables, and so on. An easy way is to use the Internet and click onto a loan calculator (http://www. bankrate.com/goocan/cgi-bin/apr.asp, for example). You will find out that a loan of $42,200 will cost about $47,600 over a three-year period at 8 percent. A loan of $42,200 will mean that every month for three years, the business will have to pay $1,322 in principal and interest. After three years of these monthly payments, the loan will be paid ($42,200 in principal and $5,400 in interest). The point is that your projected three-year cash flow can support a loan of about $42,200.

We should note that we have assumed that the first-year cash flow also applies in Years 2 and 3. As we learned in Chapter 10, forecasting is an art. If you have only one year of cash flow, you might have to make the assumption of a constant cash flow over the loan period. But you should ask yourself, Is this a reasonable assumption? For example, you might want to pay yourself a higher salary in the next few years. This increased expenditure would reduce your future cash flows. If you have historic cash flows for a particular business, you might find a trend (maybe, for example, a yearly increase or decrease of 10 percent). You might then want to adjust your projected cash flow according to this kind of thinking.

Step 5: Estimate the Value of the Business Based on Its Ability to Pay the Costs out of Its Cash Flow

In Step 4, we found out the total amount of money we could borrow. Add this to the owner's investment, and you get the total value of the businesses. The business would be able to support all the cash flow payments, if you were to pay this price AND **if your assumptions are correct!**

Example

In the case of DISCovery Books, we know from Step 4 that the business can afford a loan of $42,200. We also know that the owner has invested $30,000 in the business, so the value of the business is $72,200 ($42,200 + $30,000). This estimate is based on its cash flow and its ability to pay you a rate of return (15 percent, in this case), to pay off the loan (both principal and interest), and to cover all monthly operating costs.

3. EARNINGS-ASSETS VALUATION

In the first method—asset-based evaluation—no consideration was given to the earnings potential. In the second method—ability to pay—no consideration was given to the value of the assets. This third method—earnings-assets valuation—takes into consideration both earning potential and asset value. This valuation approach requires copies of the financial statements for the business, as it is only from these figures that a valid analysis can be made.

There are various methods for calculating an earning-assets evaluation. See, for example, the CCH "excess earnings" approach provided on their Web site (http://www.toolkit.cch.com/text/P11_2244.asp).[3] Below is another method suggested by the Business Development Bank.[4] We also encourage you to work through this approach in our end-of-chapter case study (Question 4b).

EARNINGS-ASSETS VALUATION

A business valuation approach that takes into consideration both earning potential and asset value

Earnings-Assets Pricing Formula

Step 1. Calculate the tangible net worth of the business. This is, in its simplest form, the total tangible assets (excluding goodwill, franchise fees, etc.) less total liabilities (both current and long term).

Step 2. Estimate the current earning power of this tangible net worth if this amount was invested elsewhere (stocks, bonds, term deposits). This earning power will vary with economic trends and other factors but should be based on current interest rates.

Step 3. Determine a reasonable annual salary that the owner could earn if similarly employed elsewhere. Remember to take into consideration benefits paid by the business (automotive, insurance, pensions, etc.) in determining a comparable outside salary.

Step 4. Determine the total earning capacity of the owner that would result from the net worth invested plus employment sources by adding the results of Steps 2 and 3.

Step 5. Calculate the average annual net profit of the business. This average will be the total of profit from all financial statements available (before any management salaries or cash withdrawal for partners, proprietors, taxes, etc.) divided by the number of years used in the analysis. We suggest three years minimum but preferably five years for a more accurate result.

Step 6. Calculate the extra earning power of the business by subtracting the result of Step 4 from that of Step 5. This figure represents the additional money you can expect to earn if you buy the business rather than invest an amount equal to the net worth and obtain or retain outside employment.

Step 7. Calculate the value of intangibles by multiplying the extra earning power (Step 6) by a figure that we will refer to as the "development factor." This development factor is designed to weigh such things as uniqueness of the intangibles, time needed to establish a similar business from scratch, expenses and risk of a comparable start-up, price of goodwill in similar firms, and so on.

If the business is well established and successful, a suggested factor of 5 or more might be used; a more moderately seasoned firm might rate a factor of 3, and a young but profitable business might rate a factor of only 1.

Step 8. Calculate the final price. This is arrived at by adding the tangible net worth of the business (Step 1) to the value of intangibles (Step 7).

Here is one example of how this formula works. Assume you are interested in purchasing the XYZ Company, and the asking price is $200,000. At your request, the owners of XYZ have given you the following financial statement representing the last complete year of operation. (Note that we are using only one year's statement in this example. When using this formula for real, you should attempt to obtain statements for at least three but preferably for five years.)

XYZ Company Limited
Balance Sheet
As at December 31, 20XX

Assets	
Current	
Cash	$ 180
Accounts receivable	6,560
Inventory	13,150
Total current assets	19,890
Fixed assets	
Land	5,000
Buildings	35,000

Equipment	14,500	
Furniture	1,800	
Vehicles	11,500	
Less: Accumulated depreciation	8,100	
Total fixed assets	59,700	
Total assets		$79,590
Liabilities		
Current liabilities		
Bank	$ 3,000	
Accounts payable	6,600	
Current portion—Long-term	1,100	
Total current liabilities	10,700	
Long-term liabilities		
Long-term mortgage loan	21,500	
Equipment loan	9,600	
Total long-term liabilities	31,100	
Less: Current portion	1,100	
Total long-term liabilities	30,000	
Total liabilities	40,700	

Shareholders' equity		
Share capital	10,000	
Retained earning	28,890	
Total shareholders' equity	38,890	
Total liabilities and shareholders' equity		$79,590

XYZ Company Limited
Operating Statement
For the 12 months
ended December 31, 20XX

Sales (revenue)		**$250,000**
Cost of goods sold		
Opening inventory	$ 12,000	
Purchases	151,150	
	163,150	
Closing inventory	13,150	
Total cost of goods sold		150,000
Gross profit		100,000

Operating expenses		
Advertising	1,500	
Automobile	2,400	
Bad debts	300	
Depreciation	3,700	
Equipment rental	400	
Insurance	1,200	
Interest and bank charges	4,000	
Management salaries	16,000	
Miscellaneous	400	
Office supplies	1,100	
Professional fees	800	
Taxes and licences (municipal)	300	
Telephone	800	
Utilities	2,100	

Wages and benefits	40,000	
Total operating expenses		75,000
Operating profit		25,000
Less: Income taxes[a]	6,250	
Net profit		$ 18,750

[a]Arbitrarily set at 25 percent for demonstration purposes only. Rates can vary not only provincially but also within individual businesses.

Formula Calculation (figures have been rounded)

1. Tangible net worth $39,000
2. Earning power (assume 10 percent) 3,900
3. Reasonable salary for owner 16,000
4. Earning capacity 19,900
5. Average annual net profit (operating profit before taxes, $25,000 + owner's salary, $16,000) 41,000
6. Extra earning power 21,100
7. Value of intangibles (development factor of 3) 63,300
8. Final price (63,300 + 39,000) 102,300

By applying the formula, you come up with a suggested final price of $102,300, compared to the asking price of $200,000.

Any price negotiated must, of course, be related to the new financing of the business. Your combination of personal investment and borrowed money might be very different from the position of the vendor and as such will produce a very different operating result. Your negotiations will be strongly influenced by what you can afford.

Once you are satisfied that you have given full consideration to all factors affecting the proposed acquisition and you are ready to proceed, you should formalize your offer with a purchase agreement. Be sure to seek professional help and advice in the preparation of this agreement. In the meantime, we encourage you to have some fun with business valuations. Try out a net present value valuation by clicking on the Interactive Business Valuation site in the E-Exercise in Box 13.6.

Box 13.6   E-Exercise

Net Present Value Valuation, KJE Computer solutions: http://www.dinkytown.com/java/BusinessValuation.html

A net present value (NPV) calculation of a company's worth takes into consideration future business earnings. It provides you with a cash value of the business in today's dollars. Make some assumptions about DISCovery Bookstore's future cash flows (Table 10.6, Chapter 10, page 250) over the next four years; cost of capital, and expected growth rate. Using an NPV calculation, how would these assumptions affect the value of DISCovery?

THE CONTRACT

Ultimately the sale of a business involves a combination of final price, other terms, and overall risk. You might be prepared to pay a higher price as long as other conditions (such as the seller's agreeing to take a mortgage on easy terms) are suitable, or you might opt for a lower price in which you assume more of the risks of the transaction. The precise mix will vary according to the nature of the business and the inclinations of the individuals involved.

Once you have arrived at the terms, the details should be spelled out in a contract that itemizes all aspects of the sale. The following is a summary of some standard items that are usually found in such a contract:

- a definition of what is being transferred, from whom to whom, and at what price, including an itemized breakdown of costs, so that you have a record of the value of each asset, both those you can claim for depreciation and those you cannot;
- details of any leases or liabilities that you are assuming in making the purchase;
- the method of payment (in cash, by cheque, in shares in another company, in bonds), on what date, and by what means;
- any adjustments to the price to cover financial transactions occurring between the moment the offer is signed and the closing date (this could include sale of inventory, equipment purchases, tax payments, etc.);
- guarantees by the seller of the truthfulness of information supplied and provisions for any penalties in the event that information is not accurate;
- a description of the seller's obligations in operating the business up to closing, implementing the transfer of ownership, and performing any post-sale duties or services;
- mechanisms for dealing with any losses or damages that might occur to the business between the signing of the agreement and the closing date;
- a clause restricting the ability of the seller to compete with the business once the sale is closed, or limiting the seller's freedom to start up similar ventures;
- any conditions that should be met prior to closing (such as validation of deeds, liabilities, or agreements entered into by the business);
- details of closing, including the date, time, place, and individuals effecting the transfer;
- compensation to be paid by the seller to the buyer as damages or compensation if information is found to be false;
- the amount of the security deposit the buyer put up and held in escrow for a period of time as a guarantee that all terms and conditions have been satisfied; and
- who would decide the case in the event of a dispute.[5]

EXPECT SOME PLEASANT SURPRISES

Well, you've come a long way, and you've worked hard on your research. You might be wondering if the digging was worth it. Only you can answer that. There are bargains to be found out there—businesses like Woolett's Hardware. For hunter-buyers with vision and persistence, beautiful opportunities are waiting behind ugly façades.

"I heard about Woolett's being up for sale more than a year ago. I'd just opened up my second store at the time—it's also in the hardware line—and it took me just about a year, April to April, to streamline the paperwork. Thanks to a computer and a good manager, my sanity remained intact.

"So, when I finally got over there to check things out, Woolett's had been on the market about a year and a half. One look from the street and I could see why.

"The store was a mess. The building was pre–World War II, and so was the paint. Out front, the sign was sagging. The parking lot needed lots of work; there were potholes 15 centimetres deep. The entryway was littered with scraps of paper.

"Inside, things weren't much better. The floor needed a good sweeping. The merchandise was covered with dust. And all around there was this feeling of mildew, age, and disuse. It was dark—like a cave. It was tough finding a salesperson, and when you did, you couldn't get much help. Yet, there were customers all over the place.

"After you've been in business a while, you develop a sort of sixth sense about things. And the minute I stepped into the store, I knew there was something special about it, something hidden, something the eye couldn't see right off. I knew I had to dig deeper.

"A visit to the listing real-estate broker didn't help much. 'Make us an offer,' he said. 'We just dropped the price yesterday. To $400,000.'

"'What do the numbers look like?' I asked.

"He dug into a slim manila folder. 'Last year,' he said, 'they grossed just under $600,000. The net was around $200,000.'

"'What about inventory?' I asked. 'What about loans and **liens** and accounts receivable? When can I interview the manager? And why is the owner selling?'

"'Are you just asking that,' he said, 'or is this for real?'

"'This is for my son,' I said. 'He's new to the business, and we don't want a lot of surprises.'

"'Like I said, make us an offer.'

"'Let me check the books,' I said. I deposited $500 with an escrow company, making sure I got my usual escape clause—a deposit receipt saying my offer for the business was contingent on my inspection of all assets and my approval of all financial records. Doing this has saved me tons of heartburn medicine over the years.

"The minute they got wind of a buyer, the manager and two of the employees up and quit. The back office was a mess, and it took me three days of searching to find something that would tell me I was on the right track. I found a supply of rolled steel. It was on the books at $12,000, but I knew it was worth $150,000. I took that as a buy signal.

"The next day, I made an offer: $12,000 down, with the balance to be paid out of profits over the next five years. The owner accepted, and we cleared escrow in 30 days.

"The first thing we did was clean the place up. We surfaced the parking lot with asphalt, added a coat of paint, fixed the door, and added lighting.

"Business picked up right away. My son, newly married, was settling down and learning the business. He seemed to have managerial talents. Buying this business was a pleasant surprise."

In a Nutshell

There are two good reasons to explore businesses for sale: You'll learn a lot by exploring the marketplace, and you might find a gem like Woolett's Hardware—a business that will make money right from the start.

A final note of caution is in order. Buying a business can take time, and it certainly involves new risk. In making the purchase, you are assuming new responsibilities to those who helped you finance the deal, to any employees working for the business, to its suppliers, and to its clients. Before you buy, do your homework, complete the checklist provided in Box 13.5, and make sure you have a watertight contract in place.

LIEN

A legal obligation filed against a piece of property

Key Terms

ability-to-pay valuation	earnout
adjusted book value	escrow company
asset-based valuation	goodwill
book value	inventory
bulk sales escrow	lien
business broker (business intermediary)	price/earnings (P/E) ratio
earnings-assets valuation	tangible assets

Think Points for Success

✓ Stick to what you know. Don't buy a business you know nothing about.
✓ Compare what your money could do elsewhere.
✓ Don't let a seller or a broker rush you. A business is not a used car.
✓ If your seller looks absolutely honest, check him or her out anyway.
✓ Worry less about price; work harder on terms.
✓ Most good businesses are sold behind the scenes, before they reach the open market.
✓ Make sure you're there when the physical inventory takes place. Look in those boxes yourself.
✓ Get everything in writing. Be specific.
✓ Always go through bulk sales escrow.
✓ Buying a corporation is tricky. Have an experienced lawyer and accountant help you.

Checklist Questions and Actions to Develop Your Business Plan

Buying a Business

❑ Why would you buy a business rather than start from scratch?

❑ What are the potential "icebergs" (unknowns or major risks) in buying a business?

❑ Establish the value of goodwill. Is the business worth this amount?

❑ What would be the cost involved in starting from scratch versus buying a business?

Case Study

A PASSIONATE LEAP

Case Background

"Come on. Let's be realistic. You're really risking only $10,000. It's just not that much money. We hardly even need a costly lawyer or accountant. I'll tell you what. If you move quickly, I'll even throw in the inventory I just bought. With all the goodwill you're buying, you can make your small investment back in no time. I want to see my baby prosper after I'm gone. I like you guys, and I think you will take care of my business and make me proud. I really want to go with you. But, to tell you the truth, I have a couple of other offers. If you want the deal, you'll have to get back to me in the next couple of days."

Frank, the current owner of The Copy Centre Store, had started the business 18 months earlier. Now he was ready to bail out. He'd been advertising in the Businesses for Sale section of the local newspaper. Carolyn and Mitch were hungry to get into business. They had been watching this section of their local paper, and it seemed as if they had found the perfect opportunity. Here was an owner who wanted out quickly at a "bargain-basement" price—so he claimed

They could take over Frank's business for just $10,000 cash plus $98,000 in equipment and inventory. Frank offered to finance the $98,000 and even throw in a few perks, if they would move quickly and offer their house as collateral.

That evening, they asked Uncle Jack, an experienced entrepreneur, what he thought. "You have to research the business from the inside—the books, interview the previous owner thoroughly, and talk to everybody in the center and in the business. Then, complete a total evaluation of the business from the outside—the location and so on. I'm tied up right now, but give me a few days and I will prepare a list of 'inside' and 'outside' questions that need to be answered."

Mitch and Carolyn both wanted to get into an established business. They had been looking for more than six months. Entrepreneurs move fast and take risks, they reasoned. This seemed like a perfect opportunity. Not much downside. After all, as Frank the owner had said, the most they could lose was $10,000, they thought. Deep into the night, they brainstormed. They even had a few good ideas to improve the storefront and sales.

The next day, Carolyn and Mitch made the deal—and when they told Uncle Jack later on, he went ballistic, as he has been known to do! The third day after they opened, a big truck backed up to their back door and removed all the copy machines. It seems that the previous owner had leased them and hadn't made payments in three months. This was only the start. A year later, Mitch and Carolyn were broke, and their house was gone! They learned the hard way. Passionate leaps require due diligence!

Case Study Questions

1. Reasons for Buying a Business
   a. List five reasons why an entrepreneur would buy a business rather than start his or her own.
   b. If Mitch and Carolyn had reviewed this list, would they have bought the business?

2. Investigating the Business
   As Uncle Jack advised, Mitch and Carolyn should have investigated the business from both the outside and the inside. Suppose you were Uncle Jack.
   a. Prepare a checklist of possible research questions for Mitch and Carolyn related to the outside of the business.
   b. Prepare a checklist of possible research questions for Mitch and Carolyn related to the inside of the business.

3. Red Flags
   a. Carolyn and Mitch should have listened carefully to Frank, who gave them a number of "red flags" (Box 13.4, page 351) that he was trying to sell his business quickly. What red flags did Frank raise?
   b. Go back to Box 13.4. For each red flag listed, state one reason why prospective buyers should be careful when they hear each statement.

4. Businesses Valuation
   Suppose that Mitch and Carolyn had done their financial due diligence and had calculated the following financial information:

   Total assets (market value): $50,000
   Goodwill: $10,000
   Total liabilities: $35,000
   Average annual net profit before taxes: $25,000
   Salary to owner: $22,000

Suppose, as well, that Carolyn and Mitch had also estimated that they would need a combined salary of $32,000, to pay their personal expenses. This means that the net profit given to them by Frank would be $25,000 – $10,000 = $15,000. Assume that they had worked out the earning power of Frank's assets to be 10 percent. As Frank had been in business only 18 months, they would decide to apply a developmental (or times earning) factor of 1.

a. One method of valuing a business is the adjusted book value. According to this method, what is the value of Frank's business?

b. Using the earnings-assets valuation method (page 357), how much is the business worth? Compete the following steps.

   1. Tangible net worth: _____
   2. Earning power (10 percent) _____
   3. Reasonable salary for owner(s) $32,000
   4. Earning capacity _____
   5. Average annual net profit _____
   6. Extra earning power _____
   7. Value of intangibles (developmental factor of 1) _____
   8. **Final earnings-assets valuation price** _____

c. Compare your results in (a) and (b) above. Which valuation estimate is lower? Why?

Notes

1. See "The Voice of the Market." Available at: http://www.robbinex.com/profit.shtml (accessed July 2006).
2. See CCH, "Historical Earnings Evaluation." Available at: http://www.toolkit.cch.com/text/P11_2244.asp (accessed July 2006).
3. CCH, "Assets and Earnings Valuation." Available at: http://www.toolkit.cch.com/text/P11_2246.asp (accessed July 2006).
4. Industry Canada, Strategis Web site. Available at: http://strategis.ic.gc.ca/sc_mangb/contact/engdoc/homepage.html (accessed July 2006). Reprinted by permission.
5. Industry Canada, Strategis Web site. Available at: http://strategis.ic.gc.ca/ sc_mangb/contact/engdoc/homepage.html (accessed July 2006). Reprinted by permission.

SUGGESTED READING

Blayney, Mark. *Selling your Business for All It's Worth*. Oxford, UK: How To Books, 2003.

Feldman, Stanley, Tim Sullivan, and Roger Winsby. *What Every Business Owner Should Know about Valuing Their Business*. New York: McGraw-Hill, 2002.

Klueger, Robert F. *Buying and Selling a Business: A Step-by-Step Guide*. Hoboken, NJ: John Wiley and Sons, 2004.

Linton, Heather. *Streetwise Business Valuation: Proven Methods to Easily Determine the True Value of Your Business*. Avon MA: Adams Media, 2004.

Mancuso, Anthony, and Bethany Laurence. *Buy-Sell Agreement Handbook: Plan Ahead for Change in the Ownership of Your Business*. Berkeley, CA: Nolo Books, 2003.

Sperry, Paul, and Beatrice H. Mitchell. *Complete Guide to Selling Your Business*. London, UK: Kogan Page Limited, 2004.

14

Buying a Franchise or Franchising Your Business

This chapter will introduce you to the world of franchising and help you decide if buying a franchise or becoming a franchisor is right for you.

PROPERTY.GUYS.COM

Anna Babin enjoyed her job and the professional opportunities that came with working for one of Canada's largest IT consulting firms in Ottawa. But her family roots were in Nova Scotia, and she longed to return home. "I missed my family and Nova Scotia….My husband and I wanted a simpler life for our two-year-old daughter," she recalls.

In 2003, an article in *Canadian Franchise Magazine* attracted her attention. It was about a new Canadian franchise called PropertyGuys.com. Anna and her husband had talked about a lot of ideas, but "there was something about that company that kept drawing me back to the article," she recalled. Eventually, she contacted PropertyGuys.com president Ken LeBlanc and initiated discussions to buy a franchise.

Babin did her research. She learned all about the company and its owners. PropertyGuys.com was a commission-free, "for sale by owner" marketing company that helped homeowners retain their hard-earned equity. She knew that traditional real estate agents charge a percentage-based commission regardless of how quickly the house is sold. A standard 6 percent commission on a $200,000 home would equate to $12,000 in real estate broker fees. PropertyGuys.com provided clients with the support needed to sell their homes privately. The PropertyGuys support package included selling-related help such as national marketing exposure, signage, Web listings, and legal forms. Home sellers would also get the personalized attention of a PropertyGuys.com representative—all for a pre-set fee starting in the $500 range.

After a great deal of investigation and family discussion, Anna took the plunge in 2005. She and her family are now back home with a PropertyGuys.com franchise licence covering Annapolis, Digby, Yarmouth, Shelburne, and Queens Counties; aggressive expansion plans; and a business vision to "help save her clients $3 million in accumulated real estate fees over the next five years."[1]

"YOU'RE ONLY HERE FOR A CUP OF COFFEE"

"'You're only here for a cup of coffee,' Orv Lahey, our small-business professor, told us that first day of class, a few years ago. How ironic. My name is Doug Tham, and I had a passion—and still do—for

LEARNING OPPORTUNITIES

After reading this chapter, you should be able to

- appreciate the vast world of franchising,
- understand key franchising terms and conditions in an agreement,
- understand the relationship between franchisor and franchisee,
- learn the benefits and liabilities of owning and operating a franchise,
- learn how to become a master franchisee,
- learn the process involved in purchasing a franchise,
- understand what it takes to become a franchisor, and
- decide whether buying a franchise or becoming a franchisor is the right step for you.

ACTION STEP
PREVIEW

61. Conduct secondary research on franchising.
62. Investigate the franchise system by interviewing franchisors and franchisees.

coffee and always wanted to own a coffee shop. So it was an omen that Orv came out with this nugget at our first encounter.

"I researched the market and came to the conclusion that I needed a partner, a strong partner who could secure me a good location, provide the right training, and be ready to move with the times. I didn't want to be out there alone. I wanted to be part of a strong organization. I felt I couldn't compete in the coffee business as a mom-and-pop operation. After months of investigation, I chose Second Cup.

"I've just completed my first year in business, and I can tell you that I made the right decision. Our team has exceeded sales targets, and our costs are in line. I know franchising isn't the option for everyone. You hear a lot of horror stories. But it's worked out for me.

"My manager, Aaron Cope, and I went through an intensive three-week training program

"If you are going to buy a franchise, here's my advice:

- "Get a mentor.
- "You're more likely to succeed if you stick to what you know best. Make sure you and the franchisor have the same vision.
- "Always get advice from a lawyer and an accountant. You don't have to follow it, but at least listen to them.
- "Have a business plan.
- "Teamwork is everything. If you can't work in a team, you may as well pack it in.
- "Find out how the franchisor helps franchisees sell their business. I considered this a litmus test of Second Cup's corporate culture."[2]

Our walk-through of opportunities in small business is almost finished. Decision time approaches. If you've followed the Action Steps, you've spent several months gathering data and talking to people in small business. In Chapter 13, we explored buying a business and talking to sellers. In this chapter, we look at another option: acquiring a franchised business.

Franchisees like Anna Babin of PropertyGuys.com and Doug Tham of the Second Cup have found success through buying a franchise. We learned in Chapter 6 how 1-800-GOT-JUNK? made a success as a franchisor by franchising out their business format to business people like Doug Tham and Anna Babin. In this chapter, we'll introduce you to other Canadian entrepreneurs who are "riding high" on the franchising wave.

The franchising industry is enormous. Each year, Entrepreneur.com publishes a ranking for some 500 franchises. They also publish a series of top 10 franchises in the following categories: home-based, low cost, top new, fastest growing, and top global. The top 10 global franchises are shown in Table 14.1. If you were to buy or rent a car tomorrow morning, put gas in it, buy a coffee and doughnut, purchase some paint, and then go to a fast-food restaurant for lunch, chances are you would support a franchise at every stop. According to franchise experts, here are some franchising facts.

- About 48 cents of every dollar spent in the retail sector goes to some franchise business.
- The country's franchise sector is Canada's largest employer. There are about 85,000 franchise units (franchisees) and 950 franchise systems (franchisors).
- There is one franchise outlet for every 1,200 Canadians.
- Franchise revenues are estimated to be in the $100 billion range.

- Average annual franchise sales growth during the past few years has exceeded 10 percent.
- A new franchise opens in Canada every 90 minutes, 365 days of the year.
- Over 60 percent of Canadian franchise systems are master licensees of U.S. franchisors.[3]

What is a franchise? Is a franchise for you? Should you franchise your business? When does it make business sense? Are you ready to surrender some of your independence? Is this a good first business, a steppingstone to the future entrepreneurship you seek? We'll try to help you answer these questions in this chapter.

WHAT IS A FRANCHISE?

As we discussed in Chapter 7, a franchise is a distribution system used by businesses to sell or market their products or services. It's a special kind of partnership in which one company (the **franchisor**) grants the right to sell its products or services to another company or individual (the **franchisee**).

FRANCHISE SYSTEMS

A variety of franchise business arrangements or systems exist. If you drop by Second Cup for a cup of coffee, buy a dozen doughnuts at Tim Hortons, or get your trash removed by 1-800-GOT-JUNK?, you have just experienced familiar examples of the so-called **business format franchise** system. This type of franchise is one in which the product, method of distribution, and sales and management procedures—the business format—are highly controlled. The franchisor "blueprints" every aspect of the business and then sells this business format to a franchisee. The main job of the franchisee is to staff and run the operation. This is the most popular type of franchise system—one that encompasses most businesses, from used clothing to coffee to the selling of mufflers.

FRANCHISOR (OR FRANCHISER)

The firm that sells the rights to do business under its name and continues to control the business

FRANCHISEE

The individual operator who is licensed to operate under the franchisor's rules and directives

BUSINESS FORMAT FRANCHISE

A type of franchise in which the product, method of distribution, and sales and management procedures are highly controlled

Table 14.1 Franchising—a Global Trend

Top 10 Global Franchises

Franchise	U.S. Franchises	Canadian Franchises	Foreign Franchises	Company Owned
Subway	18,280	2,032	2,742	1
Curves	7,860	726	800	0
Quizno's	2,961	289	50	2
Kumon Math & Reading Centers	1,352	341	21,800	22
KFC Corp.	4,277	715	5,275	2,999
The UPS Store	4,201	271	1,213	0
RE/MAX Int'l. Inc.	3,614	580	1,285	28
Domino's Pizza LLC	4,348	0	2,605	577
Jani-King	9023	540	1369	22
GNC Franchising Inc	1,314	0	737	3,657

Source: Entrepreneur.com, Franchise Zone: (http://www.entrepreneur.com/franzone/listings/fran500/0,5831,,00.html).

DEALERSHIP RELATIONSHIP FRANCHISE

Also called licensing or associate relationship, a type of franchise in which the franchisee buys the right to distribute a franchisor's product or service

A second type of popular franchise system is the **dealership relationship franchise** (also termed a licensing or associate relationship). Here the dealer or associate (franchisee) buys the right to distribute a franchisor's product or service. These types of licensing arrangements are less restrictive than the business format arrangement, where the key is standardization. Dealership franchisees distribute and sell the product under the franchisor's conditions but are left relatively free from any other franchisee obligations. Property Guys.com and Home Hardware are good examples of this kind of arrangement. Another example would be Coca-Cola and Pepsi, which license or franchise out the right to distribute their products to a local bottler but don't normally tell the licensees how to run their business operations.

FRANCHISE NETWORKS

A franchisor has two basic types of franchise networks available to distribute its products or services. When a franchisee deals directly with the franchisor on a one-to-one basis, this type of network is referred to as **direct franchising**. For example, in the opening vignette, Anna Babin bought the franchise rights from PropertyGuys.com to operate her franchise for several counties in Nova Scotia. PropertyGuys.com, the franchisor, will be dealing directly with her. If she has questions or problems, she deals directly with a representative of the franchisor.

DIRECT FRANCHISING

A business arrangement in which a franchisee deals directly with the franchisor

MASTER FRANCHISING

A business arrangement in which a franchisor sells the rights of an area or territory to a franchisee, who is normally required to sell (or establish) and service a specified number of franchises in its area within a specified time period

If a franchisor wants to grow quickly and still provide hands-on service, it might turn to the master franchise format. **Master franchising** is a business arrangement or network in which a franchisor sells the rights of an area or territory to a franchisee, who is usually required to sell (or establish) and service a specified number of franchises (often called sub-franchisees) in a specified time period within its area. The master franchisee pays the franchisor (franchise company) an initial territory fee for the rights to develop its area. Normally, in return, it retains at least a portion of the franchise fees and royalties fees paid over time by the sub-franchisees. These area sub-franchisees work with the Master Franchisee in the operations of their business. For example, PropertyGuys.com signed its first Master Franchise Agreement (MFA) in 2005, when Don Swanston and Matt Eldridge purchased 18 franchise units in British Columbia's Greater Vancouver area. According to this agreement, over the next two-and-a-half years, they will either resell the franchises to sub-franchisees or operate new outlets themselves. As master franchisees, they will service this area on behalf of the PropertyGuys.com. In turn, the corporate office will be able to focus on growing the business in other areas. According to Ken LeBlanc, president of PropertyGuys.com,

> It's been getting more and more difficult to deliver [franchisee services] when a vast majority of our time is spent travelling back and forth across the country and recruiting new franchisees. We are dedicated to providing our franchisees with personal, hands-on support, but our new master franchise agreements will enable us to maintain our trademark support, while continuing to realize our long-term international expansion strategy."[4]

If you want to learn more about master franchising, click on the sites shown in Box 14.1.

WHY BUY A FRANCHISE?

In theory, a successful franchise system can benefit the customer, the franchisee, and the franchisor—a win-win situation.

WHAT THE CUSTOMER GETS

Imagine that you're on a holiday. You have been driving for hours, and it's time for lunch. Do you have lunch at Wendy's or Taco Bell, or do you take a chance and pull in at a flashing "Joe's Diner" sign? If you're like the average Canadian, you'll choose a name that is familiar. Why? Because to some degree, you've been branded. You've become comfortable with a product and gained a certain attachment to it. You know what to expect, so even if it isn't perfect; you keep returning. It's hard to get out of this comfort zone.

"Customer satisfaction" and brand loyalty are the key reasons for buying a franchise. Each franchise outlet is cloned to offer a consistent standard of service and product. If the franchise system runs as planned, customers will know what to expect and how much they will pay every time. Franchises give customers a sense of security. Should a dispute arise, customers know that they can appeal to a larger organization. Franchises give the appearance that they will be around for the long run. Also, there is a good chance the "owner" will be around, and customers like to know that they can speak to the owner should the need arise.

WHAT THE FRANCHISEE RECEIVES

Let's examine what you can expect to receive when you buy a franchise. In principle, a franchise can provide

1. **brand-name recognition**—if you pick the right franchise with a high, positive consumer profile, you will have a recognizable brand;
2. **support from the corporation**—corporate services can include help with site selection, employee training, inventory control, vendor supplies and connections, a corporate-produced business plan, lease negotiations, layout assistance, and more;
3. **training**—the franchisor will teach you the business and provide ongoing training;
4. **financial support**—lenders often prefer to lend to new franchises over new start-ups;
5. **a template**—you are buying a proven business plan and strategy that work;
6. **purchasing power**—you may share in economies of scale in purchasing goods, services, and promotion;
7. **corporate monitoring and assistance**—you are likely to receive psychological hand holding and field visits from the franchisor;
8. **less risk of failure**—the failure rate of franchises is less than half of self start-ups;
9. **national/regional promotion**—you will get pre-tested promotion and marketing programs; and
10. **additional units**—you are likely to get opportunities to buy another franchise in your area.

WHAT THE FRANCHISOR ASKS OF YOU

Franchisors earn money in several ways.

1. They collect a **franchise fee** for the rights to use their name and system. This can range anywhere from $3,000 for a small service firm to more than $100,000 for a well-established name, such as that of a hotel, auto dealership, or major restaurant. The franchise fee is usually paid by the franchisee on the day the franchise agreement is signed and applies

FRANCHISE FEE

Fee paid by a franchisee for the rights to represent the franchisor in a given geographic area for a specified length of time, commonly 5 to 10 years

ROYALTY FEE

Ongoing obligation to pay the franchisor a percentage of the gross sales

for the term of the agreement (usually 5–10 years). The franchise agreement will state if an additional franchise fee is due for any subsequent renewal period.

2. They normally collect a **royalty fee**, which ranges from 2 to 15 percent of the annual gross sales. Some franchisors collect their royalties by charging a percentage on the purchase of supplies rather than on sales.

3. Some franchisors make a profit on the markup of items (such as store fixtures) that they sell directly to franchisees.

4. Some franchisors receive volume rebates or other benefits from suppliers that they don't pass on to the franchisees.

5. Some require franchisees to pay advertising and promotion fees. These generally range from 2 to 5 percent of the franchisee's gross sales. Some of these are directed toward local promotions, but most go into the national advertising fund. In some cases, depending on the age of the franchise, it might be possible to ask for some concessions in the payment of these fees.

In addition, growth and market penetration are key benefits. Franchisors can expand their business quickly with limited capital from the original owners. A number of growth options are available. Some franchisors, for example, provide incentives for their successful franchisees to own multiple units. Other aggressive franchisors have been known to sell geographic territories to master franchisors—as we discussed above in the PropertyGuys.com case.

ACTION STEP 61

Conduct secondary research on franchising

A great place to start exploring the world of franchising is the Internet. One option is to complete the E-Exercise provided in Box 14.2.

A second, more rigorous option would be to do a Web search on "buying a franchise." To narrow your search, check out the sites listed in Box 14.1. Begin with the information-related sites, then move on to the franchise databases and directories and do some comparison shopping. Which franchises are hot, and which ones are on their way out? This is a learning exercise, so record any franchising terms or good ideas you come across in the course of your search.

Next, visit the Web sites of two or three franchisors, and submit an e-mail request for a franchise information packet. (Alternatively, use the information on their sites provided that it is comprehensive enough.) Write a one-page summary identifying the advantages and disadvantages of each of your selected franchises. The Franchise Comparison Work Sheet, which can be downloaded from Entrepreneur.com (see Box 14.1), will help you do a comparative analysis.

INVESTIGATING FRANCHISE OPPORTUNITIES

According to Mac Voisin, from the highly successful M&M Meat Shops that started in Kitchener, Ontario, a franchise chain of more than 350 outlets, true entrepreneurs will die of frustration in a franchise system, because they want to do everything their way. As Voisin points out, many of you will not be comfortable operating by the franchisor's strict rules and regulations. Your entrepreneurial spirit might make it difficult for you to follow detailed rules and policies. But that doesn't mean you shouldn't keep your eyes open. You can learn a lot by examining the way good franchises work. It makes sense to evaluate franchise opportunities (especially those in your industry), because, at the very least, it will give you a better picture of the marketplace. You first step might be to attend a franchise trade fair. This is a great way to find new opportunities. If you are interested, we suggest you get in touch with the Canadian Franchise Association (Box 14.1). See if they are holding an event near you. Action Steps 61 and 62, and the E-Exercise provided in Box 14.2 will also help.

| **Box 14.1** **Bookmark This** |

Franchise Information and Resources

- **Canadian Franchise Association (CFA)**: http://www.cfa.ca
- **YouthBusiness.com**: http://www.youthbusiness.com—Click on "Franchise" to access an article titled "Why Buy a Franchise?"
- **BusinessGateway.ca**: http://businessgateway.ca/en/hi/index.cfm—Do a search on "franchising" to access government services and information.
- **Siskinds Franchise Law Group**: http://franchiselaw.ca/book.html—Download the booklet *Franchising Your Business*.
- **Franchise Comparison Work Sheet (Entrepreneur.com)**: http://www.entrepreneur.com/Home/HM_Static/1,4472,formnet_analysis,00.html—Use this

form to help you determine the attractiveness of each prospective franchise you are considering.

- **The Franchise Magazine**: http://www.thefranchisemagazine.net
- **Canadian Business Franchise**: http://www.cgb.ca

Franchise Databases and Directories

Use the following sites to search for franchising opportunities.

- **Canadian Franchise Directory**: http://www.franchisedirectory.ca
- **Canadian Franchise Association**: http://www.cfa.ca/investigate.html
- **Newbusinesscentre**: http://www.newbusinesscentre.com/Default.htm
- **FranchiseShowroom.com**: http://www.franchise-conxions.com
- **CanadianFranchise.com**: http://www.canadianfranchise.com/index.asp
- **Franchise Directory**: http://www.franchisedirect.com/directory
- **Businessnation.com, Franchise Opportunity Listings**: http://www.businessnation.com/franchises/pages/

Master Franchising

- **Entrepreneur.com, "What Is a Master Franchise?"**: http://www.entrepreneur.com/article/0,4621,316905,00.html
- **Master Franchising in Canada**: http://www.davis.ca/publications/2004-07_master_franchising_in_canada.pdf
- **Franchisezone, "Hi, I'm a Master Franchisee"**: http://www.entrepreneur.com/franzone/article/0,5847,289362——1-,00.html
- **MegaDox.com, "Master Franchise Agreement"**: http://www.megadox.com/docdetail.php/4072

Box 14.2 E-Exercise

- "Is It Smart to Buy a Franchise Right Out of College?" See what Jeff Elgin has to say in his franchise article in Entrepreneur.com (http://www.entrepreneur.com/article/0,4621,319078,00.html).
- Find a franchise that suits you. Click onto the "5 Minute Franchise Matching Service" link of Selectyourfranchise.com (http://www.selectyourfranchise.com/canada/?src=adw) and find out about
  - free service—without obligation,
  - the five steps to finding your franchise matches,
  - match criteria supplied by the franchisors themselves,
  - franchise opportunities where you live and within your budget, and
  - franchise opportunities available from $15,000 to $750,000 CAD.
- Is franchising for you? Take the online quiz at Franchise Help, « Franchise quiz »: http://www.franchisehelp.com/execfb/public.quiz
- "Buying a Franchise" quiz: http://www.business.vic.gov.au/CA256C7F0005066C/quiz1?OpenForm (please note: Questions 2 and 5 are not applicable in Canada)
- FRANInfo, "Self Test to Determine if You Are Compatible with Franchise Ownership": http://www.franinfo.com/selftst1/default.html
- Franchise Direct, "Franchisee Checklists—Evaluating Yourself": http://www.franchisedirect.com/icentre/evaluate.htm#intro
- Canada Business Service Centres, "Checklists for Franchisees": http://www.cbsc.org/servlet/ContentServer?pagename=CBSC_FE/display&c=GuideFactSheet&cid=1081945275607&lang=en

ACTION STEP 62

Investigate the franchise system by interviewing franchisors and franchisees

Franchises are everywhere: Tim Hortons, Boston Pizza, Second Cup, RE/MAX, Dale Carnegie Training, Holiday Inn, Esso, Hertz, and many, many others. You might even want to check out Property Guys.com and 1-800-GOT-JUNK? to learn more about the system, interview people on both sides of the franchise agreement.

Part A: Franchisors

Leave your chequebook at home, and interview at least three franchisors. Here are some questions to start you off.

- What is the business experience of the franchisor's directors and managers?
- How many years has the franchise been operating?
- What are the start-up and ongoing royalty fees, and other assessments?
- What level of training and service could I expect before and after I open, and what support is given?
- What is the turnover rate of the franchisees?
- Is the territory well defined?
- What are the minimum volume requirements?
- Is the franchisor a member of the Canadian Franchise Association?
- Is the franchise registered in Alberta or Ontario?
- How can the franchisor buy back or cancel the franchise?

Part B: Franchisees

Now interview at least three franchisees. Ask them the same questions, with emphasis on the type of support they receive from the franchisors.

THE FRANCHISE AGREEMENT AND SYSTEM

When you purchase a franchise, you will be required to sign a contract that could be as long as 50 pages and with numerous appendixes attached. This contract is the franchise agreement, which lays out the system you will be working within, and the rules and policies that you are bound to operate by. It goes without saying that you need to get legal advice before you sign the agreement. The typical clauses in the contract include

- definitions,
- grant and term,
- franchise royalty fee and sales taxes,
- reports,
- general services of the franchisor,
- compliance with system,
- manual,
- training,
- advertising and promotions,
- leasing of the premises,
- improvements to the premises,
- engagement in similar business and non-disclosure of information,
- trademark,
- insurance,
- indemnification,
- events of default,
- effect of termination,
- assignment,
- general provisions,
- renovations, and
- schedules related to the premises, trademark, sublease, and payments.

THE PROCESS INVOLVED IN PURCHASING A FRANCHISE

If you have explored and investigated franchising and believe it is the right fit for you, and if you have worked through the Action Steps, the process truly begins. First you must contact the franchise development office or the Web site of the franchises you are exploring. They will ask you several questions to pre-qualify you. If the franchisors believe there might be a fit, they will send you a franchise packet. These packets are full of marketing pieces meant to sell you on the franchise. Try to read between the lines. Keep in mind that you are reading advertising materials at this point and that you are at the start of the process. Many of the packets will include an application for additional information. For example, if you go to the Web site of M&M Meat Shops, and link onto franchise information (http://www.mmmeatshops.com/en/franchiseinfo/index.asp), "Confidential Qualification Report," you will get a good idea of the kind of personal detailed information a reputable franchisor will require. Another option is to link onto the Subway "Application for Additional Information" site (https://www.subway.com/applications/AdditionalInfoApp/index.aspx).

If the franchise is large, a local sales manager or master franchisee will contact you after reviewing your application. Should there be a fit, you will meet and discuss capital requirements and possible locations in more detail. At this point, you should be exploring the franchisor and franchisees, current and past, in depth. Spend time, and ask the questions we have presented throughout the chapter. Within the franchisor's packet, you will find information on capital requirements. As an example, we have featured M&M's investment requirements in Box 14.3.

Figure 14.1 Subway Application

6063128455

SUBWAY

Application for Additional Information

The filing of this Application does not obligate the applicant to purchase
or the franchisor to sell a franchise.
(Complete in Full and do not use abbreviations. Please Print Clearly or Type)
Please enter the information using either the mouse or the TAB key.
Items listed in blue are required.

(Example: 11/30/2002).   (Example: 10/31/1961).

Date ___ / ___ / _____   Citizen of _____   Date of Birth ___ / ___ / _____

Name _____   Identification/
      Last   First   Middle   Social Security # _____

Other names known by _____   Are you of legal age in your state/province
   and/or area of residence? Yes ☐ No ☐

Have you ever been convicted of a felony? Yes ☐ No ☐   Have you ever been associated directly
(Example:domestic: 555-555-5555 or international: 61-8-555-5555).   or indirectly with terrorist activities? Yes ☐ No ☐

Telephone (Home) _____   (Fax) _____   (Mobile) _____
   country & city code   country & city code   country & city code

Present Address

   Address _____

City _____   State/Province _____   Postal Code _____

Country _____   Email Address _____

Spouse's Name _____   Citizen of _____
   Last   First   Middle   Identification/
   Social Security # _____

Date of Birth ___ / ___ / _____   Is the Spouse of legal age in the state/province and/or area of residence? Yes ☐ No ☐

Other names _____   Have you ever been associated directly or indirectly
Have you ever been convicted of a felony? Yes ☐ No ☐   with terrorist activities? Yes ☐ No ☐

EDUCATIONAL BACKGROUND

Schools Attended	Years	Grade or Degree Attained

BUSINESS INFORMATION (all spaces below must be completed)

☐ Self Employed

☐ Employed By _____   No. Years _____
   Address _____

   City _____   State _____   Zip Code _____

   Telephone (Business) _____   Position _____
      country & city code

   Nature of Business _____

May you be contacted at work? Yes ☐   No ☐

REFERENCES (excluding relatives)

Name	Address	Telephone # (country & city code)

Please complete page 2   Application © 2002 Doctor's Associates Inc.

You will want to know if the franchisor provides any financing or equipment leasing. In addition, if you are interested in an area or master franchise, now is the time to explore this option. Before going any further, ask if you can work within one of the franchises for two to four weeks to get a feel for daily operations and responsibilities.

You might also want to contact the Canadian Franchise Association to determine if there is a local association of franchisees for your selected franchise in your local area. If so, contact them, and delve as deeply as necessary and for as long as you need until your questions are answered. The more contact you have with franchisees, the better equipped you will be to make a final purchase decision.

If your experience working in the franchise proves to you that you want to explore it further, you can work with the franchisor to determine what the best site or area would be for you. They should provide you with the business information to support the numbers required for a successful franchise in the selected area. Deposits might be required before the site selection process begins. At this time, we strongly advise you consult a lawyer. **Please, do not make a deposit or sign any agreement until you have had a chance to review the information with your lawyer.** You should have a lawyer who specializes in franchising to help you answer any questions you might have. Also, if you are beginning to look at offices or retail space, involve your lawyer immediately.

An accountant should also be called in to review material and point out financial issues that need to be discussed with the franchisor. Your accountant, if he or she has franchise experience, will help you assess the financial possibilities and feasibility of the venture, and might also help you compare it to other options. Use all the information you have gathered, and work through the Action Steps to develop your franchise business plan—yes, you still need a business plan.

With the advice of your accountant, lawyer, past and current franchisees, and banker, you are finally ready to negotiate with the franchisor to complete the sale. Be sure that you understand your role and the franchisor's responsibilities. Once you have negotiated your contract, you might be basically on your own, or you might have a strong franchise organization behind you helping you with site selection, store design, training, advertising, marketing, and, possibly, a grand-opening celebration. The story doesn't end on opening—it has just begun! Good luck!

Now we want you to be aware of some of the major pitfalls of franchising.

Box 14.3 M&M: The Investment Requirements

M&M Meat Shops is a franchised operation that requires a total investment of approximately $300,000. This amount excludes approximately $16,000 GST, which is 100% refundable.

Although this amount of money might be available to an applicant by way of a bank loan, M&M Meat Shops will not approve candidates unless they have approximately one-half of the total investment price ($150,000) available in unencumbered (free and clear) cash. We are of the belief that this amount of money is required so that the candidate does not enter the business with an unreasonable debt load. Experience has shown that unreasonable debt loads are detrimental to the success of the franchise.

If the funds are to be borrowed against the applicants' equity in their home, the repayment of this mortgage must be supported by a sufficient outside source of income (i.e., one spouse/partner who is otherwise employed).

The $300,000 includes

- $30,000 franchisee fee

- $229,000 (approximately) is the capital required for equipment, construction, (Contingency and Construction Management Fee) legal costs, accounting, Grand Opening advertising, miscellaneous start-up items. This amount can vary with each store, depending on what improvements are provided by the landlord. Many new shopping centre developers offer only a bare shell and it is up to the franchisee to put in the floor, ceiling, wiring, etc.

- $50,000 (approximately) is for the initial inventory and cash on hand. This amount will also vary depending on the degree of success at the Grand Opening. Since most suppliers offer 14-day payment terms, there is normally sufficient cash in the register from the sales to pay for most of the initial inventory.

Source: M&M Meat Shops, "Franchise Information" (http://www.mmmeatshops.com/en/franchiseinfo/index.asp).

BUYER BEWARE: SOME PITFALLS OF FRANCHISING

Many franchise lawyers and desperate franchisees tell the same stories, again and again. Investors are told a location makes $10,000 a week when it actually brings in $2,000; in some cases, refundable deposits are never returned; and some chains ask for deposits as high as $40,000 before giving the franchisee a contract to review.

Here are some of the more notable pitfalls that plague the franchising industry.

ENCROACHMENT

According to some franchise experts, **encroachment** is the Number 1 issue in the franchise industry. Encroachment is a situation in which franchisors compete with franchisees by putting a store nearby or operating through an alternative distribution channel, such as mail order or the Internet. For example, H&R Block now offers tax service on the Internet, you can buy a Tim Hortons coffee and doughnut at your local Esso station, and the Body Shop has retail outlets as well as mail-order distribution. What this means is that established franchisees are finding it more and more difficult to protect their territory.

ENCROACHMENT
Situation in which franchisors compete with franchisees by putting an outlet nearby or setting up alternative distribution channels, such as mail order or Internet sales

GROUND-FLOOR OPPORTUNITIES

Beware of the so-called "ground-floor" ("grow with us") franchise opportunities. A franchisor offering such an "opportunity" is experimenting with your money. If you buy a franchise, you should be buying a recognized brand name, a proven business plan, excellent field support, and experience that demonstrates the particular franchise will work in your location. Otherwise, you are better off to do it yourself. A concept is not normally considered established until it has been in business for four or five years.

RENEWAL PERIOD

Franchise agreements should stipulate the conditions for a renewal period after the contract agreement has expired. For example, if you sign an agreement for five years, your franchise fee, royalty payments, and even your protected territory could change drastically when it comes time to renew—if you have not negotiated renewal conditions beforehand. Beware of the contracts that do not provide for conditions of renewal *that are negotiable*. At the very least, you should attempt to negotiate an option to renew for a set period under the same terms and conditions as the original contract. One thing is certain: On renewal, you do not want to pay a second franchise fee, *and, again, this can be negotiated.*

VERBAL AGREEMENTS

Beware of the franchisor who makes statements such as, "It's a two-way street. We have to trust each other. We'll make you a good deal if you want to renew. After all, who knows what will happen in the future? We don't need to put this in the franchise agreement." Most well-written agreements come with a "small-print" paragraph that says something to the effect that the franchisor or it representatives are not legally responsible for any promises made prior to the signing of the agreement. *Get everything in writing.*

MINIMUM FRANCHISE LEGISLATION

As of 2006, the federal government had no franchise legislation protecting franchisees. As a result, Canada has often been termed the Wild West of the franchise industry, because almost any company can become a franchisor. In most provinces, all you need is a franchise agreement and a naïve franchisee ready to sign. There are very few legal requirements or restrictions stopping you from starting your own franchise. Alberta and Ontario are the only provinces that have put in place any substantive franchise legislation (information on this legislation is available at http://www. cfa.ca/legal.html). Outside of Alberta and Ontario, franchisors are not legally required to provide you with the following types of information about the company:

- balance sheet and income statement information,
- number of franchises,
- bankruptcy history,
- background of the owners and/or key officers,
- revenues and expenses of the franchisor, or
- turnover rate of franchisees.

SIGNING PERSONALLY

If you are going into a partnership with a franchisor, we strongly advise you to keep your legal distance. You don't want to get your personal assets mixed up with a franchisor's business. Form a company, and sign the franchise agreement in the company name. If a franchisor wants personal guarantees, be prepared to say no.

FEW FACTS

Are franchisees more successful? American statistics would support this, but there are no Canadian data. Are franchises more profitable? Again, we don't know. Most evidence is anecdotal and relies on information from franchise associations. For example, we told you at the beginning of this chapter that the average annual franchise sales growth during the past few years had exceeded 10 percent. Here we relied on information provide by those in the franchise business, and we trusted that their sources were accurate. The fact is, there are no regular government surveys on franchising in Canada, and no major survey on franchises has been conducted since the early 1990s. So beware of an ambitious franchisor who presents you with an extensive list of franchise benefits and unsubstantiated claims like "only 5 percent or 8 percent of all franchises fail."

The Canadian Franchise Association (CFA) is one of the few sources of franchise information. The organization has about 350 members, who are required to disclose certain types of information to prospective franchisees. As of 2006, you could find this disclosure information on the CFA Web site (http://www.cfa.ca/disclosure.html). This disclosure requirement, however, is not backed by government legislation. In addition you should note that even when members provide you with information, "the Canadian Franchise Association has not checked the information and does not know if it is correct." Still, check the Web site for prospective franchisors, and see if they are registered. If they are not members, find out why. If they are, you should be able to find some information. Keep in mind, though, that members are not required to file financial information about their operations. In other words, a franchisor could be close to bankruptcy, and you might not know it. You should also be aware that some franchises, like Pizza Pizza, have been asked to leave the organization.

SATURATED MARKETS

Competition has become intense among competitive franchisors, which has led to a tendency for franchisors, especially fast-food outlets, quick-printing shops, and specialty retailers, to saturate market areas, thus resulting in many failures.

POOR TRAINING

Some training programs are poor or nonexistent.

SUPPLIES STIPULATION

Some franchise agreements stipulate that you must buy your supplies from the franchisor. Problems emerge when franchisees are required to pay non-competitive prices (i.e., they are overcharged) for products supplied by the franchisor.

INSIDERS FIRST

Typically, current franchisees are offered prime locations before outsiders or first-time franchise buyers are. Rarely is a new player offered a sure thing. Invariably, new players are offered franchises that have already been passed over.

NON-REFUNDABLE DEPOSITS

Some franchisors ask for a non-refundable deposit during the time the buyer is negotiating an agreement. This is supposed to show the buyer's good faith. Be careful, even if you are presented with a request for a refundable deposit. Seek legal advice, and place the money in trust with your lawyer, not the franchisor's. Some refundable deposits were never returned.

EVALUATING A FRANCHISE

Evaluating a franchise opportunity is much like evaluating any other business that's up for sale, but because of the nature of franchisors, you need to ask some additional questions. For example,

* How long has this franchise been in business?
* Who are the officers?
* Has the franchise gone bankrupt or been convicted of any criminal offences?
* How many franchise outlets are operating right now?
* How well does this franchise compete with similar franchises?
* Where is this franchise in its life cycle? and
* What will this franchise do for me?

In Chapter 13, we provided a checklist to use in evaluating an ongoing business you are considering buying. The majority of that checklist applies to franchises as well. To supplement it, we're giving you a checklist prepared specifically for evaluating franchise opportunities (see Box 14.4). The questions will help you generate a profile of the franchise and make a wise decision.

CHOOSE YOUR PRODUCT OR SERVICE WITH CARE

As a potential franchisee, you should know everything about the product or service the franchise system delivers. Naturally, an exclusive product or service, or one that is of superior quality and value, is a good business bet, but these aren't the only criteria for judging the competitive strength of the product or service. There are good profits to be made or lost in products that are essentially not different from others in the market—except in how they are marketed. One franchise can be much the same as another, but if its marketing is superior, it can overpower the competition.

So when you try to assess the competitive strength of the product or service you're interested in, keep your focus wide. Consider everything it takes to deliver that product or service to customers. Then ask yourself how well your prospective franchisor does all of these things.

REASONS FOR NOT BUYING A FRANCHISE

Many entrepreneurs have decided against buying franchises. Here are some of the reasons they have given.

* I know the business as well as they do.
* The franchise name is not all that important.
* Why pay a franchise fee?
* Why pay a royalty and advertising fee?
* My individuality would have been stifled.
* I don't want others to tell me how to run my business.
* I didn't want a ground-floor opportunity where I'd be the guinea pig.
* There were restrictions on selling out.
* If I didn't do as I was told, I would lose my franchise.
* The specified business hours didn't suit my location.
* The franchisor's promotions and products didn't fit my customers' needs or tastes.
* They offered no territory protection.

Box 14.4 Franchise Evaluation Checklist

General

	Yes	No
1. Is the product or service		
a. considered reputable?	_____	_____
b. part of a growing market?	_____	_____
c. needed in your area?	_____	_____
d. of interest to you?	_____	_____
e. safe,	_____	_____
protected,	_____	_____
covered by guarantee?	_____	_____

2. What makes the franchisor's product/service distinctive or unique?

_____

_____

3. How long has the product/service been on the market?

_____

_____

4. What products must be purchased from the franchisor or designated supplier? Under what terms?

_____

_____

5. Is the franchise
   a. local?   _____   _____
       regional?   _____   _____
       national?   _____   _____
       international?   _____   _____
   b. full-time?   _____   _____
       part-time?   _____   _____
       possibly full-time in the future?   _____   _____

6. Existing franchises
   a. Date the company was founded
       Date the first franchise was awarded
   b. Number of franchises currently in operation or under construction
   c. References
   Franchise 1: Owner _____
              Address _____
              Telephone _____
              Date started _____
   Franchise 2: Owner _____
              Address _____
              Telephone _____
              Date started _____
   Franchise 3: Owner _____
              Address _____
              Telephone _____
              Date started _____
   d. Additional franchises planned for the next 12 months

7. Failed franchises

   a. How many failed? _____   How many in the past two years? _____
   b. Why have they failed?
   Franchisor reasons: _____

   _____

   Better Business Bureau reasons: _____

   _____

8. Franchise in local market area

   a. Has a franchise ever been awarded in this area? _____
   b. If so, and if it is still in operation: _____
       Owner _____
       Address _____
       Telephone _____
       Date started _____
   c. If so, and if it is no longer in operation:
       Person involved _____
       Address _____
       Date started _____
       Date ended _____
       Reasons for failure _____

   _____

   d. How many inquiries have there been for the franchise from the area in the past six months? _____

CAN YOU FRANCHISE YOUR IDEA AND BECOME THE FRANCHISOR?

"I wanted to be more than an employee," recalls Aileen Reid. "I worked hard and I wanted a piece of the business." But the insurance firm she worked for would not make her a partner. So after eight years of dedicated employment, she quit her job and started her own insurance company with a few credit cards and a lot of chutzpah.

Reid had always dreamed big. She wanted to grow the company fast but did not want the financial risk of owning every office, so she turned to franchising. Today her franchised company, A.P. Reid Insurance Stores Ltd., is Atlantic Canada's largest provider of group insurance, with revenues well over $12 million. "Don't let anyone tell you that you can't do it," she tells future business owners.[5]

Aileen Reid in Atlantic Canada franchised and grew her business. In the opening vignette, we saw how Ken LeBlanc made a success out of franchising PropertyGuys.com. Remember Brian Scudamore (in Chapter 6) of 1-800-GOT-JUNK? He put his company into growth mode through franchising. These successful entrepreneurs are dreamers, and they dream big.

You, too, might be able to franchise your new business some time down the road. To learn more about franchising your business, click on the sites in Box 14.5. Consider reading books by Fred DeLuca, the founder of Subway, and articles by other major franchisors. Learning from their experiences and losses can be an excellent first steppingstone in exploring becoming a franchisor. Take time to talk to others who have started franchises—both the successful and the unsuccessful!

We caution you, however, that it is not easy to build a successful franchise business. One former franchisor we know, for example, advises that franchising takes a great deal of money to start up, with no payoff guarantees, and recommends building a successful and profitable business model before attempting to sell any franchises. To franchise a business, it will also have to have a competitive advantage (as we learned in Chapter 6 and will see in our PropertyGuys case study featured at the end of this chapter), have credibility, and be teachable. Can someone learn to operate your business in 3 months or less? Also, consider the time and effort entailed in developing your franchisees, and be careful not to provide additional concessions and finances to help them financially beyond what is reasonable. Keep your idea simple, and make sure you can train franchisees within a short time. Depending on the type of business, franchisees might have only two or three days to learn the business. In addition, consider the amount of time that will be expended to assist the franchisees, not only in their start-up phase but also in the first year of operation. Personnel, as well as personal and financial resources, can be drained by demanding and unsuitable franchisees, so selecting your franchisees becomes incredibly important for initial success.

Franchisors need to be aware that not all franchise ideas are transferable to other physical locations. Also, you need to make sure the concept can be replicated and is not dependent on the product or economic cycle. In addition, the success of many businesses is based on the personalities of the owners and employees. For a franchise, the success must be dependent not on the owner's personality but on the systems and the franchise's products or services.

Before becoming a franchisor, consider whether you are willing to fulfill primarily the needs of your franchisees rather than the needs of your customers directly. Being a franchisor means working with many different personalities and setting up systems, operations, and training. In addition, you must be willing to watch others grow "your baby." Be aware that many consultants are on the prowl for companies that think they can be the next Subway, and they will do their best to convince you that you are that next company.

A FINAL WORD ABOUT FRANCHISES

Buying a franchise or franchising your business can be a rewarding experience. But we want you to be very careful and do your homework. A franchise is a partnership, and you need to make sure that you or others can work under the controls of its system. We encourage you to look at franchising as an option—the E-Exercise in Box 14.2 will help you evaluate your suitability for becoming a franchisee, or a franchisor, for that matter. Yes, remember that there is no reason why *you* cannot be the franchisor. If you can develop a winning formula, then with a little entrepreneurial flair, you can become a franchisor yourself. As we have learned, many entrepreneurs have done this, and it's another reason for learning all you can about franchising now. In the opening vignette, we discussed two successful franchises. M&M Meat Shops, Boston Pizza International, 1-800-GOT-JUNK?, and Yogen Früz World-Wide are other notable examples.

> **Box 14.5   Learn More about Becoming a Franchisor**
>
> - The Bibby Group, "Franchise Feasibility": http://www.bibbygroup.com/franchising_a_business.htm
> - Entrepreneur.com, "What Makes a Good Franchisor": http://www.entrepreneur.com/article/0,4621,303298,00.html
> - Entrepreneur.com, Business Coaches, "Franchising Your Business": http://www.entrepreneur.com/business-coaching/intro/0,6900,316501,00.html

In a Nutshell

There are many good reasons to consider buying a franchise. Notably, if the brand name is respected, you'll already be positioned in the marketplace; and if the franchisor is sharp, you'll inherit a business plan and a strong corporate partner that can work for you. It's important, however, to examine carefully the franchise's appeal with consumers; you want to get a marketing boost from the name. Depending on the franchise, you might also get other services for your money (e.g., help onsite selection and interior layout, or vendor connections), but the main thing you're buying is brand name recognition.

Just as if you were investigating an ongoing independent business, study the opportunity and franchisor thoroughly. Is a master franchise territory available? Examine the financial history, and compare what you'd make if you bought the business to what you'd make if you invested the same money elsewhere. Speak to other franchisees in the system. *If you are the first, be very careful.* Most of all, before you sign anything, get good legal and financial advice.

Finally, we want you to dream big. Consider franchising your idea or business.

Key Terms

business format franchise

dealership relationship franchise

direct franchising

encroachment

franchisee

franchise fee

franchisor (or franchiser)

master franchising

royalty fee

Think Points for Success

✓ Avoid ground-floor opportunities. "Grow with us" might really signal *"Caveat emptor"* ("Let the buyer beware").
✓ Talk to other franchisees.
✓ Consider becoming a master franchisee
✓ If you are going to buy a franchise, get professional help before you sign anything.
✓ The franchisor gets a percentage of gross sales for advertising and royalty fees whether the franchisee enjoys a profit or not.
✓ Read the proposed agreements carefully.
✓ Do you really need the security blanket of a franchise?
✓ Think about franchising your business.

Checklist Questions and Actions to Develop Your Business Plan

The Franchise Option

❏ Why have you selected a franchise as your method of start-up?
❏ What were your lawyer's comments on the franchise agreement?
❏ Do your personal vision, goals, and personality match a franchise form of ownership?
❏ Have you considered a master franchise?
❏ Is there a possibility you can franchise your business in the future?

Case Study

PROPERTYGUYS.COM

Background

In the opening vignette, we captioned Anna Babin, who bought a PropertyGuys.com franchise and returned to her roots in Atlantic Canada.

The idea for PropertyGuys.com began in 1998. Ken LeBlanc and three other young Moncton, New Brunswick, entrepreneurs had a business concept. They had done their research and found a solid market niche—consumers resented paying real estate agents' high commissions. House sellers were looking for an alternative. LeBlanc and his partners wanted to launch a commission-free real estate company. They approached the Canadian Youth Business Foundation (CYBF) and received help with their business plan, professional advice and support, and a small amount of financial assistance.

In September 2000, they opened their business as a part-time venture with four employees. The market responded, and almost overnight, the business was a success. The partners knew they had a great concept and would have to grow the business quickly if they wanted to be successful in the longer term. They chose the franchise route, and by early 2002, they had launched their franchise division. Franchising proved to be the right growth strategy. Today PropertyGuys.com is Canada's leading private sale real estate marketing company, with more than 50 licensed franchise units across the country. It's a member of the Canadian Franchise Association (CFA) and a recipient of the 2005 CYBF New Brunswick Best Business award, and has been recognized as one of the Top 25 most successful Canadian franchise systems by *Canadian Franchise Magazine*.

Case Study Resources

Additional information on this successful, high growth, Canadian franchise business can be found by linking on to the following online sources:

• PropertyGuys.com home page: http://propertyguys.com
• PropertyGuys.com, press releases, "Reversing the Brain Drain": http://propertyguys.com/corporate/press_release/2005-08-16_NS-Yarmouth.html

- PropertyGuys.com Home Page, press releases: "PropertyGuys.com Expands into Master Franchise Agreements": http://propertyguys.com/corporate/press_release/2005-05-27_HO-Master.html
- Direct Marketing News: "Case study—PropertyGuys.com, Private Sale Real Estate Marketing Company": http://www.dmn.ca/Click/articles/vol32/click32f.htm
- CNW GROUP, Signs of Changing Times: www.newswire.ca/en/releases/archive/April2005/22/c8733.html
- Checklists for Franchisees (Canada Business Service Centres) www.cbsc.org/servlet/ContentServer?pagename=CBSC_FE/display&c=GuideFactSheet&cid=1081945275607&lang=en
- Entrepreneur.com, Mark Siebert's article "How To Be a Successful Franchisor" http://www.entrepreneur.com/franchises/franchisingyourbusinesscolumnistmarksiebert/article83230.html
- Entrepreneur.com, Mark Siebert's article "Are You Ready to Franchise?" http://www.entrepreneur.com/franchises/franchisingyourbusinesscolumnistmarksiebert/article82112.html

Case Study Questions

1. The Driving Forces

   In Chapter 5, we talked about the need for a driving force, or distinctive competency. We explained that successful businesses have at least one dominant driving force.
   a. What was PropertGuys.com major driving force, or competitive strategy?
   b. A compelling vision has been a common linchpin for all of the successful small business we have highlighted in this text. And franchising is no different! According to experts in the franchise field like Mark Siebert "Virtually every successful franchisor starts with a vision of the future and the role their company will play." (http://www.entrepreneur.com/franchises/franchisingyourbusinesscolumnistmarksiebert/article83230.html).
   What was Ken LeBlanc's and the other founding partners' vision of the future and the role their company would play?
   c. What role has the Internet played in the success of PropertyGuys.com?

2. Types of Franchise Systems
   a. What is a franchise?
   b. In this chapter, we discussed two basic types of franchise systems: business format franchise and dealership relationship franchise. Briefly describe the characteristics of these two systems.
   c. Which franchise system did PropertyGuys.com use?
   d. Return to the Chapter 6, 1-800-GOT-JUNK? opening vignette on page 123. Which franchise system did 1-800-GOT-JUNK? use?

3. Franchise Networks

   To distribute its products or services, a franchisor has the options to use a direct franchise or master franchise network—or a combination of both.
   a. Distinguish between a direct and master franchise network.
   b. In the opening caption of this chapter, Anna Babin bought the franchise rights from PropertyGuys.com to operate her franchise. What type of franchise network agreement did she sign? Briefly explain why.
   c. In 2005, Don Swanston and Matt Eldridge signed a PropertyGuys.com franchise agreement for the Vancouver area (http://propertyguys.com/corporate/press_release/2005-05-27_HO-Master.html). What type of franchise network agreement was this? Briefly explain the reason for your answer.

4. Franchise Checklist

   Suppose you were Anna Babin's franchise consultant. Prepare a franchise checklist composed of what you think to be 10 of the most important franchise evaluation criteria. Based on these criteria, would you have advised Anna to buy the franchise? (Hint: You might want to start by checking out Boxes 14.1 and 14.4.)

5. You, Too, Can Be Your Own Franchisor!

PropertyGuys.com latched onto the franchising trend as a distribution method to expand quickly at minimum cost. We have also highlighted other bold entrepreneurs who have chosen the franchisor rout—like Aileen Reid of A.P. Reid Insurance Stores, and 1-800-GOT-JUNK?.

Link onto Entrepreneur.com, Mark Siebert's article "Are You Ready to Franchise?" (http://www.entrepreneur.com/article/0,4621,325405-1,00.html). According to Siebert, what are the top 10 questions to ask yourself if you're thinking of franchising your business? If you are not thinking of franchising, these same questions will also help you decide if you want to start your own business.

Notes

1. Reprinted with the kind permission of Anna Babin, PropertyGuys.com, propertyguys.com press release, "Reversing the Brain Drain." Available at: http://propertyguys.com/corporate/press_release/2005-08-16_NS-Yarmouth.html (accessed July 2006).
2. Prepared by Doug Tam, franchise owner, Second Cup, St. Laurent Mall, Ottawa, ON. Reprinted by permission.
3. See, for example, Industry Canada: "STAT-USA Market Research Reports." Available at: http://strategis.ic.gc.ca/epic/internet/inimr-ri.nsf/en/gr127348e.html. Also newbusinesscentre, "Franchise Statistics." Available at: http://www.newbusinesscentre.com/statistics.html (accessed July 2006).
4. Propertyguys.com Home Page, press releases. Available at: http://propertyguys.com/corporate/press_release/2005-05-27_HO-Master.html (accessed July 2006).
5. *Canadian Business* Online "The New Face of Franchising: Aileen Reid." Available at: http://www.canadianbusiness.com/entrepreneur/index.jsp (accessed January 2006).

SUGGESTED READING

Bond, Robert. *How Much Can I Make?: Actual Sales and Profit Potential for Your Small Business.* Oakland, CA: Source Book Publications, 2004.

Bond, Robert. *Bond's Top 100 Franchises.* Oakland, CA: Source Book Publications, 2004.

Canadian Franchise Association (CFA). The following publications and resources are available from the CFA, 2585 Skymark Avenue, Suite 300, Mississauga, ON L4W 4L5; phone: (905) 625-2896 or (800) 665-4232; fax: (905) 625-9076; Web site http://www.cfa.ca/page.aspx?url=shopbookstore.html:
- *CFA Franchise Canada Magazine*
- *CFA Franchise Canada* (The Official CFA Directory)
- *How to Franchise your Business* (Edited by Larry Weinberg & John Woodburn)
- *The Complete Information Kit for Franchise Success*
- *The Ladder to Success-How to Succeed in Business* (46-minute video featuring Ron Joyce, Cofounder of Tim Hortons)
- *Canadian Franchise Legislation* (Edward N. Levitt)
- *Franchising Your Business* (Siskinds Franchise Law Group)
- *Buying a Franchise in Canada* (Tony Wilson, B.A., L.L.B.)
- *Franchise Law* (Frank Zaid)

Childs, Michael J. *Franchise Buyer's Guide & Workbook.* CITY: Franchise One, Inc., 2002.

Keup, Erwin J. *Franchise Bible: How to Buy a Franchise.* 5th edition. New York: McGraw-Hill, 2004.

Sherman, Andrew. *Franchising and Licensing: Two Powerful Ways to Grow Your Business in Any Economy.* 3rd edition. New York: AMACOM, 2003.

Spinelli, Stephen, Sue Birley, and Robert Rosenberg. *Franchising: Pathway to Wealth Creation.* Upper Saddle River, NJ: Financial Times/Prentice Hall, 2004.

Thomas, Dave, and Michael Seid. *Franchising for Dummies.* Etobicoke, ON: John Wiley & Sons Canada, 2000.

The 2005 Franchise Annual. St. Catharines, Ontario: Info Franchise News Inc.

15

Pulling the Plan Together

In Chapter 15, we tell you how to draw on all of the materials you have generated in the earlier chapters to create your finished Business Plan—a portable showcase for your small business, as well as a personal road map to success.

You might be closer to completing your Business Plan than you think. If you have completed the Action Steps in the preceding chapters, you already have the major components of your plan. If you haven't completed them, return to Chapter 1 and work through the Action Steps. Throughout the preceding chapters, you have found gaps in the market, researched your target customer and your competition, defined your business, developed marketing and promotional ideas, and completed basic financial research and projections. As you develop your Business Plan using the Action Steps, you might recognize areas that need further attention and research. Chapter 15 provides you with the structure to put your facts, figures, ideas, dreams, passion, and intuition into a workable plan. Your Business Plan might be one of the most important documents you pull together.

We have provided you with a comprehensive online resource base, which can be found on the book's support Web site, including another example of a completed Business Plan. The emphasis for Specialty Chocolates and Candy Concession's business proposal is store operations. We also provide you with a detailed Business Plan template. Before writing your plan, you might want to review this material—especially the Business Plan template. Remember: In Chapter 1, Box 1.4, we outlined a list of Business Plan sites. Now, in Box 15.1, we have added a few more sites that might help you create a winning plan.

If you need to start with your business immediately, consider using the Fast-Start Business Plan. This might be the alternative for you, particularly if your business is not very complex and has very low capital needs. Lots of examples and templates of Fast-Start Business Plans are also contained on the book's support Web site.

If you are completing a Business Plan for a high-tech company and are seeking venture capital and angel investors, you might need to access additional Business Plans, as the specific requirements might go beyond what is covered in the basic Business Plan presented in this text. For new high-tech products, lenders and investors are most interested in how you plan to introduce a new concept and where specifically you will locate the early adopters for your product. For new ventures, the traditional channels of distribution might not work for your product, and you will therefore need to develop and substantiate your new distribution method. Again, the book's support site will help you prepare these kinds of plans.

Before you begin your plan, we want you to think about your target audience. Are you presenting this plan to a banker, a panel of investors, or family members? What are their needs? What information do they require, and in what format? Will this plan satisfy the needs of your target market? For example, if you are presenting your plan to a financial institution or a panel of potential investors, your financial statements had better satisfy

LEARNING OPPORTUNITIES

After reading this chapter, you should be able to

- gather all the information you have together into one coherent unit, which becomes a working showcase for your business;
- study a sample business plan to see how one group of entrepreneurs defined and presented their business;
- match or surpass the sample business plan in value-added information, research, and effectiveness;
- complete a PERT chart to organize the work ahead; and
- put your finished business plan to work with passion.

ACTION STEP PREVIEW

63. Write a cover letter for your plan.
64. Write an executive summary.
65. Describe your product or service.
66. Describe the market and the target customer.
67. Describe your major competitors.
68. Describe your marketing strategy.
69. Show off your location.
70. Introduce your management team.
71. Introduce your personnel.
72. Project your cash flow.
73. Project your income statement.
74. Project your balance sheet.
75. Construct a PERT chart, and go for it.

their specific needs. Any grammatical errors will certainly be frowned on. Major financial institutions, for example, are risk avoiders, so you might have to think about how you have reduced risks.

With a completed Business Plan in hand, you will also have something to present to the people who are important to your business: bankers, lenders, relatives, venture capitalists, vendors, suppliers, key employees, friends, and others. You are going to have to think about your presentation. In most cases, you are not going to have a lot of time for presentation. Some investors will give you only 5 or 10 minutes of their time. You might even want to think about your elevator pitch (Chapter 2)—a clear, concise description of your business idea, the market need, how your business will satisfy that need, and how your business, the customer, and your investors will benefit. Most entrepreneurs will have to present their plans to someone. We have provided you with a number of Web sites in Box 15.1 that can help you present your plan, depending on your target market.

The plan is portable, and you can make as many copies as needed to share with people who can help you succeed. You can either mail it to contacts across the country or post it on the various Internet sites that link investors with entrepreneurs. Be cautious. You might want to number every copy, keep a log of who was given each copy, and make a note to retrieve your copies. You don't want them to be passed around without your permission. You might also want to put a note on your plan that is not to be copied. You might even need a signed confidentiality agreement.

Planning is hard work. You will stay up nights, lose lots of sleep, and miss many meals, but in the end you will have saved time. Just as a pilot would not consider a flight without a plan, neither should you consider a business venture without a Business Plan. Once you've completed the plan, you might decide that the costs in terms of money, time, effort, stress, and risk are not justified. If this happens to you, congratulations! You have learned a valuable lesson, and it has cost you only time, not money!

Your plan should become a working, breathing, living document for your business dreams. Share your plan with others; they might have ideas, insights, or recommendations. In Chapter 6, we introduced you to networking, and in Chapter 12, we encouraged you to get a mentor and draw on the resources of an advisory team. Now is the time to get their help, before you start your business. Have them read and evaluate your plan. Review their input, and revise your plan if necessary. Business Plan reviewers sometimes ask for further details or backup data that, when added to your plan, will make it stronger and more effective. Sometimes we become so close to our Business Plan that we omit important and relevant details and information. And we remind you, keep looking for grammatical errors.

HOW TO START WRITING YOUR BUSINESS PLAN

It is now time for your passion to come to the forefront and spill out into every section of your Business Plan. If your plan doesn't shout passion and confidence, you cannot expect your Business Plan readers to read further than the executive summary. Before you begin, gather your completed Action Steps and backup data. Outline your plan, fill in the information from your Action Steps, refine the plan, ask a knowledgeable person to review it, refine it further, and prepare to present the plan to potential investors or lenders. If you are not seeking funding, now is the time to decide, "Is it profitable to go forward with this plan?"

Remember, your reader and you should be looking at where you are now, where you are going, and how you are going to get there. Planning is an ongoing process. Your Business Plan is a road map, and it should represent a fast-growing area where new roads and new opportunities and challenges constantly present themselves. If you're a creative thinker, chances are your thought processes don't always follow a linear sequence. That's great—it will help you as an entrepreneur! Nonetheless, the Action Steps in this chapter do follow a linear sequence: the sequence of the parts of a completed Business Plan. This is a matter of convenience—you will see an example of each part as it would appear in the finished product. Bear in mind, however, that we don't expect you to write each part sequentially.

The best way to begin writing a Business Plan is to start with the material with which you feel most comfortable. For example, if you really enjoyed interviewing target customers, you might begin with The Market and the Target Customers.

In this chapter, the Action Steps will serve as a checklist for keeping track of which parts of the plan you have written. For example, in practice you would probably write the cover letter last, but that is the first Action Step we present. Think of writing this first cover letter as a valuable exercise. After completing Chapter 15 and your Business Plan, rewrite your cover letter. The more cover letters you write, the easier it becomes to write them effectively.

Box 15.1   Business Plan Resources

The following online resources will help you prepare your business plan:

- **Business Plans Planning Guide** (Royal Bank of Canada): http://www.royalbank. com/sme/bigidea
- **Interactive Business Planner** (Canada Business Service Centres): http://www. cbsc.org/ibp/home_en.cfm
- **Business Plans** (Canada Business Service Centres): http://www.cbsc.org, then follow links to "business planning"
- **About's Business Plan Online:** http://sbinfocanada.about.com/cs/businessplans/ a/bizplanoutline.htm
- **Business Start-up Assistant, Preparing a Business Plan** (Canada Business): http://bsa.cbsc.org/gol/bsa/site.nsf/en/su04938.html
- **Your Roadmap: The Business Plan** (Canadian Bankers Association): http://www.cba.ca/en/viewPub.asp?fl=6&sl=23&docid=40&pg7
- **Preparing a Business Plan** (CBSC Online Small Business Workshop, Session 4): http://www.cbsc.org/servlet/ContentServer?pagename=CBSC_FE% 2FCBSC_WebPage%2FCBSC_WebPage_Temp&cid=1102594891135&c=CBSC_ WebPage&lang=eng
- **Virtual Business Plan** (BizPlanIt): http://www.bizplanit.com/free.html
- **Writing a Business Plan** (Bplans.com): http://www.bplans.com/dp
- **Scotiabusiness Plan Writer** (Scotiabank): http://www.scotiabank.com/ cda/content/0,1608,CID400_LIDen,00.html
- **Sample Business Plans:** http://www.smallbusinessfinancetips.com/ sample-business-plans.html
- **Business Plans** (SOHO-suite.com): http://www.soho-suite.com/business_ plans.html
- **Fast-Start Business Plan:** http://www.knowles5e.nelson.com

THREE-PART STRUCTURE: WORDS, NUMBERS, AND APPENDIXES

Your Business Plan tells the world what kind of business you are in and where you are going. For ease of handling, divide your plan into two sections, and provide the needed documentation in appendixes at the end.

In Section 1 use *words* to introduce your strategies for marketing and management. Try to hook your reader with the excitement of creating a business, assessing the competition, designing a marketing plan, targeting customers, finding the right location, and building a team—all those human things that most people can relate to, even if they're not in business. Clearly point out your firm's uniqueness and ability to compete and handle change.

In Section 2 and the appendix, present *numbers:* projected income statements, cash flows, and balance sheets. This section is aimed primarily at bankers, credit managers, venture capitalists, vendors, small-business investment companies, and commercial credit lenders. Projected income statements for three to five years are usually included in an appendix. At the same time, you must also make it accessible to the casual reader who is searching for the bottom line.

Support Sections 1 and 2 with *appendixes.* This is where you place résumés, maps, diagrams, photographs, tables, reprints from industry journals, letters from customers, letters from vendors, credit reports, personal financial statements, bids from contractors, and other documentation that demonstrates the viability of your plan.

Note that in most cases, material in the appendixes comes from existing sources. You are not stating anything new here; you are merely supporting what you have already said.

Appendixes vary for each type of business; for that reason, sample appendixes are not included in this book.

If you follow and complete the Action Steps in this chapter and in the past chapters, you will have in hand all the components you need to write a winning Business Plan.

OUTSIDE ASSISTANCE IN WRITING A BUSINESS PLAN

Many people ask, "Should I hire a pro to write my Business Plan?" Our response is always, "*You* are the pro!" If you don't want to put the time and effort into writing your own Business Plan, it is doubtful that you will have the energy and drive to develop a business. Also, only *you* can put the passion you feel into your plan. The information you have collected by completing the Action Steps now allows you to complete your Business Plan. We do suggest that on finishing your initial plan you look for several business owners and possible investors to review it. In addition, attorneys, marketing specialists, accountants, and manufacturing experts might improve your plan with their review; they will show you what areas need additional clarification or support data. Take all of their comments to heart, and rework your plan where necessary.

Hiring a business consultant to refine your plan is acceptable, but don't allow him or her to dream your dream! Also, if you don't have total control over input to your plan, you might embarrass yourself by not being able to explain the details of it to investors and bankers.

REMINDERS

Completing a Business Plan helps reduce the risk of failure. No plan can guarantee success, but a well-researched plan will help acknowledge issues, anticipate problems, and determine the resources available to correct them.

The plan should be easy to read, with each number and figure well documented. Use bullets, graphs, and appendixes to support the plan's strongest points. Be sure there are no typographical errors and that the plan is well written. If you are not comfortable with your writing skills, hire an editor to review your plan. Focus on the potential opportunities the business provides for investors. Tie together—with a clear, consistent message—all elements of the plan. Include possible risks as well; a business without risks does not exist.

The plan should consist of about 20 to 40 pages, with additional pages for appendixes. Make the plan easy for your reader to write notes on, and include how the reader can reach you—fax, e-mail, address, telephone, pager, and so on.

In this chapter, we illustrate the steps involved in completing a Business Plan, along with providing you samples of each step as completed by a hypothetical business, The Software School Inc. The Software School has been in operation for six months and has been self-financed by the owners, who are now seeking to expand and need additional outside financing. Read through this chapter once and then reread it, completing the Action Steps. Although the Action Steps appear in the order they would be included in your Business Plan, you should complete Action Steps 65 to 75 first, then Action Step 64 (which focuses on the Executive Summary), and finally Action Step 63, the cover letter.

ACTION STEP 63

Write a cover letter for your plan

Address your letter to a specific person who can help your business. Be brief; aim for about 200 words.

State the reason you are sending the plan. If you are asking for money, tell the person what you want it for and how much you need. One well-written paragraph should be all you need to do this.

Your purpose in writing the cover letter is to open the door gently and prepare the way for further negotiations. The cover letter is bait on your hook.

If you are putting money into the business, or if you have already donated, indicate how much.

The tone you are after in this opening move is confident and slightly formal. You want to appear neat, bright, organized, and in control of your venture.

Be certain to explain briefly how you will repay the money.

Refer to the sample letter in Box 15.2

THE COVER LETTER

To aim your plan so that it will achieve the most good, you use a cover letter. Each time you send the plan to someone, you write a special cover letter addressed to that specific reader. The cover letter introduces the excitement of your plan, and it tells the person why you are sending it to him or her.

Read the sample cover letter in Box 15.2.

Let's summarize what's good about our sample cover letter.

1. The writer is making use of a previous contact.
2. The writer tells the reader—the manager of a bank—that he is in the market for a loan. He does not put the manager on the spot by asking for money.
3. Instead, he asks for advice on where to find sources of capital.
4. The writer strikes the right tone. (To do that, he rewrote the letter several times.)

You can do as well or better—and it's worth the effort! As you draft your cover letter, remember that the reader will pass judgment on your business plan (and on your business ability) on the basis of the letter. Do you want your small business to look bright, attractive, and welcoming? Your cover letter needs to give the same impression. A good cover letter will make its readers want to become involved in your venture.

Action Step 63 will help you write your cover letter.

Box 15.2 Sample Cover Letter

In this sample cover letter, The Software School's CEO introduces his company's business plan to a potential lender.

November 24, 20XX

THE SOFTWARE SCHOOL
47 Turbo Drive
Suites 108–110
Toronto, Ontario

Mrs. Deborah Wallis
Manager, Royal Bank
1400 Market Circle
Anytown, Canada

Dear Mrs. Wallis:

We at The Software School Inc. want to extend our appreciation for the advice and guidance you have provided on revising and updating the enclosed Business Plan. Your input was helpful in the marketing area and invaluable for the financial section. Everyone here at The Software School Inc. appreciates the care you took reading over those early drafts.

We're now in the market for a loan of $50,000 (the figure you suggested) to be used for capital expenditures—microcomputers, desks, chairs, and upgrading our curriculum—and we'd appreciate any guidance you could give us concerning sources of capital. (As I'm sure you'll recall, our venture was launched without any debt whatsoever, with each of our five principals putting up $20,000 apiece. And the present Turbo Drive location already has space available for the second classroom.)

We're planning to repay the loan out of new profit over the next three years. (For more information, please refer to the financial section of our plan, beginning on page 14.)

Again, thank you very much for your help and advice. We couldn't have done it without you.

Cordially,

Derek Campbell, CEO

PRELIMINARIES

THE TABLE OF CONTENTS

Box 15.3 provides a sample table of contents to give you a quick overview of a finished Business Plan. In practice, the table of contents is prepared last.

The Executive Summary

The executive summary serves as an introduction to the Business Plan. In function, it is similar to the preface of this book: It is written to acquaint the reader with the nature of the business, to direct the reader's attention to whatever strengths the author (entrepreneur) wants to emphasize, and to make the reader want to turn the page and become involved. Because the executive summary gives perspective to the entire Business Plan, it needs to be written after the entire plan is completed. All the information should be condensed in one or two pages. Pay special attention to the *business description, current position and future outlook, management, uniqueness,* and—if funds are being sought—*funds sought, how they will be used,* and *when they will be repaid.* This summary will appear right after the table of contents (and the confidentiality statement, if one is used).

Box 15.3 Sample Table of Contents

The table of contents page of The Software School's Business Plan.

Table of Contents
Executive Summary 1

1. Description of the Business 1
   A. The Service We Provide 3
   B. The Market and Our Target Customer 4
   C. The Competition 6
   D. Marketing Strategy 8
   E. Our Location 10
   F. Management 11
   G. Human Resources 12

2. Financial Section
   H. Projected Cash Flow 16
   I. Projected Income Statement 18
   J. Projected Balance Sheet 19
   K. Other Financial Information 21

3. Final Conclusions*

Appendixes**

   1. Customer Surveys, First Six Months of Operation
   2. Letters from Mass Merchandisers
   3. Quote from IBM Supplier
   4. Personal Résumés
   5. Personal Financial Statements
   6. Credit Reports
   7. Letters of Reference
   8. Bid from Contractor
   9. Diagram of the Turbo Drive Location and Associated Costs
   10. Industry Information and Trends
   11. Detailed Competitive Analysis
   12. Target Customer Profiles
   13. Promotion Plan, Budget, and Costs
   14. Legal Documents, Licensing, and Risk Management
   15. Sources of Information and Contacts

---

* You should not leave your reader "hanging" on at the end. Wrap it up, and "tie a bow around it" with a clear, concise conclusion.

** The need for specific appendixes varies greatly from Business Plan to Business Plan. For that reason, this chapter does not include a sample of each of these appendixes. As you draft your plan, you will need to document and substantiate your business strategies; this kind of documentation is best included as appendixes.

As you write your executive summary, remember that lenders prefer "hard" numerical data and facts; they cannot take speculations about things seriously. Therefore, such phrases as "50 percent return on our original $100,000 investment"

ACTION STEP 64

Write an executive summary

Imagine that you have two minutes to explain your business venture to a complete stranger. This gives you an idea of what information you need to put into writing for your executive summary.

Practise explaining your venture to friends and strangers, limiting yourself to two minutes. Ask them to raise questions, and use their questions to guide you as you revise and hone your presentation.

When you are satisfied with your oral summary, write it down and type it up. It should not exceed three typed pages. (The Software School's executive summary, which serves as our example, was less than one page, single spaced.)

This might constitute a very small portion of your Business Plan, but it could be the most important part of it.

and "secured agreements from 17 retail computer stores" make the example in Box 15.4 a strong executive summary. They help to paint a picture of good management and solid growth potential for The Software School.

You, too, can write an effective executive summary. Action Step 64 will help you to decide which facts and numbers will portray you and your business venture as credible and promising, and then to summarize them on paper.

Box 15.4   Sample Executive Summary

The Software School Inc. provides numerical data and hard facts in its executive summary.

Executive Summary

The Software School Inc. is a user-friendly, state-of-the-art microcomputer training centre. In our first six months of operation, we demonstrated our unique and profitable way of exploiting a strong and growing market within a fast-growing industry. The Software School's sophisticated electronic classroom provides "hands-on" education that teaches computer users how to use new software programs. By January 2, 20XX, we were operating at 92 percent capacity (50 percent is break-even) and had a waiting list of 168 students.

We plan to add a second classroom to double our capacity. This expansion will allow us to attain $400,000 in sales by the end of our 18th month. At that time, our pre-tax profits will have reached almost $50,000, representing a 50 percent return on our original $100,000 investment.

Our target customers seem to have insatiable appetites for software application knowledge, and The Software School Inc. anticipates an annual compound growth rate of 50 percent over the next five years. With respect to our business-to-business market, for example, we have secured training agreements with 17 retail computer stores in the area and firm contracts for more than 700 employees from 8 industrial users.

Our competitors continue to train in the traditional style and currently show no sign of copying our unique instructional approach. Occasional price cutting by competitors has had no effect on our enrollment.

Management, led by Derek Campbell, has demonstrated how to offer superior training at competitive prices. Our plans for the future include developing additional profit centres by providing on-site counselling and training for firms throughout Southern Ontario. Research and customer surveys indicate that we have just begun to satisfy the ever-increasing need for software education. Extensive documentation is contained the Appendixes of our business plan. Note, for example, that our confidential legal documents, licensing our risk management analysis, are contained in Appendix 14.

SECTION 1: DESCRIPTION OF THE BUSINESS

You know your business, but you need to prove it with words and numbers. By the time your reader finishes your Business Plan, you should have a convert to your side. To give you examples to follow, we have reprinted key sections from the Business Plan (newly revised and updated) for The Software School, an ongoing business that is seeking financing for acquiring more equipment. Regardless of whether your business is already in existence or just starting up, the goals of Section 1 are the same: to demonstrate that you know your business and that you're a winner.

PART A: BUSINESS DESCRIPTION

Box 15.5 shows how The Software School Inc. tackled this part of Section 1.

The Software School Inc. will get its funding because the writer of the plan proves that the business is a winning concern. The writer has

1. let the facts speak for themselves,
2. supported all claims with numbers,
3. avoided hard-sell tactics,
4. refused to puff the product, and
5. projected a positive future.

The writer does a terrific selling job without appearing to be selling at all. Now it's your turn. Do Action Step 65.

ACTION STEP 65

Describe your product or service

Excite your reader about your business. Excitement is contagious. If you can get your reader going, there's a good chance you'll be offered money. Investors love hot ideas.

If this is a start-up, explain your product or service fully. What makes it unique? What industry is it in? Where does the industry fit in the big picture?

Mention numbers wherever you can. Percentages and dollar amounts are more meaningful than words like "lots" and "many."

If this is an ongoing business, your records of sales, costs, and profit and loss will substantiate your need for money.

Keep the words going and the keyboard smoking. You need to persuade the reader to keep reading.

Box 15.5 Sample Business Description

The Software School Inc. describes its business effectively in Section 1.

The Service We Provide

The Software School, a federal corporation, is a microcomputer training facility located in Toronto, between the Pearson International Airport and a high-density executive business complex. The area has a large number of microcomputer users. Now in its seventh month of operation, the school has a waiting list of 168 students (67 percent of whom have paid a deposit).

We train people in computer software systems from the "Top 10" list of best-selling microcomputer and Internet software packages. Because of their power, these systems are complex. They provide a learning hurdle, especially at first.

Students are drawn to our teaching method because it gives them hands-on experience and because we have a very knowledgeable staff. Our teaching works. Working people are busy, and a student can upgrade a given software skill by 80 percent in 8 hours. (Slower learners are guaranteed a second try, and a third, at no additional cost.) Most of our courses can be completed in one day or two evenings. In contrast, the average college course (which emphasizes concepts rather than hands-on software systems) takes 12 to 18 weeks. Our price is $100 for most courses, and so far no one has complained about the cost.

The Software School Inc. achieves this space-age learning speed with a sophisticated electronic teaching system adapted from flight simulation techniques used by airlines for training pilots. We are constantly streamlining and upgrading the system, using funds already allocated in our start-up budget.

One especially bright note: We have done far better than we had hoped. Our actual income figures average 24 percent above our original projections. Projected income for the first 6 months, with an assumed occupancy rate of 50 percent, was just over $10,000 a month. The actual occupancy has not peaked, and for the past 2 months we have operated at 92 percent capacity.

As a service business, we sell seats as well as skills and information, and as Appendix 1 shows, our promotion has generated a heavy demand for present courses such as Computer Fundamentals, Excel, and Windows 2000. At the same time, customers are asking for courses to meet their needs—for example, a course in Lotus Notes.

Until the end of our fifth month, we were open six days a week from 8 a.m. to 10 p.m. To meet demand with our current classroom facilities, we are now also open on Sundays from 9 a.m. to 6 p.m., and the Sunday classes are full.

Our Target Customer

Our primary target is the small and medium-sized businesses profiled in Appendix 12, with these characteristics:

> size—1–30 employees;
> annual sales—$250,000 to $500,000;
> type of business—light manufacturing/retail; and
> major output—paper (reports, letters, documents, etc.).

Our secondary target (profiled in detail in Appendix 12) is the home user with these characteristics:

> sex—50 percent male, 50 percent female;
> age—18–45;
> education—some college;
> owns PC—30 percent;
> has access to a computer at work—52 percent;
> lives near a computer store—73 percent;
> household income—$55,000+; and
> occupation—professional, managerial, executive, or entrepreneurial.

Company profiles on the primary, business-to-business segment and demographic/psychographic research on the secondary, business-to-consumer target market are contained in Appendix 12, "Target Customer Profiles."

PART E: LOCATION

The next part of your business plan is the one on location. You might want to review your work in Chapter 7 now.

Read how The Software School Inc. shows off its location to its advantage (Box 15.9 on page 402).

Box 15.7 Sample Competition Assessment

The Software School Inc. assesses its competition objectively.

The Competition

The Software School Inc. has four main competitors.

- **Traherne Schools.** Our oldest, most entrenched competitor. Three locations in Metro: Etobicoke, North York, and Scarborough. Traherne conducts a six-hour course, Introduction to Microprocessors, for $95. They currently run a course on desktop publishing for the Mac, and they have been planning to introduce an Internet course but to date have not done so. Traherne operates within our geographic market. Their Scarborough operation is closed on Saturdays.

- **Big Micro Computer Instruction.** Excellent classroom facilities, located in East York near the Don Valley Parkway. All instruction is tied to Macintosh machines and is free if you buy your hardware from Big Micro. Otherwise, courses usually cost around $95 and take 6 to 8 hours. The instructors try hard, but Big Micro is really in the business of pushing hardware.

- **Micro Hut Computer Centre.** Friendly salespeople with teaching skills double as teachers. Courses at Micro Hut are Microsoft related. Prices range between $100 and $200 per student/day: VisiCalc, $89; Word Processing, $149.

- **Your Micro and You.** Local facility developed by professional educators. The atmosphere of YMAY is excellent. They offer a normal range of programs and a course in using the computer in a small business, each course costing about $125. Their market seems to be divided between adults with casual interest in computers and children aged 10 to 15. These people have done it right.

- **Other competitors.** Secondary competitors are colleges, which offer a range of 6- to 12-week courses. As well, more companies today are supplying in-house training for their employees. More details on The Software School Inc.'s competitive analysis, including a SWOT analysis and competitive test matrix, are provided in Appendix 11.

Meeting the Competition

The Software School Inc. is in the computer education business. We do not sell hardware or software.

Our program of instruction is relevant. We teach software, and we are constantly on the lookout for trends that will lead us to new markets. For example, we have just added a course on how to create your own home page. Furthermore, our prices are competitive, and we teach classes seven days a week.

Our price per hour might be higher than the college courses, but time and results are important to our students. Therefore, we are seen as price competitive.

You need to paint an attractive picture of your business site and, at the same time, keep your reader interested by inspiring confidence in your choice. Location takes a tremendous amount of analysis. The Software School Inc. writer gives himself a subtle pat on the back by describing the lease arrangements and by identifying the need for a second classroom. The reader who needs more is referred to an appendix. This is smart writing.

Your plan will become very real when you showcase your physical facility. Complete Action Step 69.

ACTION STEP 69

Show off your location

The great thing about a location is that it's so tangible. A potential lender can visit your site and get a feel for what's going on.

A banker will often visit your business site. That's good news for you, because now the banker is on your turf. Clean up the place before your banker arrives.

In this section, you want to persuade potential lenders to visit your site. Describe what goes on here. Use photographs, diagrams, and illustrations to make it feel almost like home.

Box 15.8 Sample Marketing Strategy Description

The Software School Inc. takes a carefully reasoned approach in its description of its marketing strategy.

Marketing Strategy

An analysis of our competitors indicates that our prices—$99 for a one-day course, $198 for a two-day course—are between two extremes. These prices are competitive but still maintain our image of quality.

We use a wide range of strategies to let our customers know where we are: mass media advertising (newspapers, television, and radio), special promotions (press releases, brochures, newsletter, etc.), and personal selling (commissioned salespeople, networking, corporate contracts, trade shows, etc.). A promotion budget, promotion plan, and calendar of related costs are contained in Appendix 13.

Mass Media Advertising

The Software School Inc. places ads in *The Toronto Star* and smaller area newspapers to keep a continuous presence in front of our target customers. In the beginning, we used inducement (two-for-one offers, 15 percent reductions, etc.), but that is no longer necessary, as our waiting lists grow. As we continue to expand, we will develop advertising on radio and TV.

Creative Promotions/Ink/Free Ink

In our first month of operation, we sponsored a scholarship contest in the local high schools, which resulted in some very positive press. In addition, the school has been featured in several local newspapers.

We are in the information business, and toward that end we are developing three different publications: a computer handbook, a newsletter, and a brief history of the founding of The Software School. In time, we hope that this history (a how-to

ACTION STEP 70

Introduce your management team

Almost every study you read on small-business failure puts the blame on management. Use this section to highlight the positive qualities of your management team.

Focus on quality first: their experience, accomplishments, education, training, flexibility, imagination, and tenacity. Be sure you weave in experience that relates to your particular business.

Remember: Dreamers make terrific master builders, but they make lousy managers. Your banker knows this, and potential investors will sense it. A great team can help you raise money.

The key to a great team is balance.

for computer educators) will become a guide for the industry. We have also developed our own Web site (http://www.software.com).

Our mailing list grows daily. We log all incoming phone calls and e-mail with information on the callers and how they found out about us. This information helps us define our target market.

Personal Selling

Personal contact has gained us our largest accounts so far. (Please refer to letters from computer retailers in Appendix 2.) We intend to intensify our efforts along these lines. Fortunately, our directors have experience and talent in the area of personal selling.

We maintain a booth at the major computer trade shows in the area. Approximately 17 percent of our hobbyist/home user business has been generated this way.

PART F: MANAGEMENT

Management will make or break your small business. You are a member of the management team, and you want this business plan to inspire confidence in your team. Writing this section will help you focus more closely on your management team members. (If you need a refresher, review your work in Chapters 11 and 12.)

Now let's see how The Software School Inc. introduces *its* management (Box 15.10).

Nothing is more important than the people who will make your business work. Present their pedigree, and focus on their track records and accomplishments as you complete Action Step 70. It is also helpful to include résumés in an appendix.

Box 15.9 Sample Location Description

The Software School Inc. paints an attractive picture of its location.

Our Location

The Software School Inc. is currently in the first year of a three-year lease at 47 Turbo Drive, Toronto, Ontario. The facility is all on the ground floor and occupies 210 square metres.

The area, which is zoned for business use, is a hotbed of high-technology activity. Within the immediate area, there are two computer stores, one computer furniture store, one software dealer, an electronics store, and two printers, one of which does typesetting directly from software diskettes. Within a 7-kilometre radius are 27 computer dealers.

During our lease negotiations, we persuaded the landlord to make extensive improvements in the interior and to spread the cost out over the three-year term of the lease. The decor—blue carpet, white walls, and orange furniture—gives the effect of a solid, logical, somewhat plush business environment in which our target customer will be comfortable and learn quickly.

The building is divided into four areas: a reception area (30 square metres), a director's office (10 square metres), a classroom (75 square metres), and a storage area (90 square metres).

The principals envision the storage area as a second classroom. See the diagram in Appendix 9. The costs associated with this site are also contained in Appendix 9

The area is easily accessible by public transportation, and we offer free parking.

> ## Box 15.10 Sample Management Team Description
>
> The Software School Inc. shows off its winning management team.
>
> **Management**
>
> - **Derek Campbell.** Mr. Campbell was born in Stratford, Ontario, in 19XX. He took a B.Sc. degree in Industrial Engineering from McGill University and then spent five years in the Armed Forces, where he was a flight instructor, a check pilot, and a maintenance officer. While in the service, Mr. Campbell completed an M.A. degree in Marketing Management and Human Relations.
>
>   Following military service, Mr. Campbell was employed as a pilot for Air Canada. He is currently the CEO of EuroSource, a software importing company. He is the author of several articles on computers and the information age.
>
> - **Roberta Jericho.** Ms. Jericho was born in Lethbridge, Alberta, in 19XX. She has a B.Sc. degree in Geology and Physical Sciences from the University of Calgary. She has completed the Microsoft training program and has been the IT manager for EuroSource for the past five years.
>
> **Directors**
>
> - **C. Hughes Smith.** Mr. Smith was born in Halifax, Nova Scotia, in 19XX. He has a B.A. degree in Political Science and Philosophy from Dalhousie University, an M.B.A. from Stanford, and a law degree from the University of Toronto.
>
>   Mr. Smith is a senior vice president of Lowes and Lockwood, a residential home-building firm, and a partner in Graebner and Ashe, a Toronto law firm. He is the author of numerous articles in the field of corporate planning and taxes.
>
> - **Philu Carpenter.** Ms. Carpenter was born in Winnipeg, Manitoba, in 19XX. Her B.A. degree is from the University of Manitoba, and her M.B.A., with a Marketing specialty, is from the University of Western Ontario.
>
>   Ms. Carpenter spent 20 years in the corporate world (IBM, DEC, InterComp, etc.), where she worked in marketing and industrial sales. Currently a professor of Business at York University, Ms. Carpenter is the general partner in two businesses and a small-business consultant. She has written and lectured widely in the area of small business.
>
> - **Dan Masters.** Mr. Masters was born in Mississauga, Ontario, in 19XX. His degrees (B.A., M.B.A.) are from the University of Western Ontario, where he specialized in Marketing and Finance. Mr. Masters has worked for Kodak and Nortel Networks (as senior account sales executive and sales manager, respectively) for a total of 25 years.
>
>   Mr. Masters is currently a professor of Business at Seneca College. He is active in several small businesses, lectures widely, and has published numerous articles in the field of small business.
>
> - Personal résumés of all personnel are provided in Appendix 4.
>
> **Other Available Resources**
>
> The Software School Inc. has retained the legal firm of Farney and Shields and the accounting firm of Hancock and Craig. Our insurance broker is Sharon Mandel of Fireman's Fund. Our advertising agency is George Friend and Associates.

PART G: HUMAN RESOURCES

Part G of your plan shows off your human resources. For a start-up business, you're peering into the future with confidence, conducting informal job analyses for key employees who will help you to succeed. For an ongoing business, you need to list your present employees and anticipate your future personnel needs. If you have five employees now and you want to indicate growth, try to project how many jobs you'll be creating in the next five years.

ACTION STEP 71

Introduce your personnel

Describe the kinds of people you will need as employees and how they fit into your plan.

What skills will they need? How much will you have to pay them? Will there be a training period? How long? What benefits will you offer? How will you handle overtime?

If you haven't yet written job descriptions, do that now. Job descriptions will help you hire people who best match the skills required.

When you start thinking about tasks and people to do them, review your work in Chapter 12. Preparing a human resource plan is important, because it gives you one more chance to analyze job functions and develop job descriptions before you start interviewing, hiring, and paying benefits—all of which are expensive.

You'll notice that The Software School Inc. gives a very brief overview of its human resource situation (Box 15.11).

In describing their lean operation, the entrepreneurs who run The Software School Inc. keep their description brief as well. They show good sense when they express a commitment to control operating costs. Their decision reflects business discipline and foresight. If you were a potential investor in this business, wouldn't you appreciate some control on the purse strings?

Every person on your team is important. Action Step 71 will help you describe the kinds of people you will need and how you will help them be productive.

Box 15.11   Sample Human Resources Description

The Software School Inc. provides a brief overview of its human resources.

Human Resources

At the end of 6 months of operation, The Software School Inc. has 3 full-time employees and 14 part-time employees. The full-time employees include

1. a manager, salaried at $3,000 per month;
2. a receptionist, salaried at $8 per hour; and
3. a training director, salaried at $1,500 per month.

The part-time employees include three directors, who assist in the marketing function; three outside commissioned salespeople, and eight part-time instructors. According to our plan, one salesperson will become full-time at the end of the seventh month.

We will continue to hold down overhead with qualified part-time employees as long as it is feasible. We believe that running a lean operation is important to our success.

SECTION 2: FINANCIAL SECTION

GOOD NUMBERS

The Financial Section is the heart of your business plan. It is aimed at lenders—bankers, credit managers, venture capitalists, vendors, and commercial credit lenders—people who think in numbers. Lenders are professional skeptics by trade; they will not be swayed by the enthusiasm of your writing in Section 1. Your job, therefore, is to make your numbers do the talking.

In Chapter 9, you drafted your financial plan. In Chapter 10, you investigated your financial options. Now you are ready to finalize your numbers into four standard categories:

1. the opening and projected balance sheets,
2. the cash flow projection (also called a pro forma),
3. the projected income statement, and
4. other important financial information.

Examples from The Software School Inc. will serve as models for you. You can adapt them to fit your business.

The idea is to know where every dollar is going. You need to show when you'll make a profit, and you need to show that you are efficient, conservative, and in control. You'll know you've succeeded when a skeptical lender looks up from your business plan and says, "You know, these numbers look good." You might want to think about putting a financial summary right at the beginning of your financial section. You should not make the reader pore over all kinds of financials to get the necessary key information. Some plans even contain only a summary of the financial results and leave all the details for the appendixes.

GOOD NOTES

One way to spot a professional lender is to hand over your business plan and watch to see which section he or she reads first. Most lenders study the notes that accompany income and cash flow projections first. Knowing this allows you to be forewarned. Use these notes to list all assumptions, to tell potential lenders how you generated your numbers (for example, "Advertising is projected at 5 percent of sales"), and to explain specific entries (for example, "Leased equipment—Monthly lease costs on IBM microcomputers").

Make these notes easy to read, with headings that start your readers off in the upper left-hand corner and march them down the page, step by step, to the bottom line. (Some sample projection charts use tiny footnotes on the same page. We prefer *large* notes on a separate page. Notes are important, no less important than the rest of the plan.)

Creating your business plan takes a lot of time. It's only natural for you to hope that lenders will read it, get excited, and ask questions. These notes can help you accomplish that, even if you haven't started up and the numbers and assumptions are projections into the future.

PART H: PROJECTED CASH FLOW

Next, focus your attention on the projected cash flow, the lifeblood of your business. By projecting cash flow month by month, you get a picture of how healthy your business will be.

The Software School's cash flow projection is set out in Table 15.1. The notes for these numbers are reprinted in Box 15.12. If you compare the projected income statement (Table 15.2) with the cash flow projection, you will see that some items are treated differently in the tables. For example, expenses in the projected income statement are divided into monthly installments, whereas the same expenses in the cash flow projection are shown as bulk payment when due. Now look at insurance expense. In the projected income statement, we find a total expense of $960, shown as 12 monthly debits of $80 each. The same expense in the cash flow projection is shown as two payments of $480 each, falling due in the 7th and 13th months. If the entrepreneurs running the business had only $80 available to pay for insurance in the 7th month—that is what is shown in the income statement—they would be in trouble.

Profits don't pay the bills and the payroll; cash flow does. Potential lenders look at cash flow projections first. In Action Step 46, Chapter 9, you drafted your projected cash flow. Now it is time to revisit these estimates. Finalize your projected cash flow. Complete Action Step 72.

ACTION STEP 72

Project your cash flow

Get used to doing cash flow. Once a month is not too often. If you prepared a cash flow for your business back in Chapter 9, bring those numbers forward. If you skipped that step, do it now. Here's how it's done.

1. Write down all the cash you will have for one year.
2. Add net profit.
3. Add any loans.
4. Figure your total cash needs for the year.
5. Spread these numbers out across the year. You might have a lot of cash at the start of the year; you want to make sure you have enough to get all the way through.
6. Now list all disbursements. Spread these out too.
7. Now examine the figures. Is there any time during the year when you will run short of cash? It's better to know the truth now, when you're still working on paper.
8. If your cash picture looks good, drop in a couple of what-ifs. (Let's say you've budgeted $300 for utilities, and the air conditioner goes out. It will cost $200 to repair it, and the lease says it is your expense. Or let's say you see an opportunity for a sale, but you would have to hire someone to handle it for you. Can your cash flow handle such surprises?)

Box 15.12 Sample Cash Flow Projection Notes

The Software School's notes for its cash flow projection.

1. **Beginning of the month.** Cash available as the month begins.
2. **Sales.** Includes all sales by cash, cheque, or credit card at the time the class is taken. Does not include accounts receivable.

3. **Credit card expense.** Fees of 2.5 percent paid to credit card companies. Approximately 50 percent of customers use charge cards.
4. **Loans.** Loan for new course development and audiovisual equipment.
5. **Total cash available.** Sum of all money available during the month.
6. **Books.** Books for sale are ordered and paid for one month in advance of projected sale.
7. **Instructional materials.** Covers course materials purchased from licenser.
8. **Salaries.** Net salaries paid employees approximate 80 percent of gross salaries paid.
9. **Payroll taxes.** Total of amount withheld from employees, plus Income Statement payroll tax item.
10. **Advertising.** Established as 30-day accounts with all media companies.
11. **Leased equipment.** Lease payments are due the first day of each month.
12. **Licences and fees.** Licence fees are due the 15th of the following month.
13. **Legal and accounting.** Due 30 days after bill is received.
14. **Rent.** Due the first day of each month.
15. **Office supplies.** Paid at time of purchase or with subscription. No credit.
16. **Insurance.** Paid in month when expense occurs.
17. **Telephone and utilities.** Paid within 30 days of receipt of bill.
18. **Interest.** Interest only, paid each month.
19. **Loan payback.** $5,000 loan payment due every six months.
20. **Miscellaneous.** Paid in month when expense occurs.
21. **Income tax reserve.** Paid into a special tax account at the bank.
22. **Total disbursements.** Total cash expended during the month.
23. **Net cash before capital investment.** Cash balance before capital investment payments.
24. **Capital equipment.** Purchase of additional audiovisual equipment.
25. **Contracted course development.** Contract payment due for new course development.
26. **Monthly cash flow.** Cash balance after all payments at the end of the month.

PART I: PROJECTED INCOME STATEMENT

Your next task is to put together your projected income statement (sometimes called a profit and loss statement). With the information you've gathered so far, it shouldn't be too hard. In fact, it will be enjoyable—if the numbers look good.

The Software School's projected income statement is shown in Table 15.2, and the careful documentation of each item is reprinted here. For instance, if a lender wanted to know how the figures for commissions were generated, Note 6 explains that they are estimated as 10 percent of sales (Box 15.13).

Box 15.13   Sample Projected Income Statement Notes

Here are The Software School's notes for its projected income statement.

1. **Instruction.** Based on 2.5 percent occupancy growth per month, starting at 35 percent (235 students) and growing to 69 percent. Students pay $99 per course.
2. **Books.** Revenue from books sold averages approximately 1 percent of instructional sales, rounded to bring total sales to an even $100 figure.
3. **Classroom materials.** $7.50 per student.
4. **Instruction personnel.** Instructor cost is $100 per 8-hour class, starting with 25 classes and growing to 30 classes by the end of the year.
5. **Books.** Cost of books is 70 percent of selling price.
6. **Commissions.** Average 10 percent of instructional sales.

7. **Advertising.** Projected at 5 percent of sales.
8. **Credit cards.** Approximately 50 percent of sales are paid with credit cards. The cost is 2.5 percent of the sale.
9. **Salaries.** Start with three full-time employees. Bring on one additional person beginning the 10th month.
10. **Payroll taxes.** The company's share of employee taxes averages 7 percent of commissions and salaries.
11. **Leased equipment.** Monthly lease costs on IBM microcomputers.
12. **Licences and fees.** Licence (right to use copyrighted material) costs 10 percent of instruction sales.
13. **Accounting.** Average accounting and bookkeeping costs for the area and size of the business.
14. **Rent.** Based on three-year lease.
15. **Office supplies.** Estimated at 0.25 percent of sales.
16. **Dues and subscriptions.** Estimated costs for magazines, newspapers, and membership in organizations.
17. **Repair and maintenance.** Projected to be 1 percent of sales.
18. **Insurance.** Based on current insurance contract for next 12 months, payable every 6 months.
19. **Telephone and fax.** Figured at 1.5 percent of sales.
20. **Utilities.** Figured at 2 percent of sales.
21. **Depreciation.** Schedule established by accounting firm.
22. **Interest.** Loan at 13 percent, with $5,000 payments due every 6 months until paid off.
23. **Miscellaneous.** Figured at 3 percent of sales.
24. **Reserve for taxes.** Local, provincial, and federal taxes estimated at 20 percent of net profit.

Refer to Table 15.2 as you predict your income.

PART J: PROJECTED BALANCE SHEET

The professionals will look at your balance sheet (sometimes called a statement of financial position) to analyze the state of your finances at a given point in time. They are looking at things like liquidity (how easily your assets can be converted into cash) and capital structure (what sources of financing have been used, how much was borrowed, and so on). Professional lenders will use such factors to evaluate your ability to manage your business.

Table 15.3 shows two balance sheets for The Software School. Note that the first one shows its actual position at the end of its first 6 months and the second is a projection of where it will be at the end of its first 18 months. If you're just starting up, *all* figures will be projections.

In Chapter 9, Action Step 47, you drafted a projected income statement. Now it is time to add the final touches. Complete Action Step 73.

OTHER IMPORTANT FINANCIAL INFORMATION

The ratios tell you a lot about the health of your business. They allow you to compare it with industry benchmarks and also to compare your results to your objectives.

Let's talk for a minute about **return on owners' investment**. It is a bottom-line figure that shows how much is earned on the total dollars invested in the business. You have this kind of information up front if you invest money in bonds. The interest tells you your Return on Owner Investment. Imagine that you have two

ACTION STEP 73

Project your income statement

What you're driving at here is net profit—what's left in the kitty after expenses—for each month and for the year.

First, you figure your sales. The first big bite out of the figure is the cost of goods sold. (In a service business, the big cost is labour). Subtracting that gives you a figure called gross margin.

Now add up all your expenses (rent, utilities, insurance, etc.) and subtract them from the gross margin. This gives you your net profit before taxes. (Businesses pay quarterly installments.)

Subtract taxes. There's your net profit.

RETURN ON OWNERS' INVESTMENT

Net profit to owner's investment

Table 15.1 The Software School Inc. Cash Flow Projection

Cash Flow: Software School

	7th Month	8th Month	9th Month	10th Month	11th Month	12th Month	13th Month	14th Month	15 Month	16th Month	17th Month	18th Month	Total
Cash-Receipts													
Beginning of Month	$3970	$7365	$6015	$51575	$47060	$35275	$31840	$28645	$27900	$33115	$43895	$47800	$364455
Sales	23500	25200	26900	28500	30200	31900	33600	35300	38350	40100	43300	43300	400150
Less: Credit Card Expense	(295)	(315)	(335)	(355)	(380)	(400)	(420)	(440)	(480)	(500)	(540)	(540)	(5000)
Loan			60000										60000
Total Sales	$27175	$32250	$92580	$79720	$76880	$66775	$65020	$63505	$65770	$72715	$86655	$90560	$819605
Disbursements													
Books	$175	$190	$200	$210	$225	$235	$250	$305	$350	$370	$370	$385	$3265
Inst./Materials		6000			7500			9000			9000		31500
Salaries													
Instruction	2000	2000	2040	2080	2120	2160	2200	2240	2280	2320	2360	2360	26160
Administration	2640	2640	2640	3120	3600	3600	3600	3600	3600	3600	3600	3600	39840
Commissions	1730	1865	1995	2130	2255	2390	2530	2660	2795	3030	3170	3420	29970
Payroll Taxes	2045	2195	2250	2435	2690	2755	2805	2870	2925	3025	3075	3170	32240
Advertising	1080	1175	1250	1335	1410	1495	1580	1660	1750	1895	1980	2135	18745
Leased Equip.	1270	1270	1270	1270	1270	1270	1270	1270	1270	1270	1270	1270	15240
Licences/Fees	2160	2330	2495	2665	2820	2990	3160	3325	3495	3790	3960	4275	37465
Accounting/Legal	500	500	500	500	500	500	500	500	500	500	500	500	6000

Cash Flow: Software School

	7th Month	8th Month	9th Month	10th Month	11th Month	12th Month	13th Month	14th Month	15 Month	16th Month	17th Month	18th Month	Total
Rent	3890	3890	3890	3890	3890	3890	3890	3890	3890	3890	3890	3890	46680
Office Supplies	60	65	65	70	75	80	85	90	95	100	110	110	1005
Dues/Subscript.	20	20	20	20	20	20	200	20	20	20	20	20	420
Repair/Maint.	235	250	265	285	300	320	335	355	385	395	435	435	3995
Insurance	480						480						960
Telephone	325	355	380	405	430	455	480	505	530	575	600	650	5690
Utilities	430	470	505	540	570	605	640	670	705	765	800	865	7565
Interest				650	650	650	650	650	650	595	595	595	5685
Loan Payback									5000				5000
Miscellaneous	705	755	805	855	905	955	1010	1060	1150	1205	1300	1300	12005
Inc. Tax Reserve	65	265	435	200	375	565	710	935	1265	1475	1820	1820	9930
Total Disbursements	$19810	$26235	$21005	$22660	$31605	$24935	$26375	$35605	$32655	$28820	$38855	$30800	$339360
Net Cash Before Capital Invest.	$7365	$6015	$71575	$57060	$45275	$41840	$38645	$27900	$33115	$43895	$47800	$59760	$480245
Capital Equipment			10000										10000
Contracted Course Development			10000	10000	10000	10000	10000						50000
	$7365	$6015	$51575	$47060	$35275	$31840	$28645	$27900	$33115	$43895	$47800	$59760	$420245

Table 15.2 The Software School Inc. Projected Income Statement

Cash Flow: Software School

	7th Month	8th Month	9th Month	10th Month	11th Month	12th Month	13th Month	14th Month	15 Month	16th Month	17th Month	18th Month	Total
Sales													
Instruction	$23285	$24950	$26630	$28215	$29900	$31580	$33265	$34945	$37915	$39600	$42770	$42770	$395825
Books	215	250	270	285	300	320	335	355	435	500	530	530	4325
Total Sales	$23500	$25200	$26900	$28500	$30200	$31900	$33600	$35300	$38350	$40100	$43300	$43300	$400150
Cost of Instruction													
Clssrm. Matrls.	$1765	$1890	$2020	$2140	$2265	$2395	$2520	$2650	$2875	$3000	$3240	$3240	$30000
Inst./Personnel	2500	2500	2600	2600	2700	2700	2800	2800	2900	2900	3000	3000	33000
Books	150	175	190	200	210	225	235	250	305	350	370	370	3030
Total Cost/Instr/Books	4415	4565	4810	4940	5175	5320	5555	5700	6080	6250	6610	6610	66030
Gross Profit	$19085	$20635	$22090	$23560	$25025	$26580	$28045	$29600	$32270	$33850	$36690	$36690	$334120
Expenses													
Sales													
Commissions	$2330	$2495	$2665	$2820	$2990	$3160	$3325	$3495	$3790	$3960	$4275	$4275	$39580
Advertising	1175	1250	1335	1410	1495	1580	1660	1750	1895	1980	2135	2135	19800
Credit Cards	295	315	335	355	380	400	420	440	480	500	540	540	5000
Administrative													
Salaries	3300	3300	3300	4500	4500	4500	4500	4500	4500	4500	4500	4500	50400
Payroll Taxes	570	580	600	695	715	725	745	755	785	795	825	825	8615

Cash Flow: Software School

	7th Month	8th Month	9th Month	10th Month	11th Month	12th Month	13th Month	14th Month	15 Month	16th Month	17th Month	18th Month	Total
Leased Equip.	1270	1270	1270	1270	1270	1270	1270	1270	1270	1270	1270	1270	15240
Licences/Fees	2300	2495	2665	2820	2990	3160	3325	3495	3790	3960	4275	4275	39550
Accounting	500	500	500	500	500	500	500	500	500	500	500	500	6000
Rent	3890	3890	3890	3890	3890	3890	3890	3890	3890	3890	3890	3890	46680
Office Supplies	60	65	65	70	75	80	85	90	95	100	110	110	1005
Dues/Subscript.	20	20	20	20	20	20	200	20	20	20	20	20	420
Repair/Maint.	235	250	265	285	300	320	335	355	385	395	435	435	3995
Insurance	80	80	80	80	80	80	80	80	80	80	80	80	960
Telephone	355	380	405	430	455	480	505	530	575	600	650	650	6015
Utilities	470	505	540	570	605	640	670	705	765	800	865	865	8000
Depreciation	1170	1170	1170	1335	1335	1335	1335	1335	1335	1335	1335	1335	15525
Interest				650	650	650	650	650	650	595	595	595	5685
Miscellaneous	705	755	805	855	905	955	1010	1060	1150	1205	1300	1300	12005
Total Expenses	$18725	$19320	$19910	$22555	$23155	$23745	$24505	$24920	$25955	$26485	$27600	$27600	$284475
Net Profit	$360	$1315	$2180	$1005	$1870	$2835	$3540	$4680	$6315	$7365	$9090	$9090	$49645
Reserve for Taxes	65	265	435	200	375	565	710	935	1265	1475	1820	1820	9930
Net Profit After Taxes	$295	$1050	$1745	$805	$1495	$2270	$2830	$3745	$5050	$5890	$7270	$7270	$39715

Table 15.3   The Software School Inc. Balance Sheet

	Actual Balance Sheet of Software School as of September 30, 20xx (after first 6 months)		Projected Balance sheet as of September 30, 20xx (after first 18 months)	
Assets				
Cash	$3,970		$59,670	
Instruction materials and books	2,500		4,495	
Total current assets		$6,470		$64,165
Leasehold improvements	$41,000		$41,000	
Furniture	15,100		15,100	
Audio/visual	10,600		20,600	
Office equipment	3,600 $70,300		3,600 $80,300	
Less depreciation	7,020	63,280	22,545	57,755
License agreement		25,000	$25,000	
New courses		–0–	50,000	75,000
Total assets		$94,750		$196,920
Liabilities				
Instructors' salaries	$1,250		$1,500	
Administrative salaries	1,650		2,250	
Commissions	2,165		4,275	
Accounts payable	4,495		9,020	
Current liabilities		$9,560		$17,045
Long-term debt		–0–		54,970
Total liabilities		$9,560		$72,015
Net worth (owner's equity)				
Capital stock	$100,000		$100,000	
Retained earnings	(14,810)	85,190	24,905	124,905
Total liabilities and net worth		$94,750		$196,920

funds, Bond A and Bond B; Bond A pays you a 4 percent return, and Bond B pays you 25 percent. Which bond would have the better Return on Owner Investment?

You compute Return on Owner Investment for a business by dividing the net profit by investing dollars. For The Software School, the profit after taxes is $39,715 (from Table 15.2). Divide that by the owner's investment of $100,000 (from Table 15.3):

$$\$39\ 715 \div \$100,000 = 39.7 \text{ percent.}$$

Could you get 39.7 percent from a savings account or a bond fund? It's not a bad Return on Owner Investment. It would dazzle lenders and probably draw the attention of a venture capitalist.

It is also helpful to include a comparison of your ratios to industry standards. Don't forget to include your break-even analysis as well.

The Software School Inc. did not provide notes to its balance sheets because, in this case, no notes are needed. In conjunction with the income statement and the cash flow projection, all the entries in the balance sheet will make sense to your professional readers. Under some circumstances, you would want to note unusual features of a balance sheet for an actual fiscal year, but in most cases— and in most projections—this won't be necessary.

Now project a balance sheet for your business. Action Step 74 will help you.

EPILOGUE: ACT ON WHAT YOU KNOW

Well, do you feel like you're ready? You are. You have thoroughly researched your product or service, your market and target customer, your competition, your marketing strategy, and your location. You've discovered how to prepare for surprises you can't afford, how to handle numbers, how to pursue financing, when and why you should incorporate, how to build a winning team, and whether you should buy, franchise, or start on your own. You've surveyed the vistas that a small business computer training school can open up for you. And you've written it all up in a workable business plan that can be implemented.

Before you take off running, we want you to think about how you are going to implement your plan. A common and effective approach is to prepare a calendar showing week by week what has to be done and who is responsible for doing it. All too often, new entrepreneurs seriously underestimate the time it takes to get their new business off the ground. So you should spend the necessary time beforehand trying to make sure you minimize delays.

One management tool that can help you put your business plan to work is called **PERT,** an acronym for Program Evaluation and Review Technique. It's often used to establish schedules for large projects, but small businesses can use it as well.

A PERT chart is just the thing if you feel overwhelmed by the tasks of starting up and don't know where to begin. If you're a person who sometimes tries to do everything at once, PERT is also recommended. It will help you focus your energy on the right job at the right time. A sample PERT chart is provided in Table 15.4. Yours will need to be bigger and more detailed. You can use days, weeks, or months to plot the tasks ahead. (If you think you should use years, reassess your industry and business idea.)

In constructing your PERT or "to do" calendar, we want you to be very careful. Time frames are often much longer than expected. The official time for obtaining a liquor licence, for example, is three months, but enter any bureaucratic "glitch" or any opposition, and it's easily double that. The search for a suitable storefront location usually takes months; and if Yellow Pages advertising is crucial to the

ACTION STEP 74

Project your balance sheet

A projected balance sheet is simply a prediction, on paper, of what your business will be worth at the end of a certain period of time. This prediction allows you to figure your actual and projected Return on Owner Investment, which is the real bottom line.

1. Add up your assets. For convenience, divide these into current (cash, notes, receivables, etc.), fixed (land, equipment, buildings, etc.), and other (intangibles, such as patents, royalty deals, copyrights, goodwill, contracts for exclusive use, and so on). You'll need to depreciate fixed assets that wear out. For value, you show the net of cost minus the accumulated depreciation.

2. Add up your liabilities. For convenience, divide these into current (accounts payable, notes payable, accrued expenses, interest on loans, etc.), and long-term (trust deeds, bank loans, equipment loans, balloon payments, etc.).

3. Subtract the smaller figure from the larger one.

You now have a prediction of your net worth. Will you be in the red or in the black?

PERT

Acronym for Program Evaluation and Review Technique

Task	Week					
	1	2	3	4	5	6
Befriend banker	X	X	X	X	X	X
Order letterhead		X				
Select site	X					
Get business name statement	X					
Register company			X			
Select ad agency	X					
Lunch, lawyer			X			
Appointment, accountant				X		
Prepare vendor statement					X	
Make utilities deposit					X	
Review promotional material					X	
Survey phone system			X	X	X	
Order phone system						X
Hold open house						X

Table 15.4 A Sample PERT Chart

Index

Note: Page numbers beginning with the letter "M" indicate modules available on the Knowles book support site: www.knowles5e.nelson.com